Contents

Acknowledgements

We are fortunate to have many people working with us who make the task of publishing books like these a pleasure. In particular, we would like to thank the Clubs for their assistance, the Hoteliers for their support and John Alder for his juggling skills. Val for her calming demeanour during the inevitable periods of tension and the writers and photographers for such excellent material. To all of these people we owe our thanks but especially to you for buying the book. Thank you.

Andrew Finley

Robert Brand

Regional introductions photographs & illustrations

England & Wales

Regional maps – ©*MAPS IN MINUTES*™ *2001.*
©*Crown Copyright, Ordnance Survey 2001.*

Southern England – *Chart Hills*

West Country – *St. Mellion*

Midlands and East Anglia – *Royal West Norfolk*

Lancashire & The North West – *Windermere*

Yorkshire & The North East – *Bamburgh Castle*

Wales – *Harlech Castle*

Scotland

Regional maps – ©*MAPS IN MINUTES*™ *2001.*

Edinburgh & The South East - *Dunbar*

Fife - *St. Andrews*

Tayside - *Dunkeld & Birnam*

Grampian - *Stonehaven Harbour*

Highlands & Islands - *Brora*

Glasgow & South West - *Kilchurn Castle, Loch Awe*

Ireland

Regional maps Eire & Northern Ireland – ©*MAPS IN MINUTES*™ *2001.* ©*Crown Copyright, Ordnance Survey Northern Ireland 2001 Permit No. NI 1675 &* ©*Government of Ireland, Ordnance Survey Ireland.*

Dublin & The North East – *The Island Club*

Midlands – *Mount Juliet*

Northern Ireland – *Royal County Down*

North West – *Ballyliffin*

South West – *Waterville*

South East – *Old Head*

Introduction

W elcome to Golfing Gems, the leading guide to the best courses of
Britain & Ireland. *Courses featured pay no entry fee – they are selected
purely on merit.*

Designed to appeal to those golfers who are happy to explore new areas in their
love of the game, Golfing Gems guides you to over 200 wonderful clubs each of
which, we believe, is a delight to play. The courses selected may not necessarily be
the longest, their club houses may not be the most luxurious, however, they all
offer value for money and every one is representative of the great traditions of
Golf, presenting a fair and testing challenge, a courteous welcome to visitors and
the opportunity to savour beautiful scenery. The information supplied is concise
and relevant with superb photographs to give you a feel for the course and a
commentary written by leading golf writers who know the courses well.

Keep the guide close to hand; it will become an essential companion when
travelling on business or pleasure. The hotels featured have, in nearly all cases,
been recommended by the relevant golf club and we feel sure that you will find
them an excellent place to stay. Often the proprietors are keen golfers themselves
ensuring good local knowledge and a steady supply of sympathy!

Each year the listings are reviewed to ensure that the selection is a fair one.
To help us in this task, we are eager to receive any comments you may have.
Please contact us using the forms provided at the back of this book or by e-mail
via our website *www.golfingguides.net*, we will be delighted to hear from you.

Happy golfing!

International Dialling Codes

From UK to Eire	00353	(delete first 0 of local number)
From Eire to NI	0044	(delete first 0 of local number)
From USA to Eire	011353	(delete first 0 of local number)
From USA to UK	001144	(delete first 0 of local number)

Southern England

Southern England

It has been suggested that 'South of England' is more a state of mind than a geographical expression. But for present purposes it encompasses golf in Hampshire, Sussex and Kent (from the New Forest to the White Cliffs), Greater London and the Home Counties (the 'Old Smoke' and its surrounds) and Berkshire, Buckinghamshire and Oxfordshire (from the tip of the Chilterns to the edge of the Cotswolds).

Hampshire is one of those counties that is particularly adept at burying its golfing treasure. You never associate it with links golf and yet there is a very fine, almost forgotten, championship links on Hayling Island. You cannot imagine that there could be a beautiful golf course in the depths of the New Forest – until you stumble across Brokenhurst Manor, and you are convinced that all the superior heathland courses are in Surrey and Berkshire – until you have played at Liphook or Blackmoor.

Sussex and Kent are much better known for their golf. With apologies to Rye, Sussex is celebrated for its inland golf and Kent for its links courses. The jewel of West Sussex is undoubtedly Pulborough (the West Sussex Golf Club) but there are many other fine courses in the county, including the delightful Waterfall Course at Mannings Heath. East Sussex has Royal Ashdown Forest and Crowborough Beacon, two extremely pleasant moorland type courses at which you should avoid the gorse at all costs.

Kent's golfing reputation has been built around a three mile stretch of linksland between St Margaret's Bay and Pegwell Bay. Here is where you find Royal St George's, Royal Cinque Ports (Deal) and Prince's. Another fine Kent links – often overlooked – is Littlestone, situated towards Romney Marsh. Since the late 1980s several new courses have been built in Kent and Sussex, the two outstanding examples of which are Chart Hills at Biddenden and East Sussex National near Uckfield.

Good golf within Greater London itself is limited. The best course with a London post code is probably Royal Wimbledon, and the most historic is Royal Blackheath. But a magnificent stretch of golfing country lies only a

short distance to the south and west of the capital. This is the heath country of Surrey (predominantly) and Berkshire, and it is comparable in quality to the great sandbelt of Melbourne. It is a golfing kingdom of pines, heather and silver birch. The most famous heathland courses are Sunningdale, Wentworth, Walton Heath and The Berkshire, but there are at least another twenty in the vicinity, and among the finest of these are St George's Hill, The Addington, Hankley Common, New Zealand and 'the three Ws', Woking, Worplesdon and West Hill.

The scores of parkland courses that fringe the city are rather ordinary by comparison. There are, of course, a handful of exceptions. Circling clockwise from the heathland region, in southern Buckinghamshire, Stoke Poges and Denham are both decidedly worth inspecting; in Hertfordshire, Moor Park has two courses and (like Stoke Poges) a remarkably palatial clubhouse, but Ashridge may be the best 'traditional' course in the county and Hanbury Manor is the star of the modern generation. Essex has a very modest golfing reputation. The county's leading course is probably Thorndon Park, while Langley Park is the pick of the 'London absorbed' Kent courses. Further to the north of London, yet still well within striking distance, is the redoubtable Woburn Golf and Country Club on the borders of Buckinghamshire and Bedfordshire. There are now three first rate courses here with the Duke's, Duchess and Marquis Courses, and also three at Frilford Heath in Oxfordshire. With its Red, Green and Blue Courses – all heathland gems – Frilford is the outstanding golf club near Oxford. Huntercombe is another firm favourite and Tadmarton Heath enjoys splendid isolation in the far north west of the county.

ASHRIDGE	MANNINGS HEATH
BROKENHURST MANOR	PRINCE'S
CHART HILLS	ROYAL ASHDOWN FOREST
CROWBOROUGH BEACON	ST GEORGES HILL
FRILFORD HEATH	TADMARTON HEATH
HAYLING	WEST SUSSEX
LITTLESTONE	

Southern England

12

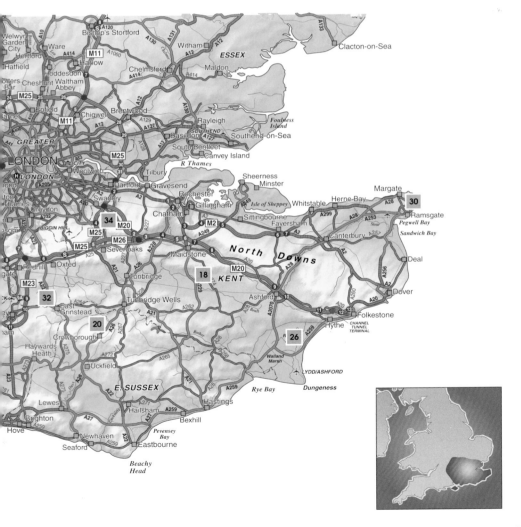

Ashridge

It is probably safe to say that the three finest ever English golfers have been Harry Vardon, Henry Cotton and Nick Faldo. Cotton's dominant period unfortunately coincided with the Second World War: he won the first of his three Open Championships in 1934 and the third in 1948. And Cotton's connection with Ashridge? For much of his 'dominant period' he was the Professional attached to the Club - Ashridge in leafy Hertfordshire was Henry Cotton's home.

Cotton joined Ashridge just five years after the Club's formation in 1932. The 18 hole golf course was laid out by Sir Guy Campbell and Colonel Hotchkin and later refined by Tom Simpson. It is one of England's loveliest courses and is always beautifully maintained. Strictly speaking it is a parkland layout, although many of the holes have a heathland feel to them. Parkland or heathland, the terrain is ideal for golf and the design makes the most of a wonderfully undulating landscape.

Ashridge has something of a reputation for 'flattering' golfers. You are certainly encouraged to play well with several fairways running through valleys which tend to gather tee shots - the first couple of holes being prime examples. Among the outstanding holes at Ashridge are the 2nd, a very handsome par five; the 9th, where the green is perched on a shelf of land overlooking the clubhouse; the 14th, which is often described as a miniature version of the Road Hole at St Andrews, and the rollercoasting 18th, with its vast, two-tiered green.

HOW TO GET THERE

5 miles north of
Berkhamsted on B4506.

Ashridge
Golf Club

COURSE INFORMATION & FACILITIES

Ashridge Golf Club
Little Gaddesden,Berkhamsted,Hertfordshire HP4 1LY
Secretary: Martin S Silver
Tel: 01442 842244 Fax: 01442 843770
Email: info@ashridgegolfclub.ltd.uk
Web: www.ashridgegolfclub.ltd.uk

Golf Professional Tel: 01442 842307

Green Fees: Weekdays — Weekends — N/A
Weekdays (day) On application. Weekends (day) N/A

Restrictions: None except weekends, but all bookings
through Secretary

CARD OF THE COURSE — PAR 72

1	2	3	4	5	6	7	8	9	Out
391	505	167	412	492	190	400	185	361	3103
Par 4	Par 5	Par 3	Par 4	Par 5	Par 3	Par 4	Par 3	Par 4	Par 35

10	11	12	13	14	15	16	17	18	In
355	165	405	476	431	513	185	482	432	3444
Par 4	Par 3	Par 4	Par 5	Par 4	Par 5	Par 3	Par 5	Par 4	Par 37

Brokenhurst Manor

*H*arry Colt provided the architecture, William the Conqueror was responsible for the backdrop, and somebody, who shall be nameless, got the spelling wrong.

Brokenhurst is located in the village of Brockenhurst! Yes, they left the 'c' out of Brockenhurst when they decided to add the 'Manor'. As for William the Conqueror, it was apparently his idea to plant the New Forest, and it is on the edge of this beautiful part of Hampshire that Brokenhurst Manor is found.

It is a wonderful and very natural setting for golf, and so when, soon after the First World War, Harry Colt was invited to lay out an 18 hole course there was really very little he needed to do. Fortunately, Colt (unlike a few modern golf course architects) knew instinctively when to apply his skills and when to leave well alone. The result, then, is an extremely natural looking golf course.

Of medium length, rather unusually the course comprises 'three loops of six', and there is a nice blend of parkland and woodland type holes. A winding stream comes into play on a number of occasions, introducing itself as early as the 2nd. This hole is one of two very good par fives, the other being the 16th. The par threes at Brokenhurst are quite varied, the pick of the bunch perhaps being the 5th, while among the most interesting of the two-shotters are the 4th (a very difficult-to-read green here), the short but tricky 14th and the dog-legged 17th.

HOW TO GET THERE

From Southampton proceed along the M27 towards Ringwood, take turning off for Lyndhurst and then follow the signs for Brockenhurst.

Brokenhurst
Manor
Golf Club

COURSE INFORMATION & FACILITIES

Brokenhurst Manor Golf Club
Sway Road, Brockenhurst,
Hants. SO42 7SG

Secretary/Manager: Paul Clifford
Tel: 01590 623332   Fax: 01590 624140

Golf Professional Bruce Parker Tel:01590 623092

Green Fees:
Weekdays — £35 Weekends — £45
Weekdays (days) £45 Weekends (day) £60

CARD OF THE COURSE — PAR 70

1	2	3	4	5	6	7	8	9	Out
316	504	173	376	163	324	377	446	459	3138
Par 4	Par 5	Par 3	Par 4	Par 3	Par 4	Par 4	Par 4	Par 4	Par 35

10	11	12	13	14	15	16	17	18	In
213	401	171	420	295	316	516	421	331	3084
Par 3	Par 4	Par 3	Par 4	Par 4	Par 4	Par 5	Par 4	Par 4	Par 35

Chart Hills

*I*magine a setting in the heart of the Kent countryside where ancient oak trees stand proud. Imagine a golf course that has clusters of fairway bunkers reminiscent of those at Royal Melbourne; where the fairways comprise a variety of sweeping dog-legs and island sanctuaries; where holes twist and tumble downhill in an almost links like fashion towards huge contoured greens, and where entry to the putting surfaces is protected by winding creeks and steep pot bunkers similar to Carnoustie and Muirfield. This is Chart Hills.

Designed by Nick Faldo and Steve Smyers, Chart Hills rivals Loch Lomond as Britain's finest new course. In terms of scenery Loch Lomond is far superior (but then it compares favourably with

almost every course on the planet), and nor does Chart Hills have the magnificent natural terrain of a Sunningdale or a Woodhall Spa; however the quality of the layout is second to none. This becomes apparent from the moment you step on to the 1st tee and confront the extraordinary 599 yards par five opening hole.

The 1st at Chart Hills incorporates many, if not most of the design features described in the first paragraph. And the challenge continues as dramatic holes are followed by more subtle ones with constant changes in direction and elevation. Among other outstanding holes at Chart Hills are the 4th, 6th, 8th and 9th and, on the back nine, perhaps the finest sequence of all, the 12th, 13th and 14th.

HOW TO GET THERE

M25 — M20. Take junction 8 on M20 and follow signs towards Leeds Castle. Pass Leeds Castle on left and keep going through Leeds Village. Turn left at T-Junction towards Tenterden (now on A274). Continue through Sutton Valence and Headcorn, after which you will pass Unigate complex on right and then Garages also on right. Take first left after garage into Weeks Lane. Club entrance is on left.

Chart Hills
Golf Course

COURSE INFORMATION & FACILITIES

Chart Hills Golf Club
Weeks Lane, Biddenden
Kent TN27 8JX

General Manager: Roger Hyder
Tel: 01580 292222 Fax: 01580 292233

Golf Professional:
Tel: 01580 292148 Fax: 01580 292118

Green Fees per 18 holes per day:
Weekdays — £60 Weekends — £65

CARD OF THE COURSE — PAR 72

1	2	3	4	5	6	7	8	9	Out
599	459	183	424	511	309	206	439	365	3495
Par 5	Par 4	Par 3	Par 4	Par 5	Par 4	Par 3	Par 4	Par 4	Par 36

10	11	12	13	14	15	16	17	18	In
453	215	536	426	402	481	482	147	449	3591
Par 4	Par 3	Par 5	Par 4	Par 4	Par 4	Par 5	Par 3	Par 4	Par 36

Crowborough Beacon

Could this be the finest prospect from any clubhouse in England? You find yourself asking this question when you stand on the terrace at Crowborough Beacon and gaze out across the course and over the Weald of Sussex and the South Downs. On a clear day in June, when there is a glimpse of the sea through Birling Gap, the answer may be, 'yes'. The creator of Sherlock Holmes must have posed this (elementary) question many times, for Sir Arther Conan Doyle was Captain of Crowborough Beacon Golf Club in 1910.

Situated 800 feet above sea level on the edge of Ashdown Forest, Crowborough is an undulating moorland course which like Gleneagles, has many heathland characteristics.

Stately pines and fir trees are scattered throughout the course and there is plenty of heather and gorse. The gorse in particular is often allowed to run riot... which is all very nice to look at but it can be a devil to play out of.

Generally speaking, Crowborough will test your accuracy more than your length off the tee: there aren't too many bunkers but the fairways are narrow and the greens invariably on the small size.

The feature holes are the par four 2nd, a sweeping 'bite off as much as you dare' dog-leg to the right with a deep gully in front of the green and the 6th, a very intimidating yet scenically spectacular par three played across a vast gorge to an angled green beautifully framed by trees and rhododendron bushes.

COURSE INFORMATION & FACILITIES

Crowborough Beacon Golf Club
Beacon Road, Crowborough,
East Sussex TN6 1UJ

Secretary: Mrs. V Harwood
Tel: 01892 661511 Professional: 01892 653877

Green Fees per 18 holes per day:
Weekdays — £25 Weekends — £30
Weekdays (day) — £40
Society Rates: from £45.25 inc lunch

CARD OF THE COURSE — PAR 71

1	2	3	4	5	6	7	8	9	Out
388	448	143	358	357	190	506	324	392	3106
Par 4	Par 4	Par 3	Par 4	Par 4	Par 3	Par 5	Par 4	Par 4	Par 35

10	11	12	13	14	15	16	17	18	In
495	328	413	141	498	366	342	144	438	3167
Par 5	Par 4	Par 4	Par 3	Par 5	Par 4	Par 4	Par 3	Par 4	Par 36

HOW TO GET THERE

From Tunbridge Wells A26 to Uckfield — drive through Crowborough, across Traffic lights Clubhouse is 1 mile on left.

From Uckfield A22 turn right onto A26, Clubhouse 5-6 miles on right.

East Grinstead A22 towards Nutley, turn left at signpost to Crowborough continue to meet A26.
Turn left onto A26 Clubhouse 1 mile on right.

Crowborough
Beacon

Frilford Heath

*O*f all the great heathland venues in Britain, Frilford Heath may be the most underrated. For some reason its courses are often overlooked by the various panels that rank the nation's best. This may have something to do with the fact that it is located in an unfashionable area for golf courses and is a little off the beaten track – Bernard Darwin once called Frilford Heath, 'A wonderful oasis in a desert of mud'. Like Little Aston, it is reached via an ancient Roman road. A second reason is that the powers within the club are probably content with its quiet profile and not inclined or adept at singing its praises. And thirdly, commentators find it difficult to determine which course is the jewel in Frilford's crown. Is it the Red Course or the Green Course? Or, since 1994, could it be the new Blue Course?

Yes, there are now 54 holes of golf at Frilford Heath. The courses, to adopt an Irishism, are similar yet different. All three are undoubtedly heathland courses, with sandy subsoil and heather running throughout. In terms of appearance the Red and Green courses resemble one another closely for both are very mature and their architectural styles similar. However the Red Course is much longer while the Green has the greater number of 'pretty' holes (including some very picturesque par threes). The Blue Course is of a similar length to the Red but has a modern design. It features several water hazards and a host of large strategically placed fairway bunkers.

HOW TO GET THERE

From North: Junction 9 off M40 to A34 and Oxford. At Botley junction on A34 take A420 towards Swindon. After approximately 5 miles on the A420 take left turn off dual carriageway onto A338 to Wantage. Frilford Heath Golf Club is about 2 miles on right. From South: Junction 8 off M40 follow A40 to Oxford. Take A34 ringroad to Botley junction, then as above

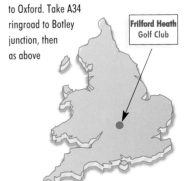

Frilford Heath
Golf Club

COURSE INFORMATION & FACILITIES

Frilford Heath Golf Club
Abingdon,
Oxon OX13 5NW

Secretary: S. Styles.
Tel: 01865 390864 Fax: 01865 390823
Email: reservations@frilfordheath.co.uk
web: www.frilfordheath.co.uk

Golf Professional Tel: 01865 390887

Green Fees:
Summer/Weekdays (day) — £50 Weekends (day) — £65
Winter/Weekdays (day) — £37.50 Weekends (day) — £52.50
Handicap Certificate required

CARD OF THE RED COURSE — PAR 73

1	2	3	4	5	6	7	8	9	Out
376	524	407	193	421	477	388	442	183	3411
Par 4	Par 5	Par 4	Par 3	Par 4	Par 5	Par 4	Par 4	Par 3	Par 36

10	11	12	13	14	15	16	17	18	In
526	147	486	361	328	394	307	358	313	3220
Par 5	Par 3	Par 5	Par 4	Par 4	Par 4	Par 4	Par 4	Par 4	Par 37

Hayling

*I*t has been called 'The poor man's Rye', but Tom Simpson, one of golf's greatest architects, once described the duneland at Hayling as, 'The best linksland in Britain'.

Founded in 1883, and very fashionable in the early part of this century, Hayling has become something of a forgotten links. Its setting is unusual rather than remote. It occupies the southern tip of Hayling Island (which is linked by road to the mainland) and stares across The Solent to the Isle of Wight. Hayling is a traditional links with firm fairways and fast greens; it is raw and rugged, although its present day moonscape appearance owes much to the fact that it was heavily bombed during the War.

The eccentric genius, Tom Simpson (you may have guessed) was largely responsible for the design of the course. A man who travelled everywhere by chauffeur driven Rolls Royce and was responsible for the amazing routing of Cruden Bay was never likely to deliver a humdrum layout, and Hayling is certainly not that. The course starts out quietly but quickly gathers momentum. The finest sequence of holes – and the most spectacular duneland – occurs between the 10th and 13th. The 10th is an interesting short par four which can be driven (a fourball once recorded scores of 1, 2, 3, and 4); the 11th is an outstanding par three with a lovely plateau green; the 12th is a mighty two-shotter running parallel to the shore, and the charming, 'up and over' 13th features a massive bunker known as 'The Widow'.

HOW TO GET THERE

From M27, (A3(M) and A27. Leave the A27 at the Havant/Hayling Island Junction and follow the main road (A3023) over Langstone Bridge onto the Island. Continue to roundabout, take second exit. Continue 1 mile to roundabout, take second exit. After 3/4 mile entrance is on left opposite Sinah Lane.

Hayling Golf Club

COURSE INFORMATION & FACILITIES

Hayling Golf Club
Links Lane, Hayling Island
Hampshire PO11 0BX.

Secretary: Chris Cavill.
Tel: 01705 464446.

Golf Professional Ray Gadd Tel: 01705 464491.

Green Fees:

Weekdays — £28. Weekends — £35.
Weekdays (day) — £33. Weekends (day) — £45.
Handicap certificate required. Some time restrictions.

CARD OF THE COURSE — PAR 71

1	2	3	4	5	6	7	8	9	Out
179	495	398	410	163	434	505	352	414	3350
Par 3	Par 5	Par 4	Par 4	Par 3	Par 4	Par 5	Par 4	Par 4	Par 36

10	11	12	13	14	15	16	17	18	In
270	157	444	341	534	430	178	432	385	3171
Par 4	Par 3	Par 4	Par 4	Par 5	Par 4	Par 3	Par 4	Par 4	Par 35

Littlestone

*T*he most commonly adopted description of Littlestone is 'overshadowed' - its qualities kept in the shade by the brighter and greater reputations of Royal St George's, Deal and Prince's, all situated further east along the Kent coast. But then Littlestone was never destined to be famous, for its location, adjacent to Romney Marsh is both stark and remote. There is an almost medieval feel to this part of Kent - an ancient, forgotten land.

Littlestone Golf Club was founded in 1888. The course was initially designed by Laidlaw Purves and revised by James Braid early this century. Although the site does incorporate an impressive range of sandhills, the course is essentially quite flat and, consequently, uneven lies and awkward stances are rarely encountered. What determines a player's strategy at Littlestone is the course's expert bunkering and the strength and direction of the wind: what you see (and feel !) at Littlestone is what you get.

The course opens benignly with a short, straightaway par four. This is followed by a testing two-shotter, but in truth the first six holes are mere appetisers. The sequence from the 7th to the 11th is full of variety and interest while the two most outstanding holes are undoubtedly the 16th and 17th. The former is a long, uphill, dog-legging par four with an elusive green that is both raised and heavily contoured; as for the 17th, it is a classic links par three, its green blending into a wonderfully natural dune setting.

HOW TO GET THERE

From Junction 10 on M20 take A2070 to Brenzett. A259 to New Romney — turn right on B2071 to Littlestone. After 1¼ miles turn left in Madeira Rd. The clubhouse is to your left front after 400 yds.

Littlestone Golf Club

COURSE INFORMATION & FACILITIES

Littlestone Golf Club
St. Andrews Road, Littlestone, New Romney, Kent TN28 8RB

Secretary: Colonel Charles Moorhouse
Tel: 01797 363355   Fax: 01l797 362740
Email: secretary@littlestonegolfclub.org.uk
Web: www.littlestonegolfclub.org.uk

Golf Professional Tel: 01797 362231

Green Fees:
Weekdays — £35 Weekends — £45
Weekdays (days) £46 Weekends (day) £55
Restrictions: Very little scope for weekend visitors.

CARD OF THE COURSE — PAR 71

1	2	3	4	5	6	7	8	9	Out
300	407	398	371	493	159	506	382	174	3190
Par 4	Par 4	Par 4	Par 4	Par 5	Par 3	Par 5	Par 4	Par 3	Par 36

10	11	12	13	14	15	16	17	18	In
417	377	393	409	187	363	469	182	499	3296
Par 4	Par 4	Par 4	Par 4	Par 3	Par 4	Par 4	Par 3	Par 5	Par 35

Mannings Heath

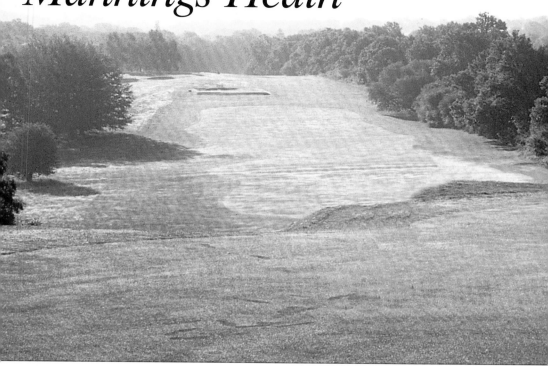

Nestling amid beautiful countryside on the edge of the Downs, Mannings Heath is one of the most attractively situated golf clubs in southern England. It was founded in 1905 and for the best part of a century has enjoyed a reputation as 'the hidden jewel of Sussex'. But two recent developments have ensured that Mannings Heath is unlikely to remain quite so 'hidden' in the future.

Within the last decade or so the Club has acquired new owners, who in turn have provided a new clubhouse. This buiding - a magnificently restored manor house known as Fullers - is arguably the finest 19th hole in the country. From a lofty perch it provides commanding views across the rolling fairways of the Waterfall Course.

The second reason is that since 1996 Mannings Heath has offered 36 holes of golf. Just as Sunningdale has an Old and a New, and East Sussex an East and a West, so Mannings Heath now has the Kingfisher Course to complement the Waterfall Course. The Club can hardly remain a 'hidden' jewel when it has so much to offer the visiting golfer.

The new course is maturing rapidly but the Waterfall Course - presently in better condition than ever - remains the premier attraction. It comprises an interesting mix of woodland, parkland and heathland holes. The terrain is naturally undulating throughout, mature trees line the majority of fairways, and water, in the form of a winding stream, affects at least half of the holes.

HOW TO GET THERE

From London: Take A24 south from Dorking. At Broadbridge Heath near Horsham turn left on to A281 towards Mannings Heath where Golf Course can be found.

Mannings Heath Golf Club

COURSE INFORMATION & FACILITIES

Mannings Heath Golf Club
Fullers, Hammerpond Road, Mannings Heath, Horsham, West Sussex RH13 6PG

General Manager: John Curtis
Tel: 01403 210228 Fax: 01403 270974

Golf Professional: Tel: 01403 210228

Green Fees:
Weekdays (18 holes) — £32. Weekends — £40
Weekdays (36 holes) — (days) £42
Weekends (36 holes) — (day) £55

CARD OF THE COURSE — PAR 68

1	2	3	4	5	6	7	8	9	Out
325	289	399	372	184	377	425	499	376	3246
Par 4	Par 4	Par 4	Par 4	Par 3	Par 4	Par 4	Par 5	Par 4	Par 36

10	11	12	13	14	15	16	17	18	In
141	368	368	486	153	247	466	487	416	3132
Par 3	Par 4	Par 4	Par 5	Par 3	Par 4	Par 5	Par 5	Par 4	Par 37

Prince's

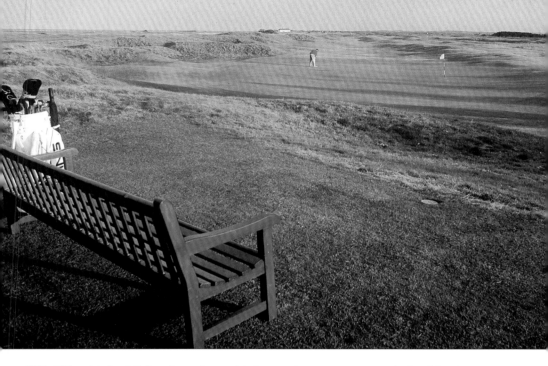

You think of Prince's and you think of Gene Sarazen. 'The Squire', as he is affectionately known, was the first golfer to win all four of the game's Major championships; he was the player who 'made' the Masters when he holed a four wood for an albatross two at the 15th en route to winning at Augusta in 1935; at the ripe old age of 71 he holed-in-one at the 8th, the famous 'Postage Stamp', during the 1973 Open Championship at Troon, and it was Sarazen who won the Championship in 1932 on the one occasion it was held at Prince's.

Situated 'next door' to Royal St George's on the Kent coast at Sandwich, Prince's has the kind of geography and terrain that made it an ideal site for war time manoeuvres; indeed in the immediate post war years there was talk of Prince's becoming a permanent military training base. But, happily for golfers, in 1950 the links was restored to its former glory – although not as an 18 hole Championship course, rather as a layout comprising 27 holes, the present day three loops of nine.

With windswept plateaued greens, rippling fairways and tangling rough, each of the nines at Prince's (the Himalayas, Shore and Dunes) presents a daunting test of traditional links golf. It is hard to say which is the best nine but a selection of the finest holes might include the 2nd, 7th and 8th from the Himalayas, the 3rd, 6th and 9th from the Shore and the 3rd, 4th and 6th from the Dunes.

COURSE INFORMATION & FACILITIES

Prince's Golf Club
Sandwich Bay, Sandwich
Kent CT13 9QB

Secretary: Ali McGuirk
Tel: 01304 611118 Fax: 01304 612000

Golf Professional Tel: 01304 613797

Green Fees per 18 holes per day:
Weekdays — £45 Weekends: £55
Weekdays (day) — £55 Weekends (day) — £65

CARD OF THE COURSE (Shore/Dunes)

1	2	3	4	5	6	7	8	9	Out
420	485	161	385	377	393	538	176	412	3347
Par 4	Par 5	Par 3	Par 4	Par 4	Par 4	Par 5	Par 3	Par 4	Par 36

10	11	12	13	14	15	16	17	18	In
440	147	484	400	406	487	363	200	416	3343
Par 4	Par 3	Par 5	Par 4	Par 4	Par 5	Par 4	Par 3	Par 4	Par 36

HOW TO GET THERE

M25, A2, M2, A2, A256 to
Sandwich.
Turn right into St George s
Road before Elf service
station, then right into
Sandown Road, through
tollgate into Sandwich Bay
Estate, then left into Kings
Avenue, turn left at Seafront
and continue
along to
Prince's.

Prince's
Golf Club

Royal Ashdown Forest

't is only at the end of a round that we realise with a pleasurable shock that there is not a single hideous rampart or so much as a pot bunker'. Bernard Darwin made the observation back in 1910 but it is one that remains true today. Royal Ashdown Forest is the one outstanding course in the British Isles that doesn't possess any bunkers. And yet, anyone anticipating a gentle ride when they visit this golf course had better think again: Royal Ashdown poses a challenge that is at once stern and stimulating.

Gloriously situated on the fringes of Ashdown Forest (the celebrated home of Winnie the Pooh), Royal Ashdown can properly be described as a moorland course. It is quite similar in appearance to the famous heathland layouts of

Berkshire and Surrey but it doesn't have their sandy subsoil. The principal hazards are an abundance of heather and gorse, a fine mix of trees – which not only frame the fairways but occasionally encroach – and a meandering brook. The natural contours of the landscape contribute greatly to a rare golfing experience.

The most cunningly conceived hole at Royal Ashdown is undoubtedly the 6th, a short par three where, thanks to the aforementioned brook, the only place to be is on the green. The par fours, however, are the real strength of Royal Ashdown and the best of these two-shot holes is arguably the 17th which features a very searching but exhilarating downhill appproach.

COURSE INFORMATION & FACILITIES

Royal Ashdown Forest Golf Club
Chapel Lane, Forest Row,
East Sussex RH18 5LR

Secretary: D J Scrivens
Tel: 01342 822018 Fax: 01342 825211

Golf Professional Tel: 01342 822247

Green Fees per 18 holes per day:
Weekdays — £42
Weekdays (day) — £45 Weekends (day) — £60

Letter of introduction required.

CARD OF THE COURSE — PAR 72

1	2	3	4	5	6	7	8	9	Out
332	384	334	356	512	128	372	501	143	3062
Par 4	Par 4	Par 4	Par 4	Par 5	Par 3	Par 4	Par 5	Par 3	Par 36

10	11	12	13	14	15	16	17	18	In
485	249	568	367	202	312	407	473	352	3415
Par 5	Par 3	Par 5	Par 4	Par 3	Par 4	Par 4	Par 4	Par 4	Par 36

HOW TO GET THERE

Four miles south of East Grinstead. Take B2110 (off A22) in Forest Row and after half mile turn right into Chapel Lane. Bear left at top of Chapel Lane. From M25 take junction 6 (A22 turn off) then as above.

Royal Ashdown
Golf Club

St. George's Hill

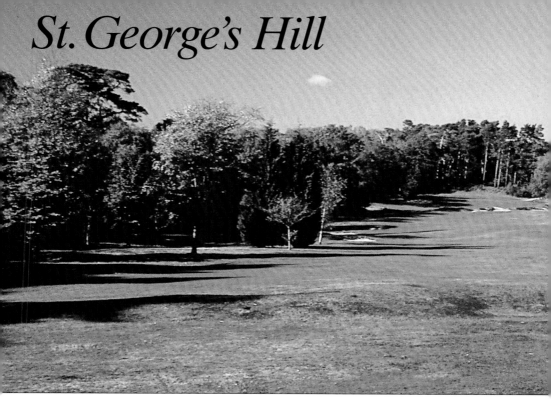

Developed before the First World War, St. George's Hill near Weybridge is England's prototype golf course and residential estate. It is also, in the opinion of many, the most enjoyable, most spectacular and potentially the best of all the Surrey heathland courses.

The last comment is a bold statement and one likely to be ridiculed by every member of Sunningdale and Walton Heath. But the claim of St. George's Hill is a valid one. In many ways it is course architect Harry Colt's masterpiece. Certainly nowhere did he have such a beautifully undulating, sweeping piece of land to work with. The terrain is classic heathland: sandy underfoot (erupting here and there), heather all around and

a magnificent spread of tall pines. To appreciate the full glory of St. George's Hill one need only stand on the terrace of the vast, imposing clubhouse. On a fine summer's evening there is no finer sight in golf. Yet, for all Colt's achievement, it is the naturally dramatic nature of the landscape that distinguishes St. George's Hill.

There are, in fact, 27 holes, for the main 18 hole layout is complemented by an excellent 'full length' nine hole course. Among the greatest holes on the main course are the 2nd (a long and beautifully flowing par four), the 8th (an heroic short hole across a heathery valley), the 10th (a rollercoasting two-shotter with an extraordinarily sloping green), the picturesque 12th (deep amid the pines) and the 14th, another stunning par three.

HOW TO GET THERE

M25 come off junction 10, take A3 signposted to London. After $\frac{1}{2}$ mile take first main exit on left A245 signposted to Woking after $1\frac{1}{2}$ miles mini roundabout B374 turn right Brooklands one mile turn right St George's Hill estate.

St. George's Hill
Golf Club

COURSE INFORMATION & FACILITIES

St. George's Hill Golf Club
Golf Club Road, St. George's Hill
Weybridge, Surrey KT13 0NL

Secretary: John Robinson
Tel: 01932 847758 Fax: 01932 821564

Golf Professional Tel: 01932 843523

Green Fees:
Weekdays — £60 Weekdays (day) — £80

CARD OF THE COURSE — PAR 70

1	2	3	4	5	6	7	8	9	Out
384	468	199	278	393	474	476	179	377	3228
Par 4	Par 4	Par 3	Par 4	Par 4	Par 4	Par 5	Par 3	Par 4	Par 35

10	11	12	13	14	15	16	17	18	In
442	113	351	431	210	539	440	422	393	3341
Par 4	Par 3	Par 4	Par 4	Par 3	Par 5	Par 4	Par 4	Par 4	Par 35

Tadmarton Heath

The Romans encamped here. During the Second World War it was a training ground for tanks. Today peace and tranquility reign. By central England standards Tadmarton Heath enjoys a wonderfully remote setting. It is located six miles from Banbury Cross in a quiet corner of north west Oxfordshire – east of the Cotswolds and north of the Chilterns.

Tadmarton Heath Golf Club was founded in 1922. Harry Vardon advised on the layout and C K Hutchison brought it to fruition. It can properly be described as a heathland course, for although there is not a great deal of heather, it is quite sandy underfoot, moreover gorse envelops the back nine. Occupying high ground (650 feet above sea level at its highest point)

Tadmarton is fairly exposed: on windy days the course sets a tough examination; on calm days it is an idyllic spot.

Unless the wind is particularly fierce, Tadmarton Heath will not test the length of your drives. It will, however, severely punish anything that strays too far from the fairway. The course begins with a loop of seven holes close to the clubhouse, which, incidentally, is a converted Cotswold stone farm building. The most interesting of the early holes is the 5th, a tightly bunkered par five, and the 7th, a charming short hole which is played across the waters of Tadmarton's celebrated Holy Well. On the back nine – deep amidst the gorse – among the most memorable holes are the impish 10th, the dog-legged 14th and the deceptively tricky 17th.

HOW TO GET THERE

M40 Junction 11. Banbury
A361 to Chipping Norton,
at Banbury Cross take B4035
to Shipston on Stour. Travel
4.5 miles. At Tadmarton turn
up hill to Wigginton Heath.
Course is on left after
1 mile.

Tadmarton Heath
Golf Club

COURSE INFORMATION & FACILITIES

Tadmarton Heath Golf Club
Wigginton, Banbury
Oxon OX15 5HL

Secretary: R E Wackrill
Tel: 01608 737278. Fax: 01608 730548

Golf Professional Tel: 01608 730047

Green Fees:
Weekdays — £28 Weekends — £30 (with Member)
Weekdays (pm) — £18

CARD OF THE COURSE — PAR 69

1	2	3	4	5	6	7	8	9	Out
328	350	155	410	484	350	139	330	440	2986
Par 4	Par 4	Par 3	Par 4	Par 5	Par 4	Par 3	Par 4	Par 4	Par 35

10	11	12	13	14	15	16	17	18	In
117	339	400	431	376	288	178	365	437	2931
Par 3	Par 4	Par 4	Par 4	Par 4	Par 4	Par 3	Par 4	Par 4	Par 34

West Sussex

Find it an extra 300 yards and you'd have a second Sunningdale; find it an extra 600 yards and you'd have another Woodhall Spa. West Sussex, or Pulborough, as it is more commonly known, is a magnificent and largely undiscovered heathland classic.

Like the Old Course at Sunningdale, West Sussex occupies a wonderfully undulating site. The climbs are never severe but the fairways continually rise and fall in thrilling fashion; they also meander their way through forests of pine, oak and silver birch, with purple heather and splashes of silver sand defining the fairways. It is a breathtakingly beautiful place. Length apart, the similarities with Woodhall Spa are equally apparent. Both courses are renowned for the quality of their bunkering. At Woodhall Spa the traps are plentiful and cavernous; at Pulborough they are plentiful and superbly positioned. Again, like Woodhall Spa, the surrouding countryside, i.e. the land immediately beyond the golf course, is unexceptional. Woodhall Spa and West Sussex are the two great oases of English golf.

There is not a weak hole on the course but among the most memorable are the 4th, the 10th (where the bunkering is reminiscent of Royal Melbourne), the 12th, 13th and 16th, and the outstanding sequence between the 5th and 7th – Pulborough's 'Amen Corner' and arguably the most scenic run of holes on any inland course in the British Isles. Yes, they are that special!

HOW TO GET THERE

1 mile South East of Pulborough on the A283 Pulborough to Storrington Road.

West Sussex
Golf Club

COURSE INFORMATION & FACILITIES

West Sussex Golf Club
Golf Club Lane, Wiggonholt
Pulborough, W. Sussex RH20 2EN

Secretary: Colin Simpson
Tel: 01798 872563 Fax: 01798 872033

Golf Professional Tel: 01798 872426

Green Fees per 18 holes per day:
Weekdays — £45 Weekends — £50
Weekdays (day) — £55 Weekends (day) — £60
Letter of introduction or handicap certificate required.

CARD OF THE COURSE — PAR 68

1	2	3	4	5	6	7	8	9	Out
485	413	365	382	144	224	440	183	351	2987
Par 5	Par 4	Par 4	Par 4	Par 3	Par 3	Par 4(5)	Par 3	Par 4	Par 34

10	11	12	13	14	15	16	17	18	In
401	448	219	382	429	143	360	441	413	3236
Par 4	Par 4(5)	Par 3	Par 4	Par 4	Par 3	Par 4	Par 4	Par 4	Par 34

West Country

The West Country

*W*ith an impish twinkle in his eye, a Cornishman will tell you that the west country starts at the Tamar and finishes at Lands End. For us it includes the counties of Cornwall and Devon, Somerset and Dorset, Gloucestershire and Wiltshire – King Arthur's Kingdom, if legend is to be believed.

A map of Cornwall resembles a miniature mirror image of Italy. You are never far from the sea in Cornwall, and you are never far from a golf course. The wilder, more rugged northern coast has many splendid holiday courses – four of the best being West Cornwall (at Lelant), Trevose, Bude & North Cornwall and, finest of all, the classic links at St Enodoc. On the south coast there is picturesque Mullion, two courses at Falmouth, two at St Austell, and, a little inland, a good parkland course at Lanhydrock near Bodmin and, beyond Saltash, St Mellion and the extraordinary course that Jack built.

With beaches to the north, beaches to the south and Dartmoor in the middle, it is little wonder that Devon is known as 'Glorious Devon'. Golfwise it has two outstanding links courses on its northern coast: historic Royal North Devon at Westward Ho! and the terrific championship links at Saunton. The moorland charms of the Manor House Hotel course at Moretonhampstead is no longer golf's best kept secret but the heathland-come-clifftop course at Budleigh Salterton (East Devon) may be just that. East Devon surely rivals the Isle of Purbeck and Bamburgh Castle as the most scenic course in England. Also on the south Devon coast, there are inspiring views from the courses at Thurlestone and Bigbury, and a short but immensely entertaining links at Dawlish Warren.

Bristol is the west country's largest city. Bordering the counties of Gloucestershire and Somerset it has an enviable location. Arguably the city's two best golf courses are found almost adjacent to one another, Long Ashton and Bristol and Clifton. Gloucestershire and Cotswold country lies to the

north of Bristol; there aren't too many courses in the county but visits to Stinchcombe Hill, Minchinhampton and Broadway will be well rewarded. The superb links at Burnham and Berrow is the main attraction for golfers in Somerset and anyone visiting the elegant Georgian (or is it Roman?) city of Bath might travel to nearby Chippenham where the courses at Castle Combe (Manor House) and Bowood both occupy beautiful settings. Stonehenge spotters may be able to slip a game in at High Post, long regarded as the top downland course in Wiltshire.

Dorset is one of England's quieter counties. Here is the home of fossils and thatched cottages. The greatest proliferation of golf courses centres around Bournemouth and Poole, where there are three first class heathland layouts: Broadstone, Parkstone and Ferndown. There is another very pretty course at Sherbourne but the most spectacularly situated is the aforementioned Isle of Purbeck Golf Club near Swanage – a golfing gem if ever there was one.

BROADSTONE
BURNHAM & BERROW
EAST DEVON
FERNDOWN
ISLE OF PURBECK
LANHYDROCK

MINCHINHAMPTON
ROYAL NORTH DEVON
SAUNTON
ST ENODOC
WEST CORNWALL

West Country

Page

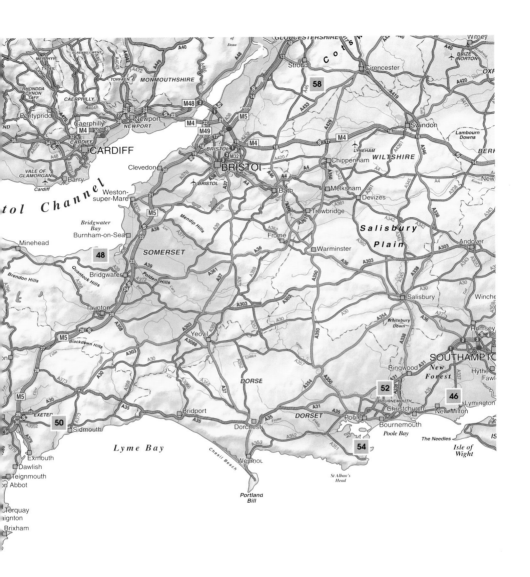

Broadstone

*A*s rich as they undoubtedly are, the
counties of Surrey and Berkshire
do not have a monopoly of the
outstanding heathland type courses in
England and Wales. There is Hollinwell near
Nottingham, Pulborough in West Sussex,
Lindrick in South Yorkshire and Woodhall
Spa in Lincolnshire. And there is also
Broadstone, a little known but spectacularly
beautiful course near Poole in Dorset.

Broadstone Golf Club was founded in
1898. Its golf course was originally laid out
by Tom Dunn but was later revised
by three outstanding architects, namely,
Willie Park Jnr, Harry Colt and Herbert
Fowler, who between them created Surrey's
three most famous heathland courses:
Sunningdale (Old), Wentworth (West) and
Walton Heath (Old). Blessed with a wealth
of heather and gorse, firs, pines and silver
birch trees, Broadstone resembles
Sunningdale the most (moreover it doesn't
have the length of a Wentworth or a Walton
Heath).

The terrain is fairly undulating and with
much of the back nine occupying high
ground there are splendid views of
Poole Harbour and the Purbeck Hills.

Broadstone boasts an impressive
collection of short holes, but it is two par
fours that are especially memorable.
With its island fairway and jealously
defended plateau green, the long 7th is one
of the toughest two-shot holes in the
country, while the Redan styled 13th, its
green angled across the line of play and
guarded by bunkers to the front and left, is
one of the most classically designed.

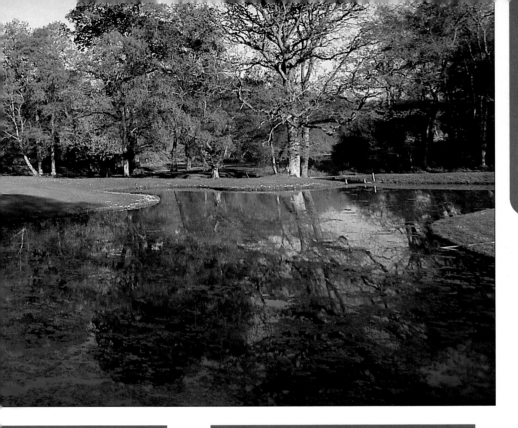

HOW TO GET THERE

From A31 take Broadstone turn off. From Poole take A349 to Broadstone.

Broadstone Golf Club

COURSE INFORMATION & FACILITIES

Broadstone (Dorset) Golf Club
Wentworth Drive
Broadstone, Dorset BH18 8DQ

Secretary: Colin Robinson
Tel/Fax: 01202 692595

Golf Professional Tel: 01202 692835

Green Fees:
Weekdays — £45 (36 hole) Weekends (Limited) — £45
Weekdays (day) — £32 (18 hole)
Letter of introduction required

CARD OF THE COURSE — PAR 70

1	2	3	4	5	6	7	8	9	Out
492	410	376	380	286	152	415	202	512	3225
Par 5	Par 4	Par 4	Par 4	Par 4	Par 3	Par 4	Par 3	Par 5	Par 36

10	11	12	13	14	15	16	17	18	In
363	169	354	440	355	194	424	408	383	3090
Par 4	Par 3	Par 4	Par 4	Par 4	Par 3	Par 4	Par 4	Par 4	Par 34

Burnham & Berrow

*L*ittle known internationally (and indeed far from famous in Great Britain), Burnham and Berrow is one of England's finest links courses. Its lack of notoriety is due largely to its geography. Burnham and Berrow is tucked away – almost concealed – behind an ancient Iron Age fort on the coast of Somerset, a county more celebrated for its cricket than its golf. But play Burnham and Berrow and you will experience much of what is so appealing about links golf.

It is difficult to classify Burnham and Berrow in that it combines old fashioned quaintness – the odd blind shot and 'humpy bumpy' fairways – with several holes that require solid hitting and precise shot-making, a layout that's deemed strong enough and good enough to host important amateur championships. In other words, it sits somewhere between St Enodoc and Saunton.

If the links' greatest attribute is the quality and consistency of its putting surfaces, the two most visibly dominant features are the towering sand dunes. which frame many of the fairways, and the ever encroaching buckthorn-studded rough – accuracy is essential at Burnham.

There are some good holes on the front nine, notably the par threes, but it is the back nine that reveals the best and true character of Burnham. It begins with a formidable tee shot over a vast sand hill at the 10th and concludes with a tough dog-legging par four in front of the homely clubhouse.

HOW TO GET THERE

At M5 junction 22; follow
B3140 for 2$\frac{1}{2}$ miles and
St Christopher's Way is on
left-hand side.

Burnham
& Berrow
Golf Club

COURSE INFORMATION & FACILITIES

Burnham & Berrow Golf Club
St Christopher's Way, Burnham-on-Sea,
Somerset. TA8 2PE.

Secretary: Mrs E.L.Sloman.
Tel: 01278 785760. Fax: 01278 795440.

Golf Professional Mark Crowther-Smith Tel: 01278 784545.

Green Fees:

Weekdays — £38. Weekends — £50.
Weekdays (day) — £38. Weekends (day) — £50.
Handicap certificate required. Restrictions apply.
Tee Reservations essential.

CARD OF THE COURSE — PAR 71

1	2	3	4	5	6	7	8	9	Out
380	421	376	511	158	434	450	494	170	3394
Par 4	Par 4	Par 4	Par 5	Par 3	Par 4	Par 4	Par 5	Par 3	Par 36

10	11	12	13	14	15	16	17	18	In
375	419	401	530	192	440	344	200	445	3365
Par 4	Par 4	Par 4	Par 5	Par 3	Par 4	Par 4	Par 3	Par 4	Par 35

East Devon

*T*he East Devon Golf Club at Budleigh Salterton is a very special place, it is where heathland golf meets the sea. Laid out on high cliffs overlooking the coast, it is hardly a links course, and yet it is not a typical clifftop course either for the terrain is not downland in nature, as at Sherringham, for instance. East Devon looks and plays like one of the celebrated Surrey heathland courses. Cloaked in heather and gorse, and with sandy, springy turf, it is a Sunningdale by the sea.

The above comment may sound like extreme flattery given that we are describing a course that is little known outside of the south west, but East Devon is one of the true hidden gems of English golf. It is not a long course but the natural hazards are plentiful; moreover, there are only two par fives and none of the par fours is especially short – even if a player once drove to the edge of the green at the downhill 450 yards-plus 9th! The accompanying scenery is captivating: the south Devon coast is at its most glorious around Budleigh while the inland views across the course towards the rolling Devonshire hills are similarly enchanting.

The best run of holes at East Devon occurs between the 6th, a superbly designed 'risk-reward' par five, and the aforementioned 9th. The 7th may be the finest hole of all. It is a medium length par four and features a drive from a spectacularly elevated tee and an uphill approach to a wonderful stage-like green.

HOW TO GET THERE

M5 Junction 30 toward
Exmouth A376 onto B3179
Budleigh Salterton to
T-Junction then turn right
onto B3180 and then
B3178. Club is situated
on the right hand side
before Town
(Links Road).

East Devon
Golf Club

COURSE INFORMATION & FACILITIES

East Devon Golf Club
North View, Budleigh
Salterton EX9 6DQ

Secretary: Bob Burley
Tel: 01395 443370

Golf Professional Tel: 01395 445195

Green Fees:
Weekdays — £27 Weekends — £35
Weekdays (day) — £35 Weekends (day) — £42

CARD OF THE COURSE — PAR 70

1	2	3	4	5	6	7	8	9	Out
348	342	414	142	363	526	392	207	469	3203
Par 4	Par 4	Par 4	Par 3	Par 4	Par 5	Par 4	Par 3	Par 4	Par 35

10	11	12	13	14	15	16	17	18	In
150	335	486	145	411	308	406	455	340	3036
Par 3	Par 4	Par 5	Par 3	Par 4	Par 4	Par 4	Par 4	Par 4	Par 35

Ferndown

*O*f the 'big three' courses in the Bournemouth-Poole region, namely Parkstone, Broadstone and Ferndown, the last named is the most widely known. This is largely the result of its staging several televised professional tournaments during the 1970s and '80s; indeed, it is difficult to think of Ferndown without thinking of Peter Alliss, which is highly appropriate since it was here that the former Ryder Cup player and celebrated commentator first learned to play the game, his father Percy having been the Club's professional.

Today Ferndown has 36 holes to entice the visiting golfer: the championship Old Course, which was designed by Harold Hilton in 1912, and the shorter Presidents Course, designed by J Hamilton Stutt in 1969 and which has nine holes but eighteen tees.

The Old Course layout is essentially one of two loops, an inner loop comprising holes 1 to 8 and the outer containing the 10th to 18th. Always immaculately groomed, its fairways are of a sandy, heathland nature and gently undulate throughout. The rough is mainly heather and this, together with the many pines, firs and silver birch trees gives the course a very attractive appearance. Included among the most testing holes are the 6th, the dog-leg 9th and the 11th – all are quite lengthy par fours – while perhaps the most picturesque hole on the course is the short 5th, where in late May and early June the rhododendrons provide a brilliant splash of colour.

COURSE INFORMATION & FACILITIES

Ferndown Golf Club
119 Golf Links Road
Ferndown, Dorset BH22 8BU

Secretary: E Robertson
Tel: 01202 874602 Fax: 01202 873926

Golf Professional: Tel: 01202 873825

Green Fees per 18 holes per day:
Weekdays — £45 Weekends — £50
Weekdays (day) — £55* Weekends (day) — £60*
*36 holes per day

Letter of introduction required

CARD OF THE COURSE — PAR 71

1	2	3	4	5	6	7	8	9	Out
396	175	398	395	206	409	480	304	427	3190
Par 4	Par 3	Par 4	Par 4	Par 3	Par 4	Par 5	Par 4	Par 4	Par 35

10	11	12	13	14	15	16	17	18	In
485	438	186	488	152	408	305	397	403	3262
Par 5	Par 4	Par 3	Par 5	Par 3	Par 4	Par 4	Par 4	Par 4	Par 36

HOW TO GET THERE

Take the A31 from Ringwood to Ferndown. Follow the A348 Ringwood Road, take 2nd on the left into Golf Links Road. Ferndown Golf Club is approximately 1½ miles on the lefthand side.

Ferndown
Golf Club

Bridge House Hotel

The Bridge House is beautifully situated on the river Stour in the picturesque Dorset countryside.

The Hotel offers an interesting and varied range of food including a carvery, a cold counter and salad bar plus a range of daily specials. All meals are complemented by a good selection of wines and real ales.

Many of the 37 bedrooms have river views and all are en-suite with full facilities.

THE BRIDGE HOUSE HOTEL
2 Ringwood Road, Longham,
Ferndown, Dorset BH22 9AN
Telephone: 01202 578828
Fax: 01202 572620
www.oldenglish.co.uk

Isle of Purbeck

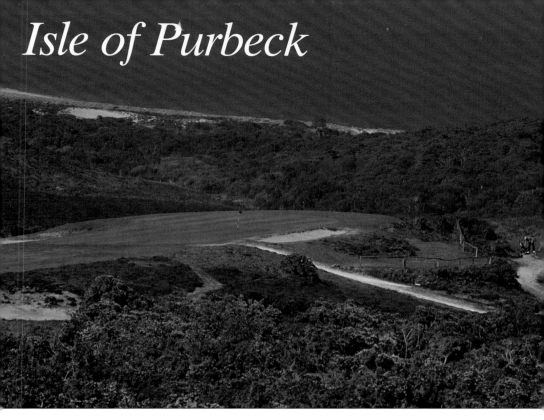

*T*he great Henry Longhurst once said, 'Golf takes us to such beautiful places'. He wasn't referring to the Isle of Purbeck when he made the remark, but he might just as well have been. The south coast possesses a number of scenic courses and yet one would be hard pushed to find one that can equal the magnificent views provided by the Isle of Purbeck. A first time visitor to the Dorset course will be convinced of this even before he reaches the 1st tee – the view from the front of clubhouse is little short of bewitching.

But the Isle of Purbeck is not merely a beautiful golf course. For one thing, the club has an extremely interesting history. Founded in 1892 – almost a decade before Sunningdale – it was once owned

by the famous children's author, Enid Blyton. The present clubhouse dates from 1966 and was built with the local Purbeck stone; incorporated into the interior walls are several fossilised dinosaur footprints.

There are 27 holes of golf at the Isle of Purbeck: the 18 hole main course, known as the Purbeck Course, and the short nine hole Dene Course. The surrounding scenery may be distracting but the quality of the golf is equally absorbing. The Purbeck Course was principally designed by master architect Harry Colt and the layout makes the most of the gently rolling, gorse studded terrain. The most talked about (and most photogenic) hole is the 5th, named 'Agglestone', where you tee off from the top of an ancient Saxon burial mound.

COURSE INFORMATION & FACILITIES

Isle of Purbeck Golf Club
Studland, Swanage
Dorset BH19 3AB

www.purbeckgolf.co.uk

Managing Director: Mrs. J Robinson.
Tel: 01929 450361 Fax: 01929 450501

Golf Professional: Ian Brake Tel: 01929 450354

Green Fees per 18 holes per day:
Weekdays — £30 Weekends — £35
Weekdays (day) — £40 Weekends (day) — £42.50

CARD OF THE COURSE — PAR 70

1	2	3	4	5	6	7	8	9	Out
371	417	302	195	404	492	355	594	147	3277
Par 4	Par 4	Par 4	Par 3	Par 4	Par 5	Par 4	Par 5	Par 3	Par 36

10	11	12	13	14	15	16	17	18	In
414	194	424	388	389	187	382	334	306	3018
Par 4	Par 3	Par 4	Par 4	Par 4	Par 3	Par 4	Par 4	Par 4	Par 34

HOW TO GET THERE

A338 towards Bournemouth. At Frizzell roundabout follow signs to Sandbanks. Take Sandbanks Ferry to Studland. Continued on B3351 through Studland towards Corfe Castle. Approx 1¹/₂ miles outside Studland.

Or A351 to Wareham and Corfe Castle. At Corfe Castle take the B3351 to Studland. The club is situated 1¹/₂ miles from Studland.

Isle of Purbeck Golf Club

★★★AA ✤ Rosette ★★★ETC Silver Award

Mortons House Hotel

Mortons House Hotel is a sixteenth century Elizabethan Manor built using stone taken from the nearby Castle, sleighted during Cromwellian times. Recently and sympathetically renovated into a fine seventeen bedroom hotel, commended for it's fine cuisine and historic surroundings.

Privately owned by two keen golfers, who play locally at the Isle Of Purbeck GC, the hotel offers it's guests the opportunity to find peace away from the Golf course, with the Swanage railway and Corfe Castle station overlooked by the hotel or the Historic Castle which can be seen from many of the bedrooms. The beauty of Studland, Kimmeridge, Lullworth and Durdle beaches should not be missed either, should time permit.

Mortons House Hotel
Corfe Castle, Dorset BH20 5EE
Tel: 01929 480988 Fax: 01929 480820 www.mortonshouse.co.uk

Lanhydrock

C ornwall and holidays are synonymous and yet, a dozen years ago, only a links golf enthusiast would have contemplated making space in the back of the car for a set of golf clubs: sand irons were invariably kept for the beach.

It was St Mellion, of course, that first attracted visiting golfers inland but several other non-links courses have appeared on the Cornish golfing map in recent years, the pick of these being Lanhydrock, near Bodmin. Actually, in terms of playing character, being situated inland is about the only real similarity between Lanhydrock and the mighty Nicklaus Course at St Mellion. Lanhydrock offers a milder, more subtle challenge – it entertains rather than examines. The setting is equally picturesque,

however, as it occupies a richly wooded valley and is surrounded by rolling, patchwork fields.

For a modern golf course the layout is refreshingly short. Its principal defences are water hazards – streams and ponds rather than lakes, a limited number of strategically placed dazzling white sand bunkers and the natural contours of a gently undulating landscape. The par four 2nd at Lanhydrock is a fine example of a very natural golf hole while the short 6th, a downhill par three played over water to a stage-like green is the most spectacular and the dog-legged 12th, which weaves a path through the ancient gnarled woods of Tregullan Moor is among the most cunningly conceived.

COURSE INFORMATION & FACILITIES

Lanhydrock Golf Club
Lostwithiel Road, Bodmin
Cornwall PL30 5AQ

General Manager: Graham Bond
Tel: 01208 73600 Fax: 01208 77325
Email: postmaster@lanhydrock-golf.co.uk

Green Fees per 18 holes per day:
Weekdays — £29 Weekends — £29
Weekdays (day) — £35 Weekends (day) — £35

CARD OF THE COURSE — PAR 71

1	2	3	4	5	6	7	8	9	Out
314	381	423	481	331	187	410	317	309	3153
Par 4	Par 4	Par 4	Par 5	Par 4	Par 3	Par 4	Par 4	Par 4	Par 36

10	11	12	13	14	15	16	17	18	In
454	185	392	407	300	167	318	201	525	2949
Par 4	Par 3	Par 4	Par 4	Par 4	Par 3	Par 4	Par 3	Par 5	Par 34

HOW TO GET THERE

Only 2 hours by car from Bristol, Lanhydrock Golf Club is accessible from all parts of the South West. It is located one mile south of Bodmin, with easy access from the B3268 via the A38/A30.

Lanhydrock
Golf Club

Minchinhampton

inchinhampton may be the most extraordinary golf club in England. It is not the only club able to offer 54 holes of golf – Frilford Heath and Wentworth also have three full length courses – but surely nowhere can provide three such contrasting golfing experiences. And which other club has two distinct venues (and two clubhouses) situated on opposite sides of the same village, some five miles apart?

The Old Course at Minchinhampton occupies one of the sites, just to the west of the Gloucestershire village, while the Avering and Cherington Courses comprise what might be termed 'New Minchinhampton', to the east. The Old Course is laid out on National Trust land and is a hundred years old; it has no bunkers and its principal architect was Mother Nature. The Avering

Course opened in the mid 1970s and is now a mature parkland layout. The Cherington has a very modern design and has only been in play since the early 1990s. Anyone managing to complete all three courses in a day could be forgiven for imagining that they had somehow participated in a fourball match with Old Tom Morris, Jack Nicklaus and Tiger Woods.

Perhaps not surprisingly, the general consensus is that the Old Course has the most charm but the Avering offers the better test of golf – the proverbial jury is still considering its verdict on the Cherington Course. Henry Cotton was a great admirer of the Old, and reckoned that the 'drop-shot' 8th was one of the finest par threes in the country.

Minchinhampton Golf Club
Minchinhampton, Stroud
Glos GL6 9BE

Secretary/Manager: David Calvert
Tel: 01453 833840 Fax: 01453 833860

Golf Professional Tel: 01453 833860

Green Fees:
New Course: Weekdays — £25 Weekends — £30
Old Course: Weekdays — £10 Weekend — £13

Handicap certificate required.

CARD OF THE OLD COURSE — PAR 71

1	2	3	4	5	6	7	8	9	Out
527	339	333	316	181	363	163	454	508	3204
Par 5	Par 4	Par 4	Par 4	Par 3	Par 4	Par 3	Par 4	Par 5	Par 36

10	11	12	13	14	15	16	17	18	In
150	423	428	493	302	197	407	360	356	3116
Par 3	Par 4	Par 4	Par 5	Par 4	Par 3	Par 4	Par 4	Par 4	Par 35

HOW TO GET THERE

M5 junction 13. M4 Junction 18 (from Bristol). M4 junction 15 (from London). Minchinhampton Golf Course is 5 miles south east of Stroud on the road between Minchinhampton and Avening.

Minchinhampton
Golf Club

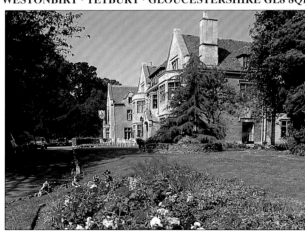

Royal North Devon

*I*magine. You are on the 1st tee of the first 'Royal' golf club you have ever played. Slightly nervously, you tee up your ball then take a few paces backwards to survey the fairway ahead. Just as you try to visualise your opening drive a sheep wanders up to your ball; it bleats a couple of times before strolling leisurely to the edge of the teeing area. There is only one place you could be.

The links at Westward Ho! is a very special place. This is the home of the Royal North Devon Golf Club, the oldest English club still playing over its original land (since 1864) and the home of the oldest ladies' golf club in the world (established in 1868). And it is surely the only golf course in the world –

never mind 'Royal Club' – where the above episode is a distinct possibility.

The 18 holes are situated on Northam Burrows, a vast and very exposed area of common land which stretches along the coast just to the north of Bideford. It is an extraordinary piece of terrain. In places it is pancake flat; in other parts the fairways ripple and undulate in a manner reminiscent of St Andrews. The hazards comprise an interesting mix of ditches, pot bunkers and, at the far end of the links, the Great Sea Rushes – giant marshland reeds unique to Westward Ho! and which can literally impale golf balls. There is also the famous sleepered Cape Bunker at the 4th which is at least 100 yards wide and quite intimidating to drive over.

HOW TO GET THERE

5 Junction 27 onto A361. Follow to
arnstaple picking up A39 to Bideford —
ross new bridge over River Torridge turn
ight at roundabout following signs to
Westward Ho!/Appledore and Northam.
ust before entering Westward Ho! Take
urning right into Beach Road and turn
ight at bottom of road
nto Golf Links Road
and the Golf
lub is
along on
our left.

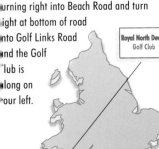

Royal North Devon
Golf Club

COURSE INFORMATION & FACILITIES

Royal North Devon Golf Club
Golf Links Road, Westward Ho!
Bideford, Devon EX39 1HD.
Secretary: Robert Fowler.
Tel: 01237 473817. Fax: 01237 423456.

Golf Professional Richard Herring
Tel: 01237 477598. Fax: 01237 423456

Green Fees:
Weekdays — £30. Weekends — £36.
Weekdays (day) — £36. Weekends (day) — £40.
Handicap certificates required. Some time restrictions.

CARD OF THE COURSE — PAR 72

1	2	3	4	5	6	7	8	9	Out
478	416	421	349	136	406	397	192	497	3292
Par 5	Par 4	Par 4	Par 4	Par 3	Par 4	Par 4	Par 3	Par 5	Par 36

10	11	12	13	14	15	16	17	18	In
373	371	423	442	201	439	143	555	414	3361
Par 4	Par 4	Par 4	Par 4/5	Par 3	Par 4	Par 3	Par 5	Par 4	Par 36

Saunton

*I*f the Open Championship is ever taken to the south west of England the two most likely venues are Burnham and Berrow in Somerset and Saunton in north Devon. Both regularly host major amateur events and both would test the world's best with a classic examination of links golf. If the setting were the determining factor, Saunton would have the edge. Separated from one of Britain's finest beaches by a vast range of sand hills, Saunton has a rugged beauty. It also has 36 holes to savour with the championship East Course and the newer, slightly shorter West Course.

While not as ancient as nearby Westward Ho!, Saunton celebrated its centenary in 1997. At first there were just nine holes and the clubhouse was a single room next to the village post office. The course was extended to 18 holes before the First World War but it wasn't until the 1930s that Saunton's reputation was really established. Most responsible was golf architect Herbert Fowler. The creator of Walton Heath, Fowler designed the East Course. Although some alterations were made in the 1950s, it remains his greatest seaside achievement.

The East begins with four strong holes, each measuring over 400 yards. The 5th is an excellent par three but perhaps the best two holes are the long 14th, with its elevated tee and ever-narrowing fairway, and the 16th, a superb par four featuring a drive over a large sandhill and an approach that must carry a deep bunker to find a bowl-shaped green.

COURSE INFORMATION & FACILITIES

Saunton Golf Club
Saunton, Near Braunton
Devon EX33 1LG.

Secretary: Trevor. C. Reynolds.
Tel: 01271 812436. Fax: 01271 814241.

Golf Professional Albert T. Mackenzie
Tel: 01271 812013. Fax: 01271 812126

Green Fees per 18 holes per day:
Weekdays — £40. Weekends — £50.
Weekdays (day) — £60. Weekends (day) — £75.
Handicap certificate required. Some time restrictions.
All green fees are inclusive of a lunch/meal voucher.

CARD OF THE COURSE — PAR 71

1	2	3	4	5	6	7	8	9	Out
478	476	402	441	122	370	428	380	392	3489
Par 4	Par 5	Par 4	Par 4	Par 3	Par 4	Par 4	Par 4	Par 4	Par 36

10	11	12	13	14	15	16	17	18	In
337	362	414	145	455	478	434	207	408	3240
Par 4	Par 4	Par 4	Par 3	Par 4	Par 5	Par 4	Par 3	Par 4	Par 35

HOW TO GET THERE

From the M5, leave at Junction 27 and follow the A361 to Barnstaple. In Barnstaple follow the A361 to Braunton and at Braunton turn left at the main traffic lights towards Saunton and Croyde. The Golf Club is about 2 miles out of Braunton on the left.

Saunton
Golf Club

St. Enodoc

Situated on the sometimes rugged, sometimes romantic coast of north Cornwall, St Enodoc is a classic and staunchly old fashioned links course: here is a land of huge sand hills, of tumbling fairways, hidden pot bunkers, awkward stances, the occasional blind shot and firm, fast greens. An exhilarating links, although not long at just over 6200 yards, it is exacting in its demand for skill and judgement and memorable for its special features.

Since 1982 there have been two 18 hole courses at St Enodoc. The main course is now named the Church Course, and the newer, shorter layout is called the Holywell Course. The main links takes its name from the little half-sunken church which is located near the far end of the course. This church threatens to come into play at the par four 10th, the most difficult hole on the course.

The drive at the 10th is dramatically downhill and it must carry almost 200 yards to find a narrow, heavily contoured fairway; off to the left is a marshy area and a stream, while to the right are steep dunes and uncomprising rough. The approach to the green is almost as daunting as the tee shot!

The other hole at St Enodoc that everyone talks about is the 6th, there players must confront the 'Himalayas', 'the highest sandhill, to the best of my belief, I have ever seen on a golf course', remarked the famous golf writer, Bernard Darwin. With holes like the 6th, it isn't hard to see why St Endoc is so often likened to Prestwick.

COURSE INFORMATION & FACILITIES

St. Enodoc Golf Club
Rock, Wadebridge
Cornwall PL27 6LD

Secretary: Colonel Ian Waters
Tel: 01208 862200 Fax: 01208 862976

Golf Professional Nick Williams
Tel/Fax: 01208 862402

Green Fees per 18 holes per day (Church Course):
Weekdays — £35 Weekends — £40
Weekdays (day) — £50 Weekends (day) — £55

Letter of introduction and Handicap Certificate required.

CARD OF THE COURSE — PAR 69

1	2	3	4	5	6	7	8	9	Out
518	438	436	292	161	378	394	155	393	3165
Par 5	Par 4	Par 4	Par 4	Par 3	Par 4	Par 4	Par 3	Par 4	Par 35

10	11	12	13	14	15	16	17	18	In
457	205	386	360	355	168	495	206	446	3078
Par 4	Par 3	Par 4	Par 4	Par 4	Par 3	Par 5	Par 3	Par 4	Par 34

HOW TO GET THERE

rom Wadebridge follow
he signs to Rock. Go right
hrough Rock until you see a
ign for St Enodoc Golf Club
n the right hand side.

St. Enodoc
Golf Club

West Cornwall

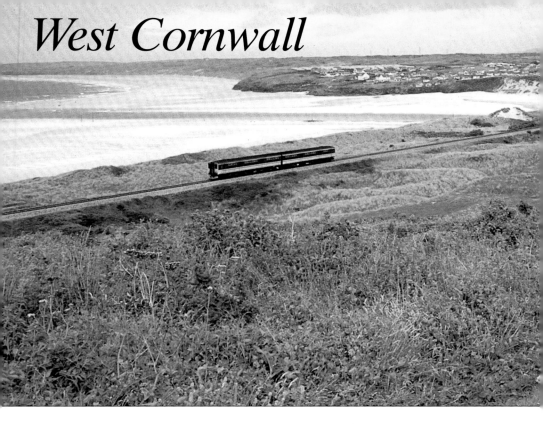

Certain clubs and courses will always be linked with famous players: Walton Heath with James Braid, Hawkstone Park with Sandy Lyle and Ashridge with Henry Cotton. So it is with the delightful West Cornwall links situated at Lelant, a tiny village near St Ives. Jim Barnes, winner of the Open Championship on both sides of the Atlantic during the 1920s was born in Lelant in 1887. 'Long Jim', as he was known (he was as tall as Nick Faldo) learned his golf at West Cornwall before emigrating to America when he was 19.

Notwithstanding the fact that St Ives is a celebrated beauty spot, a favourite haunt of fishermen and artists, the links is undeniably remote. And yet it has immense charm: the scenery is

breathtaking and the course itself bristles with character. It is quite short by modern standards - having changed little since Long Jim's day. The terrain is perfect for links golf and the greens are invariably firm and fast. Moreover, the sand hills at Lelant are not merely ornamental for, in a manner akin to Tenby in South Wales, the course careers headlong into the dunes.

The challenge begins with an extremely long par three at which the tee shot must be aimed at the spire of St Uny Church. The 2nd is a superb two-shotter, but perhaps the most memorable holes are those between the 5th and 8th where the course runs very close to the sea. The most spectacular views can be enjoyed from the 12th tee.

HOW TO GET THERE

A30 past Truro towards Penzance. Turn off Hayle by-pass towards St. Ives. Enter Lelant village, turn 1st right past The Badger Inn and follow sign to West Cornwall Golf Club. Approx 3/4 mile from A30.

West Cornwall
Golf Club

COURSE INFORMATION & FACILITIES

West Cornwall Golf Club
Church Lane, Lelant, St. Ives,
Cornwall TR26 3DZ.

Secretary: Malcolm Lack.
Tel/Fax: 01736 753401.

Golf Professional: Paul Atherton Tel: 01736 753177.
Fax: 01736 75340

Green Fees: Weekdays — £20. Weekends — £25.
Weekdays (day) — £20. Weekends (day) — £25.

Handicap certificate required.

CARD OF THE COURSE — PAR 69

1	2	3	4	5	6	7	8	9	Out
229	382	342	352	179	337	191	325	406	2743
Par 3	Par 4	Par 4	Par 4	Par 3	Par 4	Par 3	Par 4	Par 4	Par 33

10	11	12	13	14	15	16	17	18	In
331	362	494	264	446	135	521	194	394	3141
Par 4	Par 4	Par 5	Par 4	Par 4	Par 3	Par 5	Par 3	Par 4	Par 36

Midlands & East Anglia

Midlands & East Anglia

*O*ur third golfing region comprises the central chunk of England: from Elgar's 'Green and pleasant land' in the west to 'Constable Country' in the east or, if you prefer, from Shropshire to Suffolk, via the midlands.

With the likes of Little Aston near Sutton Coldfield to the north, and Copt Heath near Solihull to the south, Birmingham is surrounded by quality golf courses. And you need not travel far from England's industrial heart to unearth a few hidden gems. A little further north of Little Aston and into Staffordshire is the superb Beau Desert Golf Club at Hazel Slade, set amidst the firs of Cannock Chase. Another fine Staffordshire course is Whittington Heath near Lichfield. To the west, Shropshire boasts Patshull Park and Hawkstone Park, Herefordshire has scenic Ross-on-Wye and in Worcestershire there is classy Blackwell at Bromsgrove. South east of Birmingham, over towards Coventry, are 36 holes of wooded splendour at the Forest of Arden.

The east midlands embraces the counties of Nottinghamshire, Derbyshire, Lincolnshire, Leicestershire and Northamptonshire – plus that recently reborn smidgen of a county, Rutland. The only links course of particular note on the east coast between East Anglia and the North East is Seacroft near Skegness. Inland, however, there are plenty of gems. The two greatest courses in the east midlands are Woodhall Spa in Lincolnshire and Notts (Hollinwell). The Northamptonshire Golf Club at Church Brampton is the best course in Northants – like Woodhall Spa and Hollinwell it is resplendent with heather, pines and and gorse. Kedlestone Park near Derby provides a classic parkland test, while Leicestershire can offer a James Braid original at Luffenham Heath and an extraordinary, 'prehistoric' nine hole course at Charnwood Forest.

East Anglia is predominantly flat and, as players in these parts will tell you, predominantly windy. But the golf courses in the region are superb. Norfolk has everything from tidal marshes and sleepered bunkers at

Brancaster to a modern 'American-styled' country club at Barnham Broom. Sherringham and Royal Cromer stare across the North Sea and are two of England's finest clifftop courses. Norfolk also has an outstanding championship links at Hunstanton, a very challenging woodland course at Castle Rising (Kings Lynn) and a pretty heathland layout at Thetford.

With the exception of Royal Worlington and Newmarket, often described as 'the greatest nine hole course in the world', Suffolk's finest courses are concentrated in the south eastern corner of the county. Aldeburgh, Thorpness, Woodbridge, Felixstowe Ferry and Purdis Heath (Ipswich) are all worthy of exploration. The splendidly named Gog Magog Golf Club is the pick of the courses in Cambridgeshire.

ALDEBURGH
BEAU DESERT
BROADWAY
CHARNWOOD FOREST
COPT HEATH
HAWKSTONE PARK
KINGS LYNN
LITTLE ASTON
LUFFENHAM HEATH

NORTHAMPTONSHIRE
NOTTS
ROSS-ON-WYE
ROYAL WEST NORFOLK
SEACROFT
SHERINGHAM
WOODBRIDGE
WOODHALL SPA

Midlands & East Anglia

Page

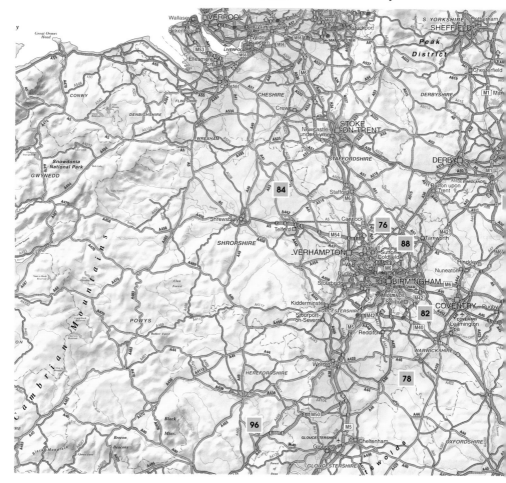

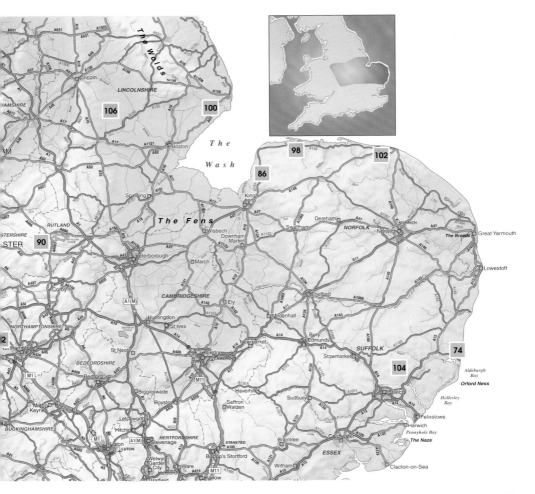

73

Aldeburgh

*T*ucked quietly away on the Suffolk coast at Aldeburgh is one of East Anglia's finest courses. The attractive town is famed for its annual music festival and Benjamin Britten once lived adjacent to the 14th fairway. Although laid out close to the sea, Aldeburgh is a essentially a heathland type course, its most conspicuous feature being the seasonal brilliance of the gorse.

To play a round at Aldeburgh is to combine charm with challenge. Visually it is a delight, and yet many golfers hold the opinion that Aldeburgh is also one of the toughest courses in England. The degree of difficulty is particularly evident on the back nine where some of the fairways are so naturally folded they wouldn't look out

of place on a links course. It is hard to judge which is the best hole as there are several outstanding candidates on this second nine. Starting home with the severely bunkered 10th and 11th, one is soon confronted by the excellent two-shot 14th. The drive here must be threaded between two towering trees; accuracy is again essential with the approach which is played over a ridge to a high plateaued green. The par threes at Aldeburgh are all good, especially perhaps the short 4th where an intimidating sleepered bunker threatens to envelop the green.

Across the road from the clubhouse there is a modest nine hole course which measures 2140 yards, par 32. It was constructed in the early 1970s and is completely free of bunkers.

COURSE INFORMATION & FACILITIES

Aldeburgh Golf Club
Saxmundham Road, Aldeburgh
Suffolk IP15 5PE

Secretary: I M Simpson
Tel: 01728 452890 Fax: 01728 452937

Golf Professional Tel: 01728 453309

Green Fees per 18 holes per day:
Weekdays — £40 Weekends — £50
Weekdays after mid-day — £30
Weekends after mid-day — £35

CARD OF THE COURSE — PAR 68

1	2	3	4	5	6	7	8	9	Out
407	367	429	127	440	431	411	165	383	3160
Par 4	Par 4	Par 4	Par 3	Par 4	Par 4	Par 4	Par 3	Par 4	Par 34
10	11	12	13	14	15	16	17	18	In
421	469	324	370	361	201	457	142	425	3170
Par 4	Par 4	Par 4	Par 4	Par 4	Par 3	Par 4	Par 3	Par 4	Par 34

HOW TO GET THERE

12 north east for Ipswich.
1094 to Aldeburgh.
lub House by A1094 at
ntry to Aldeburgh.

Aldeburgh
Golf Club

WENTWORTH
H O T E L
ALDEBURGH SUFFOLK IP15 5BD
Tel: 01728 452312 Æ Fax: 01728 454343
www.wentworth-aldeburgh.com

The hotel has the comfort and style of a Country House.
Two comfortable lounges with open fires and antique furniture
provide ample space to relax. There are 37 well equipped
bedrooms, many with views of the sea. The Restaurant serves
a daily changing menu with a variety of fresh produce.
Owned and run by the same family since 1920 and within
$1\frac{1}{2}$ miles of Aldeburgh and Thorpeness Golf Clubs we have a
long tradition of looking after golfers.

Beau Desert

Too many southern and northern based golfers have the habit of dismissing golf in central England as 'The Belfry and not much else'. How wrong they are! Not only are two of the country's greatest heathland courses situated in the east Midlands - Woodhall Spa and Hollinwell - but over to the west there is arguably England's finest parkland layout, Little Aston, and, tucked away deep in the heart of Cannock Chase, one of the country's best moorland-cum-forest layouts, the delightful Beau Desert course near Hazel Slade.

Beau Desert is a true 'hidden gem'. Secluded by a dense assortment of fir and spruce trees, few golfers outside Staffordshire appear to be aware of its charms. It is neither the longest nor toughest course in the Midlands but is certainly one of the most picturesque - more a 'beautiful oasis', then, than a 'beautiful desert'.

Founded in 1921, the course was designed by Herbert Fowler. Like all good moorland courses, the fairways play 'firm and fast' and the greens tend to be quick. At Beau Desert they are also very cleverly contoured. The front nine is the easier of the two halves, notwithstanding an extremely tough 2nd hole. The gauntlet is immediately thrown down on the back nine with a do-or-die tee shot which must be hit over a ravine. The best hole, however, is saved until last: the approach to the 18th has to be fired across a strip of heather and gorse that traverses the fairway directly in front of the green.

HOW TO GET THERE

6 Junctions 11 or 12.
ead for Cannock A460
en Hednesford A460.
gnposted after Hednesford.

Beau Desert
Golf Club

COURSE INFORMATION & FACILITIES

Beau Desert Golf Club
Rugeley Road, Hazel Slade, Cannock
Staffs WS12 5PJ

Admin. Secretary: A J R Fairfield
Tel: 01543 422626

Golf Professional Tel: 01543 422492

Green Fees:
Weekdays (day) — £38 Weekends (day) — £48

Restrictions:
Organised parties — Monday to Thursday

CARD OF THE COURSE — PAR 70

1	2	3	4	5	6	7	8	9	Out
304	458	161	352	418	400	167	377	263	2900
Par 4	Par 4	Par 3	Par 4	Par 4	Par 4	Par 3	Par 4	Par 4	Par 34

10	11	12	13	14	15	16	17	18	In
142	412	426	417	393	554	157	429	480	3410
Par 3	Par 4	Par 4	Par 4	Par 4	Par 5	Par 3	Par 4	Par 5	Par 36

Broadway

Bourton-on-Water; Moreton-in Marsh; Stow-on-the-Wold … Charming names, but like The Lake District, The Cotswolds region of England is never likely to be celebrated for its golf. Strange, then, that 1997's 'National Greenkeeper of the Year' should be based here. Cedric Gough is the Head Greenkeeper at Broadway Golf Club, an 18 hole course situated a mile or so from the village of Broadway, 'the most perfect of all Cotswold villages'.

Laid out 900 feet above sea level, and overlooking the Vale of Evesham, few courses in the country offer such commanding views. But Broadway has provided these vistas for more than a hundred years: the first nine holes were laid out in 1895. A second nine holes were added some thirty years ago. The two nines offer very contrasting experiences: the original nine has an almost links-like feel, with its humpy, hillocky ground and stone wall boundaries providing a flavour of North Berwick; the newer (back) nine is much more parkland in character.

For lovers of old fashioned golf, the most interesting run of holes at Broadway is from the 5th to the 8th, where an attractive downhill par three is followed by two extremely characterful, tumbling par fours and another fine short hole. The uphill, Stroke Index One 9th is the front nine's sting in the tail. Perhaps the two best holes on the back nine are the par three 13th, which features a quarry to the left and a three-tiered green, and the long, very challenging 16th.

COURSE INFORMATION & FACILITIES

Broadway Golf Club
Willersey Hill, Broadway
Worcestershire WR12 7LG

Secretary: Mr Brian Carnie
Tel: 01386 853683 Fax: 01386 858643

Golf Professional Tel: 01386 853275

Green Fees:
Weekdays — £30 Weekends & Bank Holidays — £36
Weekdays (day) — £35
Handicap certificate required

CARD OF THE COURSE — PAR 72

1	2	3	4	5	6	7	8	9	Out
496	274	458	510	177	366	312	126	412	3131
Par 5	Par 4	Par 4	Par 5	Par 3	Par 4	Par 4	Par 3	Par 4	Par 36
10	**11**	**12**	**13**	**14**	**15**	**16**	**17**	**18**	**In**
500	285	306	181	362	280	464	352	355	3085
Par 5	Par 4	Par 4	Par 3	Par 4	Par 4	Par 4	Par 4	Par 4	Par 36

HOW TO GET THERE

rom M5 exit at Junction 9
Evesham, follow direction
Broadway. 1¹/₂ miles east
f Broadway off A44.

Broadway
Golf Club

Charnwood Forest

*I*t is a proud boast among the members of Charnwood Forest that they belong to 'the oldest, friendliest and most picturesque golf club in Leicestershire'. They are probably right on all counts. Founded in 1890, the nine hole course is certainly the oldest in the county. It is also an undeniably hospitable club, while the location is both striking and extraordinary. Occupying an area of Special Scientific Interest, Charnwood Forest is a botanists' and geologists' haven. The landscape is positively prehistoric (680 million years old to be precise) and is characterised by craggy, volcanic outcroppings and dense, dark woodland. In summer it is place of great beauty; in winter it is eerie.

Heather, gorse and bracken – plus the occasional boulder – are the principal natural hazards on the golf course. Unusually – but not surprisingly given the terrain – there are no bunkers. However a number of dry stone walls and ditches do feature and greatly affect play. Golf here is never dull!

The course begins with a deceptively tough hole, but it is the 3rd and 4th that are more likely to be remembered due to the stone wall that crosses their fairways (à la North Berwick), threatening the drive at the 3rd and approach at the 4th. The 7th is the more challenging of the two par threes, and the dog-legged 9th makes for an heroic conclusion as players decide how much of the corner they dare attempt to cut off – a wooded copse and an Out of Bounds await the over ambitious.

COURSE INFORMATION & FACILITIES

Charnwood Forest Golf Club
Breakback Road, Woodhouse Eaves
Loughborough, Leics LE12 8TA

Hon. Secretary: James Clarke
Tel: 01509-890259
Fax: 01509-890925

Green Fees:
Weekdays — £20 Weekends — £25
Weekdays (day) — £30

CARD OF THE COURSE — PAR 69

1	2	3	4	5	6	7	8	9	Out
362	428	365	285	183	446	204	345	317	2935
Par 4	Par 4	Par 4	Par 4	Par 3	Par 4	Par 3	Par 4	Par 4	Par 34

10	11	12	13	14	15	16	17	18	In
362	464	385	312	167	476	192	350	317	3025
Par 4	Par 4	Par 3	Par 5	Par 4	Par 5	Par 4	Par 4	Par 4	Par 35

HOW TO GET THERE

1 junction 23 — then A512
Snells Nook Lane turn
ght to traffic light junction
- straight on 1 mile Golf
ourse on left hand side.
6 to Quorn then B591 to
oodhouse Eaves.

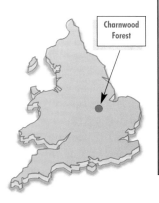

Charnwood
Forest

The Rothley Court

Rothley Court Hotel's impressive facade conceals a wealth of
creature comforts and delights. The Hotel has 32 en-suite
bedrooms, plus 3 meeting and conference rooms.
Throughout, furnishings and décor create a mood of relaxed
elegance, while personal service and facilities combine to
ensure guests want for nothing.
Chosen for its character, its charm, its historical connections
and the individuality of its rooms, Rothley Court is part of
the Old English Inns collection, which features many unique
and distinctive properties set in some of Britain's most
beautiful locations.

**WESTFIELD LANE, ROTHLEY, LEICESTER,
LEICESTERSHIRE, LE7 7LG
TEL: 0116 237 4141 FAX: 0116 237 4483**

Copt Heath

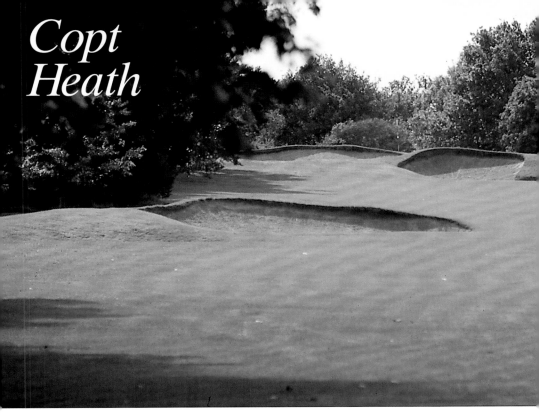

*E*ngland's second city is surrounded by good golf courses. To the north of Birmingham there is a Little Aston, Sutton Coldfield and, of course, The Belfry. Sandwell Park and Edgbaston are the best of the centrally located courses while to the west, no great distance beyond Wolverhampton is Patshull Park and to the east, towards Coventry is the Forest of Arden. Among the best courses to the south of Birmingham are Fulford Heath, Kings Norton and, perhaps the pick of the bunch, Copt Heath at Knowle.

Despite its name, Copt Heath is a classic parkland layout. Harry Vardon and Harry Colt were the joint architects, the latter being resposible for the course's superb bunkering. Although only of medium length, Copt Heath is considered sufficiently testing (and is of such quality) for it to be a regular Open Championship Qualifying course. The design places a premium on accuracy with sand, water and trees combining to provide an interesting array of hazards.

The most difficult hole is the 6th. Here you drive through an avenue of trees to a left to right sloping fairway; a ridge running across the fairway complicates the approach for you cannot see the base of the flag. The green is defended by pot bunkers and also slopes from right to left. The most picturesque hole is the short 13th, its green practically encircled by sand and water, while perhaps the most strategic is the two-shot 17th where you must avoid an out of bounds and a cleverly positioned cross bunker.

HOW TO GET THERE

42 Junction 5, 200 yards
n right towards Knowle.

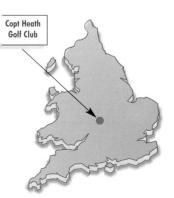

Copt Heath
Golf Club

COURSE INFORMATION & FACILITIES

Copt Heath Golf Club
Warwick Road, Knowle
Solihull, West Midlands B93 9LN

Secretary: G Hogg
Tel: 01564 772650 Fax: 01564 771022

Golf Professional Tel: 01564 726155

Green Fees:
Weekdays (day) — £40

Letter of introduction required

CARD OF THE COURSE — PAR 71

1	2	3	4	5	6	7	8	9	Out
440	454	193	358	129	403	483	336	396	3192
Par 4	Par 4	Par 3	Par 4	Par 3	Par 4	Par 5	Par 4	Par 4	Par 35

10	11	12	13	14	15	16	17	18	In
369	383	409	167	321	540	442	362	332	3325
Par 4	Par 4	Par 4	Par 3	Par 4	Par 5	Par 4	Par 4	Par 4	Par 36

Hawkstone Park

A hidden gem? Thanks to Sandy Lyle just about every golfer in the British Isles has heard of Hawkstone Park. The Open Champion of 1985 and Masters champion of 1988 has enjoyed a lifelong association with the Shropshire golf club. While there is probably no truth in the rumour that he was born adjacent to the 1st tee, he certainly grew up nearby. For many years his father Alex served as club professional and in every sense it was here that Sandy learnt his game.

But Hawkstone Park is much more than the birthplace of Sandy Lyle. It has two golf courses, the well established Hawkstone Course, which opened in 1920, and the acclaimed new Windmill Course, designed by Brian Huggett. Both are set in the beautiful grounds of the 18th century Hawkstone Park Hotel. The hotel itself is a grand affair: in a guide book of 1824 it was described as 'more like the seat of a nobleman than an hotel'. As for the grounds, they are not only beautiful – exotic plants and flowers abound – but are steeped in history and legend.

The Hawkstone Course is a traditional British parkland layout that wends its way around a 12th century castle (Hawkstone's famous Red Castle, which is reputedly linked to Arthurian legend). Many of its fairways are bordered by mature oaks and silver birch trees. By way of contrast, the Windmill Course has a very American feel to it and features a series of dramatic holes where the golfer must confront do-or-die shots over and alongside water.

COURSE INFORMATION & FACILITIES

Hawkstone Park Hotel, Golf, Historic Park & Follies
Weston-under-Redcastle
Shrewsbury, Shropshire SY4 5UY

Chairman: Mark Boler
Tel: 01939 200611 Fax: 01939 200311

Golf Professional: Paul Wesselingh

Green Fees per 18 holes per day:
Summer from: Weekdays — £30 Weekends — £38
Winter from: Weekdays — £25 Weekends — £32

CARD OF THE HAWKSTONE COURSE — PAR 72

1	2	3	4	5	6	7	8	9	Out
374	402	216	332	371	364	434	481	188	3162
Par 4	Par 4	Par 3	Par 4	Par 4	Par 4	Par 4	Par 5	Par 3	Par 35

10	11	12	13	14	15	16	17	18	In
517	438	145	373	485	315	256	383	417	3329
Par 5	Par 4	Par 3	Par 4	Par 5	Par 4	Par 4	Par 4	Par 4	Par 37

HOW TO GET THERE

f the A49 Shrewsbury-Whitchurch Road,
gnposted approximately 14 miles north
Shrewsbury.

: M54 Junction 6 — A41 Whitchurch,
gnposted from Hodnet.

: M6 Junction 15 — A53 Market Drayton
Hodnet, signposted.

Hawkstone
Park
Golf Club

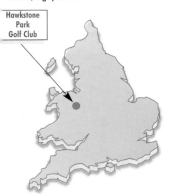

King's Lynn

The 1960s and 1970s will never be remembered as the golden age of British golf course architecture. Not too many courses were built in this period and very few are regarded as outstanding designs. The three most famous courses to have emerged from this era are probably St Pierre, Woburn and The Belfry. Undoubtedly one of the finest, but barely known outside of East Anglia, is the course at King's Lynn – or more precisely, the course at Castle Rising, the second home of the King's Lynn Golf Club.

The club was founded in 1923. Its original course was nothing special and the best decision the members ever took was to move to their present site four miles north east of the town, which they did in 1975.

Dave Thomas and Peter Alliss laid out the course at Castle Rising. It was – and is – a beautiful piece of property. Essentially, the holes were carved out of a densely wooded forest. The fairways, like emerald ribbons, weave a path in and out of the trees. It has been said (with little exaggeration) that the golfer 'enters the forest as he walks to the 1st tee and doesn't emerge until he reaches the 18th green'.

It is a very challenging golf course, demanding length as well as considerable accuracy from the tee. Among the finest holes on the front nine are the 2nd, where water threatens both the drive and the approach, the par three 3rd and the 8th. The 10th is perhaps the toughest hole on the back nine and the 15th and 16th set the mood for a strong finish.

HOW TO GET THERE

he Club is situated at
North Wootton. Take the
A149 or A148.

King's Lynn
Golf Club

COURSE INFORMATION & FACILITIES

King's Lynn Golf Club
Castle Rising, King's Lynn
Norfolk PE31 6BD

Secretary: G J Higgins
Tel: 01553 631654 Fax: 01553 631036

Golf Professional Tel: 01553 631655

Green Fees:
Weekdays — £40 Weekends — £50
Weekdays (day) — £40 Weekends (day) — £50

Handicap certificate required

CARD OF THE COURSE — PAR 72

1	2	3	4	5	6	7	8	9	Out
499	439	210	483	366	389	513	386	324	3609
Par 5	Par 4	Par 3	Par 5	Par 4	Par 4	Par 5	Par 4	Par 4	Par 38

10	11	12	13	14	15	16	17	18	In
400	367	133	397	424	359	160	383	377	3000
Par 4	Par 4	Par 3	Par 4	Par 4	Par 4	Par 3	Par 4	Par 4	Par 34

87

Little Aston

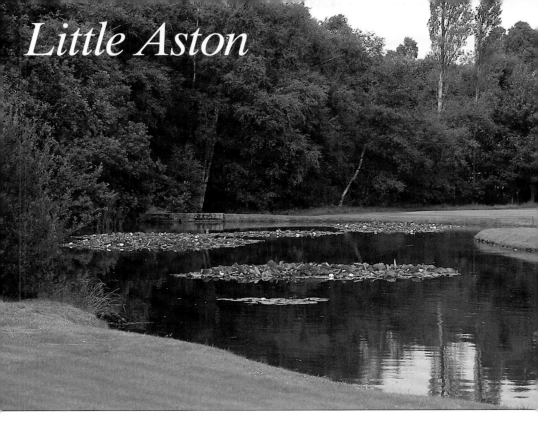

*I*n the days before The Belfry, Little Aston was the midlands' best known golf course. In the opinion of many it remains the best. Indeed, among the ranks of 'traditional' parkland courses perhaps only Stoke Poges can justifiably dispute its claim to being the finest in Britain. Located on the fringes of Sutton Coldfield, and only 10 miles from the centre of Birmingham, Little Aston enjoys a surprisingly tranquil setting. It is reached by way of an old Roman road, elegantly described by David Davies as, 'A rich and private drive of quiet perfection which epitomises the course which lies ahead'.

Little Aston was founded in 1908. The course was originally laid out by Harry Vardon and revised by Harry Colt. It was later extended to incorporate land beyond Little Aston Park, this addition providing the course with a moorland-come-heathland flavour to some of the holes. Always beautifully maintained, Little Aston is renowned for the quality of its greens and for the classical style of its bunkering. With attractive (and very natural looking) water hazards, fairways framed by silver birch trees and rhododendrons providing seasonal splashes of colour, it makes for a marvellous golfing stage.

Among the most outstanding holes at Little Aston are the par five 3rd which features a downhill drive and an approach over an intimidating cross bunker, the double dog-legging 10th – a very tough two-shotter – and the par four 17th where the sloping, pulpit green is defended by both sand and water.

COURSE INFORMATION & FACILITIES

Little Aston Golf Club
Streetly, Sutton Coldfield
West Midlands B74 3AN

Manager: A. E. Dibble.
Tel: 0121 353 2942 Fax: 0121 580 8387
Club House: 0121 353 2066
www.littleastongolf.co.uk

Golf Professional Tel: 0121 353 0330

Green Fees:
Weekdays — £50 Weekdays (Days) — £60
No visitors weekends.

CARD OF THE COURSE — PAR 72

1	2	3	4	5	6	7	8	9	Out
388	435	503	317	158	423	362	391	193	3170
Par 4	Par 4	Par 5	Par 4	Par 3	Par 4	Par 4	Par 4	Par 3	Par 35

10	11	12	13	14	15	16	17	18	In
438	394	487	160	320	548	400	366	387	3500
Par 4	Par 4	Par 5	Par 3	Par 4	Par 5	Par 4	Par 4	Par 4	Par 37

HOW TO GET THERE

miles north west of Sutton
oldfield off A454.

Little Aston
Golf Club

Luffenham Heath

*E*ven on a busy Saturday in July, Luffenham Heath exudes a sedate Tuesday afternoon ambiance. The PG Wodehouse character who claimed his concentration had been broken by 'the uproar of butterflies from an adjoining meadow' might have played his golf at Luffenham Heath. The only thing that ever caused a stir here was mother nature. Situated not far from Rutland Water, the Leicestershire golf course occupies an area of Special Scientific Interest. It is adorned by a wealth of trees, including various species of oak, pine, elm, ash, cherry and hawthorn, and is a haven for a rich variety of animal, bird, insect and plant life.

The course is rather more undulating than people imagine, although the only serious climb comes at the 7th. James Braid was the architect of Luffenham Heath, which explains why the greens are generally small and expertly defended, why there are so many cross bunkers and why several of the holes have a flavour of Gleneagles about them – the exciting downhill approach to the 4th, for instance, to a green backed by dark firs, is very reminiscent of a number of holes on the King's Course.

The wayward golfer is invariably punished at Luffenham Heath while the straight hitter is constantly teased. Among other outstanding holes are the 2nd, a difficult left to right dog-leg, the long par five 6th (especially from the elevated back tee), the exacting two-shot 13th and the dramatic vertigo-inducing par three 17th.

COURSE INFORMATION & FACILITIES

The Luffenham Heath Golf Club
Ketton, Stamford
Lincolnshire PE9 3UU

Secretary: John R Ingleby Tel: 01780 720205

Golf Professional:
Tel: 01780 720298 Fax: 01780 720298

Green Fees:
Weekdays — £35 Weekends — £40
Weekdays (day) — £35 Weekends (day) — £40
Society Rates: £35 Weekdays only.

CARD OF THE COURSE — PAR 70

1	2	3	4	5	6	7	8	9	Out
357	412	360	392	148	490	367	281	173	2980
Par 4	Par 4	Par 4	Par 4	Par 3	Par 5	Par 4	Par 4	Par 3	Par 35
10	**11**	**12**	**13**	**14**	**15**	**16**	**17**	**18**	**In**
326	440	149	472	346	393	414	200	553	3293
Par 4	Par 4	Par 3	Par 4	Par 4	Par 4	Par 4	Par 3	Par 5	Par 35

HOW TO GET THERE

om A1 5 miles west of
amford, through Ketton
nder Forsters Railway
idge. Sharp left onto
6121.

Luffenham
Heath Golf Club

Northamptonshire County

*I*n a typical display of modesty, golf architect Harry Colt once described Swinley Forest near Ascot as his 'least bad' golf course.

I guess, therefore, that he might have described his layout at Church Brampton – for the Northamptonshire County Golf Club – as 'perhaps the least acclaimed among (his) better efforts'.

Anyone who has played Northamptonshire County will find it hard to comprehend why it never seems to feature in the British 'Top 100' lists. Essentially a heathland layout (the 'Sandy Lane' address is a giveaway) and measuring close to 6500 yards, the course is not long by modern championship standards, though the quality of the hazards, particularly the brilliance of Colt's bunkering, more than compensates for any perceived lack of yardage.

The layout actually starts with a strong par four and finishes with a tough dog-legging par five. Among the most noteworthy holes in between, one should mention the 3rd, if only because it was once halved in one, the 5th, and the excellent sequence from the 10th to the 14th which are separated from the rest of the course by a railway line.

A jewel in the east midlands, if Northamptonshire County were located sixty miles to the south it would be more widely known, and, yes, would surely be rated alongside Colt's 'better efforts' amid the heathlands of Berkshire and Surrey.

HOW TO GET THERE

miles north west of
orthampton between A50
nd A428.

Northampton
Golf Club

COURSE INFORMATION & FACILITIES

Northamptonshire County Golf Club
Sandy Lane
Church Brampton, Northampton NN68AZ

Secretary: M. E. Wadley
Tel/Fax: 01604 843025

Golf Professional: Tim Rouse
Tel/Fax: 01604 842226

Green Fees:
Weekdays and Weekends - £45 per round or day
Handicap Certificate required – Restrictions apply

CARD OF THE COURSE – PAR 70

1	2	3	4	5	6	7	8	9	Out
454	519	180	334	438	204	396	312	392	3229
Par 4	Par 5	Par 3	Par 4	Par 4	Par 3	Par 4	Par 4	Par 4	Par 35

10	11	12	13	14	15	16	17	18	In
413	384	135	392	377	174	434	460	504	3273
Par 4	Par 4	Par 3	Par 4	Par 4	Par 3	Par 4	Par 4	Par 5	Par 35

Notts

avid Davies once described the Notts Golf Club at Hollinwell as 'a great gorse-filled bowl of golfing delights'. Hollinwell, as it is usually called, rivals Ganton and Woodhall Spa as Britain's premier heathland course north of London. As a test of golf it is not quite as demanding as the Yorkshire and Lincolnshire courses, for its bunkers are less punitive, but it is long (7000 yards plus from the championship tees) and invariably rewards accurate and intelligent play.

The abundance of gorse is indeed a striking feature at Hollinwell. There is plenty of heather and bracken too, and with a wealth of silver birch, oaks, pines and firs adorning the fairways it is splendid setting in which to play golf. Dominating the backdrop

are the tree-covered Robin Hood Hills which semi-circle above the course, so creating the bowl effect.

Willie Park was responsible for the excellent design. Like Woodhall Spa and Ganton, it begins with a straightforward opening hole. The 2nd, however, is a strong par four which curves towards a green framed by a giant rock known as Robin Hood's Chair. Another celebrated hole on the front nine is the 8th where you drive across an attractive pond; to the right of the tee, partly hidden by trees, is the 'Holy Well' from which the name Hollinwell derives. An outstanding run of holes commences at the 13th, 'an absolute terror' of a long par three, with the two-shot 15th being perhaps the finest hole of all.

HOW TO GET THERE

1 Junction 27 A608
rection Mansfield.
in A611 direction
ansfield. Golf Course
on right hand side of
611. From Junction 27
trance is approximately
miles.

Notts
Golf Club

COURSE INFORMATION & FACILITIES

Notts Golf Club
Derby Road, Kirkby-in-Ashfield
Nottingham NG17 7QR

Secretary: S F C Goldie
Tel: 01623 753225 Fax: 01623 753655

Golf Professional Tel: 01623 753087

Green Fees per 18 holes per day:
Weekdays — £40
Weekdays (day) — £55

CARD OF THE COURSE — PAR 72

1	2	3	4	5	6	7	8	9	Out
376	430	511	455	193	533	403	410	178	3489
Par 4	Par 4	Par 5	Par 4	Par 3	Par 5	Par 4	Par 4	Par 3	Par 36

10	11	12	13	14	15	16	17	18	In
362	365	433	236	403	440	355	490	457	3541
Par 4	Par 4	Par 4	Par 3	Par 4	Par 4	Par 4	Par 5	Par 4	Par 36

95

Ross on Wye

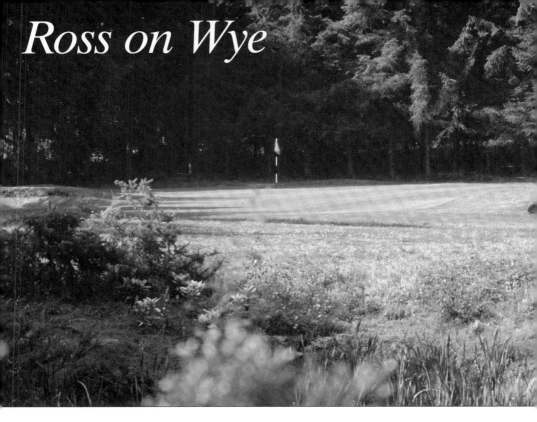

xplore the Wye Valley and you'll have a good idea as to why the English and Welsh fought so vehemently to claim the region as theirs.

The swords and shields long since put away, the Wye Valley is one of Britain's most peaceful and idyllic areas. Travel north from the Forest of Dean, past spectacular Symonds Yat (a visit here is strongly recommended) and haunted Goodrich Castle, and you reach the little market town of Ross-on Wye. Now bring out your sticks.

Ross-on-Wye Golf Club was founded in 1903. The club's present course which, despite the tranquillity is actually quite close to the M50, dates from the mid 1960s when it was laid out by C.K.

Cotton, architect of nearby St Pierre.

Ross-on-Wye is a very scenic and quite undulating woodland type golf course, its fairways bordered by a rich variety of silver birch trees, oaks and pines: you can play a round here and only rarely see another group of golfers so self-contained are the holes.

As the above comment implies, Ross-on-Wye is a course that rewards straight hitting, a feature compounded by the generally small and slick nature of the putting surfaces. Measuring close to 6500 yards, the layout includes a number of cleverly designed short par fours and, on the back nine in particular, a series of strong, 420-yards plus holes – overall, a nice balance of charm and challenge.

COURSE INFORMATION & FACILITIES

The Ross on Wye Golf Course
Gursley
Ross on Wye HR9 7UT

Secretary: Peter Plumb
Tel: 01989 720267 Fax: 01989 720212

Golf Professional: Nick Catchpole
Tel: 01989 720439

Green Fees:
Weekdays — £32   Weekends — £32
Weekdays (day) — £42   Weekends (day) — £42

Handicap Certificate required — Restrictions apply.

CARD OF THE COURSE — PAR 72

1	2	3	4	5	6	7	8	9	Out
314	453	284	352	477	534	151	495	216	3276
Par 4	Par 4	Par 4	Par 4	Par 5	Par 5	Par 3	Par 5	Par 3	Par 37
10	11	12	13	14	15	16	17	18	In
445	353	136	343	438	326	296	429	409	3175
Par 4	Par 4	Par 3	Par 4	Par 4	Par 4	Par 4	Par 4	Par 4	Par 35

HOW TO GET THERE

miles North of Ross on
ye, by M50 Junction 3.

Ross on Wye
Golf Club

Royal West Norfolk

The Royal West Norfolk Golf Club at Brancaster exudes a unique sense of tradition, history and character. This testing and most enjoyable links lies in a range of sand hills between marshland and sea. The road that leads to the course can flood at very high tide; at such times a discerning golfer may choose to leave his car in the village and walk the remainder of the journey!

Laid out in 1891, the Prince of Wales immediately bestowed patronage on the club. The Royal flavour has prevailed and there have been no fewer than four Royal Captains, most recently the Duke of Kent in 1981. The links has remained refreshingly unaltered over the years, although two greens were lost to the sea in 1939 and 1940.

A traditional out and back links layout, the character of Brancaster is exemplified by both the tidal marshes (which come into play around the 8th and 9th) and the famed wooden sleepered bunkers, many of which are cross bunkers and which are introduced as early as the 3rd. Although the shorter of the two nines, the inward half is often the more testing as it is invariably played into a stiff westerly wind. The 11th and 12th are located deep amid the dunes but the famous old 14th, where the fairway tumbles along classic linksland close to the shore, is perhaps the most difficult hole of all. After a strong finish, with sleepered bunkers both to the front and back of the 18th green, the homely nineteenth hole provides a final treat.

HOW TO GET THERE

miles east of Hunstanton.
Brancaster Village, turn
orth at Beach/Broad Lane
unction with A149. Club is
mile down this road.

Royal West
Norfolk

COURSE INFORMATION & FACILITIES

Royal West Norfolk Golf Club
Brancaster, Near King's Lynn
Norfolk PE31 8AX

Secretary: Major N A Carrington Smith
Tel: 01485 210087 Fax: 01485 210087

Golf Professional Tel: 01485 210616

Green Fees per 18 holes per day:
Weekdays — £50 summer
Weekdays (day) — £40 winter.

CARD OF THE COURSE — PAR 71

1	2	3	4	5	6	7	8	9	Out
410	449	407	128	421	186	486	478	404	3369
Par 4	Par 4	Par 4	Par 3	Par 4	Par 3	Par 5	Par 5	Par 4	Par 36

10	11	12	13	14	15	16	17	18	In
151	478	386	317	432	188	346	377	384	3059
Par 3	Par 5	Par 4	Par 4	Par 4	Par 3	Par 4	Par 4	Par 4	Par 35

Seacroft

I t is hard to believe that south east Lincolnshire was once one of the most populated areas of Great Britain. Apparently the region was buzzing in the late Middle Ages, but nowadays it has been left largely to the birds - literally so, just five miles south of Skegness at a wildlife sanctuary called (rather interestingly) Gibraltar Point. And midway between Skegness and Gibraltar Point there is a hidden, almost secret golf course named Seacroft. In actual fact, Seacroft is the finest links course on the east coast of England between Hunstanton and Seaton Carew.

Overlooking The Wash, Seacroft is a decidedly old fashioned links; its layout, crafted initially by Tom Dunn in 1892, and later revised by Sir Guy Campbell, stretches out and back à la St Andrews. The two nines occupy distinct levels with a central ridge of dunes dividing one half from the other.

The terrain is similar to that of Hunstanton and the quality of the golf is only slightly inferior. The par threes holes are particularly memorable - all four are even-numbered (something to remember when playing foursomes!) while the par fours provide plenty of variey but rarely much margin for error. As Donald Steel has observed, 'On nearly every tee, it is a case of looking down a gun barrel'. The best of the two-shot holes is probably the 13th, a reachable par five, and which in terms of character and quality is reminiscent of the much acclaimed 13th hole at Silloth-on-Solway.

COURSE INFORMATION & FACILITIES

Seacroft Golf Club
Drummond Road, Skegness,
Lincolnshire PE25 3AU

Secretary/Manager: Richard England
Tel: 01754 763020   Fax: 01754 763020
Email: enquires@seacroft-golfclub.co.uk
Web: www.seacroft-golfclub.co.uk

Golf Professional Robin Lawie Tel: 01754 763020

Green Fees:
Weekdays — £25 Weekends — £30
Weekdays (days) £35 Weekends (day) £40

Restrictions: Visitors after 9.30am.
Wednesdays — Ladies priority Day

CARD OF THE COURSE — PAR 71

1	2	3	4	5	6	7	8	9	Out
409	369	328	184	439	343	422	390	484	3368
Par 4	Par 4	Par 4	Par 3	Par 4	Par 4	Par 4	Par 4	Par 5	Par 36

10	11	12	13	14	15	16	17	18	In
153	538	210	499	175	400	313	414	409	3111
Par 3	Par 5	Par 3	Par 5	Par 3	Par 4	Par 4	Par 4	Par 4	Par 35

HOW TO GET THERE

ollow the signs to the Seafront
the Clock Tower , 20 yards
om the Clock Tower turn
ght onto Drumond Road, drive
ong approximately 1 mile. 100
rds past the Crown Hotel on
e left, The Clubhouse (a white
ilding & the first tee are
ere). Any signs for
ibraltar Point
ill take you
st the
urse.

Seacroft Golf Club

THE VINE HOTEL
SEACROFT SKEGNESS
PE25 3DB

Located only 300 yds from Seacroft Golf Course, Skegness' premier hotel offers
superb accommodation, fine wines, excellent food and Batemans award winning ales.
Set amidst tranquil gardens The Vine is the ideal place to relax after the game.
Small golf parties or societies are welcome at specially discounted rates.

Telephone: 01754 610611 Fax: 01754 769845
Web Site: http://www.skegness-resort/co.uk/vine

Sheringham

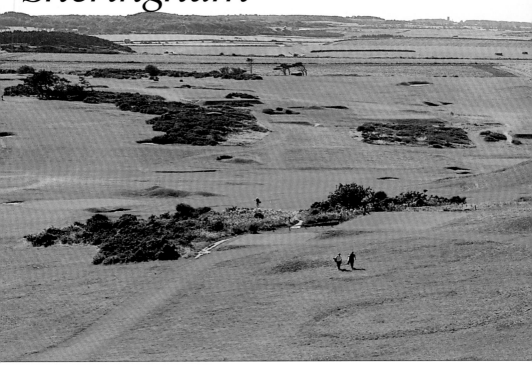

*I*f variety is the spice of golf, then
the county of Norfolk is a golfing
haven. It offers classic links golf at
Brancaster and Hunstanton, woodland
splendour at Kings Lynn, a hint of
heathland at Thetford and some superior
parkland golf at Royal Norwich. There
is also some first rate cliff top golf –
perhaps the form of golf that best
combines challenge with scenic splendour
– to be savoured at Sheringham and
Royal Cromer.

Sheringham is undoubtedly one of
Britain's finest cliff top courses. In terms
of playing quality, the layout is good
enough to have staged the English
Ladies Championship on more than one
occasion. It was here in 1920 that the
great Joyce Wethered won a famous

victory over Cecil Leitch and uttered
the immortal phrase, 'Train, what train?'
(when asked why a noisy passing loco-
motive had failed to put her off her stroke).

The golf course occupies a thin strip
of land sandwiched between the cliffs on
one side and the North Norfolk Steam
Railway line on the other. After a modest
beginning, a superb sequence of holes
commences at the 3rd. The next five
fairways – and greens – run adjacent to
the cliff edges. It is breathtaking golf
with the par four 5th being especially
spectacular. Vast seas of gorse threaten to
envelop golfers between the 8th and 14th
holes, while the railway line looms to the
right of the player as he returns towards
the clubhouse. Sheringham is a superb
test of golf – and a slicer's nightmare!

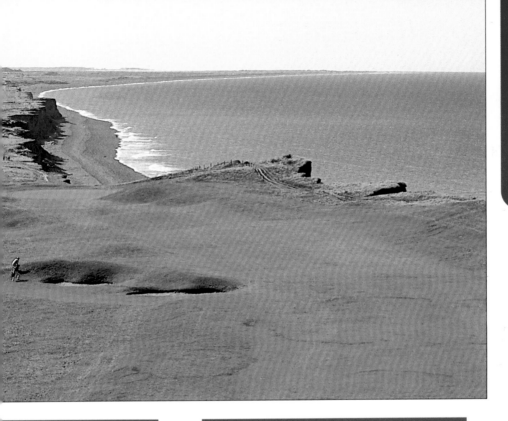

HOW TO GET THERE

alf a mile west of
heringham on A149.

Sheringham
Golf Club

COURSE INFORMATION & FACILITIES

Sheringham Golf Club
Weybourne Road
Sheringham, Norfolk NR26 8HG.

Secretary: C Davies
Tel: 01263 823488 Fax: 01263 825189

Golf Professional: 01263 822980

Green Fees per 18 holes per day:
Weekdays summer — £40 Weekends — £45
Weekdays winter — £35 Weekends — £40
Twilight after 4pm summer and after noon winter half
rate. Letter of introduction required.

CARD OF THE COURSE — PAR 70

1	2	3	4	5	6	7	8	9	Out
324	543	424	327	452	217	517	167	410	3381
Par 4	Par 5	Par 4	Par 4	Par 4	Par 3	Par 5	Par 3	Par 4	Par 36

10	11	12	13	14	15	16	17	18	In
444	163	425	351	354	195	349	405	423	3109
Par 4	Par 3	Par 4	Par 4	Par 4	Par 3	Par 4	Par 4	Par 4	Par 34

Woodbridge

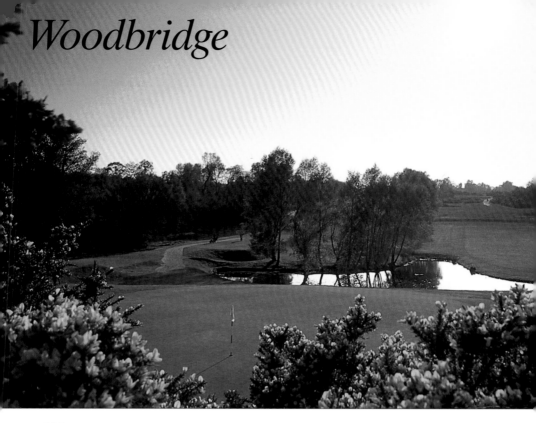

Situated in sleepy, rural Suffolk, Woodbridge is an ancient and famous little market town. Quite a stir was created here in 1939 when a hoard of 7th century Anglo-Saxon treasure was discovered in the nearby hamlet of Sutton Hoo. But history abounds in Woodbridge and the beautiful market square is jam packed with elegant Georgian buildings, and, most impressively of all, it is home to Shire Hall with its magnificent Dutch styled gabled trimmings.

Woodbridge's golf course is located two miles to the east of the town, close to the estuary of the River Deben. It is one of England's most attractive heathland courses. Very sandy underfoot and quick draining, the holes are framed by vast swathes of gorse, bracken and heather.

Woodbridge is a medium length course, designed by Fred Hawtree; it is always well maintained and is surprisingly undulating given the character of the surrounding landscape.

There really isn't a bad hole at Woodbridge but most commentators regard the rich variety of par four holes as the course's greatest strength. The 2nd provides an early example of a fine short par four: following a downhill drive, invariably struck with a long iron, you must play a deft pitch over a stream. By contrast, the long 10th requires two very big shots for it runs uphill pretty much all the way. The course possesses a particularly good back nine and the heavily bunkered, dog-legging 14th is possibly the finest two-shot hole of the round.

SUFFOLK

CARD OF THE COURSE — PAR 70

1	2	3	4	5	6	7	8	9	Out
346	329	529	330	371	401	149	514	198	3167
Par 4	Par 4	Par 5	Par 4	Par 4	Par 4	Par 3	Par 5	Par 3	Par 36

10	11	12	13	14	15	16	17	18	In
431	392	184	310	425	188	445	400	357	3132
Par 4	Par 4	Par 3	Par 4	Par 4	Par 3	Par 4	Par 4	Par 4	Par 34

HOW TO GET THERE

ave the A12 by the
1152 going to Orford.
fter passing through the
elton traffic lights and
:ross the railway crossing,
ear left at the next
undabout. The club
ntrance is 200 yards
n the
ght.

Woodbridge
Golf Club

105

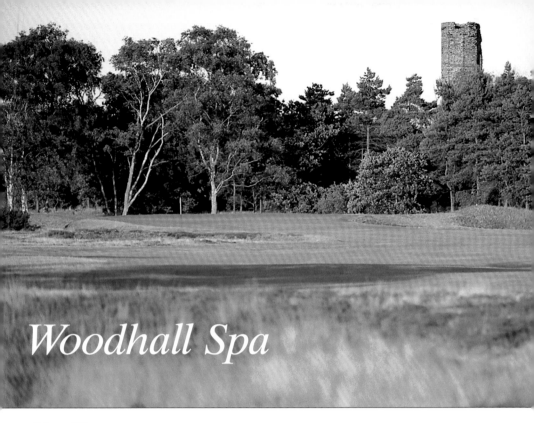

Woodhall Spa

*M*any, if not most golf course critics regard the original course at Woodhall Spa as the number one inland course in Britain. It is as scenic as Sunningdale and The Berkshire and as challenging as Ganton and Walton Heath. It has hosted many major amateur events, including both Men's and Ladies' English Amateur Championships, and would doubtless have staged several important professional tournaments if it were not so remote.

Remote? It is located half an hour's drive from Lincoln along narrow, winding roads. To find Woodhall Spa you need to be a competent map reader. But if ever a journey was worth making.... Of course, remoteness, like tranquility, is an important ingredient of charm. Walton Heath was a charming spot before they built the M25. On approaching Woodhall Spa for the first time one is not only charmed but amazed. Having driven through miles of flat, uninspiring terrain, Woodhall Spa suddenly emerges like a mirage. It is golf's most spectacular oasis: an oasis of sand, heather and pine – not to mention the remarkable wildlife that inhabits this extraordinary domain.

The course measures almost 7,000 yards from the championship tees and, like Ganton, is renowned for its cavernous bunkers. It is difficult to single out individual holes but among the finest are the 3rd and the 18th plus a wonderful sequence between the 11th and 14th. A plaque beside the green at the par three 12th records how in March 1982 two members halved the hole in one.

COURSE INFORMATION & FACILITIES

Woodhall Spa Golf Club
Woodhall Spa
Lincs LN10 6PU

Secretary: B H Fawcett
Tel: 01526 352511 Fax: 01526 352778

Golf Professional Tel: 01526 353229

Green Fees:
Weekdays — £40 Weekends — £40
Weekdays (day) — £65 Weekends (day) — £65

Letter of introduction required.

CARD OF THE COURSE — PAR 73

1	2	3	4	5	6	7	8	9	Out
363	414	420	415	155	512	438	193	562	3472
Par 4	Par 4	Par 4	Par 4	Par 3	Par 5	Par 4	Par 3	Par 5	Par 36

10	11	12	13	14	15	16	17	18	In
345	442	157	437	489	328	398	333	544	3473
Par 4	Par 4	Par 3	Par 4	Par 5	Par 4	Par 4	Par 4	Par 5	Par 37

HOW TO GET THERE

 miles South East of
ncoln on the B1191.

Woodhall Spa
Golf Club

Lancashire &
North West

Lancashire & The North West

*T*here is much keen rivalry between Merseyside and Manchester, notably in football and in music, but not in golf. There is no contest. The city of Liverpool brushes the finest stretch of linksland in England (and some would say in the entire British Isles). From the Wirral Peninsula to Blackpool, or from Hoylake to Lytham, lie a string of golfing pearls: Royal Liverpool, Wallasey, West Lancashire, Formby, Royal Birkdale, Hillside, Southport & Ainsdale, Fairhaven, Royal Lytham & St Annes and St Annes Old Links – a truly remarkable collection. Manchester excels in quantity rather than quality. But of course, there are some exceptions…

To the south of Manchester, in fact just north of Stockport, there is a very underrated golf course at Reddish Vale, and at the point where the metropolis fades into rural Cheshire, is the start of a sand belt. It is smaller, but similar in character to the heathland belt of Surrey. There is no Sunningdale or St George's Hill here, alas, but Sandiway and Delamere Forest are both very fine golf courses. On the fringes of the sand belt there is a very good new course at Tarporley, (Portal) and further to the west, close to the Welsh border is the outstanding 36 hole development at Carden Park.

Among the better golf courses to the north of Manchester are Worsley, North Manchester and Bolton Old Links. If one ventures a little further north into 'real Lancashire' there is a very good course at Pleasington near Blackburn and a very picturesque one at Clitheroe on the edge of the Forest of Bowland.

Golfers visiting the Isle of Man are rewarded with a keen selection of courses. The premier attraction on the island is undoubtedly the links at Castletown. Originally designed by Old Tom Morris, it is a stern test

of golf and it enjoys a magnificent setting on the Langness Peninsula.

Our region also encompasses the large county of Cumbria, much of which is far too mountainous for golf. The Lake District is possibly the most beautiful region of Britain. There are a handful of golf courses within the National Park and while they are essentially modest affairs, the accompanying scenery more than compensates – Windermere Golf Club is a fine example. The greatest course in Cumbria is one of Britain's ultimate hidden gems: the classic links at Silloth on Solway. It is the kind of course you play, you fall in love with, but you only tell your very closest friends about.

CASTLETOWN

CAVENDISH

DELAMERE FOREST

HILLSIDE

PLEASINGTON

REDDISH VALE

SILLOTH ON SOLWAY

WALLASEY

WINDERMERE

Lancashire &
North West

Page

Castletown

hree exraordinary individuals
helped to create and shape the
links at Castletown. The first was
Finn McCool, a legendary giant who lived
on the Antrim Coast of Northern Ireland.
He was the fellow who started (but never
finished) building the Giant's Causeway.
Finn was apparently prone to fits of
temper and one day, during a particularly
ferocious tantrum, he picked up a vast
chunk of rock and hurled it into the sea.
This rock is the Isle of Man.

It was to the southern tip of the Isle
of Man that Old Tom Morris ventured
in 1892. The four times Open Champion
was invited to lay out a golf course on the
Langness Peninsula, better known as Fort
Island. It was – and is – an amazing site:
a triangular shaped, thin strip of land

surrounded by water on three sides.
It was here, then, that Old Tom
established the original Castletown links.

By 1945 Morris's course was in need of
extensive revision. Philip Mackenzie Ross,
the architect who had performed post war
miracles at Turnberry, was commissioned
to redesign the links. An heroic site,
Mackenzie Ross believed, demanded
heroic golf holes, and this is precisely
what 'greets' the present day visitor to
Castletown. It is a thrilling round, and
one that reaches its climax on the
penultimate hole. On the par four 17th
at Castletown you are asked to drive
200 yards across the edge of a rocky
chasm (while ignoring the threat of the
sea crashing below). It is, of course,
pure Turnberry.

HOW TO GET THERE

wo miles Ronaldsway
irport. Four miles south of
ingles.

Castletown
Golf Club

COURSE INFORMATION & FACILITIES

Castletown Golf Club
Castletown Golf Links Hotel
Derbyhaven, Isle of Man IM9 1UA

Secretary: John Fowlds.
Tel: 01624 825435 Fax: 01624 824633

Golf Professional:
Tel: 01624 822211 Fax: 01624 824633

Green Fees:
Weekdays (day) — £30 Weekends (day) — £35

CARD OF THE COURSE — PAR 72

1	2	3	4	5	6	7	8	9	Out
253	391	557	377	422	384	567	164	369	3484
Par 4	Par 4	Par 5	Par 4	Par 4	Par 4	Par 5	Par 3	Par 4	Par 37

10	11	12	13	14	15	16	17	18	In
355	443	503	139	394	373	186	417	417	3227
Par 4	Par 4	Par 5	Par 3	Par 4	Par 4	Par 3	Par 4	Par 4	Par 35

Cavendish

The Peak District is the oldest (i.e. first established) and perhaps the least 'touristy' of Britain's national parks. While portions of it protrude into other counties, notably Staffordshire to the south and Cheshire to the north, most of the Peak District lies within Derbyshire. Golfers visiting the region, and who may have grown just a tad weary of trekking in the hills, should head for the town of Buxton and, more specifically, they should try to arrange a game at Cavendish Golf Club: it is an excellent golf course and they will assuredly be made to feel most welcome.

Little known outside of Derbyshire, Cavendish has many attributes, not least of which is its glorious setting. The course nestles somewhat in a valley and is framed by nearby hills and more distant mountains.

A mix of parkland and downland, the layout is the handiwork of master golf course architect, Alister Mackenzie. Mackenzie's talent is particularly in evidence in the design of the greens, many of which are two-tiered.

Selecting the best holes at Cavendish isn't easy for so many are interesting and there is plenty of variety. Most commentators, however, seem to agree that the sequence between the 8th and 11th is particularly outstanding, and many also cite the 18th as a very strong finishing hole.

HOW TO GET THERE

m Buxton take A53, second turning on
right into Carlisle Road, then second
into Watford Road, the golf club is
ated at the end of the road.

Cavendish
Golf Club

COURSE INFORMATION & FACILITIES

Cavendish Golf Club
Gadley Lane, Buxton
Derbyshire SK17 6XD

Secretary: J.D. Rushton

Tel/Fax: 01298 79708

Golf Professional: Paul Hunstone
Tel: 01288 25052

Green Fees:
Weekdays - £26 Weekends - £35
Restrictions apply.

CARD OF THE COURSE — PAR 68

1	2	3	4	5	6	7	8	9	Out
354	314	285	122	420	412	312	389	139	2747
Par 4	Par 4	Par 4	Par 3	Par 4	Par 4	Par 4	Par 4	Par 3	Par 34

10	11	12	13	14	15	16	17	18	In
422	403	350	183	496	116	403	160	441	2974
Par 4	Par 4	Par 4	Par 3	Par 5	Par 3	Par 4	Par 3	Par 4	Par 34

Delamere Forest

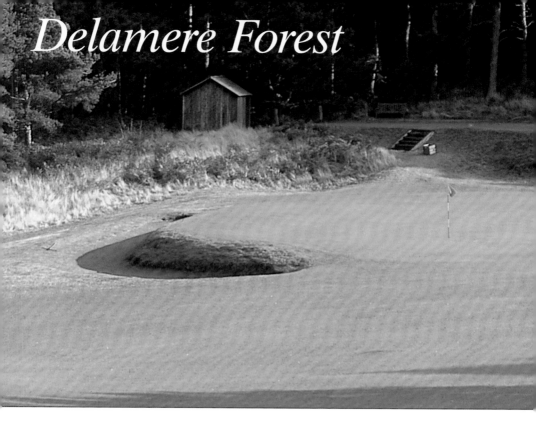

Just as a majority of the top golf courses around London are located immediately beyond its south and south western fringes, so the same can be said of Greater Manchester. Travel in a southerly or south westerly direction from the north's biggest conurbation and you quickly arrive in rural Cheshire - a county famous for its cheese and its grinning cats, but where you can also find a wealth of first rate golf courses. Probably the finest of Cheshire's 'established' courses is Delamere Forest, near Northwich.

The golf course is located on the edge of the eponymous forest (a large and beautifully wooded oasis) and is essentially heathland in nature. It doesn't feature the wonderful pine trees of a Swinley Forest but Delamere Forest has no shortage of heather and gorse. It also boasts, like Sunningdale and St George's Hill, some spectacularly undulating terrain.

Designed by Herbert Fowler (the architect of Walton Heath and The Berkshire), and opened for play in 1910, Delamere Forest could be described as a medium length course. It features plenty of stirring par four holes and in its 6th has one of the best short holes in the north west. The sharply dog-legging 14th hole is a good example of a really testing short par four, and the round concludes with a nerve wracking drive from an elevated tee - you must first flirt with an Out of Bounds - followed by a searching second to a big, undulating green - a real grandstand finish.

HOW TO GET THERE

6 to Jn18 Middlewich Rd.
54. Follow signs for
hester to crossroads B5152
Frodsham. Approx 20
iles from M6 take road
wards Frodsham (Station
oad) for about 1 mile. Golf
lub entrance
n right.

Delamere
Forest
Golf Club

COURSE INFORMATION & FACILITIES

Delamere Forest Golf Club
Delamere, Northwich,
Cheshire CW8 2JE

Secretary/Director: Graham Owen
Tel: 01606 883800 Fax: 01606 889444

Golf Professional Tel: 01606 883307

Green Fees: Weekdays — £30 Weekends — £40
Weekdays (days) £45 Weekends (day) N/A

Restrictions: None but numbers limited weekends

CARD OF THE COURSE — PAR 72

1	2	3	4	5	6	7	8	9	Out
429	442	414	213	428	147	445	418	333	3269
Par 4	Par 5	Par 4	Par 3	Par 4	Par 3	Par 5	Par 4	Par 4	Par 36

10	11	12	13	14	15	16	17	18	In
381	498	149	312	373	304	197	360	485	3059
Par 4	Par 1	Par 16	Par 4	Par 8	Par 4	Par 3	Par 4	Par 5	Par 36

Hillside

The east coast of Scotland is where golf began; the Ayrshire coast is where the Open Championship was born and yet, history aside, many believe that the greatest stretch of linksland in the British Isles is to be found on the Lancashire coast of north west England. Between Liverpool and Blackpool, a distance of 40 miles, lie a string of golfing pearls. Royal Birkdale stands proudly in the middle of this region and immediately adjacent to Birkdale is Hillside, a truly marvellous links.

In terms of international stature, Hillside is overshadowed by its illustrious neighbour – this despite the fact that it has staged many major amateur events and, in 1982, the PGA Championship. In terms of challenge, however, Hillside is every bit as good as Birkdale. The terrain is similar, of course, with massive dunes and deep bunkers the dominant features.

Hillside's strengths are the quality of its par fives and the spectacular, rollercoasting nature of its back nine – once described as being 'like Ballybunion minus the Atlantic Ocean'. The best of the early holes are the 3rd, an excellent dog-leg, and the par five 5th which features a highly unusual cross bunker. The back nine begins with an outstanding short hole played uphill to a green practicallly encircled by gaping traps. It is from here on that Hillside resembles Ballybunion. The two par fives, the 11th and 17th, are the most dramatic holes, their fairways twisting and turning along magnificent dune-lined valleys.

COURSE INFORMATION & FACILITIES

Hillside Golf Club
The Club House, Hastings Road
Hillside, Southport PR8 2LU

Secretary: J G Graham
Tel: 01704 567169 Fax: 01704 563192

Golf Professional Tel: 01704 568360

Green Fees per 18 holes per day:
Weekdays — £50 Weekends — £65
Weekdays (day) — £65

Introduction letter required.

CARD OF THE COURSE — PAR 72

1	2	3	4	5	6	7	8	9	Out
399	525	402	195	504	413	176	405	425	3444
Par 4	Par 5	Par 4	Par 3	Par 5	Par 4	Par 3	Par 4	Par 4	Par 36

10	11	12	13	14	15	16	17	18	In
147	508	368	398	400	398	199	548	440	3406
Par 3	Par 5	Par 4	Par 4	Par 4	Par 4	Par 3	Par 5	Par 4	Par 36

HOW TO GET THERE

miles south of the centre
Southport on the A565
Liverpool.

Hillside Golf Club

Pleasington

*M*ost visiting golfers heading towards the North West of England - to Lancashire specifically - have only one thought on their mind: to play some links golf. True, the Lancashire coast boasts an extraordinary array of outstanding links courses, but, let's face it, there's only so much links golf that a body can take. So when the visiting golfer has been sufficiently 'blown, buffeted and blasted' by the wind, where should he or she head for in order to 'revive, regenerate and resurge'? Pleasington is our strong recommendation.

Pleasington is as pleasant and pleasing as it sounds: Pleasington Golf Club offers inland golf at its best and most alluring. It is situated just 4 miles from Blackburn which, in keeping with many of the North's industrial towns, is surrounded by beautiful, unspoilt countryside. Pleasington's backdrop is one of rolling hills and mature woodland. In an article for Golf Monthly magazine, writer Barry Ward described the setting as 'ravishingly beautiful'.

The course comprises an interesting mix of parkland, moorland and heathland. The soil is quite sandy and in certain places heather and gorse grow in profusion. The first few holes occupy classic rolling parkland, but several of the most interesting holes are confronted towards the middle of the round as the terrain becomes more rugged. There are a couple of very good par threes within this stretch, both played from elevated tees across valleys, however, the two finest holes are arguably the par five 7th and the two-shot 12th.

HOW TO GET THERE

\6 north to Jct 28a (M65).
ake M65 to Jct 3. Take road
⊃ Blackburn from
⊃undabout. Turn right at
ghts and follow road for 3/4
nile. Turn left, signposted
'leasington Priory . Golf
lub is 300yds
n left hand
de.

Pleasington
Golf Club

COURSE INFORMATION & FACILITIES

Pleasington Golf Club
Pleasington, Blackburn,
Lancs BB2 5JF

Secretary/Manager: Mike Trickett
Tel: 01254 202177. Fax: 01254 201028

Golf Professional Tel: 01254 201630

Green Fees:
Weekdays — £36 Weekends — £42

Restrictions: Visitors welcome Mons, Weds, Fridays.

CARD OF THE COURSE — PAR 71

1	2	3	4	5	6	7	8	9	Out
385	348	330	432	343	357	527	166	488	3376
Par 4	Par 4	Par 4	Par 4	Par 4	Par 4	Par 5	Par 3	Par 5	Par 37

10	11	12	13	14	15	16	17	18	In
189	559	166	460	389	358	154	368	383	3026
Par 3	Par 5	Par 3	Par 4	Par 4	Par 4	Par 3	Par 4	Par 4	Par 34

Reddish Vale

Golfing Gems: The vast majority of courses featured in this book enjoy attractive – often extremely attractive – surroundings. Reddish Vale is an exception to the rule. Located a short distance to the north of Stockport, an historic industrial town that has long been swallowed up by Greater Manchester, Reddish Vale is what one might term 'an aesthetically challenged golf course'. For sure, there are courses set in less appealing environments; the point is made really to highlight the particular reason why we have decided to feature Reddish Vale in this guide: Architecturally speaking, Reddish Vale is something of a minor classic.

What do Augusta, Royal Melbourne, Cypress Point and Reddish Vale have in common? Precisely – all four were designed by Alister Mackenzie. There are no azaleas and dogwoods at Reddish Vale; instead the golf course sports a very rugged, even dishevelled look. Except in those places where it rubs up against town life, the golfing pallet resembles a moorland wilderness. The topography of the site is dramatic and Mackenzie's routing takes full advantage of it. Tees and greens are brilliantly, if occasionally mischievously, sited. There are one or two challenging carries but invariably (as one might expect from a Mackenzie design) the layout rewards the golfer who sensibly and successfully plots his way around.

There may be more celebrated golf courses in the south Manchester – north Cheshire area, but very few that are as thrilling to play as Reddish Vale.

HOW TO GET THERE

...nction 25 on the M60 —
...ke Tiviot Way to
...undabout at top, right
...ong Sandy Lane past the
...arousel pub, turn right just
...ast block of shops
...ignposted Reddish Vale
...olf Club) into
...outhcliffe
...oad.

Reddish Vale
Golf Club

COURSE INFORMATION & FACILITIES

Reddish Vale Golf Club
The Golf House, Southcliffe Road, South Reddish
Stockport SK5 7EE

Secretary: B J D Rendell JP
Tel: 0161 480 2359 Fax: 0161 477 8242

Golf Professional: Bob Freeman
Tel: 0161 480 3824

Green Fees:
Weekdays - £25 Weekdays (day) £30

Restrictions apply.

CARD OF THE COURSE — PAR 69

1	2	3	4	5	6	7	8	9	Out
421	179	390	166	306	240	538	393	137	2770
Par 4	Par 3	Par 4	Par 3	Par 4	Par 3	Par 5	Par 4	Par 3	Par 33

10	11	12	13	14	15	16	17	18	In
343	460	188	456	340	477	322	377	353	3316
Par 4	Par 4	Par 3	Par 4	Par 4	Par 5	Par 4	Par 4	Par 4	Par 36

Silloth on Solway

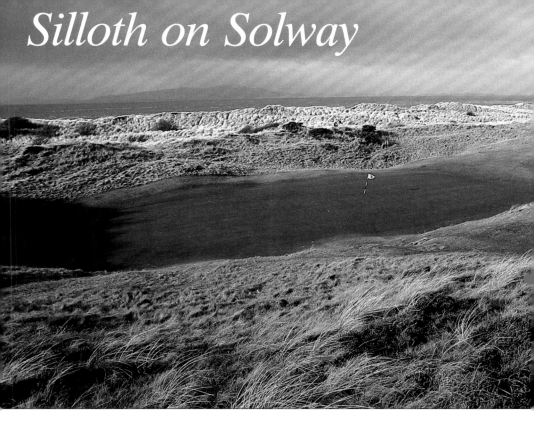

*C*ecil Leitch, one of Britain's finest ever lady golfers, once said: 'If you can play Silloth you can play anywhere'. The four times British Ladies champion should have been able to judge better than most for she grew up in Silloth and it was here that she and her four golfing sisters learned to play.

Silloth is a magnificent links and yet, despite its having staged several major championships, it remains one of Britain's lesser known (and most underrated) golfing gems. The sole reason is, of course, its remoteness, but a journey to Silloth will never disappoint, since not only does the course provide a wonderful golfing experience but the Silloth Club is one of the friendliest and most welcoming in Britain.

A cursory glance at the score card is unlikely to instil fear into the heart of the first time visitor, although anyone who has stood on the 1st tee with the wind hammering into their face will attest to how demanding a challenge this can be. The course meanders its way through and over some classic links terrain. There are occasional spectacular vantage points – the coastal views from the 4th and 6th tees being especially memorable – and the round calls for many courageous strokes. The greatest hole is the par five 13th, 'Hog's Back', which features an exceptionally narrow fairway and a severely plateaued green. If you hit a good drive it is difficult to resist going for the green in two – a failed attempt, however, spells disaster!

COURSE INFORMATION & FACILITIES

Silloth on Solway Golf Club
The Clubhouse, Silloth
Carlisle, Cumbria CA5 4BL

Secretary: John G. Proudlock.
Tel: 016973 31782.

Golf Professional Alan Mackenzie Tel: 016973 31782.

Green Fees per 18 holes per day:
Weekdays (day) — £25. Weekends (round) — £32.
Letter of introduction and handicap certificate required.
Some time restrictions.

CARD OF THE COURSE — PAR 72

1	2	3	4	5	6	7	8	9	Out
380	320	371	372	518	201	424	371	134	3091
Par 4	Par 4	Par 4	Par 4	Par 5	Par 3	Par 4	Par 4	Par 3	Par 35
10	11	12	13	14	15	16	17	18	In
318	403	204	511	512	444	200	495	438	3525
Par 4	Par 4	Par 3	Par 5	Par 5	Par 4	Par 3	Par 5	Par 4	Par 37

HOW TO GET THERE

om the South: M6 Junction
onto B5305 to Wigton,
en B5302 to Silloth.
om North East: M6
nction 43 take A69
rlisle A595/596 to Wigton
en B5302 to Silloth.

Silloth
Golf Club

Wallasey

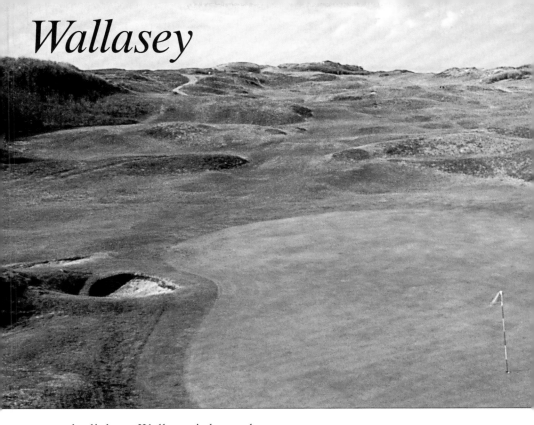

T he links at Wallasey is located on the tip of Cheshire's Wirral Peninsula; the clubhouse overlooks the mouth of the River Mersey. For golf enthusiasts the spectacular North West starts here. Given its geography, it is perhaps not surprising that the course has suffered over the years from coastal erosion. But Wallasey remains an extraordinary site. Some of the sand hills are as impressive as any to be found further north – including those at Birkdale and Hillside – and the layout of the course hurls the golfer headlong into these dunes as early as the 2nd hole. With its many elevated tees and plateau greens, the thrill factor is high at Wallasey.

Wallasey is famous as the golfing home of Dr Frank Stableford, the man who invented the Stableford points scoring system. The par three 9th hole is named after him (...four points, then, for a hole-in-one).

Unfortunately the 9th is not one of the strongest holes at Wallasey. The sequence between the 2nd and 5th is probably the best, and certainly most dramatic of the round – the view from the tee at the par five 4th is one not to be rushed – but another good run of holes comes between the 10th and 12th as the course turns back on itself and plunges once more into the dunes. The three hole finish is quite formidable, comprising a huge par three (with its elegant, shelf-like green guarded by a vast dune, the 16th may be the finest hole of all) and two crunchingly long par fours.

HOW TO GET THERE

om M53 leave Junction 1.
llow A554, signs for New
ghton. On leaving the
ur road and joining
yswater Road the
ubhouse is situated
proximately a quarter
a mile down
road on
left
nd
e.

Wallasey
Golf Club

COURSE INFORMATION & FACILITIES

 Wallasey Golf Club
Bayswater Road, Wallasey
Wirral L45 8LA.

Secretary: Mrs. L.M.Dolman.
Tel: 0151 691 1024. Fax: 0151 638 8988.

Golf Professional Mike Adams Tel: 0151 638 3888.

Green Fees:
Weekdays (round) — £39, Weekends (round) — £42.
Weekdays (day) — £42, Weekends (day) — £48.
Letter of introduction and handicap certificate required.
Some time restrictions.

CARD OF THE COURSE — PAR 72

1	2	3	4	5	6	7	8	9	Out
370	443	365	486	165	338	512	385	142	3206
Par 4	Par 4	Par 4	Par 5	Par 3	Par 4	Par 5	Par 4	Par 3	Par 36

10	11	12	13	14	15	16	17	18	In
298	340	137	476	478	358	200	453	398	3138
Par 4	Par 4	Par 3	Par 5	Par 5	Par 4	Par 3	Par 4	Par 4	Par 36

Windermere

The English Lake District: 'Where nature reveals herself in all her wildness, all her majesty'. It is not the sort of place where you would expect to stumble across a championship golf course, and indeed you will not – the land is a little too wild and majestic! However, if you should venture into Britain's favourite National Park, golf clubs in tow, you may discover one of the country's prettiest courses.

Windermere Golf Club celebrated its centenary in 1991. Its golf course has never had pretensions to becoming a 'championship course' but it has always offered an enjoyable challenge. It is short by modern standards but with its uneven, adventurous terrain – there are several blind shots – and with heather, bracken and rocky outcrops awaiting wayward shots, the par of 67 is no pushover. The accompanying views are magnificent and since the course is invariably kept in excellent condition, it isn't surprising that people have begun to describe Windermere as 'a mini Gleneagles'.

The par three 8th is generally considered to be Windermere's best hole. From the tee the green sits at eye level but in between is a deep gorse-filled ravine. The putting surface is in fact table-shaped and can be extremely difficult to hold. Distraction is the last thing a golfer needs at this hole but over the player's shoulder (as he stands on the tee) is a marvellous view of Morecambe Bay, while stretching ahead is the full mountainous splendour of the Lake District.

COURSE INFORMATION & FACILITIES

Windermere Golf Club
Cleabarrow, Windermere
Cumbria LA23 3NB

Secretary: K R Moffat
Tel: 015394 43123
Fax: 015394 43123

Golf Professional Tel: 015394 43550

Green Fees per 18 holes per day:
Weekdays — £23 Weekends — £28

CARD OF THE COURSE — PAR 67

1	2	3	4	5	6	7	8	9	Out
314	231	253	384	307	361	368	137	272	2627
Par 4	Par 3	Par 4	Par 4	Par 4	Par 4	Par 4	Par 3	Par 4	Par 34

10	11	12	13	14	15	16	17	18	In
206	266	360	316	147	190	464	352	204	2505
Par 3	Par 4	Par 4	Par 4	Par 3	Par 3	Par 5	Par 4	Par 3	Par 33

HOW TO GET THERE

ave M6 at Junction 36.
in A591. Leave A591 at
oundabout. Join B5284
ntinue for approximately
miles.

Windermere
Golf Club

Yorkshire &
North East

Yorkshire & The North East

*T*he Red Rose may have the better links courses but the White Rose has the superior inland challenges: Ganton, Alwoodley and Lindrick are the three jewels in the crown of Yorkshire golf. Our final region also includes the North East of England, a difficult-to-define area of the country, but one which probably begins somewhere amid the windswept duneland of Seaton Carew, once called the Durham and Yorkshire Golf Club.

Ganton is the greatest course in Yorkshire. An inland course with a seaside flavour, it rivals Woodhall Spa and Sunningdale as the premier non-links course in the British Isles. It is the only inland course to have staged the British Amateur Championship. Alwoodley is Alister Mackenzie's finest English creation (he is the architect who worked with Bobby Jones at Augusta); it is a very attractive heathland course with some superb bunkering. Just as Alwoodley lies to the north of Leeds, so Lindrick is situated just south of Sheffield – almost in Nottinghamshire, in fact. Lindrick's greatest hour came in 1957 when Great Britain and Ireland (as the team then was) defeated the United States in the Ryder Cup.

The above three maybe the 'jewels' but Yorkshire has a strong supporting cast. Very close to Alwoodley are Moortown (another former Ryder Cup venue) and Sandmoor. To the west of Leeds, the Bradford-Bingley-Huddersfield region is thick with courses and among the best of these is Woodsome Hall. Over to the east of Yorkshire, in fact just south of the 'border' in North Lincolnshire, is the outstanding new Forest Pines Golf Club at Broughton, near Scunthorpe. North of Leeds, Harrogate has two highly rated courses, as does the beautiful city of York with Strensall (York Golf Club) to the north and Fulford to the south. Rotherham's golf course at Thybergh Park is recommended, while for a real hidden gem, try the course at Ilkley – but don't expect to keep dry.

Seaton Carew could never be described as a scenic (or hidden) gem. Its backdrop is one of towering chimneys – or their modern equivalents – which at night appear lit up like giant torches, but it is an undeniably impressive links, the finest on the east coast between Norfolk and East Lothian. A much more serene challenge close to Durham is provided by the parkland course at Brancepeth Castle.

The immediate vicinities of Sunderland and Newcastle are not exactly endowed with golfing riches but some 20 miles west of Newcastle, and just five miles south of Hexham, is the magnificent 36 hole resort at Slaley Hall. Slaley may now be the pride of Northumberland but in the far north of the county connoisseurs of the game may be familiar with the charms of Bamburgh Castle, quite possibly the most spectacularly sited golf course in England.

ALWOODLEY	ILKLEY
BAMBURGH CASTLE	LINDRICK
BRANCEPTH CASTLE	ROTHERHAM
FULFORD	SLALEY HALL
GANTON	WOODSOME HALL

Yorkshire & North East

Page

Alwoodley

*I*n 1907 Harry met 'Ally' and the golfing world has been eternally grateful ever since. Harry Colt, already a celebrated course architect, visited Alister Mackenzie, then a medical practitioner but with a considerable interest in golf architecture, to discuss the layout of a new course at Alwoodley, just north of Leeds. Impressed by Mackenzie's ideas, Colt suggested that the two work together on the project. To cut a long story short, Mackenzie eventually became the major contributor to Alwoodley's design; he was offered more work and ultimately gave up his medical practice. Mackenzie went on to create such masterpieces as Cypress Point, Augusta and Royal Melbourne. Alwoodley remains his greatest English achievement.

Although one of the more friendly and welcoming of Britain's traditional golf clubs, Alwoodley prefers a low key profile; it has never, for instance, hosted a major professional tournament. The course is often described as a heathland layout but in truth it is part heath, part moorland in nature. It is not as sandy as Sunningdale or St. George's Hill and gorse is more prominent than heather, moreover there are far more trees than on a pure heath course, such as Walton Heath. The major feature of the design is undoubtedly the quality and boldness of the bunkering. The greens are generally large and full of subtle undulations. Among the outstanding holes are, on the front nine, the 2nd, 5th, and 8th and, on the back nine, the 11th, 14th and 18th.

HOW TO GET THERE

ve miles north of Leeds on
61 Harrogate Road.

Alwoodley
Golf Club

COURSE INFORMATION & FACILITIES

Alwoodley Golf Club
Wigton Lane
Leeds LS17 8SA

Hon. Secretary: Mr R C W Banks
Tel: 0113 2681680 Fax: 0113 2939458

Golf Professional Tel: 0113 2689603

Green Fees: Weekdays — £50 Weekends — £60
Weekdays (day) — £50 Weekends (day) — £60

CARD OF THE COURSE — PAR 72

1	2	3	4	5	6	7	8	9	Out
405	305	510	481	371	420	142	546	193	3373
Par 4	Par 4	Par 5	Par 5	Par 4	Par 4	Par 3	Par 5	Par 3	Par 37

10	11	12	13	14	15	16	17	18	In
478	168	366	396	207	405	417	437	439	3313
Par 5	Par 3	Par 4	Par 4	Par 3	Par 4	Par 4	Par 4	Par 4	Par 35

Bamburgh Castle

A publication entitled 'Golfing Gems' would be far less 'precious' if it failed to recommend a round of golf at Bamburgh Castle. This is quite possibly the most beautiful – and most beautifully situated – golf course in all England.

Tucked away on the romantic, legend-laced shores of Northumberland, the cosy village of Bamburgh is overwhelmed by its scenery. Just off the coast is Holy Island and the Lindisfarne Monastery; the Cheviot Hills provide a striking backcloth, while surveying everything from its lofty rocky perch is the majestic Bamburgh Castle, often described as Britain's most impressive Norman stronghold (in fact, the keep is Norman but parts of the castle date from the 6th century).

Rather less ancient than the castle and village is the adjoining 18 hole links of the Bamburgh Castle Golf Club. The layout of the course takes full advantage of the surroundings and provides a wealth of stunning 360 degree vistas. It is by no means the most demanding golf course you are ever likely to play, for it is fairly short, measuring well under 6000 yards from the back tees, but with gorse and heather lining almost every fairway and an abundance of wild flowers (including some rare orchids) sprinkled in the rough it is visually delightful. Among the special holes at Bamburgh Castle are the par three 8th, where you play over a plunging valley, and the par four 15th, from the tee of which can be spied no fewer than four castles.

Bamburgh Castle Golf Club
The Club House, 40 The Wynding Bamburgh,
Northumberland NE69 7DE

Secretary: Tel 01668 214321

Clubhouse: Tel 01668 214378

Green Fees per 18 holes:
Weekdays — £30. Weekends — £30
Weekdays (day) — £30
Weekends (day) — £35

CARD OF THE COURSE — PAR 68

1	2	3	4	5	6	7	8	9	Out
182	214	529	485	343	224	303	164	360	2804
Par 3	Par 3	Par 5	Par 5	Par 4	Par 3	Par 4	Par 3	Par 4	Par 34

10	11	12	13	14	15	16	17	18	In
197	343	425	413	168	417	278	257	319	2817
Par 3	Par 4	Par 4	Par 4	Par 3	Par 4	Par 4	Par 4	Par 4	Par 34

HOW TO GET THERE

eave A1 midway between
lnwick and Berwick upon
weed via B1341 or B1342
Bamburgh Village.
oceed along
e Wynding
Clubhouse.

Bamburgh Castle Golf Club

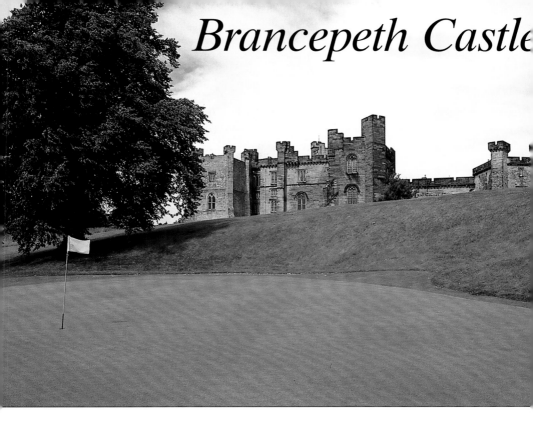

*N*ot far from the famous cathedral city of Durham is the pretty village of Brancepeth. It boasts a very fine church, an impressive castle and an extremely pleasant golf course: both church and castle watch over the golf course. In the 1920s Harry Colt was commissioned to design an 18 hole course within the grounds of a deer park belonging to Lord Boyne. Given the nature of the site and the quality of the architect, Brancepeth Castle was always likely to be a bit special.

And so it is. Only a wretched soul could ever tire of playing here. It is not the hardest golf course in the world, being of moderate length with fairly generous fairways, but the round is full of variety and interest, and of course the views are superb. The most distinctive feature of the layout is the number of shots that are required to be played across a ravine. At least eight holes call for such a stroke and the penalty for failing to rise to the occasion can be severe. Some of the Brancepeth ravines – and they are not mere ditches – are occupied by thick woodland and some by streams. Needless to say Colt positioned a number of his greens immediately beyond these natural hazards.

A selection of the best holes at Brancepeth Castle would include the 4th, a very handsome par four, the 9th, a long short hole 'of terrifying grandeur' according to Bernanrd Darwin but where there are delightful glimpses of the castle, and the short par four 14th.

CARD OF THE COURSE — PAR 70

1	2	3	4	5	6	7	8	9	Out
341	142	450	400	219	550	383	339	214	3038
Par 4	Par 3	Par 4	Par 4	Par 3	Par 5	Par 4	Par 4	Par 3	Par 34

10	11	12	13	14	15	16	17	18	In
201	439	508	408	325	156	476	380	354	3247
Par 3	Par 4	Par 5	Par 4	Par 4	Par 3	Par 5	Par 4	Par 4	Par 36

HOW TO GET THERE

ancepeth is situated four
iles south-west of Durham

Fulford

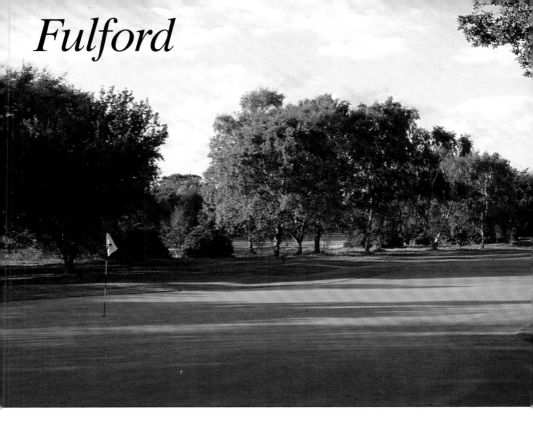

Not too many people, I suspect, would describe Bernhard Langer as a flamboyant golfer: 'Bernhard is German therefore he is cool and calculating'. And yet, here is a man who has enjoyed (and is enjoying) a very colourful career. Langer has won two Major championships, the 1985 and 1993 Masters tournaments at Augusta; he has compiled two of the finest rounds of golf ever played – his course record 62s at El Saler and Valderrama, the best two courses in Spain. And he has struck two of the most memorable 'shots' in the history of the game. One of these was at Kiawah Island – that infamous putt on the final green – and the other took place at Fulford Golf Club near York.

Playing the penultimate hole in the 1981 Benson & Hedges International event, Langer hit his approach shot into the branches of a large tree: unfortunately for Bernhard the ball remained precisely where he hit it. Seemingly unperturbed, however, Langer proceeded to climb up the tree and, after adopting a rather unorthodox (never mind precarious) stance, managed to chip the ball out of the branches and on to the green.

You think of the Postage Stamp and you think of Gene Sarazen; you think of Fulford and you think of Langer's extra-curricular activity. A high class heathland-come-parkland course that can be stretched to 6800 yards, Fulford is invariably maintained in excellent condition and is renowned for the quality (and speed) of its greens. The golf here is never dull.

iles south of York on A64.

Fulford
Golf Club

COURSE INFORMATION & FACILITIES

The Fulford Golf Club
Heslington Lane
York YO10 5DY

General Manager: R Bramley BEM
Tel/Fax: 01904 413579

Golf Professional: B. Hessay
Tel/Fax: 01904 412882

Green Fees:
Weekdays - £35 Weekends - £45
Weekdays (day) - £45

Handicap Certificate required — Restrictions apply.

CARD OF THE RED COURSE — PAR 72

1	2	3	4	5	6	7	8	9	Out
412	438	189	458	167	561	415	371	486	3497
Par 4	Par 4	Par 3	Par 4	Par 3	Par 5	Par 4	Par 4	Par 5	Par 36

10	11	12	13	14	15	16	17	18	In
165	504	321	473	175	443	361	356	480	3278
Par 3	Par 5	Par 4	Par 4	Par 3	Par 4	Par 4	Par 4	Par 5	Par 36

Ganton

*I*s it an 'inland links' or a 'links inland'? Ganton is a golfing curiosity. The course is situated nine miles from the coast and yet it possesses many of the characteristics of a seaside links. A confused identity? Make that an embarrassment of riches; Ganton is one of the greatest courses in the British Isles.

The setting is both tranquil and picturesque, with the course nestling in a quiet valley on the edge of the Vale of Pickering. Although surrounded by trees, the course itself occupies open heathland similar to Walton Heath and lies on a substratum of rich sand, hence its seaside nature.

Trees have never been encouraged to grow on the course but the gorse has been allowed to run rampant! The 'yellow peril' is a major feature of Ganton, but even more significant is the bunkering. There are more than one hundred traps at Ganton: most are deep – some are cavernous – and nearly all are superbly placed; as Patric Dickinson once observed, 'the secret of Ganton lies in its subtle use of ground and its brilliant, suggestive bunkering'.

In addition to having an outstanding golf course, the club has enjoyed a rich history. Founded in 1891, Ganton achieved near instant fame when the first professional it employed won the Open Championship of 1896. It was the first of a record six victories for one Harry Vardon. Ganton has hosted the British Amateur Championship on three occasions and in 1949 it staged the Ryder Cup. It will host the Walker Cup in 2003.

HOW TO GET THERE

miles south west of
arborough on A64.

Ganton
Golf Club

COURSE INFORMATION & FACILITIES

Ganton Golf Club
Near Scarborough,
North Yorkshire YO12 4PA

Secretary: Major R. G. Woolsey
Tel 01944 710329 Fax 01944 710922

Green Fees per 18 holes per day:
Weekdays — £48 Weekends — £53
Weekdays (day) — £48 Weekends (day) — £53

CARD OF THE COURSE — PAR 73

1	2	3	4	5	6	7	8	9	Out
373	418	334	406	157	449	435	392	504	3468
Par 4	Par 4	Par 4	Par 4	Par 3	Par 5	Par 4	Par 4	Par 5	Par 37

10	11	12	13	14	15	16	17	18	In
168	417	363	499	282	437	448	252	400	3266
Par 3	Par 4	Par 4	Par 5	Par 4	Par 4	Par 4	Par 4	Par 4	Par 36

Ilkley

There is much to see and admire in Ilkley. An attractive, prosperous spa town, it is famous for its Moor and for the song that immortalised the same. Ilkley also possesses some of the best restaurants in England, and one of the most enjoyable parkland golf courses. The River Wharfe meanders through the surrounding countryside (the area is known as Wharfedale) and it plays an extremely prominent role at Ilkley Golf Club.

It is said that the player who wins at Ilkley is the player who stays dry. In a manner reminiscent of the Manor House Hotel golf course at Moretonhampstead in Devon, the River Wharfe affects the majority of holes on the front nine, shaping several of the early challenges.

The design of the course certainly makes the most of the river, as well as the other natural features, but then the principal architect was no lesser a man than Alister Mackenzie. Mature trees frame most of the fairways and the course is invariably maintained in first class condition.

The river wastes no time in throwing down the gauntlet. At the par four 1st it threatens the left side of the fairway; at the 2nd it encircles the green. Not content with an island green, there then follows an island hole! The 3rd at Ilkley, a long and picturesque par three, lies entirely on this island that 'floats' in the River Wharfe. It makes for heroic golf and though the river is less conspicuous on the back nine, the level of quality is maintained throughout the round.

COURSE INFORMATION & FACILITIES

Ilkley Golf Club
Nesfield Road, Myddleton
Ilkley LS29 0BE

Secretary: Arthur K Hatfield
Tel: 01943 600214 Fax: 01943 816130

Golf Professional Tel: 01943 607463

Green Fees:
Weekdays – £37 Weekends – £42
Weekdays (day) – £37 Weekends (day) – £42

CARD OF THE COURSE — PAR 69

1	2	3	4	5	6	7	8	9	Out
375	150	200	490	185	476	410	340	385	3011
Par 4	Par 3	Par 3	Par 5	Par 3	Par 5	Par 4	Par 4	Par 4	Par 35

10	11	12	13	14	15	16	17	18	In
300	420	388	134	420	130	400	400	350	2942
Par 4	Par 4	Par 4	Par 3	Par 4	Par 3	Par 4	Par 4	Par 4	Par 34

WEST YORKSHIRE

HOW TO GET THERE

...om Ilkley Town Centre, at ...affic lights, take New Brook ...reet, turn left into Denton ...oad, continue over ...oundabout ...to Langbar Road ...nd turn left into ...esfield Road. ...ourse is on ...e right.

Ilkley Golf Club

Riverside Hotel

The Dalesway begins by the old bridge with delightful river walks.

The Riverside is situated on the banks of the River Wharfe in a superb riverside setting. 10 ensuite rooms with TV/Sky. Family owned and run. *Drive off in style* with a full English Breakfast. Sand wedges are served in the bar – *chip into the restaurant* where meals are served until 8.30 p.m. 19th hole is open late with hand drawn ales at sensible prices – *at the Riverside you've got the hole in one!* **We are only two minutes drive to the golf course!**

RIVERSIDE GARDENS, ILKLEY, WEST YORKS
TEL/FAX: 01943 607338

149

Lindrick

One chilly, windswept October week in 1957 established the reputation of Lindrick. Until that time very few golfers – even in the north of England – were aware of its existence, never mind quality. But this was the week that no British golf enthusiast would forget, for it was the last time an exclusively British and Irish Ryder Cup team would ever beat the mighty men from across the sea.

Lindrick occupies the best part of 200 acres of classic English Common (Lindrick Common) and is essentially heathland in nature, lying on limestone rock. Silver birch trees define many of the fairways while smatterings of gorse and a dash of heather provide seasonal splashes of colour.

Renowned for its lightening quick greens, Lindrick generally rewards accuracy and subtelty more than power. The 2nd, with its slightly uphill approach, the 8th and the 17th are among the most interesting of the two-shotters, and the 12th and 13th are possibly the most difficult. The best hole at Lindrick, however, is surely the par five 4th.
It features a blind approach to a low lying green backed by trees and behind which the River Ryton flows. The green has a magnificent stage-like setting and it was here that the boundaries of Yorkshire, Derbyshire and Nottinghamshire once merged. In ancient times the 'stage' was used for bare fist fighting, contestants and spectators being able to step swiftly into a convenient county whenever unfriendly law authorities made an appearance.

HOW TO GET THERE

om M1 Junction 31 take
57 towards Worksop.
ter approximately 5 miles
57 passes through the
olf course.

Lindrick
Golf Club

COURSE INFORMATION & FACILITIES

Lindrick Golf Club
Lindrick Common, Worksop
Nottinghamshire S81 8BH

Secretary: Lt Cdr R J M Jack RN
Tel: 01909 475282 Fax: 01909 488685

Green Fees per 18 holes per day:
Weekends — £45
Weekdays (day) — £40
Society Rates: £40

CARD OF THE COURSE — PAR 71

1	2	3	4	5	6	7	8	9	Out
402	364	165	478	431	140	439	316	436	3171
Par 4	Par 4	Par 3	Par 5	Par 4/5	Par 3	Par 4/5	Par 4	Par 4	Par 35/37

10	11	12	13	14	15	16	17	18	In
370	172	423	456	563	360	487	394	210	3435
Par 4	Par 3	Par 4	Par 4/5	Par 5	Par 4	Par 5	Par 4	Par 3	Par 36/37

Rotherham

*F*ew would dispute that the two largest and most impressive clubhouses in England are to be found in the south of the country – Stoke Poges in Buckinghamshire and Moor Park in Hertfordshire; however, the 19th hole at Thrybergh Park, home of Rotherham Golf Club, must have a strong claim to the title 'most stylish or most characterful clubhouse in Yorkshire'

The estate is ancient: Thrybergh is mentioned in the Domesday Book, and while the current mansion, a castellated Gothic building dating from 1814, the grounds are adorned with 300-400 year old trees. In fact, two chestnuts beside the 18th tee are reputed to have been planted in the late 16th century to commemorate the Lord of the Manor's contribution to repulsing the Spanish Armada in 1588.

The golf course is a youngster by comparison, though in 2003 the club will celebrate its centenary. The course was laid out originally by Sandy Herd and later revised by James Braid. There are no real weak holes at Rotherham but players often get a sense that the course is steadily building to a climax. The 16th, 17th and 18th are three of the toughest holes of the entire round. The good news is that if you survive this stretch you can celebrate in real style when you get to the 19th.

HOW TO GET THERE

1 Junction 35 towards
therham A629/A630
miles East of Rotherham.
(M) Junction A630
wards Rotherham 6 miles.

Rotherham
Golf Club

COURSE INFORMATION & FACILITIES

Rotherham Golf Club
Thrybergh Park, Doncaster Road
Thrybergh, Rotherham S65 4NU

Secretary: Gerry Smalley
Tel: 01709 850812 Fax: 01709 855288

Golf Professional: Simon Thornhill
Tel: 01709 850480 Fax: 01709 855288

Green Fees:
Weekdays - £30 Weekends - £37
Weekdays (day) - £35 Weekends (day) - £37

Restrictions apply. No visitors on Medal Days
1st Thursday & Saturday monthly.

CARD OF THE COURSE — PAR 70

1	2	3	4	5	6	7	8	9	Out
376	412	172	526	397	363	407	397	200	3250
Par 4	Par 4	Par 3	Par 5	Par 4	Par 4	Par 4	Par 4	Par 3	Par 35

10	11	12	13	14	15	16	17	18	In
476	297	366	384	169	384	151	396	454	3077
Par 5	Par 4	Par 4	Par 4	Par 3	Par 4	Par 3	Par 4	Par 4	Par 35

Slaley Hall

laley Hall was a dream of the 1980s that ran into difficulty in the early 1990s and now, at the start of the new millenium approaches, seems destined to become 'the Gleneagles of the North East'. The Slaley Hall International Golf Resort and Spa, as it proudly styles itself, combines sumptuous accommodation (including all manner of accompanying leisure facilities) with superlative golf. The golf came first with the Dave Thomas designed course opening in 1989. At that time comparisons were being made with another venue: 'Slaley Hall – the Woburn of the North'.

Thomas's layout is both extremely scenic and challenging. Situated 6 miles from Hexham in deepest, rural Northumberland, the golf course is surrounded by a dense conifer forest and with its plethora of lakes and streams has a slightly alpine feel to it. Among the many fine holes on the course one might single out the 2nd, a beautiful swinging dog-leg, and the sequence between the 11th and 13th. Slaley Hall's signature hole, however, is undoubtedly the 9th, a gorgeous par four played over water and along an avenue of tall pines and colourful rhododendrons.

In June 1997 Slaley Hall hosted its first major European PGA Tour event, the Compaq European Grand Prix. The tournament was a great success and was won by Colin Montgomerie who stormed to victory thanks to a brilliant final round of 65. A second 18 hole championship course, designed by Neil Coles, opened in the summer of 1999.

154

HOW TO GET THERE

miles west of Newcastle
on Tyne, 7 miles south of
bridge off the A68
m the south take A68 off
follow signs for
bridge. From north take
A68 (south) off
A69 follow
ns from
Pit

Slaley Hall
Golf Club

COURSE INFORMATION & FACILITIES

De Vere Slaley Hall Hotel & Golf Resort
Hexham, Northumberland
Nr. Newcastle upon Tyne NE47 0BY

Operations Manager: Mark Stancer
Tel: 01434 673350 Fax: 01434 673152

Golf Professional Gordon Robinson
Tel: 01434 673154

Green Fees:
Weekdays/Weekends — £60

CARD OF THE COURSE — PAR 72
HUNTING COURSE

1	2	3	4	5	6	7	8	9	Out
429	429	412	521	382	205	432	423	453	3686
Par 4	Par 4	Par 4	Par 5	Par 4	Par 3	Par 4	Par 4	Par 4	Par 36

10	11	12	13	14	15	16	17	18	In
362	562	531	395	179	331	395	184	463	3402
Par 4	Par 5	Par 5	Par 4	Par 3	Par 4	Par 4	Par 3	Par 4	Par 36

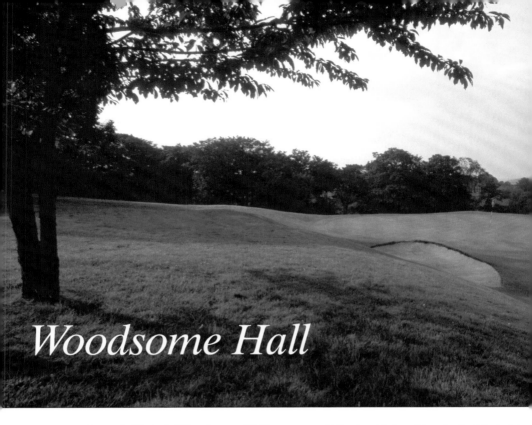

Woodsome Hall

To the uninitiated, Woodsome Hall may sound like an imaginary abode plucked from the pages of *Wind in the Willows*; for those in the know, however, it is the venue for one of the most pleasurable golf experiences in the north of England.

Actually, you do fall under a kind of spell the moment you enter the property and wend your way towards an impressive Elizabethan mansion. The grounds surrounding Woodsome Hall were shaped by Capability Brown and are resplendent with giant oaks and beech trees. Adjacent, and to an extent set right in amongst all this finery, is Woodsome Hall golf course, one of the best inland tracks in Yorkshire. Peace reigns: the nearest major town is Huddersfield 7 miles away, yet it might as well be 70 miles distant as here is a genuine retreat.

The course is invariably presented in pristine condition - the fairways sufficiently lush that the ball sits up as if on a tee peg, and the greens as slick as the proverbial marble staircase.

With its green elegantly framed by rhododendrons and beech trees, the par five 9th is often cited as the best hole at Woodsome Hall, but it's the total package that really makes this such a special destination.

COURSE INFORMATION & FACILITIES

Woodsome Hall Golf Club
Fenay Bridge
Huddersfield, HD8 0LQ

Secretary: A S Guest
Tel: 01484 602739 Fax: 01484 60826

Golf Professional: M Higginbottom
Tel: 01484 602034

Green Fees:
Weekdays — £30 Weekends — £40
Weekdays (day) — £40 Weekends (day) — £50

Handicap Certificate required — Restrictions apply.

CARD OF THE COURSE — PAR 70

1	2	3	4	5	6	7	8	9	Out
405	394	204	440	287	407	173	455	520	3285
Par 4	Par 4	Par 3	Par 4	Par 4	Par 4	Par 3	Par 4	Par 5	Par 35

10	11	12	13	14	15	16	17	18	In
158	316	331	137	374	304	499	349	343	2811
Par 3	Par 4	Par 4	Par 3	Par 4	Par 4	Par 5	Par 4	Par 4	Par 35

HOW TO GET THERE

[fro]m M1: Junction 39 or 38
[foll]ow Huddersfield signs to
[Hu]ddersfield — then A629 in the
[dir]ection of Pennistone — sign on
[rig]ht to Woodsome Hall Golf
[Cl]ub.

[fro]m M62: Junction
[24] or 25 follow
[Hu]ddersfield signs —
[tak]e A629
[dir]ection
[Pe]nnistone
[... o]ut of
[tow]n
[sig]n on
[rig]ht to
[Gol]f
[Clu]b.

Woodsome
Hall
Golf Club

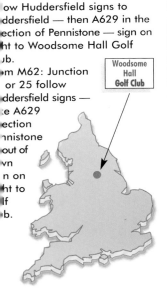

Wales

Wales

*T*he Welsh are not normally shy when it comes to singing their nation's praises. Back in the 12th century, Hywel ap Owain, Prince of Gwynedd, wrote of his homeland:

'I love its sea-marsh and its mountains,
And its fortress by its forest and its bright lands,
And its meadows and its water and its valleys,
And its white seagulls and its lovely women.'

And yet Wales has been strangely slow – almost reticent – to celebrate its golfing credentials. For too long it has allowed the reputation of its golf courses to be completely overshadowed by those of Scotland and Ireland. Where in the world are there two more scenic championship courses than Royal St David's and Royal Porthcawl? One or two courses in Scotland and Ireland are overlooked by a castle, but there is nothing to compare with the fortress setting of Harlech ... except, perhaps, at Conwy!

The Caernarvonshire Golf Club at Conwy is probably the toughest challenge in North Wales, while the course with the greatest charm is undoubtedly Aberdovey, a great favourite of the eminent golf writer, Bernard Darwin. Also in North Wales is Nefyn, a dramatic clifftop course with a setting that would do justice to California's Monterey Peninsula – 'Pebble Beach without the fog', as one wag put it. The Isle of Anglesey has some pleasant holiday golf with Bull Bay and Holyhead (Trearddur Bay) especially memorable, and there are two good links courses at Llandudno: North Wales and Maesdu.

The scenery in South Wales is generally less spectacular – there is no Mount Snowdon and only a handful of castles – but there is the Gower

Peninsula, and there is the beautiful Pembrokeshire coast. Golfers visiting the Gower should head straight for Pennard, a true hidden gem, and those touring 'Little England beyond Wales' should try to sneak a round in at Tenby. Pennard is South Wales' answer to Nefyn and Tenby is the Aberdovey of the South, a delightfully old fashioned links. Not far from Porthcawl there is a very fine downland course at Southerndown and a rugged links course at Pyle and Kenfig.

So far we have neglected inland golf in Wales. Here, alas, is not the place to do it justice; suffice to say that anyone who believes that inland golf starts and finishes at St Pierre should take a short drive to Monmouth. Better still, take a Rolls to Monmouth.

ABERDOVEY
CONWY
HOLYHEAD
NEFYN & DISTRICT
NORTH WALES
PENNARD

ROLLS OF MONMOUTH
ROYAL ST DAVIDS
SOUTHERNDOWN
TENBY

Wales

Page

St David's Head

Ramsey Island

Skomer Island

Skokholm Island

Aberdovey

*I*f golf hadn't been invented in
Scotland the chances are it would
have started in Aberdovey. Links
golf is the most natural form of the game
and nowhere does it seem so natural and
harmonious a pastime as on the mouth
of the Dovey estuary in western Wales.
The site was so perfect for golf that when
the first enthusiasts planned their course
all they felt they needed to do was to
purchase nine flower pots. They 'inserted'
the pots into nine of the most level areas
they could find and 'went golfing'. Their
course occupied a thin strip of duneland,
conveniently wedged between the shore
and a railway line. This was back in 1892,
and a romantic will tell you that not a lot
has changed since.

Writing early this century, Bernard
Darwin described Aberdovey as, 'the
course that my soul loves best of all the
courses in the world'. It is believed that
Darwin's uncle was one of the pioneering
'Aberdovey flower pot men'; his great
grandfather was the pioneering naturalist
Charles Darwin.

In addition to the Prestwickian railway
line, Aberdovey boasts numerous
old-fashioned Scottish virtues, such as
capricious undulating terrain, a blind par
three, and cows that graze on the links:
Florida, it is not. The blind par three
(actually, now no longer completely blind)
is the 3rd hole and is called 'Cader'.
Another classic challenge is provided by
the 288 yards par four 16th – a hole that
epitomises the unique character and charm
of Aberdovey.

COURSE INFORMATION & FACILITIES

Aberdovey Golf Club
Aberdovey
Gwynedd LL35 0RT.

Secretary: J. M. Griffiths.
Tel: 01654 767493. Fax: 01654 767027.

Golf Professional: John Davies Tel: 01654 767602.

Green Fees:
Weekdays — £20. Weekends — £35.
Weekdays (day) — £40. Weekends (day) — £50.
Letter of introduction and handicap certificate required.
Some time restrictions. Package deals on green fees available.

CARD OF THE COURSE - PAR 71

1	2	3	4	5	6	7	8	9	Out
441	332	173	401	193	402	482	335	160	2919
Par 4	Par 4	Par 3	Par 4	Par 3	Par 4	Par 5	Par 4	Par 3	Par 34

10	11	12	13	14	15	16	17	18	In
415	407	149	530	389	477	288	428	443	3526
Par 4	Par 4	Par 3	Par 5	Par 4	Par 5	Par 4	Par 4	Par 4	Par 37

HOW TO GET THERE

longside A493 immediately
west of Aberdovey Village.
lubhouse adjacent to
ailway station.

Aberdovey
Golf Club

Conwy

A friendly rivalry exists between the Golf Clubs of North and South Wales. Here are some of the topics of contention: 'Is Royal St David's as good as Royal Porthcawl?' 'Is Nefyn more scenic and more spectacular than Pennard?' 'Does Aberdovey possess more charm than Tenby?' And 'Is Conwy as challenging and as difficult as Ashburnham?'

So Conwy (or Caernarvonshire as it is also called) is regarded as the toughest golf course in North Wales. Laid out on the Morfa Peninsula, and originally designed by Jack Harris, Conwy is a big bear of a links. It is long – almost 7,000 yards from the championship tees – and, being generally flat, is very exposed to the elements. Much of the rough comprises thick gorse and rushes.

But Conwy has its share of beauty too (much more than Ashburnham!). From the course there are superb views of Anglesey and also of the Great Orme, towering over Llandudno. The rugged coastline around Conwy was captured on canvas in a famous series of golfing pictures by Douglas Adams, prints of which adorn clubhouses all over Britain.

Championship golf regularly comes to Conwy and in 1990 the club hosted the Home Internationals. Among the holes which test the best are the 3rd, a wonderful par four which curves along the shore and culminates in a slippery plateau green, and the 7th, a formidable two-shotter that dog-legs from left to right towards a green standing defiantly on the edge of the links, close to the beach.

COURSE INFORMATION & FACILITIES

 Conwy (Caernarvonshire) Golf Club
Beacons Way
Morfa Conwy LL32 8ER.

Secretary: D.L.Brown.
Tel: 01492 592423. Fax: 01492 593363.

Golf Professional P.Lees, Tel/Fax: 01492 593225.

Green Fees:
Weekdays (day) — £30. Weekends (day) — £37.

CARD OF THE COURSE — PAR 72

1	2	3	4	5	6	7	8	9	Out
375	147	335	393	442	177	441	435	523	3268
Par 4	Par 3	Par 4	Par 4	Par 4	Par 3	Par 4	Par 4	Par 5	Par 35

10	11	12	13	14	15	16	17	18	In
537	385	503	174	499	153	363	389	376	3379
Par 5	Par 4	Par 5	Par 3	Par 5	Par 3	Par 4	Par 4	Par 4	Par 37

HOW TO GET THERE

5 Expressway from Chester,
oceed through tunnel under
tuary, take first left, at top of
o road turn right, follow road
small roundabout, then turn
t to golf club.

5 Expressway from Bangor,
low road to sign
onwy/Marina turn left here, at
o of slip road turn left, follow
ad to small
undabout,
n left to
lf club.

Conwy
Golf Club

Holyhead

*H*olyhead, or Trearddur Bay as most people call it, is one of two superb courses on the Isle of Anglesey, the other being Bull Bay on the island's northerly tip at Amlwch. There are other courses on Anglesey, making it an ideal place for a week's holiday, but these two are unquestionably the best. Arguments as to which takes precedence frequently dominate nineteenth hole discussions in pubs around the island. Bull Bay's clifftop setting is certainly spectacular and the course provides a real test, but maybe Trearddur Bay offers the greater variety of challenge and its location on Holy Island, if not quite as impressive as Bull Bay, is sufficiently invigorating for most golfing souls.

A glance at the score card informs you that the course measures only a little over 6000 yards; moreover, from a distance, it looks relatively tame with only one serious hill to negotiate. Look a little closer, however, and you soon realise that not only are the fairways extremely narrow and quite undulating but the rough comprises much gorse, heather and bracken. And then there is the wind which whips across from the Irish Sea. The best hole may be the 3rd, a formidable par four from the front tees and a genuine par five from the back markers. Here the drive is hit straight into the crest of a hill. Once over the hill there is a gentle climb to the green; two very solid hits – usually into the wind – are required if there is to be any prospect of getting up in two.

COURSE INFORMATION & FACILITIES

Holyhead Golf Club
Trearddur Bay
Anglesey LL65 2YG

Secretary: J A Williams
Tel: 01407 763279 Fax: 01407 763279

Golf Professional Tel: 01407 762022

Green Fees:
Weekdays — £17 Weekends — £22
Weekdays (day) — £22 Weekends (day) — £28

CARD OF THE COURSE — PAR 71

1	2	3	4	5	6	7	8	9	Out
277	180	479	124	391	164	376	337	476	2794
Par 4	Par 3	Par 5	Par 3	Par 4	Par 3	Par 4	Par 4	Par 5	Par 35

10	11	12	13	14	15	16	17	18	In
478	226	517	177	268	416	448	343	383	3256
Par 5	Par 3	Par 5	Par 3	Par 4	Par 4	Par 4	Par 4	Par 4	Par 36

HOW TO GET THERE

miles from Holyhead
B4545, off A5.

Holyhead Golf Club

The Anchorage Hotel is a family run establishment situated on the Trearddur Bay road, near Holyhead. It is within easy reach of the A5 and only a short drive from the nearby, superb sandy beaches and other local attractions, including sailing and an eighteen hole golf course.

The Hotel offers a high standard of accommodation, an à la carte Restaurant open to residents and non-residents, a large and popular Lounge Bar and Dining Area serving a wide selection of Bar Meals, a pleasant Cocktail Bar and a comfortable Resident's Lounge.

FOUR MILE BRIDGE • ISLE OF ANGLESEY • GWYNEDD • LL65 2EZ

For enquiries and reservations:
Telephone: Valley (01407) 740168 Fax: (01407) 741599

Nefyn & District

Which is the most scenic seaside course in England and Wales? A shortlist of five might include the following: East Devon, The Isle of Purbeck, Pennard, Bamburgh Castle and Nefyn & District. Most first time visitors to Nefyn are left spellbound by the beauty of its setting and vow to return at the earliest opportunity.

Situated on the Lleyn Peninsula of north west Wales, Nefyn is essentially a clifftop course but is very 'linksy' in parts. There are some large sand hills in the middle of the course, and occasionally players are asked to fire a shot over the dunes, but for much of the round the course runs along the top of the cliffs – an exhilarating, if potentially perilous journey!

Measuring a little over 6500 yards from the back markers, Nefyn is not the longest of challenges, although when the wind blows it can, of course, be very tricky. On calm days, with the sea visible from every hole, it is a classic holiday course and the relaxed atmosphere at the nineteenth hole enhances this mood.

After a downhill par four opening hole, the course hugs the edge of the cliff for a spectacular series of holes; it then turns back on itself before heading off in a different direction out on to a headland where perhaps the best holes of all, numbers 11 to 18 are found. In a sandy cove just below the 12th green (and, we are told, accessible from the course), is the Ty Coch Inn. Well, if the holiday mood really takes you...

COURSE INFORMATION & FACILITIES

Nefyn & District Golf Club
Morfa Nefyn
Gwynedd LL53 6DA.

Secretary: Mr. J. B. Owens.
Tel: 01758 720966. Fax: 01758 720476.

Golf Professional Mr J Froom Tel: 01758 720102.

Green Fees per 18 holes per day:
Weekdays — £25. Weekends — £30.
Weekdays (day) — £30. Weekends (day) — £35.
Handicap certificate required. Some time restrictions.

CARD OF THE COURSE — PAR 71

1	2	3	4	5	6	7	8	9	Out
458	374	397	477	156	442	401	327	166	3198
Par 4	Par 4	Par 4	Par 5	Par 3	Par 4	Par 4	Par 4	Par 3	Par 35
10	11	12	13	14	15	16	17	18	In
415	181	349	344	401	405	367	512	376	3350
Par 4	Par 3	Par 4	Par 4	Par 4	Par 4	Par 4	Par 5	Par 4	Par 36

HOW TO GET THERE

efyn & District Golf Club
situated on the Lleyn
ninsula. It is approached
m the north on the A499
d B4417 through Nefyn
d from the south the A497
ough to Morfa Nefyn.

fyn & District
Golf Club

GWESTY
NANHORON
ARMS
HOTEL
Nefyn

*On the spectacular
Lleyn Peninsula*

*Ffordd Dewi Sant, Nefyn, Pwllheli, Gwynedd LL53 6EA
Telephone: 01758 720203*

North Wales

Alice Liddell, the girl who inspired Lewis Carroll to write Alice in Wonderland, spent 'the golden years of her childhood' on the sands of Llandudno's West Shore. Today golfers playing at North Wales try their level best to avoid visiting the same beach.

Founded in 1894, North Wales is one of two fine courses in Llandudno. The more widely known (and possibly more difficult) is Llandudno Measdu; however, for connossieurs of traditional links golf, North Wales may hold greater appeal. For one thing, it is an exceptionally scenic course – the Welsh coastline is at its most dramatic around Llandudno; it also possesses enormous character with humpy, hillocky fairways, awkward stances and the occasional blind shot. Heather and gorse lurk immediately beyond the fairways and several of the greens are defended by deep bunkers.

The links begins rather modestly but quickly plunges into some exciting duneland. The first outstanding hole at North Wales is the 5th, a par five that dog-legs into the wind along a rollercoasting, bottle-neck shaped fairway. Two of the best par fours are the 8th, where you journey through a narrow valley menaced by a railway line and the beach, and the Stroke One 11th which runs uphill into the wind, and where the beach again threatens. As for the par threes holes, the finest is the 16th: 'O.L.' it is called – a cry you may utter should your tee shot land in the deep bunker to the left of this partially hidden, bowl shaped green.

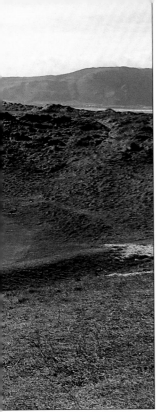

COURSE INFORMATION & FACILITIES

North Wales Golf Club (Llandudno)
72 Brynian Road, West Shore,
Llandudno, Conwy LL30 2DZ

Secretary: F Hopley
Tel: 01492 875325 Fax: 01492 875325

Golf Professional:
Tel: 01492 876878 Fax: 01492 872420

Green Fees:
Weekdays — £16 Weekends — £20
Weekdays (day) — £23 Weekends (day) — £30

CARD OF THE COURSE — PAR 71

1	2	3	4	5	6	7	8	9	Out
344	359	338	200	510	385	498	387	347	3368
Par 4	Par 4	Par 4	Par 3	Par 5	Par 4	Par 5	Par 4	Par 4	Par 37

10	11	12	13	14	15	16	17	18	In
400	420	359	182	530	334	151	120	383	2874
Par 4	Par 4	Par 4	Par 3	Par 5	Par 4	Par 3	Par 3	Par 4	Par 33

HOW TO GET THERE

rom A55 North Wales
pressway take A470 to
andudno. The Golf Course
located at the resort's
est shore.

North Wales
Golf Club

Pennard

F ounded around the turn of the century, and originally laid out by James Braid, Pennard has long enjoyed a reputation as 'Wales' best kept golfing secret'. Tom Doak, a leading American golf course architect and controversial course critic has threatened to let the proverbial cat out of the bag by describing it (in his book The Confidential Guide to Golf Courses) as 'One of my all-time favourites', adding, 'the site is one of the most spectacular I've ever seen'.

As usual, Doak is spot on: Pennard is indeed a jewel of a links. It is to be found on the Gower Peninsula, just beyond the little village of Pennard. The course is essentially a links, although, rather like Royal Porthcawl,

much of it lies on high ground, on this occasion overlooking the great sandy sweeps of Oxwich Bay and Three Cliff Bay. Delightfully old-fashioned, or as Doak puts it, 'awful quirky', Pennard is not a long course but nonetheless provides a stern challenge. The links is routinely buffeted by strong winds that roar up the Bristol Channel and much of the rough consists of thick gorse and rust coloured bracken.

The hole that everyone remembers at Pennard is the short par four 7th. Here you drive over a deep valley to find a fairway which runs alongside the ruins of a 12th century Norman castle; you then pitch to a partially concealed, sunken green – a quirky golf hole, if ever there was one.

proximately 8 miles west
Swansea via A4067 &
436.

Pennard
Golf Club

COURSE INFORMATION & FACILITIES

 Pennard Golf Club
2 Southgate Road, Southgate,
Swansea SA3 2BT.

Secretary: Morley Howell.
Tel: 01792 233131. Fax: 01792 233457.

Golf Professional M.V.Bennett Tel: 01792 233451.

Green Fees:
Weekdays — £24. Weekends — £30 (Bank Holidays).
Handicap certificate required. Some time restrictions.
Societies week-days only.

CARD OF THE COURSE — PAR 71

1	2	3	4	5	6	7	8	9	Out
449	145	365	517	165	400	351	357	437	3186
Par 4	Par 3	Par 4	Par 5	Par 3	Par 4	Par 4	Par 4	Par 4	Par 35

10	11	12	13	14	15	16	17	18	In
492	180	298	196	368	165	493	488	399	3079
Par 5	Par 3	Par 4	Par 3	Par 4	Par 3	Par 5	Par 5	Par 4	Par 36

The Rolls of Monmouth

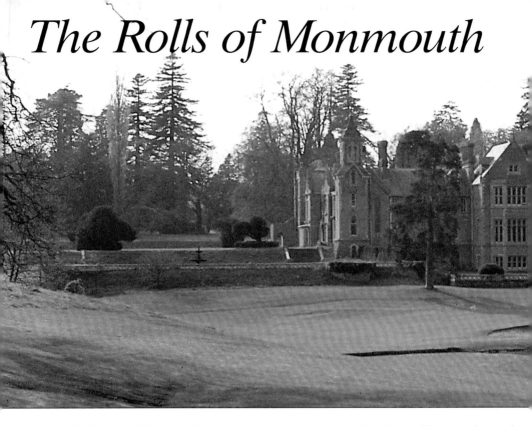

*T*he Rolls of Monmouth is one of Wales' lesser known golfing treasures. It is, after all, fairly young – the course opened as recently as 1982 – and it is situated in one of the quieter parts of Great Britain. Tucked away in rural Monmouthshire and set against a backdrop of circling hills and distant mountains, The Rolls exudes a peaceful, almost timeless atmosphere.

The course lies within the grounds of the Rolls estate, the former country home of Charles Stewart Rolls, who together with Henry Royce founded the famous Rolls Royce company. As one would imagine, Mr Rolls' abode was not exactly humble and the estate is blessed with a wonderful variety of mature trees and shrubs (which of course gives the impression that the golf course is much older than it actually is).

A championship length parkland layout, the two nines are laid out on opposite sides of the estate. On the front nine the toughest hole is undoubtedly the 6th, a par four which demands a precise drive and an even more precise approach and the most dramatic is the 7th, a long sweeping par five which twists and tumbles downhill to a green sited the far side of a stream. Two outstanding short holes, the 13th and 18th, are the highlights of the back nine. Water features on both, but while it merely helps to shape the 13th and make it a very picturesque one-shotter, it turns the 18th into an intimidating, all-or-nothing finishing hole – perfect for match play!

HOW TO GET THERE

...miles north/west of
...nmouth on the B4233
...nmouth/Abergavenny
...ad.

The Rolls of
Monmouth

COURSE INFORMATION & FACILITIES

The Rolls of Monmouth Golf Club
The Hendre
Monmouth NP5 4HG

Secretary: Mrs. Sandra Orton
Tel: 01600 715353 Fax: 01600 713115

Green Fees:
Weekdays (day) — £34 Weekends (day) — £38

CARD OF THE COURSE — PAR 72

1	2	3	4	5	6	7	8	9	Out
401	353	382	167	516	437	536	164	343	3299
Par 4	Par 4	Par 4	Par 3	Par 5	Par 4	Par 5	Par 3	Par 4	Par 36

10	11	12	13	14	15	16	17	18	In
411	331	534	190	360	443	385	556	224	3434
Par 4	Par 4	Par 5	Par 3	Par 4	Par 4	Par 4	Par 5	Par 3	Par 36

Royal St. David's

With a St Andrews in Scotland and a St George's in England, it seems only right that there should be a St David's in Wales. Along with Royal Porthcawl in the South, the Royal St David's Golf Club at Harlech is one of the principality's two greatest Championship links.

Of its many attributes, St David's is perhaps best known for its glorious setting: on the one side stretch the blue waters of Tremedog Bay, and on the other, the imperious Snowdon and the other great mountains of Snowdonia National Park; while surveying all from its lofty perch is the almost forbidding presence of Harlech Castle. The massive fortress built by Edward I has known a particularly turbulent past. It played a prominent role in the War of the Roses when a great siege took place eventually ending in surrender. The siege is commemorated in the famous song 'Men of Harlech'.

Measuring less than 6500 yards from the championship tees, St David's may not at first glance seem overly testing. However, the general consensus is that the course 'plays long'. Par is a very tight 69 and there are only two par fives on the card. Furthermore the rough can be very punishing and it is rare for there not to be a stiff westerly wind. Perhaps the most difficult holes on the course are the 10th, a long par four that is usually played into the prevailing wind, and the classic 15th which requires a lengthy, angled drive followed by a precise approach.

COURSE INFORMATION & FACILITIES

Royal St David's Golf Club
Harlech
Gwynedd LL46 2UB

Secretary: D L Morkill
Tel: 01766 780361
Fax: 01766 781110

Golf Professional John Barnet Tel: 01766 780857

Green Fees per day:
Weekdays — £38 Weekends — £44
Winter Fees: Nov/March — Day: — £28. W/E: £33

CARD OF THE COURSE — PAR 69

1	2	3	4	5	6	7	8	9	Out
436	373	463	188	393	401	484	573	173	3434
Par 4	Par 4	Par 4	Par 3	Par 4	Par 4	Par 5	Par 5	Par 3	Par 36

10	11	12	13	14	15	16	17	18	In
458	144	437	451	218	427	354	427	202	3118
Par 4	Par 3	Par 4	Par 4	Par 3	Par 4	Par 4	Par 4	Par 3	Par 33

HOW TO GET THERE

...urse is located on A496 at
...ver Harlech and directly
...ow Harlech Castle.

Royal St. David's
Golf Club

Southerndown

*A*ny golfer who thinks that the toughest courses in the British Isles are all links courses should visit Southerndown on a windy day. And anyone who does so and manages to play to his or her handicap is a bandit of the first order. Southerndown, situated 3 miles west of Bridgend, is one of Britain's most exposed courses. It occupies high ground (Ogmore Down) and overlooks the Bristol Channel. From the back tees it provides a mighty challenge - even on a calm day - yet one that is also extremely enjoyable.

Southerndown is not a links, then, rather it belongs to that golfing species known as 'downland'. Indeed, many commentators regard it as Britain's premier downland course. Although there are no sand hills to speak of, the terrain is quite sandy in nature and the course is quite undulating, with a good balance of uphill and downhill holes (the 1st climbs steadily uphill and the 18th - a superb finishing hole - tumbles back toward the sea).

Southerndown was originally designed by Willie Fernie soon after the turn of the century. Since then a number of famous architects, including Herbert Fowler, Harry Colt and, most recently, Donald Steel have made various refinements to the layout. It is expertly bunkered and in addition to an array of cleverly sited hazards, players must navigate their way over and around vast swathes of gorse, bracken and, occasionally, sheep, who from time to time wander across the fairways. Golf at Southerndown is never dull!

HOW TO GET THERE

to Jct 35. Follow signs to dgend. At 3rd roundabout e 2nd exit towards rthcawl. 2nd roundabout n left towards Llantwit ijor. After 800 yds right to gmore by Sea d Golf Club.

Southerndown
Golf Club

COURSE INFORMATION & FACILITIES

Southerndown Golf Club
Ogmore by Sea, Bridgend,
Vale of Glamorgan CF32 0QP

Chief Executive: A J Hughes
Tel: 01656 880476 Fax: 01656 880317

Golf Professional Tel: 01656 880326

Green Fees:
Weekdays — £25 Weekends — £35
Weekdays (days) £25 Weekends (day) 35

CARD OF THE COURSE — PAR 70

1	2	3	4	5	6	7	8	9	Out
367	439	400	384	166	465	220	419	355	3215
Par 4	Par 4	Par 4	Par 4	Par 3	Par 5	Par 3	Par 4	Par 4	Par 35

10	11	12	13	14	15	16	17	18	In
168	416	408	464	140	365	402	416	423	3202
Par 3	Par 4	Par 4	Par 5	Par 3	Par 4	Par 4	Par 4	Par 4	Par 35

Tenby

*A*s any toddler will tell you, some of the finest beaches in the British Isles are to be found in the south and west of Wales, and two of the finest sandy stretches in this region are to be found at the beautiful resort of Tenby in Pembrokeshire: Tenby North Beach and Tenby South Beach. Both provide magnificent views of monastic Caldey Island, while amid the dunes overlooking the glorious sweep of South Beach is the classic links of Tenby Golf Club.

Tenby lays claim to being the oldest constituted club in the Principality, having been founded in 1888. Although it has staged many important events, nowadays the links is regarded as a little too short and, like Pennard, a little too 'quaint and quirky' to host important championships.

More is the pity, for Tenby is a 19th century masterpiece – wonderfully old fashioned (and proud of it). The fairways twist and tumble with utter irregularity; the course's unpredictability is its charm and strength.

Two of the most interesting holes are the 3rd ('Dai Rees') and the 4th ('Bell'). The former features a hog's back fairway and a narrow table-shaped green guarded by deep pot bunkers. The 4th is played from an elevated tee along an undulating fairway bordered by huge dunes; the approach is blind, down to a green concealed in a dell. On the back nine the 12th is an excellent par three and the closing hole, a par four known as 'Charlie's Whiskers', bristles with character.

COURSE INFORMATION & FACILITIES

Tenby Golf Club
The Burrows, Tenby
Pembrokeshire SA70 7NP.

Secretary: J. A. Pearson.
Tel: 01834 842978.

Golf Professional: Mark Hawkey Tel: 01834 844447.

Green Fees:
Weekdays — £25. Weekends — £30.
Weekdays (day) — £25. Weekends (day) — £30.
Handicap certificate required. Some time restrictions.

CARD OF THE COURSE — PAR 69

1	2	3	4	5	6	7	8	9	Out
466	424	380	417	353	121	414	365	185	3125
Par 4	Par 4	Par 4	Par 4	Par 4	Par 3	Par 4	Par 4	Par 3	Par 34

10	11	12	13	14	15	16	17	18	In
422	410	197	287	481	371	384	172	375	3099
Par 4	Par 4	Par 3	Par 4	Par 5	Par 4	Par 4	Par 3	Par 4	Par 35

HOW TO GET THERE

4 to Carmarthen.
ad for St. Clears,
getty and then Tenby.

Tenby
Golf Club

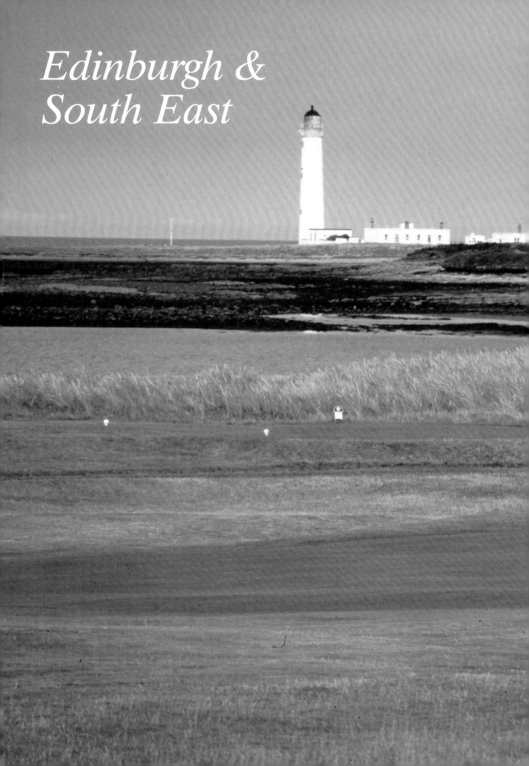

Edinburgh &
South East

Edinburgh & The South East

or a golf holiday, there are many advantages to choosing this part of Scotland. Primarily, the nation's capital, Edinburgh, is a rich cultural focal point that offers some of the best shopping, ample accommodation, fine cuisine and night-life. But, surrounded by so many fine golfing areas, Edinburgh's own golf amenities are often missed. More than any Scottish city and perhaps more than any capital in Europe, Edinburgh is one of the best-provided golf destinations. Royal Burgess and Bruntsfield Links are two highly esteemed clubs on the west side of the city whilst the well-known resort of Dalmahoy offers two fine courses. A little further out in West Lothian, Murrayfield and the courses around Musselburgh are also great venues to play. Most highly recommended is Edinburgh's flotilla of municipal courses. Not only are they well-presented with all the traditions of Scottish golf but the value-for-money is simply outstanding. Silverknowes is an impressive public parkland course rolling down to the Firth of Forth with wide fairways and wonderful greens, always in top form. On returning to the clubhouse, golfers frequently comment about the great condition of the course. Special mention must be given to the Braid Hills municipal courses. Set to the south and overlooking the city's chimney pots as well as the landmarks of Arthur's Seat and Edinburgh Castle, Braid No. 1 is one of the finest heathland courses you will find, and that says nothing of its views. Twenty miles east of Edinburgh's Princes Street is East Lothian. The courses here need little introduction, Muirfield, Gullane No. 1, North Berwick's West Links; courses to test the best golfers. But amongst them are numerous shorter courses that offer the same terrain and challenge as these more well known links. Accommodation in East Lothian is geared up to golfers, most a short distance from the clubhouses. If you want to take advantage of Edinburgh's nightlife or shopping, there is an excellent train service running through most East Lothian towns that can have you in Princes' Street and

the heart of the city within half an hour. To the south and within an hour's drive of Edinburgh, is the Scottish Borders, an area not as well known for golf but, with a rapidly growing portfolio of courses, both of holiday and championship status, this is rapidly changing. The Par 72, 6,789-yard Roxburghe course near Kelso, has recently opened and is surely a venue for international tournaments of the near future. For the touring golfer, this entire region is a bounty. In close proximity to England, golfers from the south can reach it and be playing in a few short hours. Throughout Edinburgh and the south east, there are numerous venues, some not mentioned in this edition, such as East Lothian's Whitekirk or Castle Park, recently opened and very promising. In the Borders there are others such as Duns or Eyemouth that have extended to offer 18 holes and these too are much improved. To the west of this region, and still within a short drive of the nation's capital, are courses such as West Linton or Harburn in West Calder or Ratho Park on Edinburgh's western fringe. Each offers a uniquely different environment and a singular golfing challenge. For details of the Lothian and Edinburgh's Golf Pass ring 0131 558 1072 and the Scottish Borders 'Freedom of the Fairways Passport' telephone 018907 50678.

DUNBAR

HARBURN

HAWICK

HIRSEL

LONGNIDDRY

MINTO

ROXBURGHE

WHITEKIRK

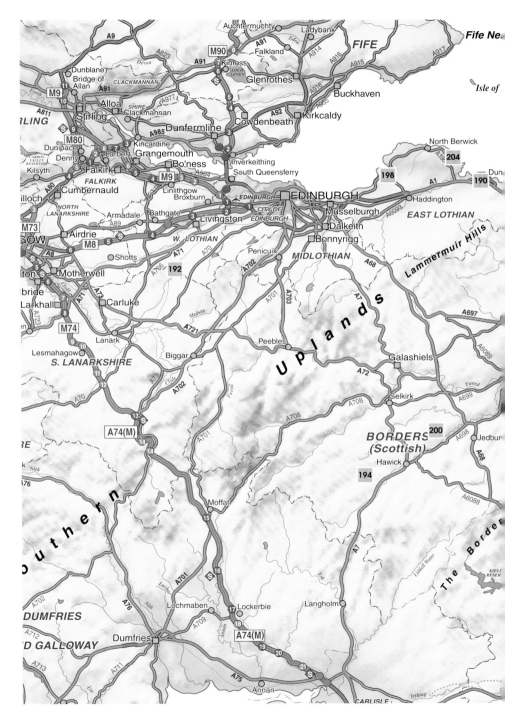

Fife Ne...

FIFE

Isle of...

Auchtermuchty
Ladybank
A91
Eden
A914

M90
Falkland
A916
A915

Kinross
LOCH
LEVEN
Glenrothes
A916

A9

A823

A91
Devon

Dunblane
Bridge of
Allan
CLACKMANNAN

M9

Alloa
SHIRE
Clackmannan

Stirling

Dunfermline

Cowdenbeath

Buckhaven

Kirkcaldy

North Berwick
A198
204

198
A1
190
Dun

RLING

M80

Kincardine

Dunipace
Denny
Larbert
Grangemouth

Bo'ness

Inverkeithing
South Queensferry

Kilsyth
FALKIRK
Falkirk

M9

A904

EDINBURGH

EDINBURGH

Haddington

EAST LOTHIAN

illoch
Cumbernauld
NORTH
LANARKSHIRE

Linlithgow
Broxburn

CITY OF
EDINBURGH

Musselburgh

M73

Armadale
A89
Bathgate

Livingston

Dalkeith

Bonnyrigg

A6093

LAMMERMUIR HILLS

GOW

Airdrie

M8
A8

Shotts

W. LOTHIAN
A70
A71

192
A702

Penicuik

MIDLOTHIAN
A68

A7

A697

ton
Motherwell

bride
Larkhall

Carluke

Medwin

A701

A703

U p l a n d s

Peebles

Galashiels
A6089

M74

Lanark

A721

A72

Tweed

Selkirk
A699

Lesmahagow
S. LANARKSHIRE

Biggar

A702

Clyde

A708
A708

BORDERS
(Scottish)

200
A698
Jedbur

A68

A74(M)

A701

Hawick

194

RE

Nith

A76

Moffat

15

A7

The   Border

KIEL
RESER

A702

uthern

A74(M)

A701

16

Langholm

Liddel Water

Lochmaben
Lockerbie

A709

18

Annan

DUMFRIES

D GALLOWAY
A712

Dumfries

A76

A711

A713

Ur

A74(M)

19
20

21

A75

Annan

Irthing

CARLISLE

Edinburgh & South East

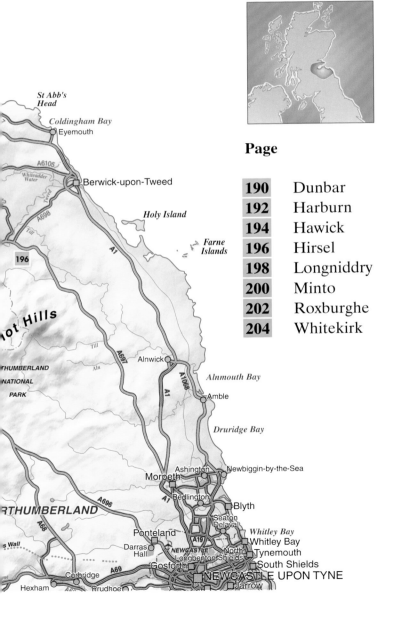

Page

St Abb's Head

Coldingham Bay
Eyemouth

A6105

Whiteadder Water

Berwick-upon-Tweed

Tweed

A698

Till

Holy Island

Farne Islands

A1

196

ot Hills

Till

A697

Aln

Alnwick

A1068

Alnmouth Bay

A1

Amble

THUMBERLAND NATIONAL PARK

Druridge Bay

Ashington

Newbiggin-by-the-Sea

Morpeth

A696

Bedlington

A1

Blyth

RTHUMBERLAND

Seaton Delaval

A68

Ponteland

Whitley Bay

A19

Whitley Bay

s Wall

Darras Hall

NEWCASTLE

North Shields

Tynemouth

Longbenton

South Shields

Gosforth

Corbridge

A69

NEWCASTLE UPON TYNE

Hexham

Prudhoe

Jarrow

Dunbar

*I*t isn't entirely clear when golf was first played at Dunbar. Whilst the Dunbar Golf Club was founded in 1856 following a meeting in the Town Hall, the Dunbar Golfing Society had been instituted in 1794. Furthermore, records indicate that some cruder form of golf had been played in the area early in the 17th century. In 1616 two men of the parish of Tyninghame were censured by the Kirk Session for 'playing at ye nyne holis' on the Lord's Day, and in 1640 an Assistant Minister of Dunbar was disgraced 'for playing at gouff.' Today 'gouff' is still played at Dunbar, although no one is likely to be censured or disgraced for doing so, and there are now 18 splendid holes.

The links is laid out on a fairly narrow tract of land, closely following the contours of the shoreline. It also features (and to an extent is bisected by) an ancient stone wall.

While Dunbar is by no means the longest of Scottish links, when the wind blows it can prove one of the toughest. This may have something to do with the fact that there is an 'Out of Bounds' on the 3rd, 4th, 5th, 6th, 7th, 8th, 9th, 16th, 17th and 18th, and the beach can come into play on no fewer than nine of the holes – straight hitting would appear to be the order of the day!

Dunbar is one of the east coast's most attractive links with some splendid views out across the sea towards Bass Rock. After two fairly gentle par fives and a spectacular par three, the course heads away from the clubhouse along the shore. Some of the finest holes occur around the turn, namely the 9th to the 12th, and the 18th provides a strong finish with the stone wall Out of Bounds running the entire length of the fairway to the right.

HOW TO GET THERE

nbar Golf Club lies to the
t of town. From the A1
m Edinburgh take the
087 into Dunbar. Signs
 will direct you to
Club from here.

COURSE INFORMATION & FACILITIES

Dunbar Golf Club
East Links, Dunbar
East Lothian EH42 1LL

Secretary: Liz Thom
Tel: 01368 862317 Fax: 01368 865202

Golf Professional: Tel: 01368 862086

Green Fees:
Weekdays (Day) — £35 Weekends (Day) — £45
Weekdays (Round) — £28 Weekends (Round) — £35
Some time restrictions

CARD OF THE COURSE — PAR 71

1	2	3	4	5	6	7	8	9	Out
474	492	173	353	147	347	382	370	506	3244
Par 5	Par 5	Par 3	Par 4	Par 3	Par 4	Par 4	Par 4	Par 5	Par 37

10	11	12	13	14	15	16	17	18	In
202	418	457	377	432	338	163	338	435	3160
Par 3	Par 4	Par 4	Par 4	Par 4	Par 4	Par 3	Par 4	Par 4	Par 34

Harburn

*I*f you are visiting Scotland's busy Central Belt and want to escape into the countryside, head for the village of West Calder, around 14 miles west of Edinburgh.

Harburn Golf Club, a couple of miles to the south of the village, is an ideal rural retreat yet only a short distance from the M8 motorway. It was at this location, the building of a great golf resort was considered. Instead the Caledonian Railway found, quite by chance, a spot further north in Perthshire and Gleneagles was created.

The Harburn clubhouse is most comfortable and with an admirable menu. The course is moorland verging on parkland with a good variety of beech, oak and pine trees.

Some may find it a bit short but it makes up for lack of length with some delightfully intricate tests. Many of the fairways slope either towards the gully and river or the railway line that passes along the course's southern flank.

The last four holes are perhaps the best, the 15th an excellent Par 3 onto a table-top green that is difficult to hold and can despatch a ball 50 feet down a ravine and into the burn.

The 16th plays over a deep gully while the 17th stretches out alongside the railway line and up to a tight green.

The final hole skirts round a hill and you are at an advantage if your left leg's shorter than your right.

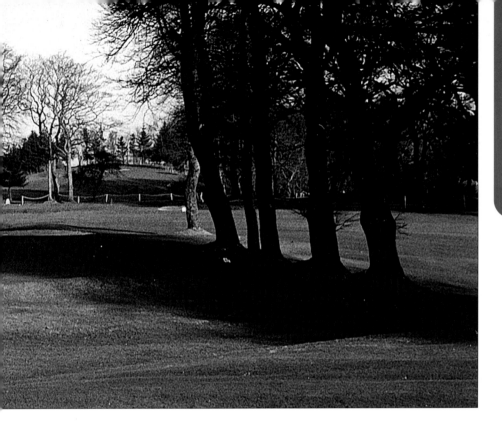

HOW TO GET THERE

Edinburgh: Take A71 to West Calder.
Course is two miles south of West
er on B7008.

Glasgow: Take M8 to Whitburn
ion. Head for West Calder then
8 to Harburn.

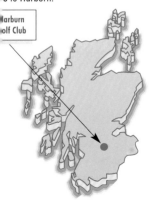

Harburn
olf Club

COURSE INFORMATION & FACILITIES

Harburn Golf Club
Harburn, West Calder
West Lothian EH55 8RS

Secretary: John McLinden
Tel: 01506 871131 Fax: 01506 870286

Golf Professional Tel: 01506 871582

Green Fees:
Weekdays — £18 Weekends — £23
Weekdays (day) — £25 Weekends (day) — £34

CARD OF THE COURSE — PAR 69

1	2	3	4	5	6	7	8	9	Out
326	385	142	480	214	334	426	383	516	3206
Par 4	Par 4	Par 3	Par 5	Par 3	Par 4	Par 4	Par 4	Par 5	Par 36

10	11	12	13	14	15	16	17	18	In
364	386	228	201	457	127	315	293	344	2715
Par 4	Par 4	Par 3	Par 3	Par 4	Par 3	Par 4	Par 4	Par 4	Par 33

Hawick

Hawick, pronounced locally as 'Hoik', is set on the banks of the Teviot River. Wool and its products have been Hawick's forte and famous names such as Pringle are the principal employers in town. You might, therefore, happen upon a photo-shoot on the 14th of Hawick's Vertish Hill course with Nick Faldo or Andrew Coultart posing in some new sweater.

But that is not the only reason the famous appear at Hawick. In 1993, Faldo and Montgomerie played a round on this testing, upland venue and both had plenty to say in the positive. Nick Faldo was no stranger as he previously played with Tony Jacklin and shot a two–under–Par 66.

Montie, on his visit, quipped that if there ever were a Himalayan Open, he would practice at Hawick. It 's not that

bad but the opening two holes do climb and are fairly tight with the road and hillside rough on either side so there is no room for mistakes. This well-respecte course then opens out to play over the top of Vertish Hill with no two holes the same. The 13th, 14th and 15th are the most beautiful with the 15th looking back down to town. The 18th is a rapidly descending Par 3, with the road out of bounds and a 'Postage Stamp' green.

Hawick, along with all the Borders courses, is a member of the excellent *"Freedom of the Fairways"* Passport, a ticket that allows cheaper access to the participating courses. A 3-day passport costs £46.00 per person and the 5-day passport costs £70.00. For more details contact the Scottish Borders Tourist Board on Tel: 01890 750678

HOW TO GET THERE

…n M6: A7 at Carlisle, head for
…burgh, at first roundabout in town
…s turn sharp right. Head up hill,
…left fork at top, continue to course.
…n Edinburgh: A7 through town
…undabout (above). Just before
…dabout turn left then
…ll as above.

Hawick
…olf Club

COURSE INFORMATION & FACILITIES

Hawick Golf Club
Vertish Hill
Hawick TD9 0NY

Secretary: Mr J Harley
Tel: 01450 374947

Green Fees:

Weekdays — £20 Weekends — £20
Weekdays (day) — £25 Weekends (day) — £25
Weekend restrictions.

CARD OF THE COURSE — PAR 68

1	2	3	4	5	6	7	8	9	Out
195	350	388	325	338	445	449	144	430	3064
Par 3	Par 4	Par 4	Par 4	Par 4	Par 4	Par 4	Par 3	Par 4	Par 34

10	11	12	13	14	15	16	17	18	In
382	390	292	198	388	437	292	276	210	2865
Par 4	Par 4	Par 4	Par 3	Par 4	Par 4	Par 4	Par 4	Par 3	Par 34

Hirsel

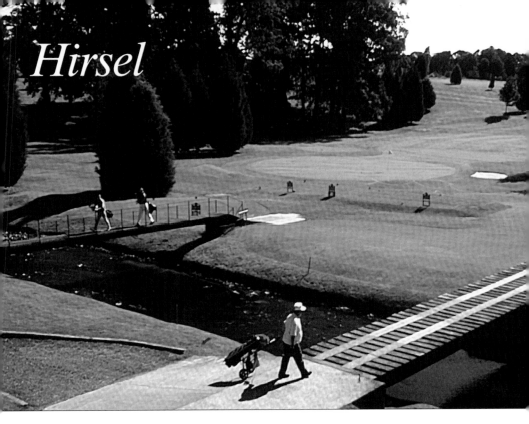

The Hirsel Golf Club is in its third year as an 18-hole course and the new section is settling in very well. With a brand new clubhouse and some delightful challenges around this glorious parkland venue, this is another very welcomed member of the Scottish Borders, 'Freedom of the Fairways' programme.

The River Leet is a major scenic feature of the course, crossing the fairways of some three holes but never presenting any real danger. The 1st dog-legs right down towards the river with high banking on either side of the corner. Mature stands of trees guard its flanks.

There is a confluence of holes at this point, rather confusing but soon untangled once you stand on the 2nd tee.

The 6th is not a long Par 4 but although straightaway, it is the toughest on the front nine, often buffeted by a cross-wind although the trees to the right belie its impetus. The following 7th is a delightfully short Par 3 playing from on high across the river to a small green.

There are some stern tests on the more open reaches of the back nine. New trees have been planted and some older specimens exist. The 9th to the 12th play over this broad-backed rise, a good mix of lengths that call for most clubs in the bag.

The Hirsel estate that houses the course is just west of Coldstream and here you also find the Homestead Museum and Craft Centre, an old farmstead building offering a rare glimpse into the common tools and crafts formerly used in this area.

COURSE INFORMATION & FACILITIES

Hirsel Golf Club
Kelso Road, Coldstream
Berwickshire TD12 4NJ

Secretary: John C Balfour
Tel: 01890-882233
Fax: 01890-882233

Green Fees:
Weekdays — £18 Weekends — £25
Weekdays (day) — £18 Weekends (day) — £25

Some time restrictions.

CARD OF THE COURSE — PAR 70

1	2	3	4	5	6	7	8	9	Out
304	290	246	320	372	357	170	345	420	2824
Par 4	Par 4	Par 3	Par 4	Par 4	Par 4	Par 3	Par 4	Par 4	Par 34

10	11	12	13	14	15	16	17	18	In
125	345	531	440	180	438	314	375	520	3268
Par 3	Par 4	Par 5	Par 4	Par 3	Par 4	Par 4	Par 4	Par 5	Par 36

HOW TO GET THERE

west end of Coldstream
the A697.

Hirsel
Golf Club

PLUM BRAES BARN

- The Roxburghe Course is 5 miles away
- 3 and 5 day Golf passes available for
  20 golf courses in the Scottish Borders
- Renowned East Lothian Golf Courses one hour drive
- Converted 2000 offering 4★★★★ accomodation
  Self-catering or B&B
- Plum Tree sleeps 2 - a charming romantic cottage!
  spiral stairs and french windows!
- Garden Bank Cottage and Cockle Kitty sleep 4-6
- 5 minutes taxi ride to Kelso for great pub grub and
  market town ambience

Longniddry

O n the south shores of the Firth of Forth, Longniddry is one of a host of courses that populate this area. It is chosen here because, in the midst of predominantly links courses such as Muirfield, Gullane Number 1 or North Berwick's West Links, Longniddry offers a slightly different character and one that many golfers enjoy.

Laid out by Harry Colt in 1921 overlooking Seton Sands, one would presume to play over the roll and pitch of a typical links layout but this is not the case.

The course presents itself in two distinct halves, the front being tighter and more enclosed with the second half being open and prey to the many winds that patrol this estuary. There are links characteristics to be found but established trees with many newer plantings coming into maturity soften this aspect making it more parkland. While variety is part of the appeal, it is the general quality of the course that makes is so popular, its fine properties endearing it to major tournaments but for its length at only 6,200 yards. Amongst the tougher holes is the 3rd, a long test on the Par 4 limit of 460 yards. There are no Par 5's at Longniddry, just long defying Par 4's. For relief, the 6th is a gorgeous, short hole played from an elevated tee with trees surrounding the green.

The course has undergone a recent programme of development and the bunker hazards are now more formidable with newly turfed facing. Another area to avoid is the thick, rough grass, in some places standing at a foot high.

COURSE INFORMATION & FACILITIES

Longniddry Golf Course
Links Road, Longniddry
East Lothian EH32 0NL

Secretary/Manager: Neil Robertson
Tel: 01875 852141 Fax: 01875 853371
Email: secretary@longniddrygolfclub.co.uk

Golf Professional Tel: 01875 852228

Green Fees:
Weekdays — £32 Weekends — £42
Weekdays (day) — £45
Handicap certificate required. Some time restrictions.

CARD OF THE COURSE — PAR 68

1	2	3	4	5	6	7	8	9	Out
396	412	459	195	314	168	427	371	373	3115
Par 4	Par 4	Par 4	Par 3	Par 4	Par 3	Par 4	Par 4	Par 4	Par 34

10	11	12	13	14	15	16	17	18	In
364	329	378	172	401	423	142	432	430	3071
Par 4	Par 4	Par 4	Par 3	Par 4	Par 4	Par 3	Par 4	Par 4	Par 34

HOW TO GET THERE

course lies to the north of Longniddry
ge, and is accessed via Links Road, in
village. Longniddry is approximately
miles north of the A1, and 17 miles
of Edinburgh City Centre.
ctions: From the A1, take the
3 to Longniddry Village.
right and first left
n Links Road).

ongniddry
Golf Club

Minto

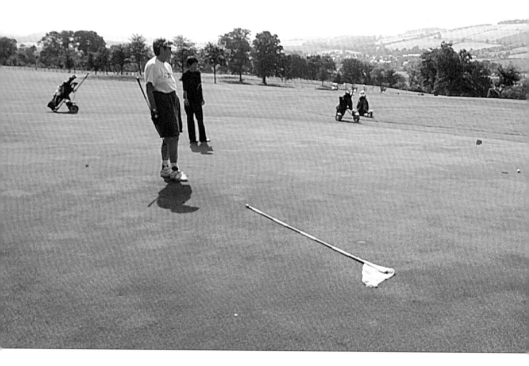

D riving through the gates to Minto Golf Club, you immediately get an impression of what this course will be like. Sympathetically laid out through the aged groves of this beautiful estate, many of Minto's holes are graced with fine arboreal specimens.

Minto is an excellent parkland course tucked away behind the village of Denholm and overlooked by the imposing Rubers Law. It plays over ambling, gentle slopes for the first ten holes before opening out into wider plains at the 11th.

The 4th is a difficult Par 3 playing across the top of the course and on the level. Here, the course opens out and the main challenge is hitting the ball into the westerly wind. Despite being built on the side of a hill, there are no steep climbs although the view from the 12th tee, on a hole they call the Everest, can give rise to sudden palpitations. This is a short par 4 that suddenly ascends just before the pin.

At the moment, there are no bunkers on the course and the rough is fairly lenient but this is changing in order to present a greater challenge. Fairways are being narrowed and bunkers strategically placed. Much of this work was completed last year. More trees are also being planted on the back nine.

Minto's clubhouse, is very modern, small but welcoming, and was built, to a large degree, by the club members.

COURSE INFORMATION & FACILITIES

Minto Golf Club
Minto
Hawick TD9 8SH

Secretary: Peter Brown
Tel: 01450 870220 & 01835 862611

Green Fees:
Weekdays — £15 Weekends — £20
Weekdays (day) — £20 Weekends (day) — £25

Some time restrictions.

CARD OF THE COURSE — PAR 68

1	2	3	4	5	6	7	8	9	Out
396	309	421	236	248	226	188	347	325	2696
Par 4	Par 4	Par 4	Par 3	Par 4	Par 3	Par 3	Par 4	Par 4	Par 33

10	11	12	13	14	15	16	17	18	In
252	369	267	311	409	355	297	122	375	2757
Par 4	Par 4	Par 4	Par 4	Par 4	Par 4	Par 4	Par 3	Par 4	Par 35

HOW TO GET THERE

orth east of Hawick on
98 (5 miles).
rn left at Denholm for
nto (1 1/4 miles), follow
ns to golf course.

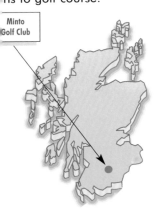

Minto
Golf Club

PLUM BRAES BARN

- The Roxburghe Course is 5 miles away
- 3 and 5 day Golf passes available for
  20 golf courses in the Scottish Borders
- Renowned East Lothian Golf Courses one hour drive
- Converted 2000 offering 4★★★★ accomodation
  Self-catering or B&B
- Plum Tree sleeps 2 - a charming romantic cottage!
  spiral stairs and french windows!
- Garden Bank Cottage and Cockle Kitty sleep 4-6
- 5 minutes taxi ride to Kelso for great pub grub and
  market town ambience

BROCHURE/BOOKING: MAGGIE STEWART, CLIFTONHILL,
EDNAM, KELSO, ROXBURGHSHIRE, SCOTLAND TD5 7QE
TEL: 01573 225028   FAX: 01573 226416
EMAIL: ARCHIE@SOL.CO.UK
WEB: www.edinburghholidaycottages.com

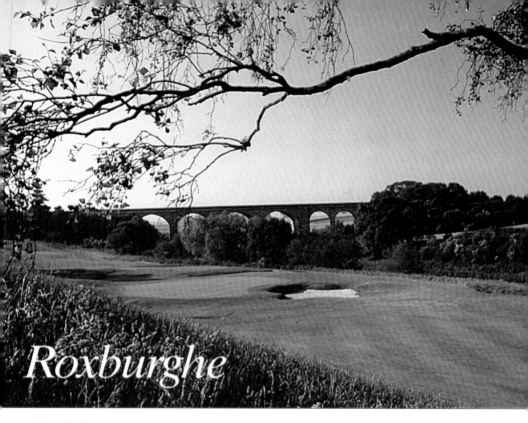

Roxburghe

*T*he Borders have long been regarded as an attractive destination for holiday-makers who may wish to take in a few golf holes along with the many other charms of this delightful area. That emphasis may have recently shifted. In 1997, the Duke of Roxburghe opened his Par 72, 6,546 yard championship golf course along the banks of the River Teviot and now there is a Borders venue to test the most ardent player.

The course architect, Welshman, Dave Thomas, must have been sharpening his pencil with delight as he set about designing a course to fit this magnificent setting. Surrounding the sumptuous Roxburghe Hotel and bound by one of the finest salmon rivers in Scotland, there are few more breathtaking settings in the whole of the country.

And it is as exquisite to play as it is to behold. Strong drivers will enjoy the open prospects off many of the elevated tees down to the clean-cut fairways. The course's defence comes mainly in the form of well-shaped, sloping greens that are adequately safeguarded by deep bunkers.

The course's signature hole is surely the Par 5, 14th, a narrow passage edged between the River Teviot and a steep, unforgiving bank. The layout requires two accurate and full-blooded strikes to gain any advantage on this inspiring and well-conceived challenge. Perhaps the most attractive aspect of the Roxburghe course is its consideration for each and every level of golfer. With several sets of teeing positions, it is a course that will satisfy the best but allow more modest golf to be similarly appreciated.

COURSE INFORMATION & FACILITIES

The Roxburghe Hotel & Golf Course
Kelso,
Roxburghshire

Email: golf@roxburghe.net
Web: www.roxboughe.net

Director of Golf: Mr Gordon Niven
Tel: 01573 450333

Green Fees:
Weekdays/Weekends — £40
Weekdays/Weekends (day) — £60

CARD OF THE COURSE — PAR 72

1	2	3	4	5	6	7	8	9	Out
385	373	352	177	537	360	486	171	384	3225
Par 4	Par 4	Par 4	Par 3	Par 5	Par 4	Par 5	Par 3	Par 4	Par 36

10	11	12	13	14	15	16	17	18	In
439	504	385	183	511	159	385	355	400	3321
Par 4	Par 5	Par 4	Par 3	Par 5	Par 3	Par 4	Par 4	Par 5	Par 36

HOW TO GET THERE

miles from Edinburgh,
ated at Heiton, three
es south west of Kelso on
A698. 55miles from
wcastle.

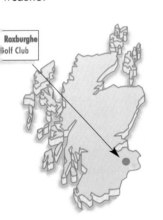

Whitekirk

*E*ast Lothian is one of Scotland's premier golf destinations with a dozen classic links courses nestling along the coast including world-renowned venues such as Muirfield. So what is a hilly little heathland like the new Whitekirk facility doing springing up amongst these sea-side leviathans.

Built four years ago, it is a course offering something a bit different. With high, rocky outcrops, deep, grassy hollows and distractingly fine views over the Firth of Forth, Whitekirk can be a welcome change to those furlongs of flat, coastal links. For those that like a lump or two with their tee times, it presents a nice alternative.

Talking about bumps, the Bass Rock, an indomitable plug of volcanic waste dominates the horizon on many holes. The first three, plain enough, skirt the south side of a hill before the course turns back into more varied terrain. The longish

Par 4, 5th is the hole everyone raves or seethes about, not only for the wonderful view but also for its portentous challenge. It is named Cameron's Test but by the way it clings to the side of the hill it might be more appropriately known as Cameron's Nest!

The front nine offers a tight test with a fair amount of gorse whereas the back nine opens out with some water hazards. Overall, the architects have made good use of the natural terrain with the course intertwining around, across, up and down hills and vales. It's not an easy layout and, in the summer, when its small greens are dried out, it would be hard to hit, hold and score on them.

One of the club's greatest assets is its restaurant. Even if you don't find time to play here, which would be a great pity, make a point of eating. It is one of the best restaurants in East Lothian.

HOW TO GET THERE

...iles off A1 Edinburgh
...wick-upon-Tweed road, on
...98 to the East of North
...wick.

Whitekirk
Golf Club

COURSE INFORMATION & FACILITIES

Whitekirk Golf Course
Nr. North Berwick,
East Lothian EH39 5PR

Email: golf@whitekirk.u-net.com

Secretary/Director: David Brodie
Tel: 01620 870300 Fax: 01620 870330

Golf Professional: Paul Wardell

Green Fees:
Weekdays — £20 Weekends — £35
Weekdays (day) — £30 Weekends (day) — £40

CARD OF THE COURSE — PAR 72

1	2	3	4	5	6	7	8	9	Out
492	276	435	359	420	167	365	149	378	3041
Par 5	Par 4	Par 4	Par 4	Par 4	Par 3	Par 4	Par 3	Par 4	Par 35

10	11	12	13	14	15	16	17	18	In
360	389	518	499	160	572	358	220	409	3485
Par 4	Par 4	Par 5	Par 5	Par 3	Par 5	Par 4	Par 3	Par 4	Par 37

The Kingdom of Fife

The Kingdom of Fife

*T*here is little doubt that the Kingdom of Fife is the epicentre of the traditions of the game of golf. The streets of the 'Auld Grey Toon', St Andrews, reflect the ages through which the game has developed. Its ancient cathedral, towers and closes have witnessed the generations that have established and advanced the game. 600 years ago, 'gowf' was already a popular pastime for the town's inhabitants, playing for free over the wide links or 'common land' on the north edge of town. Today, its citizens still enjoy the advantage of cheap golf on the five, essentially municipal, links courses that are still owned by the people of St Andrews. For the visitor too St Andrews represents good value, particularly if they take time to explore the courses less in demand than the famous Old. The Jubilee, the Eden and the New offer many of the flavours of the Old but each with its own traits. The Strathtyrum is the newer on the wide links and an easier proposition although, in a wind it can test the best. With the addition of the superlative Duke's course, two miles inland, St Andrews is a now the consummate golfing centre. With such a focus in the 'Auld Grey Toon', it is a wonder golfers ever discover the rest of Fife's golfing gems. But those that venture south along the coast, north and towards the Tay or inland to Ladybank or Dunfermline will unfold one of the richest golfing counties in Great Britain. Around the shores of the Firth of Forth to the East Neuk, are a string of golfing jewels. King James IV remarked that Fife was a "Kingdom fringed with gold" referring to the busy, trading sea-ports of the East Neuk. But today, it is a kingdom fringed with golf. The north of Fife is also plentiful with venues such as Scotscraig or the new Drumoig complex, home of the National Golf Centre. Shorter courses such as St Michael's have been encouraged to extend their number of holes to create equally inviting tests. Most Fife towns have a golf course nearby, worthy of attention. Thornton has an excellent parkland, flat but very demanding if the wind blows. Balbirnie Park is laid out amidst a wooded estate while the

courses in Kirkcaldy, both member's club and municipal, are most enjoyable. There are the Open qualifying courses such as at Lundin, Ladybank and Leven and the pay–and–play venues such as at Charleton. With so much variety and number it would be difficult to cover the majority of Fife's courses even in several visits. For non-golfing excursions, apart from St Andrews' obvious attractions, the East Neuk villages are highly recommended. If children are looking for a day out, Deep Sea World in North Queensferry is an award winning underwater adventure while Dunfermline, and villages such as Falkland and Culross offer a rich taste of the Kingdom's history.

BALBIRNIE PARK
CRAIL
DRUMOIG
ELIE
LADYBANK

LUNDIN
SCOTSCRAIG
ST ANDREWS-DUKES
ST ANDREWS-JUBILEE

The Kingdom of Fife

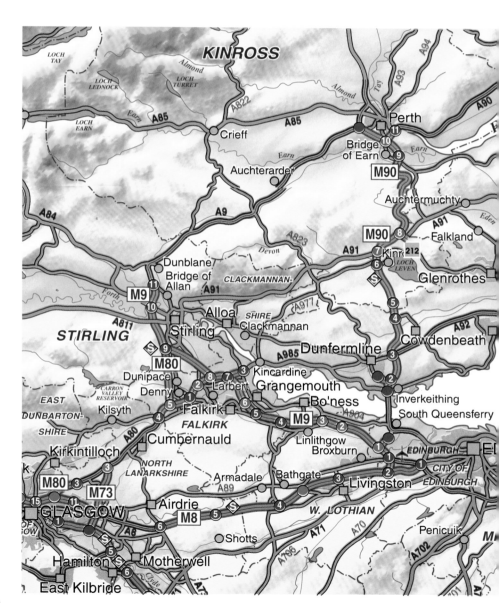

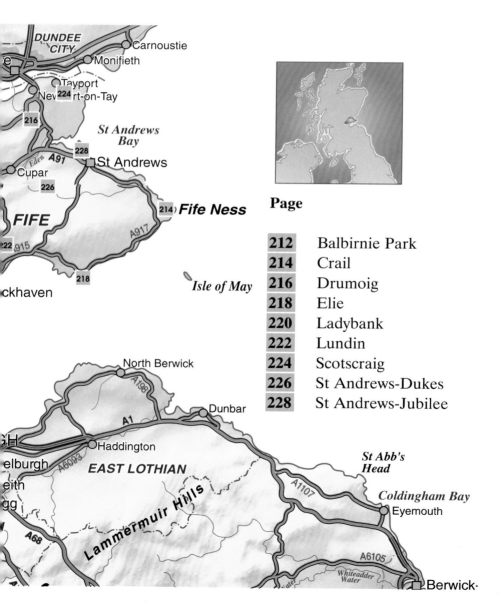

DUNDEE CITY

e

Carnoustie

Monifieth

Tayport

Nev **224** rt-on-Tay

216

St Andrews Bay

228

A91 St Andrews

Eden

Cupar

226

FIFE

22 915

A917

214) *Fife Ness*

218

ckhaven

Isle of May

Page

North Berwick

A198

Dunbar

A1

iH

Haddington

St Abb's Head

elburgh

A6093

eith

EAST LOTHIAN

A1107

gg

Lammermuir Hills

Coldingham Bay

Eyemouth

A68

A6105

Whiteadder Water

Berwick·

Balbirnie Park

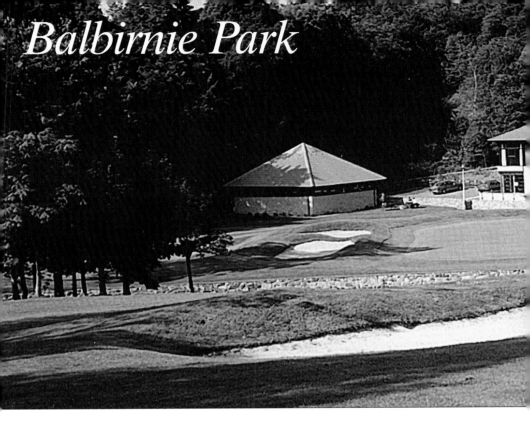

Balbirnie Park Golf Club appears to have been around for as long as the leafy, well-manicured estate it is set in. In fact it is a relatively new facility of 15 years that makes excellent use of the mature, tree-lined estate surrounding Balbirnie House Hotel.

Situated in the heart of Fife, it is an excellent example of rolling parkland, a little hilly on some of the green approaches but never too strenuous. For those that have perhaps experienced the Kingdom's many links courses, it provides an excellent option. The course's layout rewards straight hitters and can frustrate those that don't. Trees and thicker vegetation edging the fairways and behind the greens form its main defence but as long as these are avoided, golfers should play close to their handicap.

Off the back tees, Balbirnie measures 6,214 yards and 6,012 (Par 71) from the visitor tees. The gradual climbs that are encountered on two or three of the early holes make it seem longer but generally it is a fine length for a good, stretching round.

The 12th forms a worthy challenge, a Par 4 with a rather tight fairway while the premier test is left to the last with the Par 5 18th requiring two strokes of at least 200 yards with a blind second. A picturesque but hazardous burn runs right in front of green forcing a carry for an attack on the flag. Balbirnie's clubhouse has recently been extended and refurbished throughout making it a welcome and comfortable conclusion to lively round of golf.

HOW TO GET THERE

Travelling from Edinburgh: take the A92 north to Glenrothes. From town take the A911 towards Leven. After 2 miles at Markinch take left to Balbirnie Park.

Balbirnie Park Golf Club

COURSE INFORMATION & FACILITIES

Balbirnie Park Golf Club
The Clubhouse, Balbirnie Park, Glenrothes, Fife KY7 6NR

Club Administrator: Steve Oliver
Tel: 01592 612095 Fax: 01592 612383

Green Fees:
Weekdays — £25 Weekends — £30
Weekdays (day) — £33 Weekends (day) — £40

Restrictions: Total number of visitors at weekend: 24
Prior booking essential

CARD OF THE COURSE — PAR 71

1	2	3	4	5	6	7	8	9	Out
397	336	357	199	295	478	166	422	356	3006
Par 4	Par 4	Par 4	Par 3	Par 4	Par 5	Par 3	Par 4	Par 4	Par 35

10	11	12	13	14	15	16	17	18	In
493	175	390	336	206	412	395	319	482	3208
Par 5	Par 3	Par 4	Par 4	Par 3	Par 4	Par 4	Par 4	Par 5	Par 36

Crail

On 23rd February 1786 eleven gentlemen assembled at the Golf Inn in Crail and together formed the Crail Golfing Society. The records of that historic day are still preserved; indeed, the seventh oldest golf club in the world possesses a complete set of minutes from the date of its inception.

The records reveal that the original members took their golf seriously. Their golfing attire included scarlet jackets with yellow buttons and after a day on the links they would adjourn to the Golf Inn for 'happy evenings with accustomed hilarity and good fellowship.'

The Crail Golfing Society initially played on a narrow strip of land at Sauchope, before moving to Fifeness and the Balcomie Links in 1895. Having now entered its third century, it clearly remains a progressive club for it has recently constructed a second 18 hole course, the Craighead Links, which was designed by one of America's most talented and traditionally oriented golf architects, Gil Hanse.

With 36 holes to savour, Crail has become a 'must visit' venue for golfers exploring the kingdom of Fife. None are likely to be disappointed. The Balcomie Links remains one of Scotland's most sporting and attractive links with views of the sea from every hole. The Craighead Links is a little longer and more challenging. It too is beautifully situated and, best of all, it looks and plays like a century old links.

FIFE

CARD OF THE COURSE — PAR 69

1	2	3	4	5	6	7	8	9	Out
328	494	184	346	459	186	349	442	306	3094
Par 4	Par 5	Par 3	Par 4	Par 4	Par 3	Par 4	Par 4	Par 4	Par 35

10	11	12	13	14	15	16	17	18	In
336	496	528	219	150	270	163	463	203	2828
Par 4	Par 5	Par 5	Par 3	Par 3	Par 4	Par 3	Par 4	Par 3	Par 34

HOW TO GET THERE

om Edinburgh follow A92
Kirkaldy, then the A915
Leven. Take B942 to
enweem. Follow
 A917 to Crail.
m Dundee take
1 onto St Andrews,
n the A917 to Crail

Crail
Golf Club

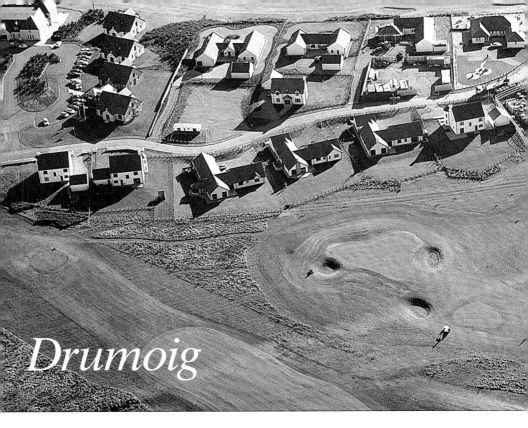

Drumoig

rumoig Golf Club and Hotel is a new course and golfing complex that has opened only 8 miles north of St Andrews.

As the base for the newly-formed Scottish National Golf Centre and Scottish Golf Union, the course is obliged to be of the highest championship standard.

Already it is gaining such acclaim. Of necessity, it is long – 7,000 yards off the back tees but even from the forward boxes it plays all its length and requires conscientious application of the big clubs.

A 25-foot quarry accentuates the course's signature holes. The 5th is a Par 5, usually into the prevailing wind, which often requires two woods and a 5 iron. It is a strenuous test, created mainly by nature except for the pot bunker placed just in front of the green.

On the other side of the quarry, the 13th creates another dilemma where a drive and wedge can get you to the green but this is a much smaller target and it is here you can come unstuck.

The 9th and 10th have created an American effect where water threatens off the tees but it also offers a stirring view of the Fife countryside. There is little doubt that Drumoig will become one of Scotland's premier venues, much as Loch Lomond has, so play it soon. At present, it is easy to get tee times, even at weekends and green fees are most reasonable.

COURSE INFORMATION & FACILITIES

Drumoig Hotel & Golf Course
Drumoig, Leuchars
St. Andrews, Fife KY16 0BE
Tel: 01382 541800 Fax: 01382 542211

General Manager: Christopher Walker
Tel: 01382 541800 Fax:01382 542211
E-mail: drumoig@sol.co.uk
Web: www.drumoigleisure.com

Green Fees:
Weekdays — £25 Weekends — £30
Weekdays (Day) — £45 Weekends (Day) — £55
Society Rates: Reduced rates for groups

CARD OF THE COURSE — PAR 71

1	2	3	4	5	6	7	8	9	Out
432	218	563	214	565	430	379	358	434	3593
Par 4	Par 3	Par 5	Par 3	Par 5	Par 4	Par 4	Par 4	Par 4	Par 36

10	11	12	13	14	15	16	17	18	In
396	340	422	300	202	582	190	539	220	3191
Par 4	Par 4	Par 4	Par 4	Par 3	Par 5	Par 3	Par 5	Par 3	Par 35

DRUMOIG HOTEL GOLF RESORT

Drumoig Hotel golf course is ideally situated within the Kingdom of Fife, overlooking our superb 18 hole Championship Course. There are over 100 courses less than a hours drive away and Drumoig is also home to the Scottish National Golf Centre.

The AA three star Hotel has 29 bedrooms including 5 Executive suites, all rooms have en-suite facilities, satellite colour TV, direct dialling telephones and tea and coffee making facilities.

The Hotel boasts two Restaurants with fine dining, comfortable lounge bar and prides itself on friendly and attentive service.

Drumoig, By Leuchars,
St Andrews, Fife. KY16 0BE
Tel: 01382 541800 Fax: 01382 542244
E-mail: drumoig@sol.co.uk
Website: www.drumoigleisure.com

HOW TO GET THERE

...moig is on the A91) St. Andrews to
...dee Road. From Glasgow or Edinburgh
... north on the M90 from the Forth Bridge,
...at junction 2A following
...s for Glenrothes. Remain on
...heading for Tay Bridge.
...before Tay Bridge, at Forgan
...dabout, head right on
...ndrews road.
...moig is
...n hill
...he
...hand

Drumoig Golf Club

Elie

A short distance east of Lundin Links lies Elie, jutting out into the mouth of the River Forth. The grand title of The Golf House Club gives an indication of the historical significance of this as a golfing venue, a point seemingly reinforced by the immense cliffs which guard the west end of the course. These rocks mingle beautifully with the course at the 10th and 11th holes whilst lending a domineering backdrop to the 13th green.

The strengths of the course go well beyond the interest at its periphery, however, as it provides a good test of links golf. There are no holes of great length on the course, the 466-yard 12th being the longest as it stretches out around a sandy beach. However, use of the smoothly rounded hill on the 1st and 2nd fairways, dog-legs on seven of the holes and some clever bunker layouts ensure a good array of shot opportunities and dilemmas.

Subtlety might be an appropriate word for this course, many smaller features of the design capturing one's admiration. It is to be savoured for the delicacy and finesse that is required to play it well. An especially enjoyable hole in this respect is the 5th. There are only a few bunkers to be wary of here but their positions, allied to the rolling fairway and the psychological influence of playing close to the buildings of Elie itself, work together to make this hole more difficult than it may at first appear.

This is a course for the connoisseur of the game, a round here undeniably complementing any visit to this most sacred of golfing counties.

HOW TO GET THERE

— leave M90 at junction 3 take the A92
rkcaldy/Glenrothes. At Glenrothes turn
at second roundabout (Preston
ndabout) A911 to Leven: A911 to Upper
o where A911 becomes A917: ¾ miles
of Upper Largo turn right at signpost for
At junction turn right for ¼ mile then
right into Golf Course

Elie
Golf Club

COURSE INFORMATION & FACILITIES

The Golf House Club
Elie, Golf Course Lane
Elie, Fife KY9 1AS

Secretary: Alexander Sneddon
Tel:01333 330301 Fax: 01333 330895

Golf Professional: Robin Wilson
Tel:01333 330895

Green Fees:
Weekdays — £32 Weekends — £40
Weekdays (day) £45 Weekends (day) £55

Handicap Certificate required — Restrictions apply

CARD OF THE RED COURSE — PAR 70

1	2	3	4	5	6	7	8	9	Out
420	284	214	378	365	316	252	382	440	3051
Par 4	Par 4	Par 3	Par 4	Par 4	Par 4	Par 4	Par 4	Par 4	Par 35

10	11	12	13	14	15	16	17	18	In
288	131	466	380	414	338	407	439	359	3222
Par 4	Par 3	Par 4	Par 4	Par 4	Par 4	Par 4	Par 4	Par 4	Par 35

Ladybank

Set at the heart of Fife's Kingdom, Ladybank Golf Club plays over heathland avenues delineated by Scots Pine, Silver Birch and shrouds of heather.

Its standard is exceptional, used as an Open Qualifier but usually it is a quiet and peaceful place where you can play without distraction. Set in a natural amphitheatre surrounded by the Howe of Fife with the Lomond Hills to the southwest, red squirrels, now quite rare in the area, live in the trees.

Old Tom Morris designed the first six holes before it was extended to a full layout. Being inland and well protected by the flanks of firs, wind is not so much of a factor. If you stray into the trees and heather you are punished, but staying straight and not trying to cut corners can profit.

The 2nd gets the game underway, a long Par 5 of 548 yards calling for full strikes all the way. The 9th is a 401-yard dog-leg. At around 180 yards off the tee there stands a huge Scots Pine, which will interfere with ambitious drives. Take an iron off the tee for position and deal with a long second shot to the green. Oh, by the way, there is a large dip in front of the green, which must be carried.

On the back nine, the 14th stands out 463 yards off the championship tees and usually into the prevailing wind with 200 yards to cover just to get on to the fairway

FIFE

HOW TO GET THERE

dybank Golf Club is
uated north of
enrothes on the A914

adybank
Golf Club

COURSE INFORMATION & FACILITIES

Ladybank Golf Club
Annsmuir, Ladybank
Cupar, Fife KY15 7RA

Secretary: D R Allan
Tel: 01337 830814 Fax: 01337 831505

Golf Professional:
Tel: 01337 830725

Green Fees:
Weekdays — £30 Weekends — £35. (Limited)
Weekdays (day) — £40

CARD OF THE COURSE — PAR 71

1	2	3	4	5	6	7	8	9	Out
374	548	391	166	344	372	543	159	401	3298
Par 4	Par 5	Par 4	Par 3	Par 4	Par 4	Par 5	Par 3	Par 4	Par 36

10	11	12	13	14	15	16	17	18	In
165	407	200	528	417	390	398	387	408	3343
Par 3	Par 4	Par 3	Par 5	Par 4	Par 4	Par 4	Par 4	Par 4	Par 35

Lundin

*I*t might be said that a keen golfer could spend a lifetime in Fife without fear of boredom and certainly with an assurance that he or she is surrounded by one of the best concentrations of links golf courses in the world. St Andrews, with its rich golfing history, is well known but there is much, much more to links golf in this small Kingdom sandwiched between the Tay and Forth estuaries.

On the south coast of Fife, Lundin makes good use of the sand dunes and water hazards nature has provided, these providing the backbone to both its technical interest and visual appeal. After a series of par four's along the edge of Largo Bay, the short 5th is a good example of how this works, thick gorse and a meandering burn crossing a rolling approach which almost hides the green.

The course provides significant variety as well. In particular, at the 12th hole a significant change occurs as play is taken up to the highest point of the course. The 13th runs parallel to the coastline in what is almost a parkland setting, before the steep 14th returns players back down to the main links below for the closing holes.

The high standards at Lundin were officially acknowledged by the Royal and Ancient Golf Club of St Andrews in 2000 when the course again provided one of the four final qualifying venues for The Open Championship. This honour is well deserved due to the superb golf offered here to the visitor who wishes to play what is a truly excellent example of a Fife links course.

COURSE INFORMATION & FACILITIES

Lundin Golf Club
Golf Road, Lundin Links
Fife KY8 6BA

Secretary: D R Thomson
Tel: 01333 320202 Fax: 01333 329743

Golf Professional: D K Webster
Tel: 01333 320051

Green Fees:
Weekdays - £32   Weekends - £40 (Sat. pm only)
Weekdays (day) - £40
Restrictions apply.

CARD OF THE COURSE — PAR 71

1	2	3	4	5	6	7	8	9	Out
424	346	335	452	140	330	273	364	555	3219
Par 4	Par 4	Par 4	Par 4	Par 3	Par 4	Par 4	Par 4	Par 5	Par 36

10	11	12	13	14	15	16	17	18	In
353	466	150	512	175	418	314	345	442	3175
Par 4	Par 4	Par 3	Par 5	Par 3	Par 4	Par 4	Par 4	Par 4	Par 35

HOW TO GET THERE

n Edinburgh: M90 over Forth Bridge, A92
ards Kirkcaldy, A915 to Leven. Continue
ugh Leven to Lundin Links and then turn
ight after 30mph sign.
n St. Andrews: South on A915 to Upper
o, then right towards Lundin Links, turn
past shops and then take the first right
d turn.

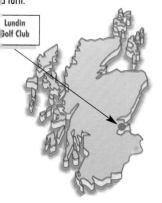

Lundin
Golf Club

Scotscraig

cotscraig Golf Club is situated just ten miles north of St Andrews in the charming North Fife village of Tayport. Established in 1817, when there were only twelve other golf clubs in existence, Scotscraig emanates a sense of tradition and hospitality to its many visitors. The present course was laid out by James Braid in the 1920's and is an Open Qualifying venue when the Open is held at St Andrews.

This is one of those enigmatic courses, not a true links nor heathland, nor even park but an interesting combination of all. Its fairways, especially on the front nine, billow with the knobbly characteristics of land that was once washed with rolling sea waves. From the 1st, you will find fairways that are not over-generous but accommodating enough to the simple, straight strike. Many find it preferable to use irons off the tees throughout the front half.

The 4th hole, a Par 4 of 366 yards, presents the course at its most challenging with a strategic decision whether to drive to get close to the green or lay up safely, but then face a long lob to a very difficult target.

The back nine is more in tune with an inland course. A new green at the 14th has made it a genuine three-shotter at over 500 yards. Generally speaking, Scotscraig is a test of accuracy rather than length and will reward the player who studies the form and plans each stroke with the next in mind. Catering in the clubhouse's Playfair Room or Maitland-Dougall Lounge is of a particularly high standard.

COURSE INFORMATION & FACILITIES

Scotscraig Golf Club
Golf Road, Tayport, Fife,
Scotland DD6 9DZ

Secretary: B D Liddle
Tel: 01382 552515 Fax: 01382 553130

Golf Professional
Tel: 01382 552855 Fax: 01382 553130

Green Fees:
Weekdays — £30 Weekends: £35
Weekdays (day) — £40 Weekends (day) — £45

CARD OF THE COURSE — PAR 71

1	2	3	4	5	6	7	8	9	Out
402	374	214	366	402	150	401	387	484	3180
Par 4	Par 4	Par 3	Par 4	Par 4	Par 3	Par 4	Par 4	Par 5	Par 35

10	11	12	13	14	15	16	17	18	In
404	459	389	165	523	175	479	380	396	3370
Par 4	Par 4	Par 4	Par 3	Par 5	Par 3	Par 5	Par 4	Par 4	Par 36

OW TO GET THERE

es north of St Andrews. Follow the A919 &
o Tayport or 4 miles south-east of Dundee
e Tay Road Bridge. Following the B945
Tayport. From Tayport,
ute to the club is well
sted. Nearest airports:
e (5 miles), Edinburgh
les), nearest train
: Leuchars
les.

Scotscraig
Golf Club

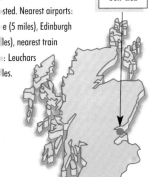

St Andrews (The Dukes)

The Duke's course is a relatively new layout overlooking St Andrews. It is classed as a blend of inland and links; the front nine weaves through woodland with flat greens, while the back offers links-like rolling fairways and undulating greens.

One of the best challenges on the front nine is the 2nd which curves through woods, a slight dog-leg right best played up the left to gain sight of the green.

The 8th called 'Fair Dunt' is a Par 3, 212 yards usually into the westerly prevailing wind with a large pot bunker at front centre, so its as important to err on the long side rather than short.

The back nine has spectacular views over St Andrews, the golf courses and sea. To the north the Grampian Mountains come into prospect especially from the 13th aptly entitled, 'Braw View'.

The 14th, a 472–yard Par 4, is where designer Peter Thomson discovered a natural spring and decided to incorporat it into the hole. It emanates at a stone mound around 200 yards off the tee ther streams to the right. The best approach here is to drive right, giving the shortest distance to the pin, but beware of water and the large beech tree that can block out the green.

The 18th is the exceptional finish to this fine course. It rises gradually from tee to green with a large oak tree on the right at 280 yards. The two tiered green can be tricky so add an extra club length to be sure of safely reaching it.

COURSE INFORMATION & FACILITIES

The Duke's Golf Course
Craigtoun,
St Andrews, Fife KY16 9SP
Secretary: Stephen Toon
Tel: 01334 474371
Fax: 01334 477668
Green Fees:
Summer — £60
Winter — £25

CARD OF THE COURSE — PAR 72

1	2	3	4	5	6	7	8	9	Out
517	448	156	439	375	565	467	212	415	3594
Par 5	Par 4	Par 3	Par 4	Par 4	Par 5	Par 4	Par 3	Par 4	Par 36

10	11	12	13	14	15	16	17	18	In
429	610	212	397	472	533	429	191	404	3677
Par 4	Par 5	Par 3	Par 4	Par 4	Par 5	Par 4	Par 3	Par 4	Par 36

HOW TO GET THERE

towards St Andrews. At Guardbridge
ge (approx 3½ miles) continue through
ge and take right turn signposted
thkinness. Head for Strathkinness
ge and after passing through go
junction towards Craigtoun. At next
ion turn left following sign
raigtoun. The Duke's is
ut half mile
he right.

he Duke's
Golf Club

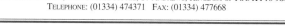

St. Andrews
(Jubilee)

For the golfing visitor to St Andrews who may not wish to endure the ballot or expense of the Old Course there are plenty of sound alternatives.

The Strathtyrum is the easiest of the 18-hole layouts, the Eden a moderate test and the New, quite demanding with, some would say, as much character than the Old without the quirkiness.

The Jubilee course, now in its 100th year and named to coincide with Queen Victoria's Diamond Jubilee, was originally only 12 holes long and then regarded as 'the Ladies course'. It was later lengthened and in recent years has undergone some major structural changes. It was not without its critics and quite rightly so but, with some excellent adaptions by Donald Steel; the Jubilee is now emerging as an excellent test. Its centenary means that many golfers are discovering it for the fine challenge that it now is. There are two overall factors to the course, its length and its open aspect to the West Sands and North Sea.

Lying on the southern flank of the peninsula that contains all the St Andrews links courses, the Jubilee catches the full effect of wind and weather. Adding this to its 6,800 yards, many are surprised how rigorous a course it can be.

It opens with a poor Par 4 but at the 2nd the new flavour of the course begins with a sprightly dog-leg to a tiered and well-protected green. There are many more such lively holes ahead and, coupled with its prodigious span, most golfers come off the Jubilee well tested.

COURSE INFORMATION & FACILITIES

St. Andrews Links
Fife
KY16 9SF

Secretary:
A J R McGregor
Tel: 01334 466666
Fax: 01334 466664
e-mail: linktrust@standrews.org.uk

Green Fees:
Weekdays — £35/28 (high/low season)

FIFE

CARD OF THE COURSE (Jubilee) — PAR 72

1	2	3	4	5	6	7	8	9	Out
454	336	546	371	162	498	373	369	192	3301
Par 4	Par 4	Par 5	Par 4	Par 3	Par 5	Par 4	Par 4	Par 3	Par 36

10	11	12	13	14	15	16	17	18	In
411	497	538	188	438	356	428	211	437	3504
Par 4	Par 5	Par 5	Par 3	Par 4	Par 4	Par 4	Par 3	Par 4	Par 36

HOW TO GET THERE

n Edinburgh and the south: Travel north
he M90 over the Forth Bridge. Leave
Motorway at Junction 3 and follow the
to its junction with the A914 north of
rothes. Take the A914 to the next
dabout, turn right and continue on
A91 through Cupar to St Andrews.
n Perth and the north: Travel south
he M90 and exit at Junction 7.
e through Milnathort and
inue on the A91 through
termuchty
Cupar

ndrews.

. Andrews
Golf Club

ST. ANDREWS GOLF HOTEL

STB 4 STAR DELUXE   AA 3 STAR 2 ROSETTES
Upholding the traditions of offering a warm and friendly welcome,
superb food and very comfortable accommodation.

On the Cliff overlooking St. Andrew's Bay and Links.
Luxurious Bedrooms. Fine Restaurant. Bistro Bar.
Owned and run by the Hughes Family.
We specialise in arranging Golfing Holidays.
40 The Scores, St. Andrews, Fife KY16 9AS
Telephone: (01334) 472611 Facsimile: (01334) 472188
email: reception@standrews-golf.co.uk
web: www.standrews-golf.co.uk

229

Tayside

Tayside

*T*ayside is one most diverse areas of Scotland. From the East Coast bordering the North Sea to the highland heartland, it covers the important counties of Perthshire and Angus. Dundee is its largest city while Perth, Montrose and Kinross are busy centres. With the Highland Boundary Fault running southwest through both Angus and Perthshire, there is a backdrop of beautiful, heather-clad hills to the courses, while in Perthshire itself, many of the courses nestle in secluded upland glens. The Gleneagles complex is an elegant example of moorland put to its best use. With three spectacular 18–hole courses, a nine–hole, 'Wee Course' and an excellent teaching and practice area, there is plenty of golf here, although it is strictly for guests of the Gleneagles Hotel. The newest Monarch course is more American in character but the two older courses are delightful James Braid layouts. Blairgowrie is also a magnet for golfers with the Rosemount course being the best known; however, the neighbouring Lansdowne course is very testing especially off the back tees. The Vale of Strathmore has become, in recent years, a compact parcel of excellent golf courses and a good base from which to stay and play any of these splendid layouts. From Blairgowrie through Alyth to Kirriemuir and Forfar, it would be possible to spend a week here sampling each of these excellent venues and, in non-golfing time, visit famous Glamis Castle, birthplace and ancestral home of HRH the Queen Mother or head into the peaceful Angus Glens. The coast offers some of Tayside's best stretches of golf with Carnoustie at the heart of a dozen links layouts fringing the North Sea coast. Nearby are the Panmure or Monifieth courses, offering the highest standards and traditions of the game. Further north are the links courses of Montrose; the Medal being the superior, a course not unlike the reputable dune-shadowed links of the Aberdeen area. The city of Dundee, a good base for touring both Fife and Tayside, has three of its own courses with Downfield on the city's northern boundary, the best

known. Two good municipal layouts are found at Caird Park and Camperdown Park. For diversion, the cities of Dundee or Perth offer good shopping centres with Crieff, Montrose or Blairgowrie presenting speciality outlets with the best of Scottish woollens and many other gift ideas of a uniquely Scottish flavour.

ALYTH	FORFAR
BLAIRGOWRIE	KILLIN
CARNOUSTIE-BURNSIDE	KIRRIEMUIR
CRIEFF	LETHAM GRANGE
DOWNFIELD	MONTROSE
DUNKELD & BIRNAM	PANMURE
EDZELL	TAYMOUTH CASTLE

Tayside

Page

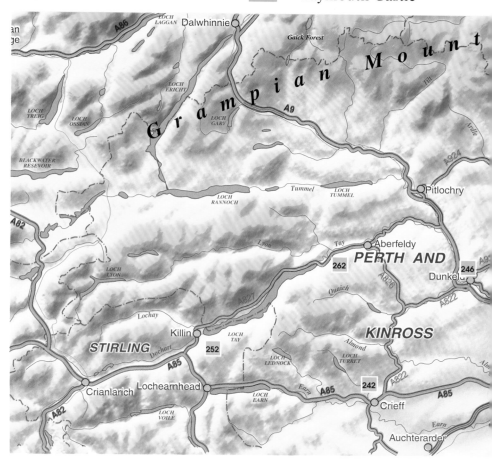

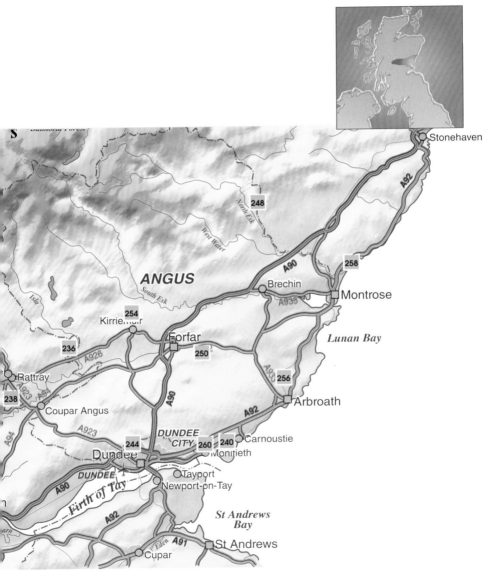

Stonehaven

248

North Esk

West Water

A92

A90

258

South Esk

Brechin

A935

Montrose

ANGUS

Lunan Bay

254

Kirriemuir

236

Forfar

250

A926

256

A933

Rattray

A923 *A94*

238

Coupar Angus

Arbroath

A94

A923

A92

Carnoustie

DUNDEE CITY

244

260 **240**

Monifieth

Dundee

DUNDEE

Tayport

A90

Newport-on-Tay

Firth of Tay

A92

St Andrews Bay

R Eden **A91**

St Andrews

Cupar

Alyth

The verdant Vale of Strathmore stretches through Perthshire and Angus, east towards Montrose on the coast and has become a hidden valley of golf where there are now a dozen delightful courses all within easy driving distance.

At its centre is Alyth Golf Club, a well-conceived heathland layout established over 100 years ago, the original 9 holes by Old Tom Morris, later extended and refined by James Braid. The combination of tree-lined fairways and diverse, rolling terrain makes this a superior test with a configuration that demands constant attention.

Therefore, the emphasis is on precision rather than distance although both are needed at the course's most demanding stretch, the 9th, 10th & 11th, two long par 4's followed by a par 5. With a tight tee shot in every instance, this is the area to make or break a card.

On the front nine, the 5th is the hole everyone remembers with two stretches of burn intersecting the dog-legged fairway. The temptation is to fly towards the green and carry both burns but the canny club golfer, having been in the burn or OOB many times, prefers to go for the island and lob a safe 8 or 9-iron onto the tabletop green.

Alyth's most demanding aspect, however, might be its tranquil setting. Within the pines, sliver birch and heather and overlooking the nearby hills, it is easy to lose yourself in the joys of a good game of golf with a layout so conceived that you barely notice other groups of golfers.

COURSE INFORMATION & FACILITIES

Alyth Golf Club
Pitcrocknie
Alyth PH11 8HT
Email: mansec@alythgolf.freeserve.co.uk
Web: www.alythgolfclub.co.uk

Managing Director: J Docherty
Tel: 01828 632268 Fax: 01828 633491

Golf Professional Tel: 01828 632411

Green Fees:
Weekdays — 1 Round £22. Day ticket £33
Weekends — 1 Round £30. Day ticket £45
Buggies for hire.

CARD OF THE COURSE — PAR 70

1	2	3	4	5	6	7	8	9	Out
398	417	155	368	325	388	130	255	456	2892
Par 4	Par 4	Par 3	Par 4	Par 4	Par 4	Par 3	Par 4	Par 4	Par 34

10	11	12	13	14	15	16	17	18	In
436	504	308	318	198	446	545	202	356	3313
Par 4	Par 5	Par 54	Par 4	Par 3	Par 4	Par 5	Par 3	Par 4	Par 36

HOW TO GET THERE

...h lies 5 miles north-east ...Blairgowrie on the A926.

Alyth
Golf Club

Blairgowrie

B lairgowrie Golf Club's Rosemount course is popular with visitors. Those who have played the links at Carnoustie and St Andrews often turn towards Blairgowrie and the pine-lined fairways of its Rosemount course to enjoy one of the country's finest inland tracts.

There is nothing dramatic about the course; in fact, after the wilds of links courses, some might find it a little demure. Tucked away with perfectly trimmed, pine avenues in a moorland setting, it is pristine and well-ordered in every way.

As with so many Scottish courses, James Braid had much to do with the design. The first four holes are hedged with heavy heather and pine, the 1st green with a tight entrance, while the 5th opens out – slightly. The most memorable holes are perhaps the closing with the 16th being one of those psychological pickles, slightly uphill, out of bounds down the left and a stand of trees in the middle distance. On the outer limits of a Par 4, it needs a good tee shot to play this hole effectively.

The 17th is a Par 3 over a wide gully with a fine, two-tiered green. Plays long and, at worst, hope for assistance from the back-banking otherwise there is bitter adversity for the short shot.

The 18th is a good driving hole with most danger from the copse of trees on the right. There are yawning cross-bunkers ahead of the green but these should not come into play if you have driven well.

COURSE INFORMATION & FACILITIES

Blairgowrie Golf Club
Rosemount
Blairgowrie PH10 6LG

Managing Secretary: John N Simpson
Tel: 01250 872622 Fax: 01250 875451

Golf Professional Tel: 01250 873116

Green Fees: (Rosemount)
Weekdays — £50 Weekends — £55
Weekdays (day) — £70 Weekends (day) — £85
Some time restrictions.

CARD OF THE COURSE — PAR 72

1	2	3	4	5	6	7	8	9	Out
444	339	220	408	551	189	373	368	326	3218
Par 4	Par 4	Par 3	Par 4	Par 5	Par 3	Par 4	Par 4	Par 4	Par 35

10	11	12	13	14	15	16	17	18	In
507	500	293	401	512	129	475	165	390	3372
Par 5	Par 5	Par 4	Par 4	Par 5	Par 3	Par 4	Par 3	Par 4	Par 37

HOW TO GET THERE

m Aberdeen/Dundee:
left off Coupar
gust/Blairgowrie road.
m Perth: Turn right off
3 on entering Rosemount.

irgowrie
olf Club

Burnside Carnoustie

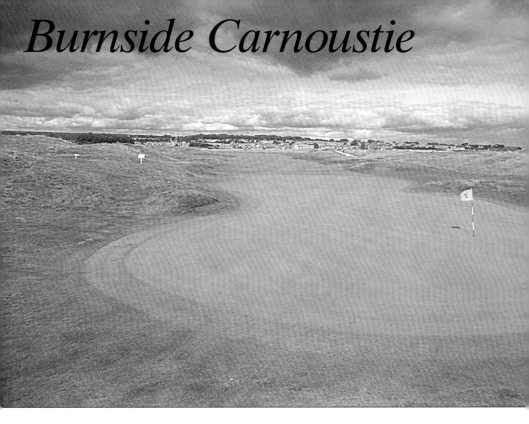

Mention of the Championship Course at Carnoustie undoubtedly conjures up mixed feelings of trepidation and excitement in the minds of many golfers. Known as one of the toughest challenges in professional golf, this is however only one of three eighteen hole courses situated on the links of this small seaside town on the east coast of Scotland.

The Burnside Course lies immediately adjacent to its famous neighbour and their holes are closely interlocked. A 'burn' is the Scots word for a stream and, as its name suggests, moving water plays an important role on the course. At the short 5th, for example, a burn almost encircles the green like a giant horseshoe leaving little room for error.

Between the water hazards and the rough, Burnside provides a good examination of skill,

even if it is not quite as demanding as the Championship Course. A good variety of short holes, dog-legs and greens of varying shapes and widths collude to give much to occupy the minds of visitors. Those coming in the latter part of the summer will also be rewarded with large areas of purple heather between many of the fairways, a resplendent splash of colour that provides a kind of warmth even when a chill wind is blowing in from the sea.

Several holes have rolling fairways similar to those found on many of famous links courses, with deep depressions in front of some of the greens and dunes clumped together giving a mottled appearance to the landscape in early morning or late evening sunlight. These reflections of such noble golfing locations make Burnside a truly worthy cohabitant of the Carnoustie Links.

COURSE INFORMATION & FACILITIES

Carnoustie Golf Links
Links Parade, Carnoustie, Angus. DD7 7JE

Secretary: John Martin
Tel: 01241 853789 Fax: 01241 852720

Golf Professional: Lee Vannet
Tel: 01241 853789   Fax: 01241 852050

Green Fees:
Championship Course: £70
Burnside Course: £25
Buddon Links: £20

CARD OF THE COURSE (Championship) — PAR 72

1	2	3	4	5	6	7	8	9	Out
401	435	337	375	387	520	394	167	413	3429
Par 4	Par 4	Par 4	Par 4	Par 4	Par 5	Par 4	Par 3	Par 4	Par 36

10	11	12	13	14	15	16	17	18	In
446	362	479	161	483	459	245	433	444	3512
Par 4	Par 4	Par 5	Par 3	Par 5	Par 4	Par 3	Par 4	Par 4	Par 36

HOW TO GET THERE

...urse is situated at ...rnoustie, north east ...m Dundee.

Carnoustie
Golf Links

THE
CARLOGIE
HOUSE HOTEL

Friendly family run country house hotel amid superb surroundings half a mile north of Carnoustie. An ideal centre for golfing on any of the fine local links and parkland courses and the many attractions of Angus. A great atmosphere, good food and personal attention are all found at Carlogie. All rooms are individual, en-suite with TV. Tee times available on Carnoustie Championship Course. Try to beat the record 20 on our newly created 9 hole putting course.

CARLOGIE HOUSE HOTEL
Carlogie Road, Carnoustie, Angus DD7 6LD
Tel: 01241 853185 Fax: 01241 856528
E-mail: carlogie@lineone.net
www.carlogie-house-hotel.com

Crieff

Crieff's Ferntower course is laid out over the hill above the rotunda pro-shop and the magnificent clubhouse. Just 17 miles from Perth and 10 miles north of Gleneagles, it is considered one of Perthshire's best courses.

It is an easy climbing course laid out in such a way that the inclines are gradual and the intent on the hole ahead foregoes any weariness in the legs. The clean, Highland air and uplifting views over the Strathearn Valley also help.

There are three Par 5's, two of them on the front nine and these sum up the nature of a round on the Ferntower. Tee shots are important throughout this course, both for accuracy and distance.

With lush, generous fairways and forgiving fringes, it is advisable to work with a driver otherwise the 6,400 yards of often-uphill lies, can prove rather stretching.

The 7th hole is from the original layout before John Stark extended the course in 1980. It is a long Par 4, usually playing into the wind and sloping right to left The green is fairly accommodating to allow for the hole's 454 yards. Stop here to appreciate the views back down to the valley.

The 12th is one of the newer holes, again, a long Par 4 of 467 yards with a soft dog-leg right, this time usually playing downwind and downhill so it is foreshortened but then this is a more difficult green, set into a conifer wood.

COURSE INFORMATION & FACILITIES

Crieff Golf Club — Ferntower Course
Ferntower
Perth Road, Crieff

Managing Secretary: J S Miller
Tel: 01764 652397 Fax: 01764 653803

Golf Professional & Bookings:
Tel: 01764 652909 Fax: 01764 655096

Green Fees per 18 holes per day:
Weekdays from — £20 Weekends — £28
Weekdays (day) from — £28 Weekends (day) — £37

CARD OF THE COURSE — PAR 71

1	2	3	4	5	6	7	8	9	Out
163	380	418	124	532	482	454	303	511	3367
Par 3	Par 4	Par 4	Par 3	Par 5	Par 5	Par 4	Par 4	Par 5	Par 37

10	11	12	13	14	15	16	17	18	In
414	379	467	191	353	377	412	139	303	3035
Par 4	Par 4	Par 4	Par 3	Par 4	Par 4	Par 4	Par 3	Par 4	Par 34

CRIEFF HYDRO HOTEL

Set in a 900 acre estate, Crieff Hydro is a 4 star resort with a myriad of leisure activities to entertain you on and off the golf course.

With its own 18 hole course from 2002, driving range, practice green and bunkers Crieff Hydro's golf facilities are perfect to warm up or for the novice golfer.

Your golfing day begins with the legendary Crieff Hydro buffet breakfast and, whatever your tee time, the Brasserie's AA rosette winning food will await your return. To soothe any aching muscles there is a spa bath, steam room, sauna and our salon offering aromatherapy and sports massage.

Crieff Hydro Ltd, Crieff, Perthshire, Scotland PH7 3LQ
Tel 01764 655555 Fax: 01764 653087
Email: enquiries@crieffhydro.com
Web: www.crieffhydro.com

HOW TO GET THERE

...ion: A85 15 miles to the west of
...on the main Perth-Crieff Road.
...the south take the A9 north,
...at junction signposted
...Muthill, Crieff which
...ile north of the
...ldie Little Chef and
...es.

Crieff
Golf Club

Downfield

Downfield Golf Club has consistently been rated as one of the finest inland courses in Scotland. Despite this, it isn't as well known as it should be and, perhaps because it is tucked out of the way a little, fewer touring golfers find there way there.

Chosen as a qualifying course for the 1999 Open at Carnoustie, its luxurious fairways will then, no doubt, be heaped with praise but anyone who wishes to savour a truly great parkland course beforehand should seek Downfield out.

James Braid laid out the original tract in an area now occupied by a 1960's housing development. In 1963, the present course was fashioned by one of the club members. Out of the original holes, the 10th, 11th and 12th still exists,

only slightly altered. Parts of the 15th and 16th are also of the Braid design but the rest of the course was built more recently

The most challenging hole is the 4th, the greatest of the par 5's, with the Gelly Burn running diagonally across the fairway near the green. The 11th is a beautiful Par 5, 448 yards off the medal tee with a pond defending the green at around 40 yards out. A ditch, hidden between the pond and the green can mean double-trouble to those who don't know of its existence. Gary Player reckoned the 12th was one of the best par 3's he had ever seen, a short hole through the trees.

In a country know for its links courses Downfield stands apart as one of the finest parklands.

COURSE INFORMATION & FACILITIES

DownField Golf Club
Turnberry Avenue,
Dundee DD2 3Qp

Secretary: Margaret Stewart
Tel: 01382 825595 Fax: 01382 813111

Golf Professional Tel: 01382 889246

Green Fees:
Weekdays — £44 Weekends — £34
Weekdays (day) — £46
Some time restrictions

CARD OF THE COURSE — PAR 73

1	2	3	4	5	6	7	8	9	Out
425	408	228	538	393	177	491	407	414	3481
Par 4	Par 4	Par 3	Par 5	Par 4	Par 3	Par 5	Par 4	Par 4	Par 36

10	11	12	13	14	15	16	17	18	In
434	498	182	480	515	326	352	151	384	3322
Par 4	Par 5	Par 3	Par 5	Par 5	Par 4	Par 4	Par 3	Par 4	Par 37

HOW TO GET THERE

n Dundee Ring Road (Kingsway) take
at A923 Coupar Angus Road. At next
dabout take right turn into Faraday
et then first left into Harrison Road.
ill and turn left at T-Junction. Follow
nahoy Drive for approx. 400 yards then
sharp turn left into Downfield Golf Club.

ownfield
olf Club

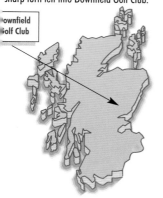

Dunkeld & Birnam

D unkeld is another focal point in the historic and scenic fabric of Perthshire. It was the centre of Scottish ecclesiastical life in the ninth century and now its ancient Cathedral remains, set in spacious parkland leading down to the River Tay.

A scenic 9-hole golf course is found high above the town with marvellous views of Birnam Hill and the Loch of Lowes to the east. The 3rd presents a deserving challenge on a moderate climb with rough and fields to the left and a distinct lean of the fairway towards this. Nearer the green stands a defensive rocky outcrop, which must be cleared with a sturdy second stroke to reach the blind green; not an easy task. Once you have delivered yourself from this dogged test, no matter what the outcome, take a

minute to appreciate the view from this loft outlook. Below is the remarkable Loch of Lowes where ospreys breed each year, zealously watched over by the RSPB and many bird-watchers who visit the public hide On the course, there are several wide gullies to cross and hills to ascend but each hole is a peach to play. The 5th is an easy Par 4 if you make landfall across the broad chasm.

The 7th plays over the access road and u one more slope while the green stays hidden upon another crest. Again, the advantage goes to a sound tee shot that clears the first precipice but, even then, it is a high lob with much danger before and aft the airy green. Dunkeld & Birnam Golf Club is part of the Highland Perthshire Ticket so play is possib here for an entire week for the price of, say round of drinks at Gleneagles.

CARD OF THE COURSE — PAR 70

1	2	3	4	5	6	7	8	9	Out
285	281	140	442	376	303	271	393	367	2858
Par 4	Par 3	Par 3	Par 5	Par 4	Par 4	Par 4	Par 4	Par 4	Par 36

10	11	12	13	14	15	16	17	18	In
508	141	274	325	417	396	274	195	123	2653
Par 5	Par 3	Par 4	Par 4	Par 4	Par 4	Par 4	Par 3	Par 3	Par 34

HOW TO GET THERE

ave A9 and proceed
ough Dunkeld. Turn right
to the A923 Blairgowrie
ad. Golf course
nposted at top
the hill.

Dunkeld & Birnam
Golf Club

Edzell

art of the appeal of a golfing holiday in Scotland is to truly get-away-from it-all into the magnificent landscapes that this country is so famous for.

Edzell Golf Club is set far enough away from the well-spiked trails around St Andrews, Carnoustie or Ayrshire yet is easily accessible within an hour's drive from St Andrews or Aberdeen.

Where the foothills of the Grampian Mountains merge into the Vale of Strathmore, Edzell Golf Club plays over a varying parkland/heathland terrain well blended with mature trees. The course sets out over notable rises, the fine turf delighting golfers who have not experienced it before. Edzell is renowned for the quality of turf on fairways and greens.

The course's rhythm is unlike most in that you are tested at the 2nd hole with a Par 4 of 446 yards. All that can be done here is ensure that you are warmed up and psychologically prepared before you play.

Paramount on the back nine is the 14th hole known as Majuba, a battle in the Boer War. This is an uphill Par 3, heavily guarded but try to avoid leaving a downhill putt on the sloping surface. There is OOB to the rear in the form of the old railway as well as to the right.

Edzell's course is a concord of all that nature offers in this part of the world, heather, and fir trees, squirrels, deer, pheasants and finches. The clubhouse, though much modified and extended, still retains all the character of its 100-year vintage.

COURSE INFORMATION & FACILITIES

The Edzell Golf Club
High Street, Edzell
Brechin, Tayside DD9 7TF

Secretary: Ian Farquhar
Tel: 01356 647283 Fax: 01356 648094

Golf Professional:
Tel: 01356 648462

Green Fees:
Weekdays — £22 Weekends — £28
Weekdays (Day) — £32 Weekends (Day) — £42

CARD OF THE COURSE — PAR 71

1	2	3	4	5	6	7	8	9	Out
312	446	310	370	429	178	385	354	478	3262
Par 4	Par 4	Par 4	Par 4	Par 4	Par 3	Par 4	Par 4	Par 5	Par 36

10	11	12	13	14	15	16	17	18	In
369	433	361	415	155	338	316	191	508	3086
Par 4	Par 4	Par 4	Par 4	Par 3	Par 4	Par 4	Par 3	Par 5	Par 35

HOW TO GET THERE

ravelling 1 mile north of
echin on A94 take B966
to Edzell. Continue
3 miles to Edzell
lage. Club
trance is just
yond arch on
tering village.

The Edzell
Golf Club

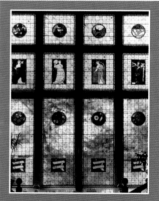

Situated in the heart of Scotland's golfing country, the Links Hotel is a fine Edwardian townhouse, with all 25 guest rooms decorated to the highest standards. Dining, both informal and formal, is highly prized, with the restaurant offering a la carte and fixed price dinner menues, created using only the freshest Scottish produce. Close to Edzell and only minutes from the Montrose Medal Course - the ninth oldest golf course in the world - the location of the Links Hotel allows you to enjoy the splendour of over 50 golf courses within a 45-minute drive, all with spectacular views and their individual charateristics, including the Carnoustie Links course, which was the venue of the 1999 Open Golf Championship.

Website: www.linkshotel.com

Mid Links, Montrose,
Angus DD10 8RL
Tel: +44 (0) 1674 671000
Fax: +44 (0) 1674 672698
e-mail: reception@linkshotel.com

Forfar

The enduring memory most golfers leave Forfar Golf Club with, is of the greatly undulating fairways that they have negotiated.

Situated many miles from the sea, Forfar Golf Club was used for the drying of flax, and the rolling swells that now cross many fairways result from this process. Meanwhile, a rich growth of conifer and larch trees form the avenues that are Forfar's other main characteristic.

James Braid was responsible for the present course layout in 1926. The 6,000 yards are admirably carved in 80 acres and, surprisingly, there are no crossovers or fairways running too close.

On the front nine, the outstanding hole is the 5th, a Par 3 with its tee set back into the trees. It is a long carry with a menacing bank of gorse ahead of the green. Most use a 3 or 4-iron to avoid the penalties of landing short.

The 12th is a tough Par 4 where three good shots are needed to get on. Slightly dog-legged left with well-bunkered fairways, the need for accuracy prevails to a difficult sloping green.

Beware of unfair bounces that can come off the ridges running up, for instance, the 14th fairway. The 15th, 'Braid's Best', is the signature hole, a dog-leg right, although not as long as 12th. With the green sitting on the side of a slope, the ideal shots to approach this are a fade off the tee and fade for the second

If you can keep out of the trees and bunkers at Forfar, you should score well

COURSE INFORMATION & FACILITIES

Forfar Golf Club
Cunninghill, Arbroath
Forfar DD8 2RL

Secretary: W Baird
Tel: 01307 463773 Fax: 01307 468495

Golf Professional Tel: 01307 465683

Green Fees:
Weekdays — £17 Weekends — £22
Weekdays (day) — £25 Weekends (day) — £30

CARD OF THE COURSE — PAR 69

1	2	3	4	5	6	7	8	9	Out
341	354	381	393	200	376	404	395	164	3008
Par 4	Par 4	Par 4	Par 4	Par 3	Par 4	Par 4	Par 4	Par 3	Par 34

10	11	12	13	14	15	16	17	18	In
359	352	444	154	478	412	153	344	348	3044
Par 4	Par 4	Par 4	Par 3	Par 5	Par 4	Par 3	Par 4	Par 4	Par 35

HOW TO GET THERE

ve the A90 at the Coupar
us Junction to Forfar.
ow the road through Forfar
ping straight on at both
of traffic lights. Take
roath Road A932 out of
far. Club is one mile further
he right just past
Auchterforfar
ction.

Forfar
olf Club

Killin

There are still some real bargains to be found in the world of golf and the Perthshire Highland Ticket must be one of the best. For the price of one round on more expensive courses, you could have five days of golf on some of the most beautiful of Scotland's Highland gems.

Killin Golf Club is, arguably, the most beautiful of the five nine hole courses that participate in this programme, perched on the foothills of Ben Lawers and looking over the charming Highland village of the same name.

Apart from the Par 5, 9th of 514 yards off the back tee, none of the holes is long but there is plenty of interest in each. The 4th offers the trickiest test with a blind tee shot to the marker then a second blind shot to the green. A novel touch is the old hand-operated fire bell half way up the fairway to let the following group know you are clear.

The 5th is an 87-yard, par 3 with a dyke so close in front of the pin, it take a very high lob to clear it and still hold the small green.

Coming back down to the floor of the course, the 9th is said to be one of the most scenic holes in Scotland with the dramatic Breadalbane Hills tranquil in the background. Once you have traversed this course you will relish going again. The Perthshire Highland Ticket is now structured so that you can play all your golf on the one course or sample any of the other nearby gems.

COURSE INFORMATION & FACILITIES

Killin Golf Club
Killin, Perthshire
FK21 8TY

Secretary: Colin Scott
Tel: 01567 820829

Club House:
Tel: 01567 820312

Green Fees:
Weekdays — £12 Weekends — £12
Weekdays (Day) — £15 Weekends (Day) — £15

CARD OF THE COURSE — PAR 66

1	2	3	4	5	6	7	8	9	Out
288	211	206	361	97	327	340	159	519	2508
Par 4	Par 3	Par 3	Par 4	Par 3	Par 4	Par 4	Par 3	Par 5	Par 33

10	11	12	13	14	15	16	17	18	In
288	211	206	361	97	327	340	159	519	2508
Par 4	Par 3	Par 3	Par 4	Par 3	Par 4	Par 4	Par 3	Par 5	Par 33

HOW TO GET THERE

A9 Perth-Inverness Road — take A827 from uic through Aberfeldy and Kenmorg along Loch Golf Club on left as you drop into Killin. From M9 g to Perth — exit Jct 10 (A84) to Callander and nhead. A85 Lochernhead to Crianlarich via Lix 827 Lix Toll turn right through Killin. Course on From Oban (A85) or Fort n (A82) — take A85 to Tyndrum to Tyndrum. Take A82 to arich then A85 to Lix, turn to A827 at Lix — h Killin, on

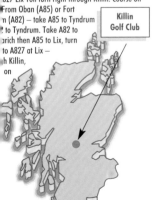

Killin Golf Club

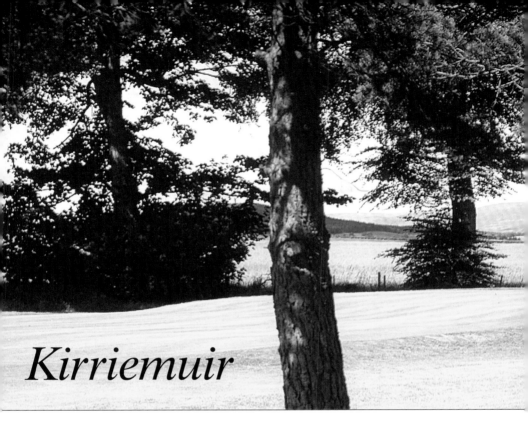

Kirriemuir

One of the most compact parcels of golfing land is to be found at the foot of the beautiful Angus Glens. Here, above the town of Kirriemuir, James Braid met the challenge of fitting 18 holes into just 77 acres. The result is a testing and entertaining heathland/parkland.

With an overall length of 5,550 yards, Kirrie is a fine length for most golfers with plenty variety on the front nine and some challenging tests on the tighter back.

The front seven holes play across open ground of a more parkland nature and, apart from some pines, do not pose too many problems.

It is the thicker vegetation of the back 9 that dogs the timid off the tees. There are trees, gorse, broom and heather along many of the fairways so accuracy as well as length is beneficial.

The finish at Kirriemuir has to be its most challenging aspect. The 17th is a long Par 3 with a couple of majestic tree on either side of the fairway. When in full bloom, they can get in the way if, in a wind, you want to start the ball left.

The 18th presents an uphill Par 4 with a blocking tree to the right and a massive gully just before the green. You would be happy to come off with par here.

HOW TO GET THERE

...ted to the north of Kirriemuir and ...y accessible from main Dundee/ ...deen dual carriageway (A94). Head ...centre of town — ...w one way system ...urn left at ... Roods", continue right ...p of road (2 miles) ...you have ...ed

Kirriemuir
Golf Club

COURSE INFORMATION & FACILITIES

Kirriemuir Golf Club
Northmuir, Kirriemuir
Angus DD8 4LN

Secretary: C Gowrie
Tel: 01575 572144 Fax: 01575 574608

Golf Professional:
Tel: 01575 573317 Fax: 01575 574608

Green Fees per 18 holes per day:
Weekdays — £20 Weekends —£25
Weekdays (Day) — £25 Weekends (Day) — £30

By prior arrangement

CARD OF THE COURSE — PAR 68

1	2	3	4	5	6	7	8	9	Out
373	147	414	335	277	384	301	154	352	2737
Par 4	Par 3	Par 4	Par 4	Par 4	Par 4	Par 4	Par 3	Par 4	Par 34

10	11	12	13	14	15	16	17	18	In
330	325	388	391	352	285	119	195	388	2773
Par 4	Par 4	Par 4	Par 4	Par 4	Par 4	Par 3	Par 3	Par 4	Par 34

Letham Grange Old Course

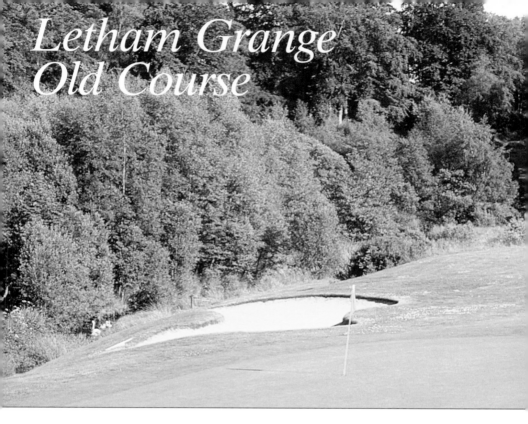

*T*ucked away in beautiful Angus countryside northwest of Arbroath, Letham Grange actually sports two courses surrounding a fine country house hotel.

Every golf course has something to offer – Letham Grange Old Course perhaps more than most. Recalling a round here conjures a sense of the great variety of environments and many testing predicaments this course presents.

The 'Old', with no two holes the same, is surely one of the more demanding parklands in Scotland. The most common factor on the course is the burn that appears on no less than thirteen holes coming into play, in one form or another, on most of them. The course plays all of its 6,632 yards and if it has been damp with no roll to the fairways, it demands fair and punctilious blows to reach greens in regulation.

The 2nd hole is memorable mainly for its lovely pond and weir, ideal for photographs but don't get too carried away with aesthetics because many good strikes fall short of the green with little margin between it and the pond. The following two holes form an excellent run making this perhaps the best part of the course. The 3rd is a stretching Par 5 dog-legging left while the 4th plays from an elevated tee to a safe landing area ahead of a long lob across another wide pond.

For those not used to it, Letham Old can be a fair old plod on foot therefore the Pro Shop offers rental golf carts to make it more manageable. Just make sure you don't crash into one of the many 'Stones of Good Fortune' peppered around the area and blessed by a Zen Buddhist priest. The New Course is a fair bit easier, at only 5,528, a good 1000 yards shorter that the Old with none of the hazards. It's good fun and testing enough with six Par 3's.

OW TO GET THERE

...ling from Edinburgh: Take the M90 to
...g, then follow the A9/M9 to Perth and
...he A90 to Dundee. Take the A92 to
...ath and then the A933 towards
...in. Take the 1st right after Colliston for
...m Grange.

...am Grange
...ld Course
...Golf Club

COURSE INFORMATION & FACILITIES

Letham Grange Old Course
Colliston, By Arbroath
Angus DD11 4RL

Secretary/Golf Professional: Steven Moir
Tel: 01241 890 377 Fax: 01241 890 725

Green Fees:
Weekdays — £24 Weekends — £33
Weekdays (day) — £36 Weekends (day) — £66

Restrictions:
None apart for members priority times (vary)

CARD OF THE COURSE — PAR 73

1	2	3	4	5	6	7	8	9	Out
397	166	550	381	435	184	342	485	189	3129
Par 4	Par 3	Par 5	Par 4	Par 4	Par 3	Par 4	Par 5	Par 3	Par 35

10	11	12	13	14	15	16	17	18	In
406	511	402	342	334	476	398	154	480	3503
Par 4	Par 5	Par 4	Par 4	Par 4	Par 5	Par 4	Par 3	Par 5	Par 38

Montrose

*I*t's a little known fact that Montrose Medal is the fifth oldest course in the world. Golf has been played here since 1562. Only 20 miles north of Carnoustie, this is a veritable example of Scottish links as well as a qualifier for the 1999 Open.

Whereas Carnoustie's fairways are wide and long, Montrose combines whins, dunes and long wispy grass, as well as some singular links terrain, to make golf here both unique and most challenging. It is a rare day, when the wind is not a factor.

Throughout the course there are excellent links features, typified, for instance, at the 2nd where the undulations are successive and pronounced.

The Par 3, 3rd plays across a deep gully to a table-top green to quicken the pulse.

The features Ben Crenshaw found especially on the Par 3, 16th intrigued him when he last visited. At 235 yards and often playing into the prevailing wind, it presents a foreboding tee shot. But it is the manifold undulations on the green that make the hole so precarious for putting.

From the 16th, the course remains challenging to the end. The 17th is a difficult Par 4 at 418 yards onto a raised green with OOB all the way up the right side. The 18th, while more direct, can catch a strong gust from the west and send a ball off into treacherously long grass. With six bunkers surrounding the green and OOB behind it, this relatively straight hole can sneak up and sink a good score.

CARD OF THE COURSE — PAR 71

1	2	3	4	5	6	7	8	9	Out
393	388	155	365	292	490	370	331	443	3227
Par 4	Par 4	Par 3	Par 4	Par 4	Par 5	Par 4	Par 4	Par 4	Par 36

10	11	12	13	14	15	16	17	18	In
379	441	150	320	416	542	233	416	346	3243
Par 4	Par 4	Par 3	Par 4	Par 4	Par 5	Par 3	Par 4	Par 4	Par 35

OW TO GET THERE

trose lies 35 miles from
dee and 40 miles from
rdeen Airports. By road
n the south follow the
, turn off at Brechin and
w the A935 to Montrose.

Montrose
dal Course

Panmure

anmure is a course that could be overlooked by golfers heading for the more conspicuous links at Carnoustie. And yet it is a course of great repute, full of Scottish golfing gusto and, having been involved with the development of the game since the 19th century, teeming with tradition.

On the course, it gets tight and tough especially in the summer months when the rough is high. Wind, as with all coastal courses, is another consideration.

For the first two holes, easy openers, there is little to remark on. The 3rd, 4th, and 5th offer more interest and are ideal warmers for the challenge to come.

The 6th is a classic in Scottish golf. A 387 yard, Par 4, there is little room for mistakes here. Off the tee, the ideal line may be left but there is a huge, safe landing area to the right where the 6th and 7th fairways merge.

Choosing this route has a major drawback. From here, it is a 4-iron or 3-wood to reach the elevated green and with the surrounding conditions as they are, only the greatest of good fortune would keep you from the heather and gorse or even worse, the railway line at the rear. The sole advice is to take an iron off the tee, stay as left as you dare and then you have a chance.

The rest of the course plays through some fascinating landscapes. Serpentine burn guards the 12th green while the 14th, well-bunkered all the way, needs two good strikes to see the green with a nasty old railway line to the right.

HOW TO GET THERE

m the South and West: Follow A90
nd Dundee to the last roundabout on the
sway. Follow A92 for Arbroath for about
miles. Turn right for Barry (T-junction).
inue straight over
roads, turn right at first
ion. **From the North:**
w A92 south of Arbroath,
ut 2 miles after Muirdrum
ge, turn left
arry
unction),
 as
e.

Panmure
Golf Club

COURSE INFORMATION & FACILITIES

Panmure Golf Club
Barry, By Carnoustie
Angus DD7 7RT

Secretary: Major Graeme Paton.
Tel: 01241 855120 Fax: 01241 859737

Golf Professional: Niel Mackintosh
Tel: 01241 852460 Fax: 01241 859737

Green Fees:
Round — £33 Day — £50
Some time restrictions.

CARD OF THE COURSE — PAR 70

1	2	3	4	5	6	7	8	9	Out
289	488	398	348	147	387	418	360	174	3009
Par 4	Par 5	Par 4	Par 4	Par 3	Par 4	Par 4	Par 4	Par 3	Par 35

10	11	12	13	14	15	16	17	18	In
416	171	363	398	535	234	382	401	408	3308
Par 4	Par 3	Par 4	Par 4	Par 5	Par 3	Par 4	Par 4	Par 4	Par 35

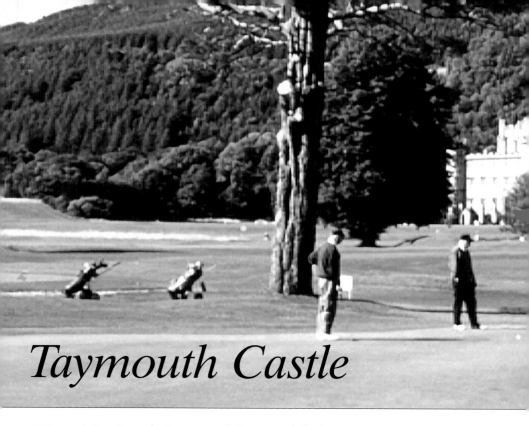

Taymouth Castle

Driving through the gates of the Breadalbane Estate, the grey, castellated turrets of Taymouth Castle leap into view, surely a escape for a multi-millionaire or a world-class resort with its own golf course.

The location, castle and course certainly merit such a lofted status but, for humble touring golfers, they are certainly glad it remains down to earth and open to the travelling public.

Immediately to the west lies Loch Tay with the picturesque village of Kenmore at its mouth and the Tay, one of Scotland's most famous salmon rivers, beginning its sojourn east to the sea. Overlooking the loch and golf course is Ben Lawers and other smaller peaks but

it is the easternmost bowl of the valley, surrounded by woods and frequented by deer, on which the course is formed. The golfing terrain is, therefore, relatively flat

James Braid designed the course in the 1920's. Braid's policy of leading player gently into the arena before testing them, holds true here with two short par 4's, a longer one then a delightful Par 3 at the 4th. The 5th is a demanding Par 5 of 543 yards and from there the contest is on.

Generally, the fairways are generous but the configuration and length make it challenging enough for a good golfer. Should a ball go off-line, the wispy rough can make it disappear into the fringe, never to be found again.

HOW TO GET THERE

...ow A9 Inverness road
...ough Perth. Turn off 5 miles
...th of Pitloche, following
...erfeldy signs follow road
...ough Aberfeldy heading for
...n. Golf Course is 5 miles
of Aberfeldy.

...mouth Castle
...olf Course

COURSE INFORMATION & FACILITIES

Taymouth Castle Golf Course
Taymouth Castle, Kenmore
Perthshire PH15 2NT

Director of Golf: Gillian Spence
Tel: 01887 830228 Fax: 01887 830830

Green Fees per 18 holes per day:
Weekdays — £20 Weekends — £24
Weekdays (Day) — £30 Weekends (Day) — £38

CARD OF THE COURSE — PAR 69/72

1	2	3	4	5	6	7	8	9	Out
296	306	420	170	543	365	283	383	377	3143
Par 4	Par 4	Par 4	Par 3	Par 5	Par 4	Par 4	Par 4	Par 4	Par 36

10	11	12	13	14	15	16	17	18	In
182	452	444	298	190	410	174	330	443	2923
Par 3	Par 4	Par 4	Par 4	Par 3	Par 4	Par 3	Par 4	Par 4	Par 33

Grampian

Grampian

*T*he Grampian region is synonymous with castles, fishing and whisky. From Stonehaven, through Royal Deeside and north to the Moray Firth, the area embodies many of the elements that Scotland is famed for. As a golf destination it has renowned venues such as Royal Aberdeen and Cruden Bay, two of the most distinctive examples of links golf. Royal Aberdeen's front nine has long been recognised as one of the finest collections of outward holes while Cruden Bay, with its wild, sea dunes and dramatic setting, captures the heart of every earnest golfer. Recently, the area has launched an initiative to highlight the large selection of golf opportunities in addition to these two prime candidates. With currently 25 golf establishments participating in the project as well as some of the best hotels and golf holiday companies, the Grampian Golf Classics campaign is highlighting the area's many diverse golfing facets. Royal Deeside has long been an escape from the pell-mell of daily life and it was Queen Victoria who brought its invigorating environment to the attention of rest of the world. Today, the Royal Family still considers Balmoral as their main retreat from the pressures of court and capital. The consequent world-wide attention has by no means detracted from the area's attraction and visitors still enjoy the peace and tranquillity that existed here much as it must have in the Victorian era. With splendid accommodation and a wealth of fine eating establishments, Royal Deeside is complete for any visitor. For the golfer, it is therefore doubly rewarding. From Braemar in the west to the outskirts of Aberdeen, there are a dozen courses of the uppermost standard set in one of the most beautiful valleys in Scotland. The city of Aberdeen has become one of Europe's great centres and is still thriving after years of the North Sea oil boom. Industry has brought business people from all over the world that have discovered the golfing bounty that lies throughout this area and within the city. On the city's outskirts, Westhill Golf Club offers special packages for the

visiting businessman or tourist while facilities such as King's Links Golf Centre can fine tune a player's swing with a host of modern teaching equipment and the most skilled teaching professionals. The northeast coast around Peterhead and Fraserburgh is often uncharted territory for golfers but they are missing some testing links. Further east, the going gets a little easier although the Alistair Mackenzie greens at Duff House Royal will make up for any easy scoring on the wide fairways. Inland, Grampian is equally blessed but there is one hazard you might have not anticipated. This is whisky country and most of Scotland's distillers are found in the valley of the River Spey. With a free dram on offer at many of these establishments, driving of any kind can become a rather unsteady affair.

ABOYNE
BALLATER
BRAEMAR
CRUDEN BAY
CULLEN
DUFFTOWN

ELGIN
FORRES
MORAY
MURCAR
NEWMACHAR
TARLAND

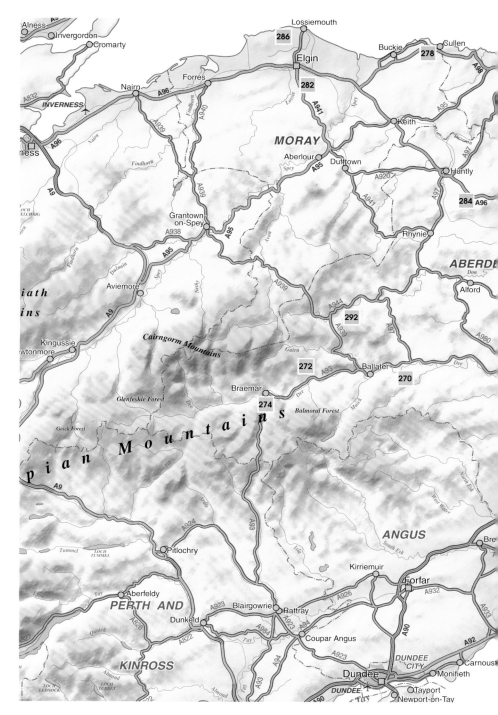

Grampian

Page

Aboyne

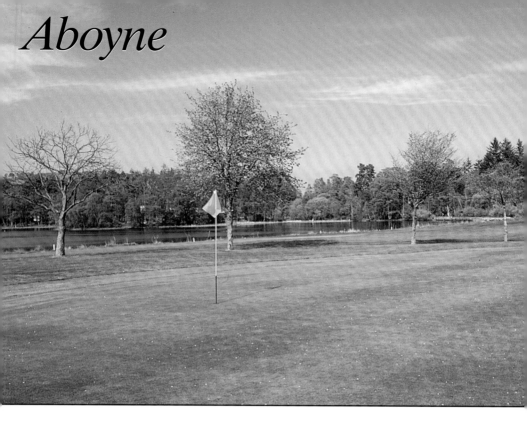

M idway between Aberdeen and Braemar, Aboyne gives the player an experience of both fairly level parkland golf and a taste of the surrounding hillside.

On a course where many of the holes are dog-legs, accurate tee shot placement is crucial. Possibly the most demanding hole of this type, and carrying a Stroke Index of 1, is the 367 yard 13th. The hole is a seemingly endless right to left curve that requires the ball to be positioned as far to the right from the tee as possible to allow a good sight in to the flag. Sloping away to that side, and heavily ribbed, the fairway design makes this difficult, however, whilst gorse bushes near the green add to the hazards.

Another exciting dog-leg is the 15th.

From the tee, golfers are forced to judge just how much of the pond in front of them it is safe to cut across. Try to take too much and there is a risk the ball will not carry the water; play left to minimise its effect, however, and the second shot becomes much longer whilst a cleverly positioned tree in the centre of the fairway can hamper the view to the green

Aboyne has an admirable variety of holes to savour. Not only is the quality of layout high, however, as so too is the greenkeeping. The greens are as smooth and manicured as one could possibly hope for in the location. At 5,607 yards, it is not a long course but unquestionably provides a serious challenge with plenty of attractions and a few surprises along the way.

COURSE INFORMATION & FACILITIES

Aboyne Golf Club
Formaston Park, Aboyne
Aberdeenshire AB34 5HP

Secretary: Mairi MacLean
Tel: 013398 86328 Fax: 013398 87592

Golf Professional: Innes Wright
Tel: 013398 86328 Fax: 013398 87592

Green Fees:
Weekdays - £19 Weekends - £23
Weekdays (day) £25 Weekends (day) £30

CARD OF THE COURSE - PAR 68

1	2	3	4	5	6	7	8	9	Out
236	379	380	160	395	345	483	166	389	2933
Par 3	Par 4	Par 4	Par 3	Par 4	Par 4	Par 5	Par 3	Par 4	Par 34

10	11	12	13	14	15	16	17	18	In
499	388	178	377	180	377	431	351	230	3011
Par 5	Par 4	Par 3	Par 4	Par 3	Par 4	Par 4	Par 4	Par 3	Par 34

HOW TO GET THERE

miles west of Aberdeen on
A93.

Aboyne
Golf Club

271

Ballater

I n the Victorian rush to discover and explore everything Scottish, Ballater Golf Club was founded in 1892. Originally a nine hole course, it was in 1905 that land became available to construct a further nine holes and the following year, a commemorative match was staged between the two notables of the time, James Braid and Harry Vardon.

Built in a bowl of the River Dee and surrounded by some glorious hillsides, Ballater is protected from bad weather and enjoys its own microclimate. 40 miles away in Aberdeen it can be pouring rain while Ballater is bone dry.

The course looks quite flat from the clubhouse but treading the fairways reveals subtle rolls and humps that can interfere with a well-struck ball. It is a fair test of golf but what it lacks in challenge it makes up in beauty. Favoured holes include the first six. Starting with a relatively easy par 5 to get going, reachable in two, a birdie here is quite possible.

The par 3, 5th stands as one of the best holes in golf in this region if not all of Scotland. With a large bunker on the front right and a ten-foot drop along the left, you have to hit the green and stay otherwise it could take a 4, 5 or even a 6 to get down.

Ballater, with its royal neighbours, is also a great place to dine. Per head of population there are more good eating-houses here than anywhere else in Britain.

COURSE INFORMATION & FACILITIES

Ballater Golf Club
Victoria Road
Aberdeenshire AB35 5QX

Secretary: A E Barclay
Tel: 013397 55567. Fax: 013397 55057

Golf Professional: Bill Yule
Tel: 013397 55658

Green Fees:
Weekdays — £18 Weekends — £21
Weekdays (day) — £27 Weekends (day) — £31

CARD OF THE COURSE — PAR 67

1	2	3	4	5	6	7	8	9	Out
394	413	180	409	177	338	457	324	208	2900
Par 4	Par 4	Par 3	Par 4	Par 3	Par 4	Par 4	Par 4	Par 3	Par 33

10	11	12	13	14	15	16	17	18	In
375	420	365	157	310	337	318	153	303	2738
Par 4	Par 4	Par 4	Par 3	Par 4	Par 4	Par 4	Par 3	Par 4	Par 34

THE LOCH KINORD HOTEL

The Loch Kinord Hotel is Perfectly Situated for guests to
participate in and experience the unique availability of outdoor
activities in the surrounding locality.
For the golfer, there are six courses all within 30 minutes drive
from the hotel, including the famous Ballater, Aboyne and
Braemar golf clubs. Visitors are made more than welcome.

**Ballater Road, Dinnet, Royal Deeside,
Aberdeenshire Scotland AB34 5JY
Tel: 013398 85229 Fax: 013398 87007
E-mail: golf@lochkinord.com
Web: www.lochkinord.com**

OW TO GET THERE

A93 approx. 42 miles
t of Aberdeen. Turn left
illage at Victoria Road,
:eed to the very end.

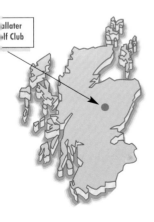

allater
lf Club

273

Braemar

A s one of the highest golf courses in the United Kingdom, set in the heart of the Grampian Mountains, one could be forgiven for expecting Braemar to be a steep, hillside course. Straddling the delightful sparkling Clunie Water, however, the course is generally flat and low-lying although the grandeur of the surrounding heather-clad hills is nonetheless breathtaking. It is certainly easy to see why Queen Victoria chose Balmoral, just a few miles to the east, as her Highland retreat.

The Clubhouse, reopened in April 2000, provides an impressive view of the inviting, wide fairway belonging to the opening hole. The 2nd then runs alongside the river to a most majestic, raised green. When at the course, the writer was lucky enough to observe a red deer hind browsing next to the fairway here, oblivious to the game going on beside her. It was a wonderful sight that brought home the close integration of nature and golf.

One feature that will please many visitors is that bunkers do not feature at Braemar. Instead, mounds of soil have been created on which the grass has been allowed to grow to the height of light rough. Be warned, however, as these grassy hillocks can prove an effective punishment for inaccuracy, particularly difficult to play from when wet and lush.

Whether it is the Highland air, the scenery or the nature of the golf, there something about Braemar that delights. For somewhere that is so remote, it is self-evident why the area is so popular with golfers and royalty alike.

HOW TO GET THERE

m Perth follow signs for
emar A93 - From Aberdeen
ow signs for A93 Braemar.
ce in Braemar the course is
nposted from the main road.
n left opposite Fife Arms Hotel
l follow Rive Clunie for
roximately ³₄ mile
of village.

Braemar
Golf Resort

COURSE INFORMATION & FACILITIES

Braemar Golf Club
Cluniebank Road, Braemar
Aberdeenshire AB35 5XX

Secretary: John Pennet
Tel: 01224 704471 Fax: 013397 41618

Greens fees: Weekdays - £16 Weekends £19
Weekends (day) - £19 Weekends (day) - £24

CARD OF THE COURSE - PAR 64

1	2	3	4	5	6	7	8	9	Out
337	369	144	369	231	103	207	253	257	2270
Par 4	Par 4	Par 3	Par 4	Par 3	Par 3	Par 3	Par 4	Par 4	Par 32

10	11	12	13	14	15	16	17	18	In
409	206	334	158	310	397	261	245	122	2442
Par 4	Par 3	Par 4	Par 3	Par 4	Par 4	Par 4	Par 3	Par 3	Par 32

Cruden Bay

Cruden Bay is the Ballybunion of Scotland. Really? OK, so it's nowhere near as famous as the great Irish links, and the club does not boast 36 holes, but in terms of character, visual appeal and an ability to set golfers' pulses racing, Cruden Bay is Scotland's nearest equivalent. Oh, and I nearly forgot, Tom Watson raves about the place.

A few years back the five times British Open Champion, whose regular visit to Ballybunion in the 1980s ensured that club's worldwide popularity, dropped in on Cruden Bay practically unannounced. The second he set eyes on the links he would have been mesmerised, for the view from the elevated clubhouse rivals any in the golfing world. The sand dunes at Cruden Bay are vast and impressive; beyond the dunes is a stunning beach.

The golf course tumbles in and out of the dunes and, for several holes, runs right alongside the beach. It is thrilling, cavalier golf, and immensely entertaining.

If there is a criticism of Cruden Bay then it might be said that it is a little quirky, that there are a few too many blind shots. Perhaps in this regard, the links more closely resembles Lahinch. Also, the 1st, 17th and 18th holes are similar to several at Royal Dornoch, with rippling fairways, plateau greens and rampant gorse. A confused identity, or an embarrassment of riches?

Located 23 miles north of Aberdeen and 7 miles south of Peterhead, Cruden Bay is not the most accessible of links courses. But it offers one of the world's truly great golfing experiences.

HOW TO GET THERE

m Aberdeen
e A90 Peterhead Road to Little
ef at Foveran. Turn right on A975
ough Newburgh. 10 miles to Cruden
, Golf Club is first on the right.

m Peterhead
e A90 Aberdeen Road.
n left at sign post for
den Bay Straight through
 village and Golf
b is on
 left.

ruden Bay
Golf Club

COURSE INFORMATION & FACILITIES

Cruden Bay Golf Club
Aulton Road, Peterhead AB42 0NN
Secretary/Manager:
Mrs. Rosemary Pittendrigh
Tel: 01779 812285 Fax: 01779 812945

Golf Professional:
Tel: 01779 812414 Fax: 01779 812414
Email: cbaygc@aol.com
Web: www.crudenbaygolfclub.co.uk

Green Fees:
Weekdays — £45 Weekends — £55
Weekdays (day) — £60

CARD OF THE COURSE — PAR 70

1	2	3	4	5	6	7	8	9	Out
416	339	286	193	454	529	392	258	462	3329
Par 4	Par 4	Par 4	Par 3	Par 4	Par 5	Par 4	Par 4	Par 4	Par 36

10	11	12	13	14	15	16	17	18	In
385	149	320	550	397	239	182	428	416	3066
Par 4	Par 3	Par 4	Par 5	Par 4	Par 3	Par 3	Par 4	Par 4	Par 34

Cullen

*B*uilt around the huge, dominating cliffs protecting Cullen Bay, this course is an unusual example of links golf. The scent of the sea together with the continual rustle of breaking waves are perhaps nothing out of the ordinary but the way the course locks in to the cliff-face provides both some interesting golf and spectacular scenery.

The first real taste of this comes at the 2nd. At only 130 yards, the tee shot here has to climb above a steep escarpment to a green where the flag (most unusually for a par three) is hidden by the top of the cliff-face. The next four holes then sit along the top of the cliffs, with deep gorges forming treacherous obstacles at the 4th and 6th.

The panorama which opens up at the 7th tee must be one of the most awe-inspiring in golf. Teeing up here to return to the links below, one's attention i firstly taken by the massive weathered sandstone rocks that rise from the centre of the course. Sweeping views of virtually every hole then capture the gaze and it is likely the visitor will be tempted to spend far longer admiring these scenes than the etiquette of the game permits.

Once down on the links again, much of the course is fairly flat, the greens blendin: in to the fairways. Few bunkers have been constructed in the sandy soil whilst raised tees help the perspective. Notable aspects include the rolling fairways at the 11th and 15th, whilst high, sandstone rocks eat into the fairways at the 12th and 13th resulting in particularly intriguing shots to these greens.

MORAY

CARD OF THE COURSE — PAR 63

1	2	3	4	5	6	7	8	9	Out
344	130	236	129	360	172	231	275	194	2071
Par 4	Par 3	Par 3	Par 3	Par 4	Par 3	Par 3	Par 4	Par 3	Par 30

10	11	12	13	14	15	16	17	18	In
309	245	182	149	207	510	348	262	327	2539
Par 4	Par 3	Par 3	Par 3	Par 3	Par 5	Par 4	Par 4	Par 4	Par 33

HOW TO GET THERE

f A98 midway between
erdeen and Inverness, on
iry Firth coast.

Cullen
Golf Club

Dufftown

*S*et on a steep hillside in an area famous for its whisky distilling, Dufftown golf course rewards the visitor with both a challenge and some of the most stunning views from any golf course in Scotland.

The turf is in good condition for the altitude and exposure although a good degree of accuracy is required to hold some fairly severely sloping fairways. At only 5,308 yards from the white pegs, this is a course that favours precision rather than length.

The 5th is a cheeky test of nerve. At only 143 yards, the hole is both short and atypically flat but runs tight against the heather on the golfer's left; a large bunker tucked close in to the right of the narrow green leaves little room for error. Another short hole of note is Fittie Burn. The name of the par three 7th is perhaps an understatement, however, a huge, deep gully swallowing any short ball greedily.

If there is a view to strike a real sense of awe into the heart of the golfer, however, it is that from the 10th medal tee. A short heather bed lined by enormous larch trees provides a launch pad for the most spectacular long, steep drop down to the green, a barely visible mark in the distance. The sight of the distillery in the valley below may set even the most resolute teetotaller wishing for wee dram here to steady his swing.

COURSE INFORMATION & FACILITIES

Dufftown Golf Club
Tomintoul Road, Dufftown
Banffshire AA55 5BS

Secretary: Mrs Marion Swan
Tel: 01340 820325

Green Fees:
Weekdays - £12 Weekends - £12
Weekdays (day) - £15 Weekends (day) - £15

CARD OF THE COURSE — PAR 67

1	2	3	4	5	6	7	8	9	Out
288	285	333	367	143	345	103	276	305	2445
Par 4	Par 4	Par 4	Par 4	Par 3	Par 4	Par 3	Par 4	Par 4	Par 34

10	11	12	13	14	15	16	17	18	In
462	290	222	359	397	200	325	411	197	2863
Par 4	Par 4	Par 3	Par 4	Par 4	Par 3	Par 4	Par 4	Par 3	Par 33

HOW TO GET THERE

le south of Dufftown on B9009 on right
d side of road.

Dufftown
Golf Club

Aberlour Hotel

Located in the centre of Aberlour village, the hotel offers
easy access to the Spey Valley, Grampian Mountains and
the Moray Firth coast. This is an ideal location for
fishing, walking, golfing and touring the Malt Whisky and
Castle trails.

Aberlour Hotel
Charlestown of Aberlour, Moray. AB38 9QB
Tel: 01340 871287 Fax: 01340 871218
E-mail: ABERLOUR_HOTEL@hotmail.com

Elgin

*E*lgin Golf Club's excellent parkland course is a contrast to the many fine links courses found elsewhere along the Moray Firth.

Although much of Elgin itself is located on the flat Moray coastal plain, the golf course is positioned in a more hilly area on the southern edge of the town. At the start of the round, a couple of gently downhill par 4's are followed by two relatively flat holes set among a charming birchwood: these help to settle a player before some more testing holes on the slopes that follow.

Judgement of length is, of course, a critical factor in these latter holes. The 5th is a good example of this, the second half of the fairway swooping gracefully up to an elevated green, requiring approach

shots to be carefully calculated. Several greens, such as those at the 6th and 15th, are built into the sloping ground, producing tricky landing areas and cross slopes that can carry misdirected balls well away from their intended targets.

Do not be mistaken, however, for there are ample rewards for the climbs and test involved in playing this course. The scent of the birch and pine trees and generous fairways on many of the holes are obvious examples. One of the best treats, however, is provided at the 10th green in the extreme north-west corner of the course. Whilst the wave-like mounds around the green can pose a challenge to the golf, a sensational view of the town of Elgin is surely adequate compensation.

HOW TO GET THERE

...south of Elgin City. Turn onto Birnie
...d from A941.

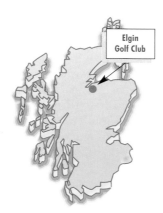

Elgin
Golf Club

COURSE INFORMATION & FACILITIES

Elgin Golf Club
Hardhillock
Birnie Road Elgin, Moray IV30 8SX

Secretary: David Black
Tel: 01343 542338 Fax: 01343 542341

Golf Professional: Ian Rodger
Tel: 01343 542884

Green Fees:
Weekdays - £23 Weekends - £29
Weekdays (day) - £30 Weekends (day) - £35

Restrictions apply

CARD OF THE RED COURSE — PAR 69

1	2	3	4	5	6	7	8	9	Out
459	438	368	155	484	222	167	453	408	3154
Par 4	Par 4	Par 4	Par 3	Par 5	Par 3	Par 3	Par 4	Par 4	Par 34

10	11	12	13	14	15	16	17	18	In
438	375	278	325	462	188	417	334	445	3262
Par 4	Par 4	Par 4	Par 4	Par 4	Par 3	Par 4	Par 4	Par 4	Par 35

Forres

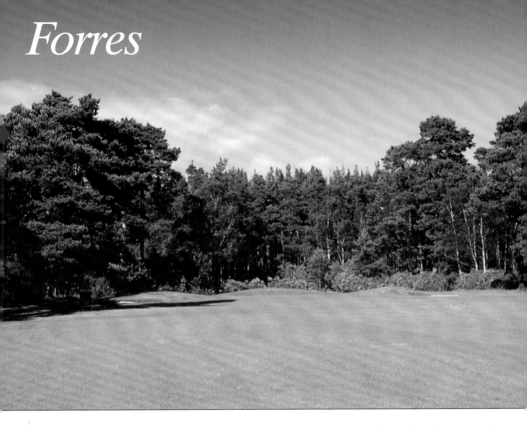

*O*nly a short drive away from Nairn to the west (host to the Walker Cup in 1999), the Moray Golf Club at Lossiemouth to the east and a host of other superb courses in the area, Forres is an excellent base for a golfing break. At the foot of Cluny Hill on the southern edge of the town, however, Forres itself boasts an excellent parkland course.

The first four holes have a hilly theme which is reflected elsewhere on the course, albeit in the main less severely. There are some outstanding tee positions to enjoy whilst undulating ground presents testing approaches to some of the greens. Granite blocks at each tee provide well laid out hole information, including a plan- a welcome touch on what is generally a well-presented course.

A test of both accuracy and judgement is required at the 16th, a short par four which nevertheless requires a difficult decision to be made at the tee. The fairway is split lengthways by a large clump of gorse leaving a high section to the golfer's left and a low area to the right. The approach shot from the right is certainly easier but the landing area is very much smaller here and is made even more treacherous by the pond that borders the fairway. Take the much higher left-hand route and finding a decent lie from the tee should be less difficult; however, several bunkers and a hollow in front of the green make the green a much more intimidating target from this direction. The hole typifies the choices that must be made on what is an entertaining and thought-inducing example of inland golf.

COURSE INFORMATION & FACILITIES

Forres Golf Course
Forres Moray IV35 0RD

Golf Profession/Manager: Sandy Aird
Tel/Fax: 01309 672250

Green Fees:
Weekdays — £18 Weekends — £18
Weekdays (day) — £25 Weekends (day) — £25

CARD OF THE COURSE — PAR 70

1	2	3	4	5	6	7	8	9	Out
306	337	323	379	142	505	202	368	482	3044
Par 4	Par 4	Par 4	Par 4	Par 3	Par 5	Par 3	Par 4	Par 5	Par 36

10	11	12	13	14	15	16	17	18	In
248	455	430	398	427	383	322	159	370	3192
Par 3	Par 4	Par 4	Par 4	Par 4	Par 4	Par 4	Par 3	Par 4	Par 34

HOW TO GET THERE

res Golf Club is situated on
A96 between Inverness
d Aberdeen.

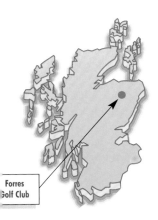

Forres
Golf Club

KNOCKOMIE HOTEL

Knockomie has been in the process of gradual refinement and
redefinition for some 150 years, with major renovations in 1914
when an Arts and Crafts house was created. In 1993 a new wing
was added to create a 15 bedroom hotel, having opened as a hotel
in 1987, although paying guests were recorded as early as the
1840's when Lord Cockburn called on his circuit journeys.
Nowadays we welcome guests to come and savour our food and
wine and maybe the odd malt whisky or two!! After all you are on
the Malt Whisky Trail now.

Grantown Road, Forres, Moray IV36 2SG
Tel: 01309 673146 Fax: 01309 673290
stay@knockomie.co.uk
www.knockomie.co.uk

Moray

The high dunes to the right of the first fairway on this well respected links at Lossiemouth on the Moray coast may invoke expectations of hilly terrain to follow. Other than influencing the 1st, 17th and 18th fairways, however, this landscape does not play a dominant role here.

Do not be mistaken, though, for this is very definitely a true links course, originally designed by no less than Tom Morris, a true master of links golf himself. The course brings out the importance of planning, keeping aware of the multitude of things that can happen in the golfing environment. The 12th hole, a right to left dog-leg running west to east, demonstrates how the effect of the sea, for example, can have a significant influence on how a links hole can play, a breeze from the left hampering attempts at accurate ball positioning.

Some narrow and interesting fairway layouts and bunker patterns provide something new at virtually every hole. The sunken greens at the 2nd, 5th and 16th are potential surprises that demand special care to avoid an unwelcome kick from the greenside banking. Aesthetic aspects to the course are also in abundance. Visitors are also unlikely to forget the dramatic end to the course as the 18th hole sweeps across some large dunes on its way up to a high green beside the imposing Clubhouse. Look out too for the 6th where a lighthouse in the distance sits as an impressive backdrop to the green.

The course is indeed rich in most facets and is well deserving of its substantial reputation.

HOW TO GET THERE

...iles North of Elgin. Follow
... from Aberdeen or Inveresss,
...e turn off for Lossiemouth in
...n.

...rdeen - 90 mins.
...rness - 45 mins.
...rn - 30 mins.

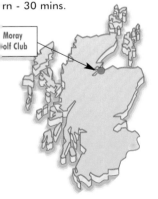

Moray
...olf Club

COURSE INFORMATION & FACILITIES

Moray Golf Club
Stotfield Road, Lossiemouth,
Moray. IV31 6QS

Secretary: Boyd Russell
Tel: 01343 812018. Fax: 01343 815102.

Golf Professional: Alistair Thomson
Tel: 01343 813330.

Green Fees:
Weekdays - £30, Weekends - £40.
Weekdays (day) - £40, Weekends (day) - £60
Handicap certificate required.

CARD OF THE COURSE — PAR 71

1	2	3	4	5	6	7	8	9	Out
332	494	397	197	416	145	434	452	310	3177
Par 4	Par 5	Par 4	Par 3	Par 4	Par 3	Par 4	Par 4	Par 4	Par 35

10	11	12	13	14	15	16	17	18	In
312	423	389	415	409	184	351	506	406	3395
Par 4	Par 4	Par 4	Par 4	Par 4	Par 3	Par 4	Par 5	Par 4	Par 36

Murcar

A yrshire, Fife and Lothian may be more obvious locations for a links golfing holiday, but the North East of Scotland - the Grampian region, if you like - shouldn't be overlooked. Aberdeen is the major city here and it has much to offer in the way of quality links golf.
In particular two outstanding links courses lie adjacent to one another just north of the city (on the same side as the Airport), namely Royal Aberdeen and Murcar. And some 45 minutes drive north of these two championship links is Cruden Bay, 'the Ballybunion of Scotland.'

Royal Aberdeen is better known than Murcar; how much this has to do with the former's 'Royal' prefix is hard to judge, but on a hole-by-hole analysis many consider Murcar to be its equal.

In any event, both are decidedly worth investigating.

Established in 1909, Murcar is an uncompromising links. It's not long, but it's tough. According to Golf Monthly writer, Barry Ward, "the faiways are tighter than a taxman's purse and hemme with fearsome rough." The terrain is fairl undulating throughout - some fairways ar decidedly humpy and hillocky - and there are one or two blind shots. Several tees are elevated and provide impressive sea views.

The par four 7th is the best and most exhilarating hole at Murcar. From a high tee overlooking the shore, you must drive over a burn and then thread your second shot between dunes to a well defended plateau green.

COURSE INFORMATION & FACILITIES

Murcar Golf Club
Bridge of Don
Aberdeen AB23 8BD

Secretary: D Corstrophine
Tel: 01224 704354 Fax: 01224 704354

Golf Professional Tel: 01224 704370

Green Fees:
Weekdays — £30 Weekends — £35
Weekdays (day) — £40 Weekends (day) — £45

Handicap certificates required.

CARD OF THE COURSE — PAR 71

1	2	3	4	5	6	7	8	9	Out
322	367	401	489	162	447	423	383	323	3317
Par 4	Par 4	Par 4	Par 5	Par 3	Par 4	Par 4	Par 4	Par 4	Par 36

10	11	12	13	14	15	16	17	18	In
402	338	155	386	482	351	160	367	329	2970
Par 4	Par 4	Par 3	Par 4	Par 5	Par 4	Par 3	Par 4	Par 4	Par 35

HOW TO GET THERE

prox 5 miles from centre
Aberdeen to N.E. off A90
erhead/Fraserburgh Road.

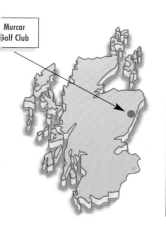

Murcar
Golf Club

THISTLE ABERDEEN CALEDONIAN HOTEL

One of the best known hotels in Aberdeen, centrally located overlooking Union Terrace Gardens.

- Centrally located, this traditional stylish hotel overlooks Union Terrace Gardens. It holds a well earned reputation for good food and warm hospitality making it a popular choice for both business and leisure guests.
- 77 Bedrooms
- The Terrace Restaurant – Our Table d'hôte and A la Carte menus offer an extensive choice of locally produced food with a wide selection of fine wines & beverages to accompany your dinner
- Café Bar – creates a lively atmosphere for you to enjoy a meal or a drink with an exciting choice of dishes on our bar menu
- Cocktail Lounge
- Limited Car Parking

UNION TERRACE · ABERDEEN AB10 1WE
TEL: 01224 640233 · FAX: 01224 641627
A Thistle Hotel

289

Newmachar

N ewmachar Golf Club is a fairy
story of how one man, local police
sergeant, Charlie Keith, had a
dream of a golf course closer to
his village and the reality, some 12 years
later, has, no doubt, well surpassed his
original vision.

Now with two exceptional 18-hole
layouts, a magnificent clubhouse and one
of the largest practice/teaching facilities
in Scotland, Newmachar is one of the
main golf complexes in the northeast.

Only 15 minutes from Aberdeen city
centre and 10 minutes from Aberdeen's
Dyce Airport, it is in a prime position to
be included on a tour of the area's premier
courses including Royal Aberdeen and
Cruden Bay.

The Hawkshill course, designed by
Dave Thomas, is the original and a
much-varied test of every element of
the game. Several holes resemble US
style courses with water carries being
the prominent hazard.

But it is the woodland holes, more
akin to Rosemount or Gleneagles, that
offer most pleasure with many tight drive
and tricky turns. Unless each stoke is
played judiciously, this can be a trying
examination for every level of player.

As testament to the calibre of the
Hawkshill, the Scottish Seniors Open has
recently been held here and is scheduled
to return. The new Swailend course is a
wider, rolling and altogether easier test
but, at 6,300 yards and with over 15, 000
trees planted, there is still plenty room
for challenge.

ABERDEEN

OW TO GET THERE

miles north of Aberdeen
main A947.
rdeen/Banff Road —
h is signposted.

machar
f Club

COURSE INFORMATION & FACILITIES

Newmachar Golf Club
Swailend, Newmachar
Aberdeen AB21 7UU

Manager: George A. McIntosh
Tel: 01651 863002 Fax: 01651 863055

Golf Professional Tel: 01651 862127

Green Fees: Hawkshill Course
Weekdays — £30 Weekends — £40
Weekdays (day) — £45

CARD OF THE COURSE — PAR 72
HAWKSHILL (CHAMPIONSHIP)

1	2	3	4	5	6	7	8	9	Out
390	543	331	378	320	170	405	493	181	3211
Par 4	Par 5	Par 4	Par 4	Par 4	Par 3	Par 4	Par 5	Par 3	Par 36

10	11	12	13	14	15	16	17	18	In
337	381	428	399	362	210	504	432	359	3412
Par 4	Par 4	Par 4	Par 4	Par 4	Par 3	Par 5	Par 4	Par 4	Par 36

Tarland

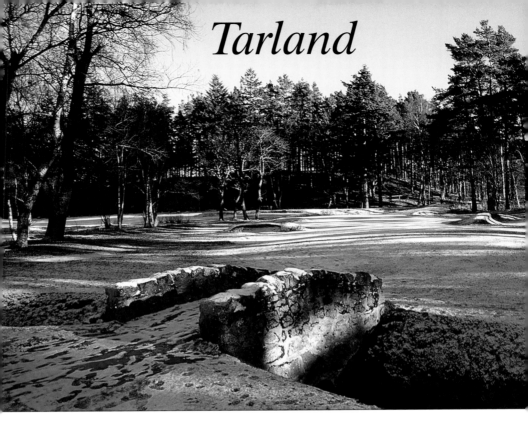

arland Golf Club, set on the northern slopes of the Dee Valley, is only nine holes and appears quite elementary on a score card map. Playing over the course is an entirely different experience. Each of its nine holes offers a different golfing encounter.

The 1st is an easy start but not without its hazards, either from a fade that rolls into the rough to the right or by playing a second shot too long over the green and into the large, waiting bunker.

It is the 4th and 5th holes that are the most notable on this course. At a stretch of the imagination, the 4th has shades of Augusta with a burn and bridge crossing before a pine-surrounded green.

The 5th is a long Par 3 of 238 yards with high trees infringing on the left

and a rough road and more trees to the right so this is a very demanding shot

The remaining holes travel back and forth on a more open area but there is plenty adventure in each of them.

The course records stands at only one under Par so this gives some indication of the calibre of the club. Good golfers enjoy it and average golfers are happy with the easy walking and lovely views.

Part of the attraction at Tarland, although by no means a measure of its quality, is the extraordinarily cheap cost of a day's golf. For the price of a glove, you can play till your heart's content. The little clubhouse is very friendly, comfortable and serves good meals through the season.

COURSE INFORMATION & FACILITIES

Tarland Golf Club
Aberdeen Road
Tarland, Aboyne

Secretary: Mrs L O Ward
Tel: 013398 81000

Green Fees:
Weekdays (day) — £14
Weekends (day) — £18

ABERDEENSHIRE

CARD OF THE COURSE — PAR 67

1	2	3	4	5	6	7	8	9	Out
309	350	171	373	236	450	172	437	398	2896
Par 4	Par 4	Par 3	Par 4	Par 3	Par 4	Par 3	Par 4	Par 4	Par 33

10	11	12	13	14	15	16	17	18	In
311	350	221	379	208	415	211	486	398	2979
Par 4	Par 4	Par 3	Par 4	Par 3	Par 4	Par 3	Par 5	Par 4	Par 33

OW TO GET THERE

th off the A93 —
al Deeside Route

arland
olf Club

Highlands & Islands

Highlands & Islands

*C*rossing the great, mountainous barrier of the Drumochter Pass into the Highland region, there is a feeling of entering another country, quite separate from the lowlands to the south. With the mighty Grampian and Cairngorm Mountains as their defence and boundary, the Highlands were partly cut off from the rest of Scotland for many centuries. In this way, they developed their own character and culture which survives today. The golf courses here are also unique, embodying the scenery and constitution of the land on which they are built. Following the A9 or Great North Road from the south, the Victorian towns of Newtonmore and Kingussie appear nestled beneath the Monadhliath Mountains. Not only are these ideal golf destinations but they are relaxing and revitalising Highland communities in their own right, worth spending time to become acquainted with. A little further north is the renowned Boat of Garten Golf Club, perhaps the course that best captures the essence of Highland golf. Here, from the 2nd tee, the view is breathtaking. Grantown-on-Spey is another excellent test while Carrbridge and Nethybridge offer two holiday layouts that are by no means easy. The town of Inverness is a good base for touring the Highlands with Loch Ness, Urquhart Castle and many more attractions all within easy driving distance. Inverness Golf Club is a plush parkland overlooking the town and the Beauly Firth. East of Inverness is the town of Nairn, referred to as the 'Brighton of the North' because of its warm climate. Here are two excellent tests, the Nairn Golf Club being the venue for 1999's Walker Cup. North of Inverness, the golf courses form a chain along the coast that makes for an ideal golf-tour itinerary. These include Fortrose and Rosemarkie, Tain, Royal Dornoch, Golspie and Brora. The Carnegie Club at Dornoch also offers one of the best new courses in Scotland however it is mainly for the guests of Skibo Castle and otherwise rather expensive. Further north, John o' Groats beckons with courses at nearby Reay and Wick. It is the Northern Isles

of Orkney and Shetland that offer surprisingly good links, some such as at Whalsay, the most northerly in the UK, and a must for the true golf course bagger. The most northerly course on the mainland is found at Durness near Cape Wrath on the northwest corner. The West Coast of the Highlands does not offer so much golf, just the most spectacular scenery you have probably ever seen. However, it is worth seeking out Gairloch Golf Club near the town of the same name. Traigh Golf Club on the road to the Isles is also worth diverting for if you are approaching Skye via that route. The Isle of Skye and the Western Isles have several fine courses, ideal if you have come to this region for their many attractions and wish to play. The holiday capital of Fort William, sheltered under towering Ben Nevis offers golf at Fort William Golf Club or Spean Bridge. Island golf may not be hugely popular but many are happy to keep it that way. The views from Barra, Colonsay or Tiree over the Atlantic Ocean and their deserted beaches is enough to make a keen hacker drop his clubs and just stare.

ABERNETHY	GOLSPIE
BOAT OF GARTEN	GRANTOWN ON SPEY
BRORA	KINGUSSIE
CARRBRIDGE	NAIRN DUNBAR
DURNESS	NEWTONMORE
FORT AUGUSTUS	ROYAL DORNOCH
FORTROSE & ROSEMARKIE	STRATHPEFFER
FORT WILLIAMS	TAIN

Highlands & Islands

The Minch

The Little Minch

Greenstone Point

Rudha Reidh

Gairloch

Red Point

Rona

Uig

LOCH SNIZORT

Dunvegan Head

Sound of Raasay

Inner Sound

Lochcarron

Neist Point

Dunvegan

Portree

Raasay

Scalpay

Crowlin Islands

Pabay

Kyle of Lochalsh

Kyleakin

Isle of Skye

Soay

Canna

Sound of Canna

Cuillin Sound

Rum

Ardvasar

Sound of Sleat

Mallaig

Sound of Rum

Eigg

Muck

Sound of Arisaig

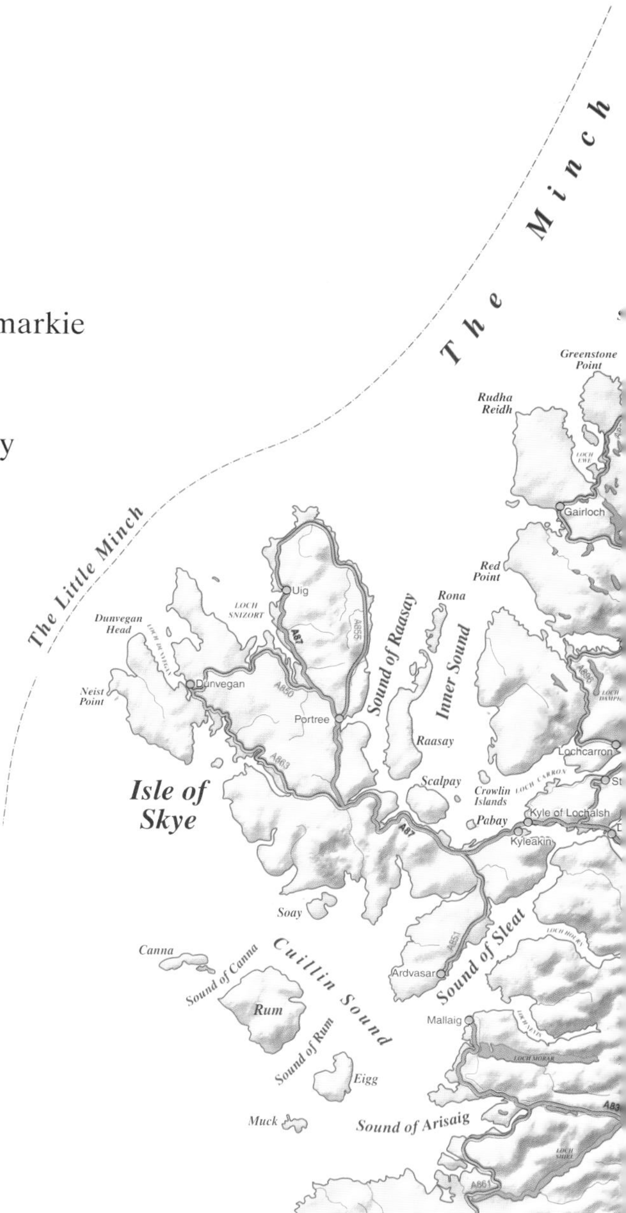

Cape Wrath
Faraid Head
Whiten Head
Pentland Firth
Dunnet Head
Island of Stroma
Duncansby Head
John O'Groats
The Parph
Scrabster
Thurso
Castletown
308
ness
Bettyhill
Melvich
Tongue
Noss Head
WICK
Wick
Altnaharra
Kinbrace
Lairg
Helmsdale
304
316
Unapool
Lochinver
326 Dornoch
Dornoch Firth
Tain
Tarbat Ness
330
Ullapool
Bonar Bridge
Alness Invergordon
Cromarty
Moray Firth
Elgin
Buckie
Cul
328 Dingwall
Garve
Achnasheen
Nairn **322** Forres
312
INVERNESS
MORAY
Aberlour
Dufftown
Keith
Inverness
Cannich Drumnadrochit
HIGHLAND
Grantown-on-Spey
318
Rhynie
Invermoriston
310
Monadhliath Mountains
306
Aviemore
302
300
Ballater
Invergarry
320 Kingussie
Newtonmore
Laggan
Cairngorm Mountains
Braemar
Spean Bridge
324 Dalwhinnie
Glenfeshie Forest
Balmoral Forest
314
Fort William
Grampian Mountains

299

Abernethy

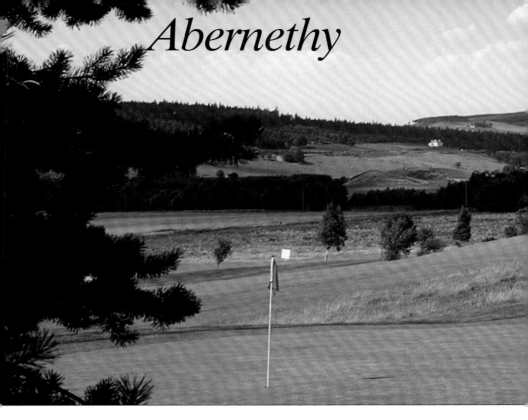

With the Abernethy Forest and Glenmore Forest Park nearby, it is no surprise that woodland plays an important role on this golf course. Located at the north end of the village of Nethy Bridge in an area renowned for its remnants of the Caledonian pine forest, the Scots Pine woodland tight along the edge of several of the fairways are an ominous presence.

Dramatic though the woodland is, there is much more to this entertaining 9 hole course. The par three 2nd, for example, is measured at only 113 yards from the yellow markers although feels significantly longer. From a slightly raised tee, golfers play over a fence, a small pond and reedy area and a tarred road lined with further fencing before finally reaching a deep, tiered green. Even then there are more obstacles to negotiate as three bunkers close in to the green snap up short or wide shots.

A more unusual feature of the course is the War Memorial sited in the centre of the 8th fairway. For those enjoying a relaxing game of golf, it is a sobering reminder of more serious times and adds to the sense of privilege one feels at being able to play golf in such a beautiful area.

Abernethy renders a challenge and a few unusual shots- and emotions. It offer golf that is both diverse and memorable with the added advantage for the visitor of being in an area that offers a cluster of some excellent inland courses.

HOW TO GET THERE

70 Grantown on Spey to
~ylumb Bridge road the club
¹₄ mile north of Nethy
idge.

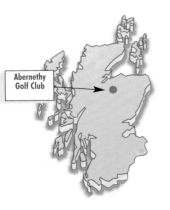

Abernethy
Golf Club

COURSE INFORMATION & FACILITIES

Abernethy Golf Club
Nethy Bridge
Inverness-shire PH25 3ED

Secretary: R.H. Robbie
Tel: 01479 821305 Fax: 01479 821196

Green Fees:
Weekdays (day) - £12. Weekends (day) - £16
Time/Day restrictions apply.

CARD OF THE COURSE - PAR 66

1	2	3	4	5	6	7	8	9	Out
301	115	304	315	217	303	414	231	319	2519
Par 4	Par 3	Par 4	Par 4	Par 3	Par 4	Par 4	Par 3	Par 4	Par 33

10	11	12	13	14	15	16	17	18	In
301	115	304	315	217	303	414	231	319	2519
Par 4	Par 3	Par 4	Par 4	Par 3	Par 4	Par 4	Par 3	Par 4	Par 33

Boat of Garten

*T*he Boat of Garten Golf Club has a reputation, which it admirably upholds, of possessing one of the most breathtaking settings of any course in Scotland. It also adds the nostalgic touch of the Strathspey Steam Railway running along its western flank.

The view from the 2nd tee includes the craggy peaks of the Cairngorm Mountains acting as its backdrop to the green. Its fairway bends from the tee to a mildly sloping green.

For the first three holes, the "Boat" is relatively plain sailing but, despite the waft of pine and heather and the evocative smell of steam trains, the 4th may make you feel a little queasy. All the way to the putting surface, one of the Boat of Garten's most notable features comes into play. Wild undulations intersect the fairway causing havoc with rolling balls.

The 6th fairway is lined with pine and birch and turns right towards the green. There is no way through the trees, only forward to drop the ball within striking distance of the green. Another tight 200 yards will get you home but the green can toss the ball over its lumpy back and off down a steep-sided bank.

After this hole, it pays to settle and enjoy the scenery, which is peerless. From the height of the 12th tee there is a fine view south and the River Spey can be looked down upon from the 14th tee. The Boat's closing hole is one of the most formidable. In a wind it can require two mighty blows to come near to the elevated green which is very difficult to hit and hold.

HOW TO GET THERE

...t of Garten lies east
...he A9, 5 miles north
...viemore and is well
...posted from the
...n road.

of Garten
olf Club

COURSE INFORMATION & FACILITIES

Boat of Garten Golf Club
Inverness-shire
PH24 3BQ

Secretary: Paddy Smyth
Tel: 01479 831282 Fax: 01479 831523

Golf Professional Tel: 01479 831282

Green Fees: Rounds: Weekdays — £21 Weekends — £26
Weekdays (day) — £26 Weekends (day) — £31
Handicap certificates required

CARD OF THE COURSE — PAR 69

1	2	3	4	5	6	7	8	9	Out
188	360	163	514	333	403	386	355	154	2856
Par 3	Par 4	Par 3	Par 5	Par 4	Par 4	Par 4	Par 4	Par 3	Par 34

10	11	12	13	14	15	16	17	18	In
271	379	349	432	323	307	168	344	437	3010
Par 4	Par 4	Par 4	Par 4	Par 4	Par 4	Par 3	Par 4	Par 4	Par 35

Brora

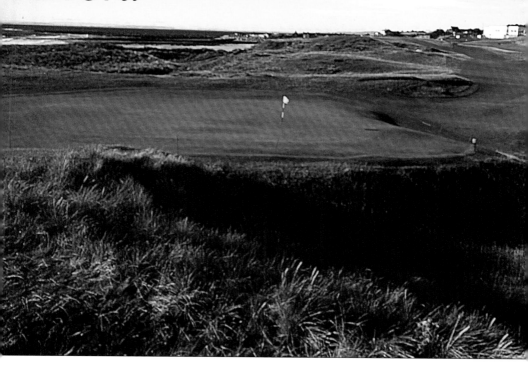

rora is known as a brisk course,
both for its breezes and the speed of
play it enjoys. Little shelter is found
for the cows and sheep that are allowed to
wander the fairways and the same applies to
golfers who tend to march smartly around
this course in old Scottish style.

It was Old Tom Morris who
established the original few holes here
in 1891 while, in the 1920's, James
Braid upgraded the links, maintaining
a traditional character with little rough
or man-made hazards and allowing the
natural aspects of the land to come
forward into play.

On this true links layout, there is a
certain flavour of St Andrews Old Course
with prescribed routes offering the best
green approach. On the 12th, a drive

down the right of the undulating fairway
will flirt with OOB but leave a more
positive view of the green.

The 9th is one of the most visually
rewarding with the green terminating just
before the beach and bay with the hills of
Sutherland in the background. The greens
which are always in such supreme conditio
are surrounded by electric fences used to
protect them from the grazing animals.

This was Braid's most northerly course
and the town of Brora and more specifically, the Royal Marine Hotel in Golf Road
is the base of the James Braid Golfing
Society. This organisation is dedicated to
the memory and principles of the great
player and course architect who includes
Gleneagles, Carnoustie and Royal Musselburgh as his work as well as some 200 othe

COURSE INFORMATION & FACILITIES

Brora Golf Club
Golf Road, Brora
Sutherland KW9 6QS

Secretary: James Fraser
Tel: 01408 621417
Fax: 01408 622157

Golf Professional Tel: 01408 621473

Green Fees:
Weekdays — £20 Weekends — £25
Weekdays (day) — £30 Weekends (day) — £35

CARD OF THE COURSE — PAR 69

1	2	3	4	5	6	7	8	9	Out
297	344	447	325	428	174	350	501	162	3028
Par 4	Par 4	Par 4	Par 4	Par 4	Par 3	Par 4	Par 5	Par 3	Par 35

10	11	12	13	14	15	16	17	18	In
435	412	362	125	334	430	345	438	201	3082
Par 4	Par 4	Par 4	Par 3	Par 4	Par 4	Par 4	Par 4	Par 3	Par 34

HOW TO GET THERE

ra is situated on main A9
miles north of Inverness.
 golf course is on the coast
he heart of the
age. From the
th turn right just
r the bridge and
ow the river to the
ch Car Park which
oins
 Club
use.

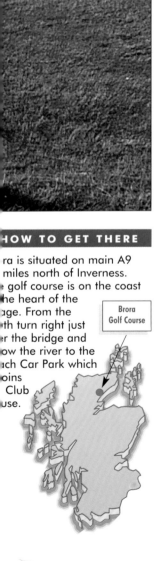

Brora
Golf Course

Carrbridge

*T*eeing off at the first hole Carrbridge, one's first impression may be that there is little of the drama of the surrounding Cairngorm and Monadhliath mountains reflected in this well-kept 9 hole course, 25 miles or so south of Inverness.

The visitor is gently introduced to three rolling holes before the Highland surroundings are more conspicuously reflected in the miniaturised mountain setting that is the remainder of the course. On holing out at the 3rd green, the golfer climbs on to a small ridge for the 4th tee and is faced with a wide, deep gully stretching all the way to the green in the distance. Valley, the name of this hole, sums it up nicely.

The 7th hole, crossing the same gully in the opposite direction, is perhaps even more spectacular. The tee is positioned in such a way that the flag on the green is silhouetted against the lower slopes of the Cairngorms mountain range beyond. The peaks of the hills often keep patches of snow well through the summer which can give an Alpine air to this wonderful view.

There is a feeling of satisfaction having played Carrbridge. The golfer samples the hilly setting but most will not be exhausted by it. This is a very attractive golf course in one of the most beautiful parts of the country; and being only nine holes in length, there is an excellent excuse for playing it twice.

OW TO GET THERE

97 miles north of Aviemore, 25 miles of Inverness.

Carrbridge
Golf Course

COURSE INFORMATION & FACILITIES

Carrbridge Golf Club
Inverness Road, Carrbridge
Inverness-shire PH23 3AU

Secretary: Mrs Anne Baird
Tel: 01479 841623 Web: www.carrbridgegolf.com

Green Fees:
Weekdays (day) - £12 Weekends (day) - £15
June/July/August — Weekdays (day) - £13
Weekends (day) - £15
Restrictions apply

CARD OF THE COURSE — PAR 71

1	2	3	4	5	6	7	8	9	Out
480	334	342	331	258	270	262	174	231	2682
Par 5	Par 4	Par 4	Par 4	Par 4	Par 4	Par 4	Par 3	Par 3	Par 35

10	11	12	13	14	15	16	17	18	In
480	334	342	331	258	270	262	174	269	2720
Par 5	Par 4	Par 4	Par 4	Par 4	Par 4	Par 4	Par 3	Par 4	Par 36

Durness

There are certain courses in Scotland which may only have nine holes, are far from the hubbub of modern life and may not present the stiffest of challenges. But they still sit very high on the 'must to be played' list.

At the northernmost corner of the Scottish mainland, Durness Golf Club is 300 miles from Edwardian elegance of Edinburgh and a short boat ride from Cape Wrath. You don't get much more remote than this but you also don't get much more beautiful.

It's a simple affair, nine holes carefully placed along the Faraid Head peninsula set behind the ancient Baloakeil Church, the most northern course on the Scottish mainland.

Just one of the wonderful things about Durness Golf Club, as well as most northerly Scottish courses, is that it can be light here well into the night. In fact, at the height of the summer, although it might be freezing and blowing a gale, the sun only really disappears between midnight and 2am.

This makes for some very pleasant evening rounds and Durness is one of the most fantastic courses to play at this time. Puffins and gannets are plentiful around this peninsula

The ultimate hole here and one of the most exciting anywhere must be the 9th or 18th, playing over the Atlantic Ocean.

COURSE INFORMATION & FACILITIES

Durness Golf Club
Balnakeil, Durness
Lairg, Sutherland IV27 4PN

Secretary: Lucy Mackay
Tel: 01971 511364

Green Fees:
Weekdays (day) — £15
Weekends (day) — £15

CARD OF THE COURSE — PAR 70

1	2	3	4	5	6	7	8	9	Out
296	321	408	287	344	443	178	377	108	2762
Par 4	Par 4	Par 4	Par 4	Par 4	Par 5	Par 3	Par 4	Par 3	Par 35

10	11	12	13	14	15	16	17	18	In
282	311	391	323	312	505	154	360	155	2793
Par 4	Par 4	Par 4	Par 4	Par 4	Par 5	Par 3	Par 4	Par 3	Par 35

HOW TO GET THERE

e club is 57 miles North
st of Lairg on the A838.

Durness
olf Club

Fort Augustus

*L*och Ness is famed throughout the world for the legendary monster that is said to live there. Popular with tourists who come in the hope of catching a glimpse of this elusive creature, the village of Fort Augustus at the southern end of the Loch is less well known for its challenging 9-hole golf course.

Occupying a level, low-lying area between the Caledonian Canal and the main road south to Fort William the large tracts of heather lining many of the fairways are perhaps the most notable feature of the course. Although attractive when in flower, the wiry nature of heather does makes it a difficult type of rough from which to play, this; allied to the narrowness of some of the fairways, ensures that your accuracy will be put to the test.

Alternative tee positions for the second

nine bring a surprisingly different perspective to some of the holes. For example, the par three 4th measures 172 yards from an elevated tee; played again as the 13th, the tee is set at approximately the same level as the green and, at only 150 yards, is a significantly different proposition. Meanwhile, at the 7th/16th, a fence crossing the fairway can have a dramatic effect on a player's choice of shot from what appear at first fairly similar tee positions.

Finally, one word of caution for those with higher handicaps. An intriguing aspect of the course are the sheep which wander the course, assisting the greenkeeping staff to trim the fairways. Remember to take care, therefore, when playing in their direction-these woolly golfing spectators are unlikely to respond to the shouts of 'fore' that follow a wayward shot!

HOW TO GET THERE

west of Fort Augustus on the A82.

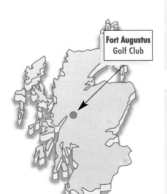

Fort Augustus
Golf Club

COURSE INFORMATION & FACILITIES

Fort Augustus Golf Club
Market Hill, Fort Augustus
Inverness-shire

Secretary: Hugh Fraser
Tel/Fax: 01320 366309

Green Fees:
Weekdays — £10 Weekends — £10
Weekdays (day) — £10 Weekends (day) — £10

CARD OF THE RED COURSE — PAR 67

1	2	3	4	5	6	7	8	9	Out
321	438	349	172	160	550	233	352	131	2706
Par 4	Par 4	Par 4	Par 3	Par 3	Par 5	Par 3	Par 4	Par 3	Par 33

10	11	12	13	14	15	16	17	18	In
313	455	363	150	193	493	253	336	192	2748
Par 4	Par 4	Par 4	Par 3	Par 3	Par 5	Par 4	Par 4	Par 3	Par 34

Fortrose & Rosemarkie

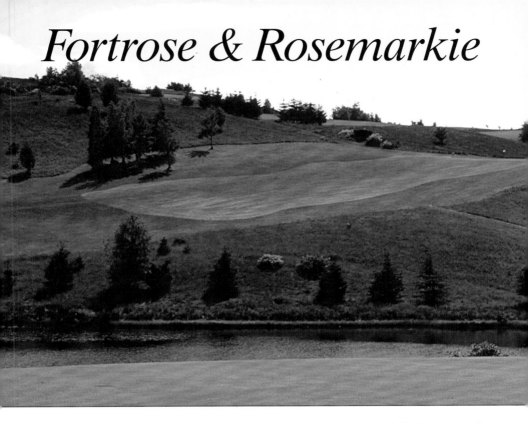

F ortrose and Rosemarkie Golf course covers a thin, wizened peninsula jutting out from the Black Isle into the Moray Firth. This is a picturesque and pastoral part of Scotland but the course presents some vigorous challenges.

The beach and water surrounding the course are not 'out of bounds' and a single-track road, also 'in bounds', dissects the course for its length. You play the ball as it lies on these hazards or lift and drop for a penalty stroke.

When Fortrose and Rosemarkie looks lovely and docile beware of that snarling tiger, the wind. There are only two holes that go with or against it, the 9th and the 5th, while the rest are crossed by the prevailing south-westerlies.

Although it is put down as a traditional Scottish links course there are not many of what you would call 'links holes'. The 4th is most typical and a very good hole with links type undulations. The 17th is an excellent driving hole with restricting bunkers on the left and a jungle of rough and whins on the right. The main difficulty throughout the course is the small greens.

At the tip of Chanonry Point, just beyond the golf course, stands a memorial stone to the legendary Brahan Seer who was burned in a barrel of oil here for revealing too much detail of the Count of Seaforth's extra-marital activities. The Point provides one of the best places to see the Moray Firth's school of bottlenose dolphins who regularly make an appearance.

HOW TO GET THERE

north of Inverness to
e Roundabout. A832 to
trose (east direction).
n right at Fortrose Police
tion to Golf Club.

rtrose &
semarkie

COURSE INFORMATION & FACILITIES

Fortrose & Rosemarkie Golf Club
Ness Road East, Fortrose, Ross-Shire
Scotland IV10 8SE
Secretary/Treasurer: Margaret Collier
Tel: 01381 620529
Fax: 01381 620529
Green Fees:
Weekdays — £17 Weekends — £23
Weekdays (day) — £25 Weekends (day) — £30
Some time restrictions

CARD OF THE COURSE — PAR 71

1	2	3	4	5	6	7	8	9	Out
331	412	303	455	132	469	303	389	196	2990
Par 4	Par 4	Par 4	Par 5	Par 3	Par 5	Par 4	Par 4	Par 3	Par 36

10	11	12	13	14	15	16	17	18	In
322	381	394	308	267	293	336	355	212	2868
Par 4	Par 4	Par 4	Par 4	Par 4	Par 4	Par 4	Par 4	Par 3	Par 35

Fort William

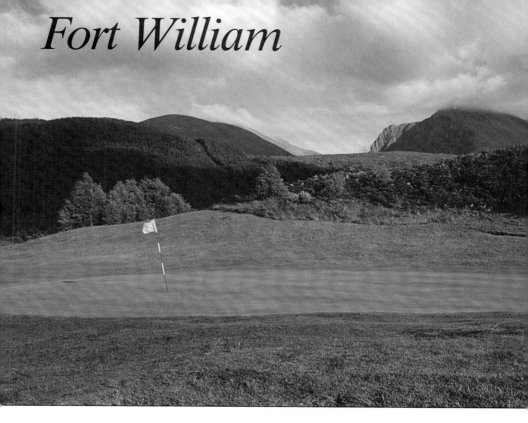

*I*t is undoubtedly an advantage for a golf course to offer something different.

In the case of Fort William, the course lies directly below the towering mass of Ben Nevis- the highest mountain in the British Isles. This awesome geological giant has an almost humbling presence that persists throughout the majority of the eighteen holes.

Despite its location, the majority of the course is not on a significant slope. However, some natural and man-made hummocks and depressions combine with ridges formed by drainage systems within the peat-rich soil to give the fairways at times a links feel. This is reflected particularly in several holes on the back nine, such as the 13th where large mounds on the fairway resemble the sand dunes found at some of the well-known courses on the Scottish east coast.

At the 14th, a few moments after setting off from the tee, the fairway suddenly drops away, opening up tremendous views across Fort William to Loch Linnhe and the mountains beyond. After returning uphill at the 15th, the 16th, Corrie, maintains this theme with a short but steep fall to a green set in a rocky basket which must surely have given the hole its name.

The tremendous scale of the environment should not be thought of as overwhelming however. The course introduces several delicate par three holes at the 3rd and 6th within attractive, partly enclosed tree-lined settings. These provide a well-planned contrast to the magnificence of the rugged but grand Highland scenery which makes this such a truly spectacular part of Scotland.

COURSE INFORMATION & FACILITIES

Fort William Golf Course
Torlundy, Fort William
Inverness-shire PH33 6SN

Secretary: Gordon Bales
Tel/Fax: 01397 704464

Green Fees:
Weekdays — £15 Weekends — £15
Weekdays (day) — £18 Weekends (day) — £18
Restrictions apply

CARD OF THE RED COURSE — PAR 68

1	2	3	4	5	6	7	8	9	Out
339	385	110	566	482	125	464	372	527	3370
Par 4	Par 4	Par 3	Par 5	Par 5	Par 3	Par 4	Par 4	Par 5	Par 37

10	11	12	13	14	15	16	17	18	In
479	387	183	284	407	262	156	357	332	2847
Par 5	Par 4	Par 3	Par 4	Par 4	Par 4	Par 3	Par 4	Par 4	Par 35

HOW TO GET THERE

miles north of Fort William on A82.

Fort William
Golf Course

Golspie

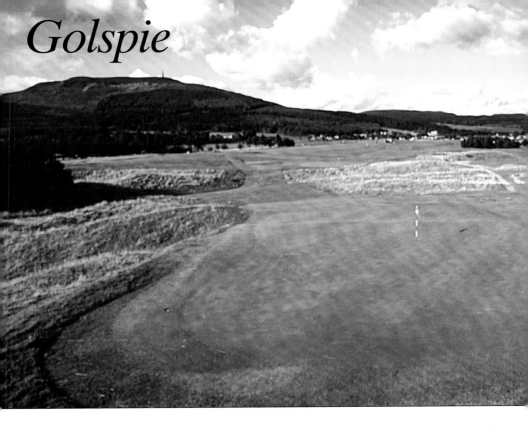

*I*f you would like to experience most of Scotland's golfing conditions, captured in one course, head for Golspie on the Sutherland coast, 10 miles north of Dornoch.

From the clubhouse, the course sets out as a pan-flat meadow, not quite parkland but of the same sort of loam. Then, at the 3rd, it turns back along the beach for a firm taste of links.

At the 6th you migrate toward the heathland section in Ferry Wood, a newer area that was laid out by James Braid in 1926. This is an attractive corner, surrounded by pine trees and heather rough. It comprises of the 8th, 9th and 10th. Visitors enjoy the contrast here although some complain of nervousness playing over the pond at the 10th.

Playing along the road on the 11th to the 14th is, once again, pastureland where the rough, sparse as it is, is all the harder to escape from. Then onto the final stretch which has the bumps and springy turf of links. The 16th is perhaps the most memorable of these, a short hole of 176 yards playing over a depression to a two tiered green with a sentinel bunker on the front left. There are several lengthy Par 4' on the card and one decent Par 5, the 4th, which plays along the beach. All of these are greatly enhanced by the wind and can prove genuine tests.

Golspie's 5, 800 yards can seem innocuous on a good day but, more often than not, the wind is coming off the sea over the Sutherland hills turning Golspie into a much more weighty challenge.

COURSE INFORMATION & FACILITIES

Golspie Golf Club
Ferry Road
Golspie KW10 6ST

Secretary/Administrator: Mrs Marie MacLeod
Tel: 01408-633266
Fax: 01408-633339

Green Fees:
Weekdays — £18 Weekends — £20
Weekdays (day) — £20 Weekends (day) — £25

CARD OF THE COURSE — PAR 68

1	2	3	4	5	6	7	8	9	Out
425	175	367	527	292	156	284	408	412	3046
Par 4	Par 3	Par 4	Par 5	Par 4	Par 3	Par 4	Par 4	Par 4	Par 35

10	11	12	13	14	15	16	17	18	In
148	345	338	329	425	420	177	217	445	2844
Par 3	Par 4	Par 4	Par 4	Par 4	Par 4	Par 3	Par 3	Par 4	Par 33

HOW TO GET THERE

miles north of Dornoch
d five miles south of Brora
the A9. Five minute drive
m the village (Golspie).
nple parking at the clubhouse.

Golspie
Golf Club

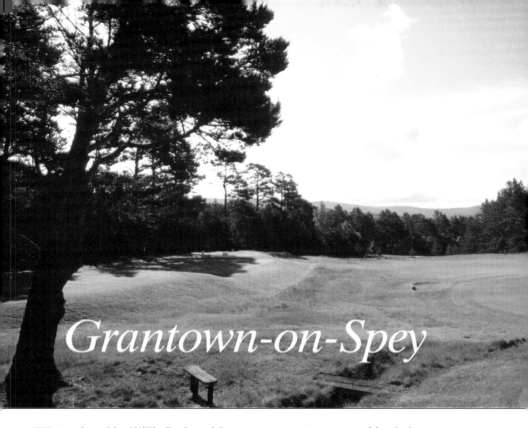

Grantown-on-Spey

esigned by Willie Park and James Braid, names which have enriched the history of Scottish golf, Grantown-On-Spey is endowed with a golf course of variety in an exquisite setting.

A relatively flat start to the course eases one into a series of six holes in a beautiful, scented woodland environment. Grand old Scots Pine trees, branches cascading irregularly around thick trunks give the golfer a feeling of the pinewoods that once would have filled the valley.

A steep, uphill tee shot makes the short 8th feel deceptively long. Playing across a blanket of heather, the green is cunningly crafted- relatively flat but surrounded by small hillocks and protected by a wide bunker across its entrance. Watch out for the mound at the right edge of the green which can bring balls even slightly right of

centre to a sudden halt.

The next hole, by contrast, is a much more open affair. From the tee, the hole falls away dramatically to a distant green providing a superb vista of the hills on the opposite side of the Spey valley and inviting players to unleash a full tee shot.

The final six holes of the course, whilst not interspersed with the same generous numbers of mature Scots Pine, offer entertaining golf of a different kind. The rolling landscape with its' significant dips and rises keeps golfers on their toes, whilst the neat whitewashed clubhouse remains ever watchful as if challenging them to meet its neat perfection.

It could be said Grantown-On-Spey is three golf courses rolled into one- if so, it must also be true that all three are worthy of praise.

COURSE INFORMATION & FACILITIES

Grantown on Spey Golf Club
Golf Course Road, Grantown on Spey
Morayshire PH26 3HY

Secretary: Jim Matheson
Tel: 01479 872079 Fax: 01479 873725

Green Fees:
Weekday (day) - £20 Weekends (day) - £25
Evenings after 5pm - £10 Restrictions apply

No visitors before 10am at weekends

MORAY

CARD OF THE COURSE — PAR 70

1	2	3	4	5	6	7	8	9	Out
287	441	401	308	359	475	380	161	275	3087
Par 4	Par 4	Par 4	Par 4	Par 4	Par 5	Par 4	Par 3	Par 4	Par 36

10	11	12	13	14	15	16	17	18	In
367	191	413	295	388	265	137	277	290	2623
Par 4	Par 3	Par 4	Par 4	Par 4	Par 4	Par 3	Par 4	Par 4	Par 34

OW TO GET THERE

m the A9 at Aviemore take
A95 to Grantown on
y. Pass through the town
are and turn right
osite the police
ion. The course is
ated on the north
corner of the
n near the
mmar
ool.

Grantown
on Spey
Golf Club

Woodside Avenue Grantown-on-Spey

TEL: **01479 872152**

The Seafield Lodge dates back to 1879, and over the years has been extended and modernised to offer the discerning visitor a welcoming home from home. Each of our comfortably appointed bedrooms has en-suite facilities, television, direct dial telephone, hairdryer and tea and coffee-making facilities. There are also two suites, The Trout and The Salmon, which may be used as family rooms, each having a separate sitting room, bedroom with a king sized bed and bathroom with spa bath.

SEAFIELD LODGE HOTEL
WOODSIDE AVENUE
GRANTOWN-ON-SPEY
MORAY PH26 3IN
SCOTLAND
TEL: 01479 872152
FAX: 01479 872340

Whether you choose the Seafield Restaurant or the Lodge Bar you are assured of a dining experience of the highest standard and one which you will remember as a highlight of your Highland holiday.

Kingussie

*T*he Highlands of Scotland must be one of the most romantic places to come and golf and there are many splendid courses to choose from, all within a half-hour's drive of each other.

Kingussie Golf Club is particularly popular with holiday golfers. It is not overly demanding at only 5,555 yards yet there are one or two climbs either to elevated tees or high greens but it is the elevation and views over to the Cairngorms, with the sultry Monadhliath Mountains to the west, that give this course its appeal.

The name Kingussie is derived from Gaelic meaning 'the Head of the Pinewood' and it is out of the pinewoods and onto the foothills of the

Monadhlaiths that Kingussie's fairways rise. Looking back from the 4th green yo can take full advantage of the promonto so pack a camera. The following three holes play over this level so there is plenty time to admire the vista.

Kingussie suits most levels of golfer with fairly straight-forward fairways and room to recover a badly angled tee shot. The longer Par 4's are the most difficult but not overly so. Three of the six Par 3 cross the road and the Gynack Burn and are good fun especially the 15th at only 100 yards.

Kingussie's clubhouse has an air of conviviality and is well-worth becoming aquainted with after a round or for an evening meal.

COURSE INFORMATION & FACILITIES

Kingussie Golf Club
Kingussie
Inverness-shire PH21 1LR

Secretary:
Norman MacWilliam
Tel: 01540 661600 Fax: 01540 662066

Green Fees:
Weekdays — £16 Weekends — £18
Weekdays (Day) — £20 Weekends (Day) — £25

CARD OF THE COURSE — PAR 66

1	2	3	4	5	6	7	8	9	Out
230	429	352	468	321	325	144	128	426	2823
Par 3	Par 4	Par 4	Par 5	Par 4	Par 4	Par 3	Par 3	Par 4	Par 33

10	11	12	13	14	15	16	17	18	In
180	336	393	418	436	105	200	385	279	2732
Par 3	Par 4	Par 4	Par 4	Par 4	Par 3	Par 3	Par 4	Par 4	Par 33

HOW TO GET THERE

er Kingussie from north.
n right at Duke of
rdon Hotel and continue
end of road.

ingussie
olf Club

321

Nairn Dunbar

*I*t is perhaps of little consequence to advise that, at Nairn Dunbar, accuracy is paramount. Golfers, whatever their self-restraint, will always be tempted to snatch a few more yards off the tee, if they think they can. But they will, if they are at all sensible, only make that mistake once here!

Nairn Dunbar is a course whose fairways are flanked by gorse, scrub trees and rough. Ladies do well, not only because there is never any carry from the tee to fairway but, in adversity, they tend to knock it safely up the middle.

The course, which has three new holes taking away some of the raised sections of the old, presents a great variation on a relatively flat linksland. With a sandy subsoil and excellent greens, it offers a savoury taste of this type of Scottish golf.

On the front nine, the 4th, 5th and 6th are quite difficult with the 9th, a new Par 5

playing down to the edge of Culbin Forest Bird Reserve.

But it is the 7th that stands out on the outward half, a shortish Par 4 with a small loch on the left-hand side, its fairway lined with thick gorse. It is a slight dog-leg to a difficult green, which may require a 2-iron c even a wedge, but both would prove equally difficult to hit and hold this green.

The 10th is a 414-yard Par 4 called Westward Ho! the most challenging on the course, also varyingly described as the 'Hole from Hell'. A carry is required to traverse a burn with OOB and gorse bushe lining the dog-legged fairway. Pot bunkers guard the green, as does the burn, which turns and runs up the left side. Replete wit a comfortable new clubhouse overlooking the course, this is the place to count your good fortune in playing Nairn Dunbar – or lick your wounds.

COURSE INFORMATION & FACILITIES

Nairn Dunbar Golf Club
Lochloy Road
Nairn IV12 5AE

Secretary: Mr Scott Falcomer
Tel: 01667 452741 Fax: 01667 456897
Golf Professional: David Torrance
Tel: 01667 453964
Email:nairndunbar.golfclub@tesco.net

Green Fees:
Weekdays — £30 Weekends — £35
Weekdays (Day) — £38 Weekends (Day) — £48

CARD OF THE COURSE — PAR 72

1	2	3	4	5	6	7	8	9	Out
418	333	189	448	453	419	395	163	501	3319
Par 4	Par 4	Par 3	Par 4	Par 4	Par 4	Par 4	Par 3	Par 5	Par 35

10	11	12	13	14	15	16	17	18	In
414	126	381	529	346	161	503	442	499	3401
Par 4	Par 3	Par 4	Par 5	Par 4	Par 3	Par 5	Par 4	Par 5	Par 37

HOW TO GET THERE

course lies half mile east
Nairn Town. Nairn lies on
A96 Inverness-Aberdeen
or road.

n Dunbar
lf Club

Newtonmore

Newtonmore is a Highland course popular with groups and societies that travel up from the south to enjoy its flat fairways. Mainly set out on the plains of the River Spey, it makes for an easy walk. At least, that is the theory.

A flat, Highland course is not so much of a contradiction either, as Newtonmore is surrounded by glorious mountains. After the first two delightful openers, both birdie opportunities from the back tees, the course drops down dramatically to the floor of the valley. It is here you first encounter Newtonmore's premier defence, the long swathes of grass and wild flowers that border many holes. So scientifically significant is this rough that they have become sites of special interest to botanists and are protected as such. Here, whilst

searching for your ball, you will come acro several species of small, rare, wild orchid. There are also wild pansies and acres of buttercups, lovely to look at but you shoul dread sending a ball anywhere near, as it too will become rare.

Although flat, these Speyside holes car cause a lot of problems particularly with a wind blowing up the valley. There are many substantial stands of trees dividing the fairways that can present difficulties b it is always the rough that will cost strokes

In splendid condition, Newtonmore's fairways and greens will succumb to the straight and steady player as length is not often a prerequisite. There is said to be a high percentage of left-handed golfers at Newtonmore Golf Club who play the gam of shinty in these parts.

HOW TO GET THERE

th: From Perth turn off A9 road
ile north of Newtonmore.
th: from Inverness turn
at Kingussie junction and take
A86 3 miles to Newtonmore.
course is in the centre
Newtonmore Village.

wtonmore
olf Club

COURSE INFORMATION & FACILITIES

Newtonmore Golf Club
Golf Course Road, Newtonmore
Highland PH20 1AT

Web: www.newtonmore.com/golfclub/

Secretary: G Spinks
Tel: 01540 673878 Fax: 01540 673878

Golf Professional Tel: 01540 673611

Green Fees:
Weekdays — £15 Weekends — £17
Weekdays (day) — £18 Weekends (day) — £23

CARD OF THE COURSE — PAR 70

1	2	3	4	5	6	7	8	9	Out
252	373	409	303	373	332	403	163	365	2973
Par 4	Par 4	Par 4	Par 4	Par 4	Par 4	Par 4	Par 3	Par 4	Par 35

10	11	12	13	14	15	16	17	18	In
518	254	417	392	406	155	389	194	331	3056
Par 5	Par 4	Par 4	Par 4	Par 4	Par 3	Par 4	Par 3	Par 4	Par 35

Royal Dornoch

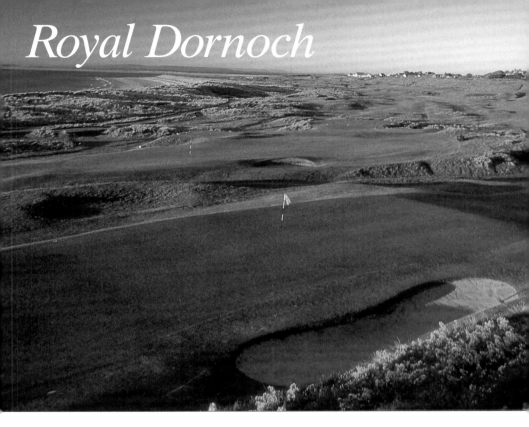

Dornoch is a magical place. It was here in the 18th century that Janet Horne, 'the last witch in Scotland' was summarily executed. And Royal Dornoch would appear to be a magical links, for it has long been casting a spell over some of the greatest golfers who ever lived.

Dornoch is geographically challenged. It is 50 miles beyond Inverness and 600 miles from London; but this fact didn't deter the Great Triumvirate, Messrs. Vardon, Taylor and Braid from visiting the links in the early years of this century. Nor did it discourage Joyce Wethered who made regular trips from the South of England. In more recent times, Tom Watson, Ben Crenshaw, Greg Norman and Nick Faldo have all embarked on what is a seemingly irresistible pilgrimage.

So what is the charm of Royal Dornoch? Firstly, there is the setting. Dornoch may be 'miles from anywhere' but this merely adds to the mystique. The links is bordered by the Dornoch Firth and a sweep of pristine white sand. Much of the golf course is blanketed in gorse and when this flowers in early summer it is a glorious sight. Then there's Dornoch remarkable history. It is the third oldest links in the world; golf has been played here since the early 1600s.

Finally there's the quality and character of the links itself. Dornoch is often described as the most natural golf course in the world. Renowned for its magnificently contoured greens, many of which sit on natural plateaux, the golf course flows wonderfully from tee to green. Yes, Dornoch is a classic, as well a enchanting links.

SUTHERLAND

COURSE INFORMATION & FACILITIES

Royal Dornoch Golf Club
Golf Road
Dornoch IV25 3LW

Secretary: John S Duncan
Tel: 01862 810219 Fax: 01862 810792

Golf Professional:
Tel: 01862 810902 Fax: 01862 811095

Green Fees:
Weekdays — £57 Weekends — £67
Handicap certificates required.
Early booking advised.

CARD OF THE COURSE — PAR 70

1	2	3	4	5	6	7	8	9	Out
331	177	414	427	354	163	463	396	496	3221
Par 4	Par 3	Par 4	Par 4	Par 4	Par 3	Par 4	Par 4	Par 5	Par 35

10	11	12	13	14	15	16	17	18	In
147	446	507	166	445	319	402	405	456	3293
Par 3	Par 4	Par 5	Par 3	Par 4	Par 4	Par 4	Par 4	Par 4	Par 35

HOW TO GET THERE

[5] miles north of Inverness
[o]f A9. 1-2 miles after
[D]ornoch Firth Bridge.
[Tu]rn right off town square
[th]en after 100 yards turn
[lef]t to Clubhouse.

Royal Dornoch
Golf Club

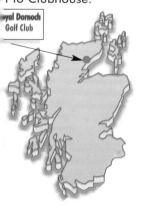

The Eagle Hotel is an ideal base for your holiday in the Highlands of Scotland. This Grade II Listed Building offers 9 en suite rooms with all amenities. Or you can stay at The Bank House which has 3 luxury rooms with whirlpool baths, ceiling fans and genuine antique furniture. Both properties have recently been completly refurbished and the proprietors Paul and Irene Hart, who are both keen golfers, are confident you will be delighted. Offering home cooked bar meals in a friendly pub atmosphere, golf courses all around and a beautiful clean beach, Dornoch is not to be missed.

The Eagle Hotel
Castle Street, Dornoch, Sutherland IV25 3SR
Telephone: (01862) 810008 Fax: (01862) 811355
e-mail:paul@eagledornoch.co.uk

327

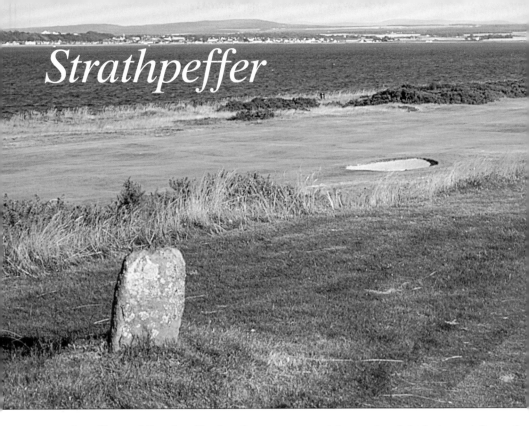

Strathpeffer

The village of Strathpeffer is a few miles due east of Dingwall, a popular spa town of the 1800's and still a quiet resort with plenty of comfortable hotels. It is the kind of place that attracts coach parties and elderly tourers but don't let them near the golf course.

High above the town, the car-park and clubhouse look over the valley below. There is a standing joke about parties that arrive seeking a day ticket. The starter keeps them right and sells a round.

Strathpeffer, you might have guessed, is hilly. From the 1st tee it is downhill all the way before zig-zagging back up and down the hill. Looking down on to the 1st green, there is a burn at 150 yards and trees tight on the right but apart from tha the views are lovely.

Back up the hill, the 9th, a Par 4 of 430 yards, shows a lot of rough on both sides and through the summer months the fairway is further narrowed by ticklish semi-rough.

There are a couple of blind holes on the back nine, most notably the 15th, 'The Ord' a big 421 yarder with a marker on the top of hill that should be reached. This isn't always the case so it's blind into the serious marsh on the right hand side and gorse on the left.

The 18th is a hard green to putt on, sloping right to left but it is the views all the way to the Cromarty Firth and Dingwall that really conclude this round.

HOW TO GET THERE

minutes north of
erness on the A9.
niles west of Dingwall,
mile north of village
uare (signposted).

rathpeffer
iolf Club

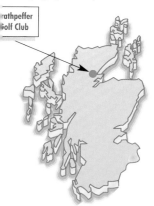

COURSE INFORMATION & FACILITIES

Strathpeffer Spa Golf Club
Strathpeffer, Ross-Shire
Scotland IV14 9AS

Secretary: Mr. Norman Roxburgh.
Tel: 01997 421396 Fax: 01997 421011
Bookings: 01997 421219/421011

Green Fees:
Weekdays — £14 Weekends — £14
Weekdays (day) — £20 Weekends (day) — £20
Some time restrictions.

CARD OF THE COURSE — PAR 65

1	2	3	4	5	6	7	8	9	Out
297	257	199	211	120	183	287	316	430	2300
Par 4	Par 4	Par 3	Par 3	Par 3	Par 3	Par 4	Par 4	Par 4	Par 32

10	11	12	13	14	15	16	17	18	In
162	231	279	306	151	419	369	271	306	2494
Par 3	Par 3	Par 4	Par 4	Par 3	Par 4	Par 4	Par 4	Par 4	Par 33

Tain

*T*ain Golf Club plays over a parcel of land on the east side of town where the alluvial deposits of the River Aldie merge with the sands of the Dornoch Firth.

This is the longest course in Ross-shire yet you are advised to hold back the driver and save yourself torn clothes and hands searching for golf balls in the whins.

The best holes on the front nine are the 2nd, 3rd and 4th.

The Aldie Burns runs through the 2nd which stands at 391 yards off the medal tees but it is a very deceiving layout with a large ridge running through it then a drop of 20 foot approaching the river. This leaves another 70 yards into green.

The 3rd at 435 yards is the hardest hole on the course; a dog-leg left which is reachable in two, but far safer to take three. Gorse lines the left-hand side with OOB on the right. The 4th has gorse all the way up both sides, and although the fairway is generous, this 499 yarder is a daunting task. Keep the ball on the fairway.

At the 11th we meet the Alps, a Par 4 of only 380 yards with a hidden green behind two 30-foot mountains. The green stands about 30 yards behind these.

The tidiest hole is perhaps the 16th where the burn bends around this Par 3 target.

Whisky connoisseurs will be happy to stop at Tain, home of famous Glenmorangie malt.

HOW TO GET THERE

...m South: 35 miles north of Inverness,
...first right on by-pass, follow road to
...centre, turn right onto Castle Brae
...past Gow's Bakery).

...m North: 9 miles south of Dornoch,
...first left on by-pass, follow road
...town centre, turn left onto
...e Brae
...before
...'s
...ery).
...e at
...le
...se
...ell
...posted.

Tain
Golf Club

COURSE INFORMATION & FACILITIES

Tain Golf Club
Chapel Road, Tain
Ross-shire IV19 1JE

Email: tgc@cali.co.uk
Web: www.mywebaddress.net/taingolfclub

Secretary:
Kathleen D. Ross.
Tel: 01862 892314 Fax: 01862 892099

Green Fees:
Weekdays — £30 Weekends — £36
Weekdays (day) — £36 Weekends (day) — £46

CARD OF THE COURSE — PAR 70

1	2	3	4	5	6	7	8	9	Out
382	391	435	542	181	309	377	189	355	3161
Par 4	Par 4	Par 4	Par 5	Par 3	Par 4	Par 4	Par 3	Par 4	Par 35

10	11	12	13	14	15	16	17	18	In
403	380	386	501	438	346	147	215	427	3243
Par 4	Par 4	Par 4	Par 5	Par 4	Par 4	Par 3	Par 3	Par 4	Par 35

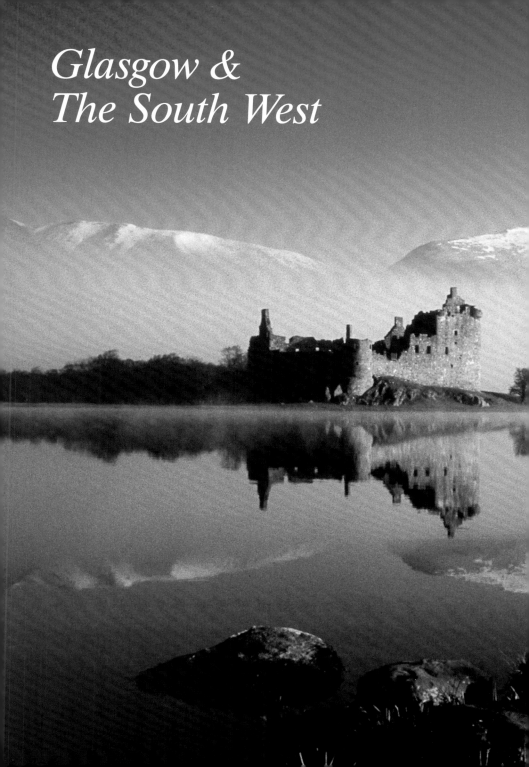

Glasgow &
The South West

Glasgow & The South West

While most visiting golfers make a bee-line for Ayrshire's flourishing golf coast, it might enlighten then to know that the Greater Glasgow and Clyde Valley area has over 80 parkland, moorland and heathland courses waiting to welcome them. From championship venues to testing 9-hole challenges, there is golf for every level of player. Combined with the abundant cultural attractions in and around the city, Glasgow presents an ideal base for a complete golfing holiday. The city is not without its golfing history and Glasgow Green was an early location for former golfers to hone their skills with 'niblick and mashie'. Now the game has spread throughout and around the city. Haggs Castle on Glasgow's south side, was the venue for the Glasgow Classic, later to become known as the Bell's Scottish Open. More recently, a new prestigious event has emerged on the banks of one of Scotland's most celebrated beauty spots. The Loch Lomond World Invitational attracts golf's greatest players to a course that, in its few short years of existence, has become known the world over for its quality and visual splendour. There are numerous other venues within a short drive of Glasgow, some of which are mentioned in the following pages, but suffice to say, a golfer would not be disappointed to bring their clubs to Glasgow. Off the fairways, the city has over 30 galleries and museums most of which are free as well as some of the friendliest pubs and clubs. There are theatres, festivals and numerous local events that are certain to make a visit most memorable. Further out from the city are the courses that surround the River Clyde such as Helensburgh, Gourock and across the water to Bute. Rothesay Golf Club on Bute has exceptional views of the surrounding hills and the Clyde Estuary. Travelling south, most serious golfers will make their way to Machrihannish on the Kintyre peninsula at least once in their lives although when they stand on the 1st tee they might wonder why! The island of Islay has one of Scotland's most special links that many golfers make a

special effort to reach. Machrie is an archetypal links that lingers as long as the aftertaste of Islay's superlative single malts. Nearby, Arran has many enjoyable venues for holiday golfers augmenting their encounter of this idyllic island. For a shorter crossing to another Clyde Estuary island, try Great Cumbria, just off the coast near Larks where there is a lovely little 18-hole course. Although the game of golf took root on the east coast of Scotland, it quickly migrated west to the well-suited coastal fringe of Ayrshire. The first Open championship was held at Old Prestwick course on the Ayrshire coast in 1860. Now there are three Open championship venues here with Royal Troon and Turnberry's Ailsa course regularly hosting this most prestigious golf event. But Ayrshire too has many excellent courses to be discovered. Western Gailes and Troon's Kilmarnock Barrassie are already firm favourites on the golfing trail but so too should be Belleisle and Troon's Lochgreen, both municipal courses that are as testing as they are cheap. Carrying on south from Turnberry you enter Galloway and the courses along the Solway Firth. Again, there are Portpatrick, Powfoot, Stranraer and Southerness but check out Wigtownshire County or Dumfries & County for courses of a different character. One to play now and keep an eye on as it develops into 18 holes, is the splendid little course at Brighouse Bay south of Kirkcudbright. In its spectacular setting on wonderful, undulating headland, this could become the premier course of the southwest.

BRUNSTON CASTLE

GLASGOW GAILES

HAGGS CASTLE

IRVINE-BOGSIDE

LANARK

MACHRIHANISH

NEWTON STEWART

PORTPATRICK (DUNKSEY)

POWFOOT

SOUTHERNESS

STRANRAER

THE MACHRIE

Glasgow & The South West

Page

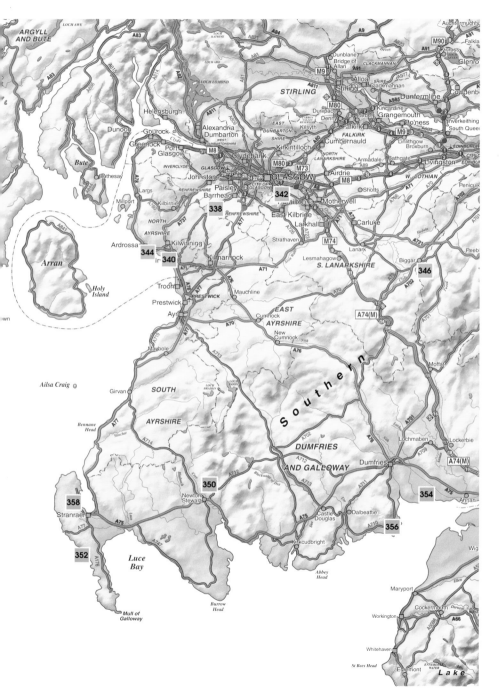

Brunston Castle

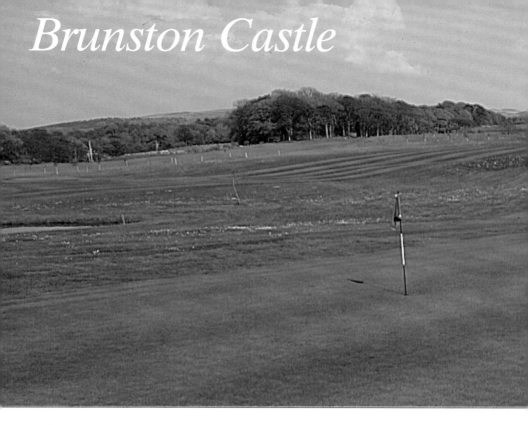

S ituated six miles east of Turnberry and the Ayrshire coast, Brunston Castle Golf Club is a relatively new layout opened in 1992, an exceptional course well worth seeking out. Sheltered in a valley surrounding the River Girvan, Donald Steel, the course architect, has made a praiseworthy job of this rich parkland layout.

The opening holes play out and back on the river valley and are straight forward enough to the prudent player. The fairly wide river comes into play on the 7th, stroke index 1, where the narrow fairway runs parallel with the river pulling anything left off the tee into thick grass lining the banks or, worse still into the river itself. To further endanger the tee shot there is a strategic sand trap to the right of the

fairway at around 220 yards off the tee. The only useful tee shot here is straight and up the middle.

The back nine runs over the valley side with the 12th, 13th, and 14th skirting its slopes. Back on level ground the Par 3, 17th is an impressive venture for intermediate players who will find an intimidating 184-yard carry over a duck pond. The pond horseshoes front left and right of a green that slopes toward the water demanding a confident stroke to the heart of the green to avoid making a splash. The closing hole climbs 20 to 30 feet back up towards the clubhouse.

The view from the clubhouse restaurant over the course is commendable, as is the standard of its catering.

HOW TO GET THERE

m Glasgow to Ayr.
e the A77 trunk road
th heading to Maybole,
n turn left taking the
23 to Crosshill, turn right
Dailly.

ton Castle
lf Club

COURSE INFORMATION & FACILITIES

Brunston Castle Golf Club
Golf Course Road, Dailly,
Girvan, Ayrshire. KA26 9GD
General Manager: Peter McCloy
Tel: 01465 811471 Fax: 01465 811545
Green Fees:
Weekdays — £26 Weekends — £30
Weekdays (day) — £40 Weekends (day) — £45
Restrictions:
Saturday and Sunday: No parties until after 10am and
between 12.30 and 1.30pm

CARD OF THE COURSE — PAR 72

1	2	3	4	5	6	7	8	9	Out
414	413	384	338	215	533	408	176	497	3378
Par 4	Par 4	Par 4	Par 4	Par 3	Par 5	Par 4	Par 3	Par 5	Par 36

10	11	12	13	14	15	16	17	18	In
323	362	426	519	355	351	397	184	386	3303
Par 4	Par 4	Par 4	Par 5	Par 4	Par 4	Par 4	Par 3	Par 4	Par 36

Glasgow Gailes

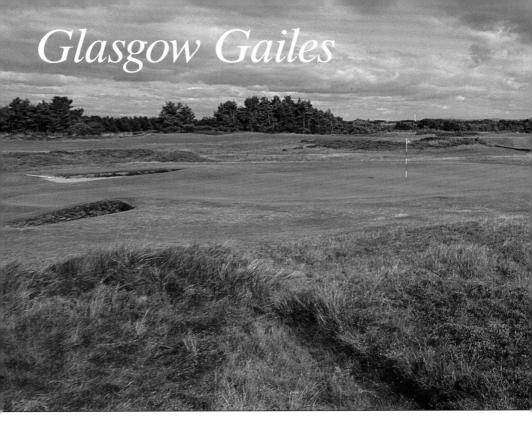

*I*t might seem confusing that a course called Glasgow Gailes is more than 30 miles from the city. The explanation is that in 1892 Glasgow Golf Club, decided to open a second facility for its members on the Ayrshire coast. The public course that they had been playing over in Alexandra Park in Glasgow had become a little too popular, hence the move.

The now exclusive Glasgow Golf Club also plays at Killermont in Bearsden in Glasgow, a course without provision for visitors. But its sister course on the Ayrshire coast makes guests most welcome.

Laid out on the coast, just south of the town of Irvine, Glasgow Gailes has the added benefit of remaining free of frost throughout the year due to the temperate effects of the Gulf Stream.

The course is lined with heather and gorse, which form the major fairway hazards. But it is the luxurious greens, beautiful to behold amidst the hoary growth, that provide much of the action and adversity on this course. Apart from the 7th and 10th which are similar, no two holes are the same at Gailes. Each hole presents something singular in its design and challenge. The 14th is a worthy Par 5 526 yards off the Medal tees. Two humps stand sentinel 70 yards short of the green, which can be reached with two good shots onto the large putting area.

With recent improvements to the clubhouse, Glasgow Gailes is as good as any of the courses to be found on this wonderful stretch of coast and should b included on an Ayrshire itinerary.

HOW TO GET THERE

...from Glasgow to Kilmarnock.
...o Irvine.
...towards Ayr and leave at the first exit.
...Marine Drive. Glasgow Gailes is off
...he Drive to the right.

Glasgow
Golf Club

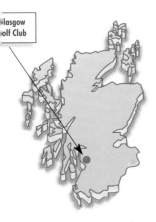

COURSE INFORMATION & FACILITIES

Glasgow Golf Club
Gailes, Irvine
Ayrshire KA11 5AE

Secretary: D W Deas
Tel: 0141 942 2011 Fax: 0141 942 0770

Golf Professional Tel: 01294 311561
Clubhouse Tel: 01294 311258

Green Fees:
Weekdays — £42 Weekends (afternoons only) — £55
Weekdays (day) — £50

CARD OF THE COURSE — PAR 71

1	2	3	4	5	6	7	8	9	Out
345	349	427	430	536	152	403	342	307	3291
Par 4	Par 4	Par 4	Par 4	Par 5	Par 3	Par 4	Par 4	Par 4	Par 36

10	11	12	13	14	15	16	17	18	In
422	419	182	334	526	152	413	365	435	3248
Par 4	Par 4	Par 3	Par 4	Par 5	Par 3	Par 4	Par 4	Par 4	Par 35

Haggs Castle

*I*t is no small accolade for Haggs Castle Golf Club that it has hosted several events on the European Tour, back in the 1980's including the Bell's Scottish Open in 1986.

Situated on the south side of Glasgow and very accessible for the motorway system, it is one of the best inland courses available so near to the city.

Its holes are carved from very pleasant parkland with a variety of dog-legs both right and left through tree-lined fairways. Another challenging feature is its small greens that are fairly well bunkered.

The 10th, 11th, and 14th are excellent holes that appeal for the demand off the tee. With out of bounds very much a factor on the 10th and 11th great care is required with the drive. The 14th is a

dog-leg left through an avenue of trees and into the wind, this can require a three iron or wood.

The closing stretch is slightly kinder with the 18th, one of the easier Par 5's on the course reachable in two for the better player.

For those with interest in some of Glasgow's many cultural features, the club is also very well placed. The baronial Haggs Castle is a free museum located nearby. Built in 1585, it is a period museum for children, centering on educational activities. Nearby also is the much-praised Museum of Education at Scotland Street School. Continuing along the A77 is Pollock Country Park in which is contained the famous Burrell Collection.

HOW TO GET THERE

3, M77 Junction 1 — end
road turn left and then
mediately right.

ggs Castle
Golf Club

COURSE INFORMATION & FACILITIES

Haggs Castle Golf Club
70 Dumbreck Road
Glasgow G41 4SN

Secretary: Alan Williams.
Tel: 0141 427 1157 Fax: 0141 427 1157

Golf Professional Tel: 0141 427 3355

Green Fees:
Weekdays — £30
Weekdays (Day) — £40

CARD OF THE COURSE — PAR 72

1	2	3	4	5	6	7	8	9	Out
470	171	358	496	402	321	188	320	406	3132
Par 5	Par 3	Par 4	Par 5	Par 4	Par 4	Par 3	Par 4	Par 4	Par 36

10	11	12	13	14	15	16	17	18	In
451	158	432	323	426	336	353	343	472	3294
Par 4	Par 3	Par 4	Par 4	Par 4	Par 4	Par 4	Par 4	Par 5	Par 36

Irvine

I rvine 'Bogside' Golf Club nestles near some of the big names in Ayrshire with Royal Troon and Old Prestwick being 'just doon the road'. There is no doubt that this stretch of Scottish coastline was ideal for the game of golf and the locals have made excellent use of the linksland.

One of the additional bonuses for the area is that most courses play all year round with the benign waters of the Gulf Stream keeping the greens frost-free.

Built between the town, a racecourse and the muddy River Irvine, Bogside's situation isn't quite perfect but when you behold the sensual terrain that this course plays over, you then notice little else.

The 6th is a remarkable Par 4 that flies over the crest of a hill before dropping 40 ft from the promontory on to the fairway. Club players lay up and then take a long iron onto the green. At 411 yards, it's not a monster but each stoke needs to be precisely and fearlessly struck.

The ground rolls and bobs over ancient dune terrain, divided by gorse and lots of heather. Every hole is an individual. Even in the heart of winter the greens are reasonable but, during the season, they are sensational.

If it's a calm day you can score well but perched as it is on a wide, open rise with wind caressing every corner, its Par 71 offers an SSS of 73.

COURSE INFORMATION & FACILITIES

The Irvine Golf Club
Bogside
North Ayrshire KA12 8SN

Secretary: W J McMahon
Tel: 01294 278209

Golf Professional Tel: 01294 275626

Green Fees:
Weekdays — £30 Weekends — £45
Weekdays (day) — £45

CARD OF THE COURSE — PAR 71

1	2	3	4	5	6	7	8	9	Out
418	476	358	289	279	411	322	165	456	3174
Par 4	Par 5	Par 4	Par 4	Par 4	Par 4	Par 4	Par 3	Par 4	Par 36

10	11	12	13	14	15	16	17	18	In
373	465	368	429	382	337	156	391	333	3234
Par 4	Par 4	Par 4	Par 4	Par 4	Par 4	Par 3	Par 4	Par 4	Par 35

HOW TO GET THERE

Kilmarnock: A71 to Warrix interchange
(roundabout). Take 3rd turning onto A78. After approx.
...es take Eglinton exit. Take 1st left and continue to next
...about. Take 2nd turning into Irvine. Continue into
... for approx 1 mile. Turn right into Sandy Road,
...ed for approx. 200 yards. At bend turn left onto
...ssified road. Club is along this road on right.
Barrhead/Irvine Road: Continue on A736 until
...ng at Sourlie roundabout. Take 2nd turning and
...ed to next roundabout. Take 4th turning
...ong Drive. Proceed for approx. 2 miles
...t roundabout (Eglinton interchange),
...as above.
Greenock/Irvine
or Ayr/Irvine
...: Continue
...8 to Irvine/
...ining
...
...gton
...hange,
...as above.

Irvine
Golf Club

MONTGREENAN MANSION HOUSE HOTEL

Conjure up the image of a country golfing break and Montgreenan will
meet your expectations... a grand Georgian house from the outside,
the interior provides perfectly proportioned rooms for friends to
meet and relax, at the bar, in the AA rosette winning Restaurant or by
the many fire sides.

While at Montgreenan loosen your swing on the 4 hole practice
course or indulge in the gentle pursuits, associated with any fine
country house, croquet, tennis, putting, snooker and billiards.

Montgreenan Mansion House Hotel, Montgreenan Estate,
Near Kilwinning, Ayrshire KA13 7QZ
Tel: 01294 557733 Fax: 01294 850397
www.montgreenanhotel.com
e-mail: info@montgreenanhotel.com

Lanark

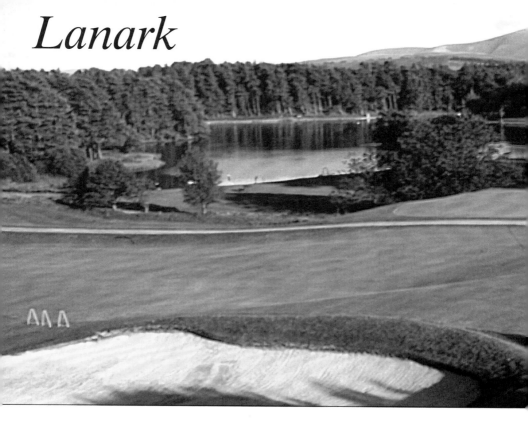

*L*anark's course has a far-flung reputation spread mainly by word of mouth and good golfers from around the world make their way here, especially when an Open Championship is held in nearby Ayrshire.

Over the past twenty years a regular Open qualifying course, Lanark offers many of the conditions found on a links course with sandy subsoil and a healthy moorland loam. The 'Moor' as it was referred to, was cattle grazing land and this, no doubt, has contributed to the vigorous tone of the turf.

The course went through various evolutions until 1897 when Old Tom Morris was hired for three days to upgrade it to an 18-hole tract. He was paid the grand sum of £3/10 shillings

for the work, a munificent sum as his usual rate was only £1.00 a day.

Ben Sayers later made his contributio and, in the 1920's, James Braid added length and bunkers.

Tinto is the name of the 8th, a 530-yard Par 5 that offers little resistanc to well-placed balls unlike some of the more deceptive Par 4's.

The 10th is a 152-yard, Par 3 looking through a channel of trees to an elevated green which is set off by three large bunkers. Tintock Tap is the mountain seen away in the distance. The 18th, at 216 yards is an unusual Par 3 finish with a plaza of a green directly beneath the clubhouse window with its attentive onlookers. Wave if you make par.

HOW TO GET THERE

n M74 take the A73, follow signs for
ark. Follow signs for town centre, turn
t before Somerfield store onto Whitelees
d (3/4 mile to course). From M8 take the
at Newhouse, follow signs for Lanark.
on A73 and turn left just past Somerfield
e onto Whitelees Road.

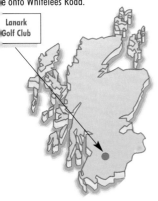

Lanark
Golf Club

COURSE INFORMATION & FACILITIES

Lanark Golf Club
The Moor, Whitelees Road
Lanark ML11 7RX

Secretary: George Cuthill
Tel: 01555 663219 Fax: 01555 663219

Golf Professional:
Tel: 01555 661456 Fax: 01555 661456

Green Fees:
Weekdays — £25 Weekdays (Day) — £38
No weekend visitors.

CARD OF THE COURSE — PAR 70

1	2	3	4	5	6	7	8	9	Out
360	467	409	457	318	377	141	530	360	3419
Par 4	Par 4	Par 4	Par 4	Par 4	Par 4	Par 3	Par 5	Par 4	Par 36

10	11	12	13	14	15	16	17	18	In
152	397	362	362	399	470	337	309	216	3004
Par 3	Par 4	Par 4	Par 4	Par 4	Par 4	Par 4	Par 4	Par 3	Par 34

Machrihanish

Situated on the south western tip of the Mull of Kintyre, Machrihanish is perhaps the most geographically remote of all the great courses in the British Isles. And yet, if ever a journey was worth the effort …..

For the lover of traditional links golf, Machrihanish has everything. The layout has altered quite a bit since the late 19th century when it was designed by 'Old' Tom Morris, but the natural character of the course remains. Not only are the fairways among the most naturally undulating in the British Isles, but the greens are some of the most amazingly contoured – awkward stances and blind shots are very much a feature of Machrihanish.

There is nothing blind, however, about the course's legendary opening hole – from the tee the challenge ahead is very visible. It is a long par four of 423 yards and the only way of ensuring that the green can be reached in two shots is by hitting a full-blooded drive across the waters of Machrihanish Bay. From the back tees a 200 yard carry is called for. 'Intimidating' is the description: 'Death or Glory' is the result.

After the 1st the rest must be easy? Not a chance! If the opening hole tests the drive, several of the following holes will test the approach shot, particularly perhaps the 2nd, 7th and 14th. Machrihanish has its own 'Postage Stamp' hole, the 4th – just 123 yards – and there are successive short holes at the 15th and 16th. The course starts to wind down at the 17th and pars here are frequently followed by birdies at the 18th and, of course, considerable celebration at the 19th.

COURSE INFORMATION & FACILITIES

The Machrihanish Golf Club
Machrihanish, Campbeltown
Argyll PA28 6PT

Email: machrihanishgolf@ic24.net

Secretary: Anna Anderson
Tel: 01586 810213 Fax: 01586-810221

Golf Professional Tel: 01586-810277
(for bookings)

Green Fees:
Weekdays — £28 Saturday — £35
Weekdays (day) — £45 Saturday (day) — £55

CARD OF THE COURSE — PAR 70

1	2	3	4	5	6	7	8	9	Out
428	394	374	122	385	301	428	339	353	3124
Par 4	Par 4	Par 4	Par 3	Par 4	Par 4	Par 4	Par 4	Par 4	Par 35

10	11	12	13	14	15	16	17	18	In
503	197	513	370	438	168	231	368	313	3101
Par 5	Par 3	Par 5	Par 4	Par 4	Par 3	Par 3	Par 4	Par 4	Par 35

HOW TO GET THERE

pproximately three hours ve from Glasgow. The ost direct route is by the 2 to Tarbet on Loch mond, then the A83 via eraray and Lochgilphead.

Machrihanish
Golf Club

Newton Stewart

*A*lthough this seems an easy enough course that is ideal for holiday golf outing, Newton Stewart comes with its own set of idiosyncrasies that any golfer will enjoy.

Laid out around a hilly area, it is a pleasant piece of rustic parkland with very little earnest climbing. Apart from the hike from the 2nd green to the 3rd tee there is only a modest elevation all the way up to the 10th.

The course is set up for golfers to enjoy themselves and not get hung-up in rough although there are patches of gorse that will catch really wild shots.

The 1st and 2nd fairways are edged with OOB while holes such as the 4th and 5th can be approached on either fairway. The 7th has OOB on the left

but there is plenty of room for manoeuvre along this stretch.

The course's apex comes at the turn. Around this corner, the 9th plays up the side of a pond, a Par 4 of 340 yards with a stream running diagonally across the fairway. The green is off-set and there is a choice of playing across the dyke or taking the easy route. The Par 3, 10th, called the Gushet is one of the original holes playing over a burn with the pond on the left.

The town of Newton Stewart sits on the banks of the River Cree. Game fishing is popular in this area. The best access point into Galloway Forest Park, famous for hills, lochs, moorland and forest that are a haven for wildlife, is via the A714 north of Newton Stewart to Glen Trool village then on to Glen Trool Lodge.

COURSE INFORMATION & FACILITIES

Newton Stewart Golf Club
Kirroughtree Avenue, Newton Stewart Dumfries & Galloway D68 6PF

Secretary: M Large
Tel: 01671 4402177

Clubhouse Tel: 01671 402172

Green Fees:
Weekdays — £20 Weekends — £23
Weekdays (day) — £23 Weekends (day) — £25
Society Rates: On Request.

CARD OF THE COURSE — PAR 69

1	2	3	4	5	6	7	8	9	Out
346	360	177	371	426	175	353	383	337	2928
Par 4	Par 4	Par 3	Par 4	Par 4	Par 3	Par 4	Par 4	Par 4	Par 34

10	11	12	13	14	15	16	17	18	In
152	520	197	523	405	328	345	164	325	2959
Par 3	Par 5	Par 3	Par 5	Par 4	Par 4	Par 4	Par 3	Par 4	Par 35

HOW TO GET THERE

wton Stewart is on the
5 Euroroute Carlisle to
anraer. The course itself
very easily reached from
A75.

> rton Stewart
> Golf Club

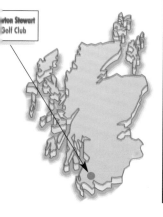

Portpatrick

*T*he village of Portpartick is a quintessential holiday retreat with enchanting lanes and cottages built around a tranquil little harbour.

The course sits above the town on a headland with steep cliffs marking its western perimeter. Perched out in the Irish Sea on a long, rocky-shored annex of land known as the Rhinns of Galloway, Portpatrick (Dunskey) Golf Club catches the best of the Gulf Stream's warmth; and its wind. It presents a variety of terrain, caught between rolling moorland and seaside heath. The rough is a devastating combination of lush green grass and gorse and it has an ally in the near-ever-present gusts, which aid in the regular abduction of golf balls.

Dunskey is known for its tricky par 3's.

The 7th is a good short hole at 165 yards with a ledge to the left that may gather some errant shots but it is ultimately safer to stray right if anywhere.

The 15th is of only 100 yards but it can be the toughest hole on the course with little room for error on a hidden and wind-dried green. The 13th is a plac to catch your breath before it gets taken away again – by the fantastic views from this hole. The panorama of the green sitting above Sandeel Bay makes the puls quicken as will the hike up to the 14th.

Dunskey is not a long course but that does not mean a lot in such a wind-buffeted corner of Scotland. Pro-ams are regularly staged over its curvaceous tracts but they have never managed to beat the 63 course record.

COURSE INFORMATION & FACILITIES

Portpatrick (Dunskey) Golf Club
Portpatrick
Wigtownshire DG9 8TB

Secretary: Mr J A Horberry
Tel: 01776 810273 Fax: 01776 810811

Green Fees:
Weekdays — £20 Weekends — £25
Weekdays (day) — £30 Weekends (day) — £35

Handicap Certificate required.

Some time restrictions.

CARD OF THE COURSE — PAR 70

1	2	3	4	5	6	7	8	9	Out
393	375	544	160	405	382	165	377	311	3112
Par 4	Par 4	Par 5	Par 3	Par 4	Par 4	Par 3	Par 4	Par 4	Par 35
10	11	12	13	14	15	16	17	18	In
329	163	388	293	293	101	393	301	535	2796
Par 4	Par 3	Par 4	Par 4	Par 4	Par 3	Par 4	Par 4	Par 5	Par 35

HOW TO GET THERE

South: M6 - A75 to
raer/Portpatrick, signposted
Glenluce By-Pass. On entering
illage fork right at War Memorial
ook for signpost.
North: A77 to Stranraer and
atrick. Then as above.

rtpatrick
olf Club

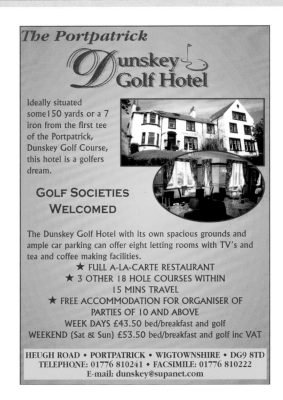
353

Powfoot

*W*andering your way from the town of Annan through the village of Cummertrees you overlook the terminal end of the Solway Firth, you have arrived at Powfoot Golf Club.

This is a prominent links course in the southwest, distinguished as a championship venue which plays through a veritable sea of gorse.

There are actually only 14 holes that are true links while the back four holes are more parkland in nature. As with most Braid designs, the start is temperate, a hole to iron out the snatches and cracks.

You will need poise for hole 2, a 474 yard Par 5 which faces south overlooking the water. It is tight after the tee shot but, unless the wind is blasting out of the west, a steady blow should see you onto the green

The 3rd plays along the shore in a west to east direction as does the 4th then it is into the thick of this compact layout with nothing but blooming gorse to be seen.

As with many links courses, it is not possible to view some bunkers from the tee so it is expedient to study a course plan. The 7th green approach is thick wi them, eight in all, making this pure targe golf on a Par 3 as the top of the flag is a that is usually visible.

This part of the southwest enjoys its own weather and is sometimes referred to as the Costa del Solway. Catering at Powfoot is of the homemade variety, usually offering some traditional Scottish cuisine and the homemade sou is worth investigating.

OW TO GET THERE

M6 north from Carlisle until A75
urn off for Stranraer/Dumfries.
road to Annan/Dumfries until 2nd
ff for Annan, continue and take first
o Cummertrees and Powfoot on
After approx. 3 miles ignore first
r Powfoot, continue until passing
railway bridge then turn
left on road leading to
ourse.

wfoot
f Club

COURSE INFORMATION & FACILITIES

Powfoot Golf Club
Annan
Dumfriesshire DG12 5QE

Manager:
Tel: 01461 700276 Fax: 01461 700276

Golf Professional Tel: 01461 700327

Green Fees:
Weekdays — £23 Weekends — £23
Weekdays (day) — £30 Weekly Ticket £90

Some time restrictions.

CARD OF THE COURSE — PAR 71

1	2	3	4	5	6	7	8	9	Out
349	474	442	357	272	349	154	360	402	3159
Par 4	Par 5	Par 4	Par 4	Par 4	Par 4	Par 3	Par 4	Par 4	Par 36

10	11	12	13	14	15	16	17	18	In
428	313	156	339	498	200	427	332	403	3096
Par 4	Par 4	Par 3	Par 4	Par 5	Par 3	Par 4	Par 4	Par 4	Par 35

Southerness

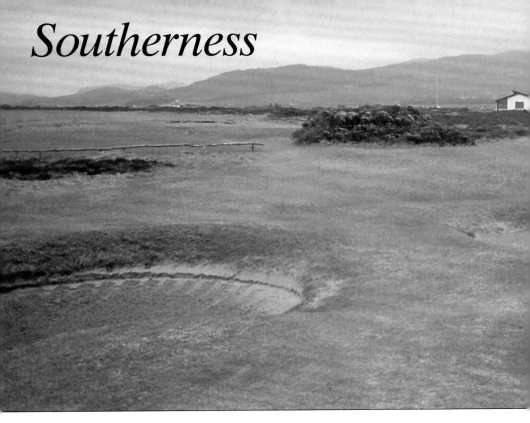

*T*wo of Britain's greatest and least explored links courses stare at one another across the Solway Firth – one is on the English side at Silloth and the other lies north of the border at Southerness. As close as they appear on the map, the only way of travelling from one to the other is by a fairly lengthy drive around the coast via Gretna Green. Before the war a bridge crossed the Solway, but before the war Southerness didn't have a golf course.

Situated 16 miles south of Dumfries, Southerness is the only true championship links in Great Britain to have been built since 1945. Quite a contrast to Ireland where the likes of Tralee, Carne and The European have all been constructed within the last 20 years.

So golf came to Southerness about 500 years after it came to St Andrews, but one cannot help wondering why it took so long, after all, the much more remote golfing outposts of Dornoch and Machrihanish took root in the dim and distant past and a more natural and pleasanter site for the links it is hard to imagine. Sandy terrain, rampant heather dense bracken and prickly golden gorse a present themselves in abundance here; as for that matter do firm, fast fairways and subtly contoured greens.

The 12th is undoubtedly the best hole Southerness: a well positioned drive here essential as the second shot must be fired towards a narrow green which sits on a plateau and looks down over a beautiful beach; deep bunkers guard the green from right and a pond will gleefully swallow an shot that strays left of centre.

HOW TO GET THERE

ve A75 at Dumfries and
ow A710 signposted
way Coast and follow for
miles south. Southerness
ignposted (approx. 1 mile).

Southerness
Golf Club

COURSE INFORMATION & FACILITIES

Southerness Golf Club
Kirkbean
Dumfries DG2 8AZ

Secretary: I A Robin
Tel: 01387 880677 Fax: 01387 880644

Green Fees:

Weekdays — £35 Weekends — £45

Weekdays (day) — £35 Weekends (day) — £45
Handicap certificates required

CARD OF THE COURSE — PAR 69

1	2	3	4	5	6	7	8	9	Out
393	450	408	169	496	405	215	371	435	3342
Par 4	Par 4	Par 4	Par 3	Par 5	Par 4	Par 3	Par 4	Par 4	Par 35

10	11	12	13	14	15	16	17	18	In
168	390	421	467	458	217	433	175	495	3224
Par 3	Par 4	Par 4	Par 4	Par 4	Par 3	Par 4	Par 3	Par 5	Par 34

Stranraer

tranraer, like some of its near neighbours, deserves more attention than it gets but this corner of Scotland, despite such great courses, remains fairly quiet.

This is a superb championship layout with the further distinction of being the last course to be designed by James Braid before his death. In fact, he never got to see the finished result. Many players will tell you this is one of his best.

In spite of the fact that it is on the shores of a saltwater loch, Stranraer does not pertain, to being a links course.

Laid out on farmland with many stands of mature trees, it is best described as parkland with fairly undulating ground

There are four holes that are played along the loch shore; these dropping down quite dramatically from the escarpment that hold the rest of the course.

The 5th is the signature hole looking over Loch Ryan north to Ailsa Craig, the island of Arran and beyond. From an elevated tee, this Par 4 plays down to a tight fairway pinched between the loch and steep, heavily roughed banking. If you miss all this and don't get caught in the two right-side bunkers, you have hit a good tee shot.

The 15th is a Par 3, and although it is only 165 yards, accuracy is paramount. The ground slopes away steeply on both sides of the green, severely on the shore side.

From the relatively new, two story clubhouse with its panoramic lounge area, you can enjoy views of a large part of the course.

HOW TO GET THERE

e course can be
proached from Stranraer
taking the A718 road to
rkcolm

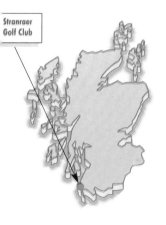

Stranraer
Golf Club

COURSE INFORMATION & FACILITIES

Stranraer Golf Club
Creachmore, Leswalt
Stranraer DG9 0LF

Secretary: Bryce C Kelly
Tel: 01776 870245 Fax: 01776 870445

Green Fees:
Weekdays — £20 Weekends — £28
Weekdays (day) — £29 Weekends (day) — £35
Some time restrictions.

CARD OF THE COURSE — PAR 70

1	2	3	4	5	6	7	8	9	Out
319	338	420	324	397	160	381	315	458	3112
Par 4	Par 4	Par 4	Par 4	Par 4	Par 3	Par 4	Par 4	Par 4	Par 35

10	11	12	13	14	15	16	17	18	In
346	377	185	335	513	165	470	462	343	3196
Par 4	Par 4	Par 3	Par 4	Par 5	Par 3	Par 4	Par 4	Par 4	Par 35

The Machrie

Scotland is famous for many things, and two of its greatest gifts to mankind are golf and whisky. The origins of each are uncertain, lost in the mists of time, but a place where both can be sampled in their purest form is on the Hebridean island of Islay. This is the home of Laphroaig, Bowmore, Bunnahabhainn and, yes, The Machrie Golf Club.

You can fly to Islay from Glasgow (a 35 minute flight) or you can drive halfway down the Kintyre peninsula and take a two hour ferry journey to Port Ellen - it depends how quickly you wish to prepare yourself for another world.

Machrie does seem caught in a golfing timewarp. Here is where you half expect to bump into Old Tom Morris. It is an old fashioned links course and is set amid gorgeous and spectacular surroundings.

There are at least a dozen blind shots at Machrie, so those who like their golf laid out on a plate are advised not to board the ferry or the plane. There are several sunken greens and elevated tees; most of the fairways twist and tumble violently and occasionally you are required to play shots that you are unlikely to face on any other golf course.

If asked to select the best holes at Machrie you might pick the 3rd, the 6th, the 7th and the 13th. But, really, the entire golf links is unforgettable.

COURSE INFORMATION & FACILITIES

The Machrie Hotel & Golf Links
Port Ellen, Isle of Islay
Argyll PA42 7AN

Email: machrie@machrie.com
Web: machrie.com

Manager: Mr Ian Brown
Tel: 01496 302310
Fax: 01496 302404

Green Fees: Non-residents
Weekdays — £25 Weekends — £30
Weekdays (day) — £35 Weekends (day) — £40

CARD OF THE COURSE — PAR 71

1	2	3	4	5	6	7	8	9	Out
308	508	319	390	163	344	395	337	392	3156
Par 4	Par 5	Par 4	Par 4	Par 3	Par 4	Par 4	Par 4	Par 4	Par 36

10	11	12	13	14	15	16	17	18	In
156	357	174	488	423	335	411	352	402	3098
Par 3	Par 4	Par 3	Par 5	Par 4	Par 4	Par 4	Par 4	Par 4	Par 35

HOW TO GET THERE

plane from Glasgow Airport, flight time
minutes. By ferry from Kennacraig,
yll, crossing time 2 hours Glasgow is
ut 110 miles by road from Kennacraig.
course is minutes from each terminal
rtesy coach will collect hotel
dents.

e Machrie
Golf Club

The Machrie Hotel provides a warm and friendly service and
has the added advantage of having an inspiring golf course
on the doorstep.
With both superior and standard rooms and 15 twin bedroom lodges, we
can cater for both the individual golfer or larger groups on a fully inclusive
or self-catering basis.
With snooker, pool and croquet at the hotel and six operational malt
whisky distilleries on the island, and of course, the golf, there is always
something to do. For details of the hotel and
golfing packages available contact:
The Machrie Hotel, Port Ellen, Isle of Islay PA42 7AN
Tel: 01496 302310 · Fax: 01496 302404
Website: www.machrie.com
E-mail: machrie@machrie.com

Northern Ireland

Northern Ireland

ead any list of top 100 courses in the British Isles, and you will find two of Northern Ireland's courses well up the rankings. Indeed, play Royal County Down and Royal Portrush and they will shoot to the top of your personal list of best courses. Portrush and County Down are two courses worthy of their Royal status, for they are man-sized golf courses, championship layouts in every sense of the word. This is links golf at its best, with everything you expect to find on seaside courses - blind shots, deep pot bunkers, fast running fairways, undulating greens and strong winds. Not golf for the fainthearted, to be sure. These two magnificent layouts have been on the itinerary of nearly every visiting golfer down through the years, and they can get quite busy during the summer months. Don't despair, though, for there are plenty of great courses throughout the region to keep every level of golfer happy.

The stretch of shoreline along the Antrim Coast is simply spectacular. It's along this coastline that you will find the Giant's Causeway, a fascinating geological formation that appears to be steps either leading into or coming from the sea. Legend has it that the Irish Giant Finn McCool built these steps to help him make his way to the Scottish isle of Staffa to woo a female giant on that island. The Giant's Causeway is just a few miles away from Royal Portrush and is a must sight to visit while in the area. Make sure you take the walk down to see the rock formations close up. Although there is a very good visitor centre which tells the whole story, there is no substitute for getting up close because the Causeway has to be seen to believed. Something else that has to be seen to believed is the links course at Portstewart. To stand on the first tee is to experience one of the best views in all of golf. Portstewart has benefitted from new holes created in the dunes which transformed the original course from a good links to a great one. Portstewart and Portrush are just two of four good links on this stretch of the Antrim Coast. The other two are

Castlerock and Ballycastle. These four layouts are used for the annual Black Bush Causeway Coast Tournament, a 72-hole stableford event sponsored by Bushmills Distillery, makers of Black Bush. And if you can squeeze in a visit to the Distillery in the little town by the same name, then your trip will be complete.

The Antrim Coast and its fabulous courses are only an hour's drive away from the city of Belfast and good parkland courses such as Malone, Belvoir Park, Royal Belfast and Malone. Not much further away you will find Lisburn and also Clandeboye, and its two good courses. In fact, you could enjoy a round at a fine course in and around Belfast, enjoy a leisurely lunch and an equally leisurely drive and, in the height of summer at least, still be back on the Antrim coast for another round before a late tea. What more could you want for in life?

One of the most scenic yet least explored areas of Northern Ireland is the Ards Peninsula. Peculiarly shaped and jutting out into the Irish Sea, it was once described as the 'Proboscis of Ulster'. The best golf course on the peninsula is the James Braid designed Kirkistown Castle course at Cloughey. Another hidden gem on the east coast is Ardglass. Somewhat reminiscent of the best clifftop courses in Cornwall, Ardglass is well worth inspecting en route to Royal County Down.

ARDGLASS	MALONE
BELVOIR PARK	PORTSTEWART
CASTLEROCK	ROYAL BELFAST
CLANDEBOYE	ROYAL COUNTY DOWN
KIRKISTOWN CASTLE	ROYAL PORTRUSH
LISBURN	WARRENPOINT

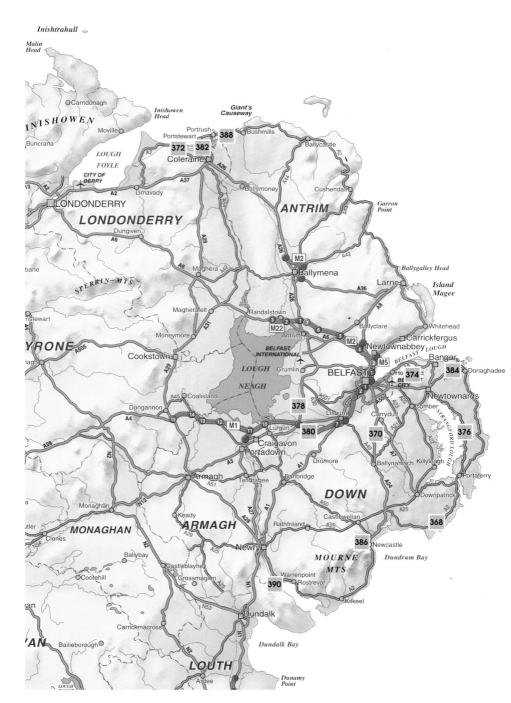

Inishtrahull

Malin
Head

INISHOWEN

Carndonagh

Moville

Buncrana

Inishowen
Head

Giant's
Causeway

Portrush

Portstewart **388** Bushmills

372 **382**
Coleraine

Ballycastle

Cushendall

Garron
Point

Ballygalley Head

Island
Magee

LOUGH
FOYLE

CITY OF
DERRY

LONDONDERRY

LONDONDERRY

Limavady

A2

A37

A26

Ballymoney

ANTRIM

Larne

Whitehead

Dungiven

A6

Maghera

M2
Ballymena

A36

A8

SPERRIN-MTS

Magherafelt

Randalstown

M22 Antrim

Ballyclare

M2

Carrickfergus

Newtownabbey LOUGH

Bangor

384 Donaghadee

TYRONE

Moneymore

Cookstown

BELFAST
INTERNATIONAL

Crumlin

BELFAST

374

BELFAST
CITY

Newtownards

LOUGH
NEAGH

378

Dungannon

A4

Coalisland

M1

Lurgan

Craigavon
Portadown

380

Lisburn

Carryduff

Comber

370

376

Portaferry

Armagh

Tandragee

Banbridge

Dromore

Ballynahinch

Killyleagh

Monaghan

Keady

Crossmaglen

Rathfriland

Castlewellan

DOWN

Downpatrick

368

Clones

Ballybay

Castleblayney

Newry

MOURNE
MTS

386 Newcastle

Dundrum Bay

Cootehill

Warrenpoint
Rostrevor

390

Kilkeel

Carrickmacross

Dundalk

Dundalk Bay

Bailieborough

LOUTH

Ardee

Dunamy
Point

Northern Ireland

Page

Ardglass

The lovely links course of Ardglass lies not too far from Royal County Down, and while it may not be the test that Down is, it's a lot of fun.

Like it's Royal counterpart, Ardglass is a links, offers good views of the Irish Sea and the Mourne Mountains, and has some testing holes. Indeed, you're presented with a test almost right away, when you step onto the second tee. This is a par-3 of just 173-yards, but the danger here is the Irish Sea. Hit short or left and you'll be looking for your swimming trunks to play your next shot.

The second is just one of five par-3s on the Ardglass layout. Three of these one shotters call for fairly easy short iron or wedge approach shots. The 9th hole doesn't. At 205-yards it calls for a full blooded 3-wood or 2-iron, depending on how far you hit the ball.

Ardglass is fairly short, just nudging the 6,000 yard mark, but don't let that fool you. The wind often blows here, as it does at County Down, making a mockery of the yardage indicated on the card.

Like many Irish courses, there are remnants of a bygone age in evidence at Ardglass. Beside the clubhouse lie the remains of a Norman Castle built in 1177. The course hasn't quite been around that long, but it dates to 1896 when nine holes were constructed beside the sea. Nine more holes were added in 1971 to make it a proper course.

On a good day you can see the Isle of Man clearly; if you can't then you may be in for a tough round.

HOW TO GET THERE

...roximately 7 miles from ...vnpatrick on B1.

Ardglass Golf Club

COURSE INFORMATION & FACILITIES

Ardglass Golf Club
Castle Place, Ardglass,
Co. Down

Secretary: Miss Debbie Polly
Tel: 02844 841219 Fax: 02844 841841

Golf Professional Tel: 02844 841022

Green Fees:
Weekdays — £18 Weekends — £24
Weekdays (day) — £18 Weekends (day) — £24

CARD OF THE COURSE — PAR 70

1	2	3	4	5	6	7	8	9	Out
292	173	269	351	135	485	507	394	205	2811
Par 4	Par 3	Par 4	Par 4	Par 3	Par 5	Par 5	Par 4	Par 3	Par 35

10	11	12	13	14	15	16	17	18	In
430	180	371	362	480	384	361	114	321	3003
Par 4	Par 3	Par 4	Par 4	Par 5	Par 4	Par 4	Par 3	Par 4	Par 35

Belvoir Park

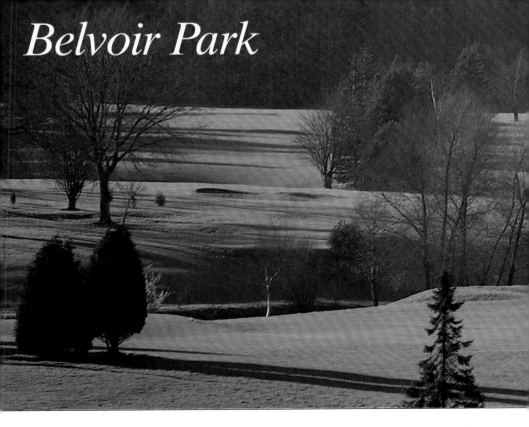

*T*his Belfast course was given the best start possible in life – it was designed by the inimitable Harry Colt.

Colt is responsible for many great layouts throughout the British Isles and around the world, including Swinley Forest, Sunningdale's New Course, Wentworth, The Eden Course at St Andrews, St George's Hill, Royal Portrush – he even had a hand in Pine Valley, recognised as the world's best. He didn't disappoint at Belvoir Park.

Harry Bradshaw once called Belvoir Park "the finest inland course I've ever played on." Mind you he could afford to be generous in his praise – he had just won the 1949 Irish Open Championship held here.

Four years later, the championship came back to Belvoir. This time it was won by Eric Brown. The Scottish Ryder Cup star holed in one at the long, par-3 16th on his way to

victory. You may not ace the 16th, nor any of the other four par-3s, but you will remember them later. The fourth is a 192-yard tester surrounded by trees, so it pays to hit the green. Fourteen is a cracker, as they would say in Ireland, calling for a medium iron over a big hollow to a raised green.

While the par-3s remain in the mind, don't think the par-4s and 5s are a pushover. They're not. You'll find a good mix of long holes, too.

Belvoir Park is a horticulturists delight, with a variety of different types of trees and bushes, including larch, fir, pine and cypress, to name only a few of the variety.

Sadly, Belvoir Park has faded somewhat into obscurity due to the troubles that have plagued this part of Ireland. Too bad, because this Colt gem should be on everyone's 'must play' list.

HOW TO GET THERE

...iles south from city
...tre. A24 to Newcastle.
...ance to golf club off
...rch Road,
...wtownbreda,
...traffic lights
...osite
...sburys.

Belvoir Park Golf Club

COURSE INFORMATION & FACILITIES

Belvoir Park Golf Club
73 Church Road,
Newtownbreda, Belfast

Secretary/Manager: Kenneth H Graham
Tel: 01232-491693 Fax: 01232-646113

Golf Professional Tel: 01232-646714

Green Fees:
Weekdays — £33 Weekends (not Sat.) — £38
Weekdays (day) — £33 Weekends (day) — £38

CARD OF THE COURSE — PAR 72

1	2	3	4	5	6	7	8	9	Out
278	406	435	192	509	390	439	137	488	3274
Par 4	Par 4	Par 4	Par 3	Par 5	Par 4	Par 4	Par 3	Par 5	Par 36

10	11	12	13	14	15	16	17	18	In
476	179	463	402	175	497	204	449	397	3242
Par 5	Par 3	Par 4	Par 4	Par 3	Par 5	Par 3	Par 4	Par 4	Par 35

Castlerock

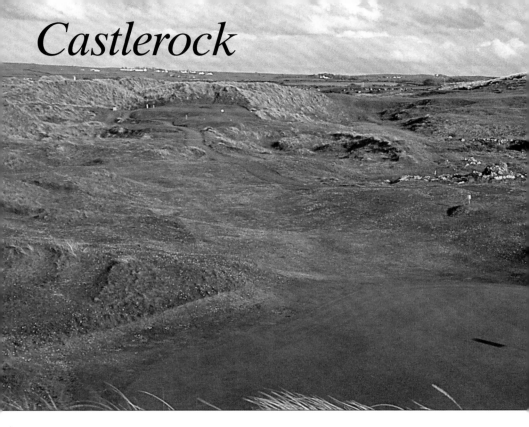

Not far from the glorious links of Royal Portrush, and where the River Bann enters the Atlantic Ocean, lies a gem of a links.

Castlerock Golf Club was founded back in 1901 when it was established as a nine hole layout. The club expanded the course to 18 holes in 1908, calling upon Ben Sayers to create a golf course worthy enough to sit near Portrush. Sayers is better known as a clubmaker, but the North Berwick man could also play. He participated in every Open Championship between 1880 and 1923, finishing second in 1888, third in 1889 and fifth in 1894.

While Sayers gave the game of golf clubs with names like the Jigger and the Dreadnought, perhaps his best contribution to golf architecture was to design the links at Castlerock. Good greens are the order of the

day here. In the height of summer, when th course is hard and dry, the putting surfaces can be treacherously quick. Given that you often have to bounce the ball in on the approach shot, getting close to the flags call for a delicate touch.

The best known hole at Castlerock is the 4th called 'Leg o' Mutton', a 200 yard par three with a railway line to the right, a burn the left and a raised green. A three here is good score as this is a green that is typically hard to hold. Among other outstanding hol at Castlerock are the par four 8th, the 9th (which is precisely the same length as the 4t and, on the back nine, the exhilarating downhill par five 17th.

Revisions to Sayers' layout were made by Harry Colt in 1925, and by Eddie Hackett in the `60s.

HOW TO GET THERE

...iles west of Coleraine, on
A2. Clearly signposted
...m lodge road
...ndabout
...eraine.

Castlerock
Golf Club

COURSE INFORMATION & FACILITIES

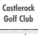

Castlerock Golf Club
65 Circular Road, Castlerock,
Co. Londonderry. BT51 4TJ

Secretary: Mark Steen
Tel: 02870 848314. Fax: 02870 849440.

Golf Professional: Robert Kelly
Tel: 02870 848314. Fax: 02870 849440.

Green Fees:
Weekdays — £30. Weekends — £40.
Weekdays (day) — £45. Weekends (day) — N/A

CARD OF THE COURSE — PAR 72

1	2	3	4	5	6	7	8	9	Out
348	375	509	200	477	347	409	411	200	3276
Par 4	Par 4	Par 5	Par 3	Par 5	Par 4	Par 4	Par 4	Par 3	Par 36

10	11	12	13	14	15	16	17	18	In
391	509	430	379	192	518	157	493	342	3411
Par 4	Par 5	Par 4	Par 4	Par 3	Par 5	Par 3	Par 5	Par 4	Par 37

Clandeboye

*I*t would be hard to find a golf course more pleasing to the eye than Clandeboye when the gorse is in full bloom. Here you are treated to a dazzling sea of yellow on many holes; in fact, the gorse runs for approximately 100 yards down the first hole, elegantly foreshadowing what's to come.

There are two courses at Clandeboye, the Ava and the Dufferin. The latter is the longer course, and the one that gets most of the tournaments and high praise. So it should, it is a challenging test for all handicap levels. It plays to a par of 71, stretching to 6,559 yards, and has been considered good enough to have hosted the Irish Professional Championship twice.

The Dufferin offers good views of Belfast Lough. Given the difficulty of some of the holes, that's just as well, for eventually you may be glad you're at least walking around in pleasant surroundings.

Good holes include the 6th, known as Rathgill, a 521-yard, par-5 which calls for an important decision on the tee. A stream about 250 yards out lies waiting for a good tee shot. Only the longest of hitters will consider trying to fly the ball over the stream while average golfers may do well to take a fairway wood just in case they hit one out of the screws. Trees to the right do not help those of have a penchant for the right hand side of the golf course.

The 18th is a strong finishing hole at 433 yards, which often calls for more club on the approach shot than seems the case.

While the Ava is some 500 or so yards shorter than its big brother, don't think it's a pushover. It isn't. Playing to your handicap harder than you think on this little beauty.

HOW TO GET THERE

al carriageway from Belfast
Bangor (past Belfast City
port), opposite Bangor
metery take Rathgael Road,
roundabout take
t exit right to
wtownards.

COURSE INFORMATION & FACILITIES

Clandeboye Golf Club
51 Tower Road, Conlig,
Newtownards, Co. Down

General Manager: William Donald.
Tel: 01247-27167 Fax: 01247-473711

Golf Professional Tel: 01247-271750

Green Fees:
Weekdays — (Dufferin) £25 (Ava) £20
Weekends — (Dufferin) £30 (Ava) £25 After 3pm

CARD OF THE COURSE (AVA) — PAR 71

1	2	3	4	5	6	7	8	9	Out
388	172	417	389	183	521	360	452	392	2904
Par 4	Par 3	Par 4	Par 4	Par 3	Par 5	Par 4	Par 4	Par 4	Par 35

10	11	12	13	14	15	16	17	18	In
415	153	490	360	167	445	392	375	433	3230
Par 4	Par 3	Par 5	Par 4	Par 3	Par 5	Par 4	Par 4	Par 4	Par 36

Kirkistown Castle

In a country that has '40 Shades of Green' there are not surprisingly numerous areas of outstanding natural beauty. One of the least explored of these is the Ards Peninsula on the east coast of Northern Ireland. Here is a true haven for wildlife - Strangford Lough divides much of the peninsula from the mainland and it is effectively one giant bird sanctuary.

Kirkistown Castle Golf Club is situated near the foot of the peninsula, beside the small town of Cloughey. A broad, sweeping beach and some sand dunes separate the golf course from the Irish Sea. It is an almost hauntingly quiet location - an atmosphere added to, of course, by the presence of the eponymous 17th century Castle.

James Braid was the principal architect of Kirkistown Castle. It seems he was very taken with the land he had to shape for he is reputed to have commented wistfully, "If only I had this within 50 miles of London". There is a very open, exposed feel to the golf course, the major natural features being a few isolated stands of trees and some gorse bushes. It is laid out in two loops of nine, which means that many rounds begin at the par four 10th, the toughest hole on the course. It measures almost 450 yards from the back tees and has an out of bounds to the left, some subtle bunkering on the right and a well guarded plateau green ...potential nightmares, then, in a haunted setting!

HOW TO GET THERE

...low the main Portaferry
...d out of Newtownards.
...tside Kircubbin turn off
...in road for Cloughey. We
... in the centre of Cloughey.

Londonderry
Donegal Northern
Ireland Belfast
Galway Dublin
Eire
Shannon
Wexford
Waterford
Tralee
Cork

Kirkistown
Castle
Golf Club

COURSE INFORMATION & FACILITIES

Kirkistown Castle Golf Club
142 Main Road, Cloughey,
Co. Down

Secretary/Manager: George Graham
Tel: 012477-71233 Fax: 012477-71699

Golf Professional: 012477-71004

Green Fees:

Weekdays — £13 Weekends — £20

CARD OF THE COURSE — PAR 69

1	2	3	4	5	6	7	8	9	Out
470	370	276	136	358	389	272	135	350	2756
Par 5	Par 4	Par 4	Par 3	Par 4	Par 4	Par 4	Par 3	Par 4	Par 35

10	11	12	13	14	15	16	17	18	In
397	116	398	401	176	321	150	404	477	2840
Par 4	Par 3	Par 4	Par 4	Par 3	Par 4	Par 3	Par 4	Par 5	Par 34

Lisburn

*F*or some years now (and according to most course ranking tables that are published) Malone and Belvoir Park have vied with one another for the unofficial title of 'best inland course in Northern Ireland'. Recently, however, a third contender has emerged and it is one whose claim to the top spot should be taken very seriously.

Lisburn, which is located in County Antrim and is just a short distance south west of Belfast, is a fairly new parkland layout having been designed by FW Hawtree and opened in 1973. It occupies a beautiful site and one which each year becomes even more beautiful as the spectacularly landscaped course continues to mature.

Lisburn has a perfectly balanced layout, the course comprising two loops of nine, each with two par threes, two par fives and five par fours. Moreover, the skilful routing of the course ensures considerable variety and continual changes in elevation and direction. Although Lisburn is a championship length course and has no shortage of hazards, it will yield to (and reward) outstanding golf. In the 1989 Ulster Professional Championship, David Feherty put together rounds of 65-64-68 65 - and duly won the tournament by 18 shots!

There are many good holes at Lisburn, but perhaps the most memorable sequence occurs at the end of the round: the 16th is a strong dog-leg to the left, the 17th a big dog-leg to the right, and the 18th is an exhilarating downhill par three.

HOW TO GET THERE

llow M1 south from Belfast
Lisburn, join Hillsborough/
blin road at roundabout.
er 300 yds turn right to
burn Golf Club.

Lisburn
Golf Club

COURSE INFORMATION & FACILITIES

Lisburn Golf Club
68 Eglantine Road, Lisburn BT27 5RQ
Co. Antrim

Secretary/Manager: G. E. McVeigh
Tel: 01846 677216 Fax: 01846 603608

Golf Professional: 01846 677217

Green Fees:
Weekdays — £25 Weekends — £30
Society Rates — £24

CARD OF THE COURSE — PAR 72

1	2	3	4	5	6	7	8	9	Out
479	360	375	157	349	164	465	500	370	3219
Par 5	Par 4	Par 4	Par 3	Par 4	Par 3	Par 4	Par 5	Par 4	Par 36

10	11	12	13	14	15	16	17	18	In
461	401	493	160	505	367	375	449	217	3428
Par 4	Par 4	Par 5	Par 3	Par 5	Par 4	Par 4	Par 4	Par 3	Par 36

379

Malone

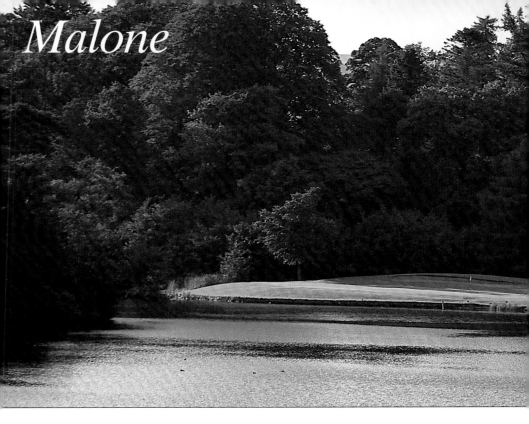

*I*t's hard to believe you could find such a beautiful golf course so close to the city of Belfast. Yet just a few miles from the city centre you will find Malone, an excellent course set on rolling parkland with mature trees and a picturesque lake. It's a place where you would happily have a picnic on a fine summer's day.

Malone has been the venue for many tournaments over the years, including the Irish Amateur Championship, the Irish Professional Championship and the Irish Ladies Amateur Championship. As recently as 1994 it hosted the Irish Senior Masters, won by Tommy Horton. It's fitting that these tournaments have been played over this course, because Malone is a good test of golf.

Although the course only measures 6,599 yards to a par of 71, it will demand your best game to play to your handicap. You'll find a good mix of long and short

holes. For example there are par-4s of 468 yards (the 7th) and 425-yards (the 18th). However, there are also par-4s that measure as little as 309-yards (the 16th), 366-yards (the 8th) and 365-yards (the 9th). Don't think the shorter ones are easier than the longer though, for they demand accuracy and a deft touch.

Best hole on the course is the delightful little par-3 15th. This hole only stretches 132 yards, a mere flick for most. However, it's a flick that has to be played across a beautiful lake. Many good scores have been ruined by the sight of the lake's shimmering surface.

The same lake comes into play on the 18th, as it lies on the left hand side of the par-4 finishing hole. You'll need an accurate tee shot and an equally accurate approach to conquer a hole that is one of the better closing holes in parkland golf.

HOW TO GET THERE

lmoral (A55) exit from M1 —
low signs for the Outer Ring
d Newcastle. At Malone
undabout take Upper Malone
ad exit to Sir Thomas and
dy Dixon Park — Golf Club
opposite.

Malone
Golf Club

COURSE INFORMATION & FACILITIES

Malone Golf Club
240 Upper Malone Road, Dunmurry,
Belfast

Club Manager: Nick Agate
Tel: 01232-612758 Fax: 01232-431394

Golf Professional Tel: 01232-614917

Green Fees:
Weekdays — £32 Weekends & Wednesdays — £37
Restrictions apply

CARD OF THE COURSE — PAR 71

1	2	3	4	5	6	7	8	9	Out
382	505	522	158	440	195	468	366	365	3401
Par 4	Par 5	Par 5	Par 3	Par 4	Par 3	Par 4	Par 4	Par 4	Par 36

10	11	12	13	14	15	16	17	18	In
404	394	193	397	419	132	309	525	425	3198
Par 4	Par 4	Par 3	Par 4	Par 4	Par 3	Par 4	Par 5	Par 4	Par 35

Portstewart

*U*ntil quite recent times Portstewart was widely regarded as 'a good links with an exceptional opening hole.' Rather like Machrihanish on Scotland's Mull of Kintyre (which as the crow flies is no great distance), Portstewart's remaining holes were somewhat overlooked on account of the astonishing start.

Nowadays, Portstewart is viewed in a very different light – the 'exceptional' tag is not limited to the 1st hole. The reason for the seachange in perception can be summarised in two words: 'Thistly Hollow.'

Until the late 1980s golfers would play the famous 1st (a left to right dog-leg that features a dramatic downhill tee shot), then gaze up into the vast range of sandhills known as Thistly Hollow behind the 1st

green and contemplate how amazing it would be if only the club could build some holes in amongst those dunes. Well, it happened! Seven new holes were constructed and the result is that Portstewart can now boast one of the finest front nines in golf. The pick of these 'new' holes may be the 3rd, a strong par three that might have been plucked from Royal Birkdale; the beautifully flowing par five 4th; the heroic two-shot 5th, and the 'Postage Stamp' like 6th.

Portstewart is situated only a few miles west of Portrush, and to the west of Portstewart is Castlerock. Together they make a superb trio; throw in the spectacular scenery of the Giant's Causeway Coast and you have a magnificent golfing destination.

COURSE INFORMATION & FACILITIES

Portstewart Golf Club
Strand Head, Portstewart.
Co Londonderry

Manager: Michael Moss.
Tel: 01265 833839. Fax: 01265 834097.

Golf Professional Alan Hunter Tel/Fax: 01265 832601.

Green Fees:
Weekdays — £45. Weekends — £65.
Weekdays (day) — £65.
Letter of introduction and handicap certificate required.
Time restrictions apply.

CARD OF THE COURSE — PAR 72

1	2	3	4	5	6	7	8	9	Out
425	366	207	535	456	140	511	384	352	3376
Par 4	Par 4	Par 3	Par 5	Par 4	Par 3	Par 5	Par 4	Par 4	Par 36

10	11	12	13	14	15	16	17	18	In
393	370	166	500	485	169	422	434	464	3403
Par 4	Par 4	Par 3	Par 5	Par 5	Par 3	Par 4	Par 4	Par 4	Par 36

HOW TO GET THERE

ow signs for Portstewart —
e there follow signs for
nd Beach. Golf Club is
ated on left overlooking
beach.

Royal Belfast

Founded in 1881, Royal Belfast is the oldest golf club in Ireland. Its course is situated at Craigavad to the east of the city on the southern shores of Belfast Lough. The club's home has not always been here - there were two previous sites - but since 1925 it has enjoyed this spectacular location. The course was designed by Harry Colt, the same architect who transformed the links at Royal Portrush.

The land at Craigavad tilts consistently towards the Lough. This slope was used to expert effect in Colt's routing which includes no fewer than 13 distinct changes of direction. There is a good mix of uphill and downhill holes as well as left and right angled dog-legs. On the higher parts of the course golf is played along mature tree-lined avenues with occasional glimpses of the Lough, while down on the waterfront there is a very open, almost links feel to some of the holes.

The round begins with two very handsome par fours. After touring the fringes of the property, the course turns towards the Lough at the 5th and 6th. The 7th, an outstanding par three, swing uphill but the 8th charges back down again to a green situated close to the shore. On the back nine, both the 10th and 11th possess enormous character, th latter being an intimidating short hole played over rocky, gorse-studded terrain and the course builds to a strong finish with the 18th, a beautifully landscaped par five, providing a fitting finale.

HOW TO GET THERE

...ow A2 to Bangor pass ...loden Hotel. Turn left at ...t set of traffic lights, take ...t fork in road. Signposted.

Royal Belfast
Golf Club

COURSE INFORMATION & FACILITIES

The Royal Belfast Golf Club
Station Road, Craigavad, Hollywood,
Co. Down

Secretary/Manager: Mrs S. H. Morrison
Tel: 01232 428165 Fax: 01232 421404

Golf Professional: 01232 428586

Green Fees:
Weekdays — £30 Weekends — £40
Restrictions: Saturdays not available before 4.30pm.

CARD OF THE COURSE — PAR 72

1	2	3	4	5	6	7	8	9	Out
411	405	356	137	547	347	161	390	405	3159
Par 4	Par 4	Par 4	Par 3	Par 5	Par 4	Par 3	Par 4	Par 4	Par 35

10	11	12	13	14	15	16	17	18	In
303	170	477	361	183	407	476	192	507	3076
Par 4	Par 3	Par 4	Par 4	Par 3	Par 4	Par 5	Par 3	Par 5	Par 35

Royal County Down

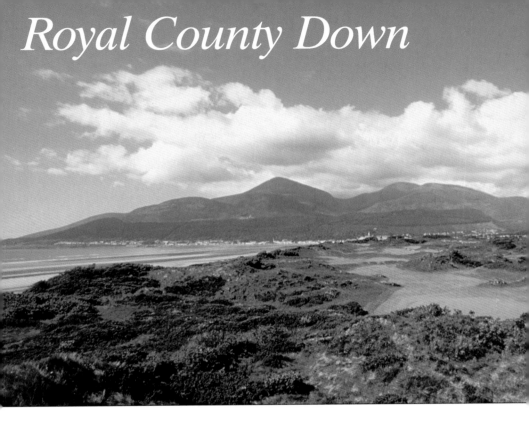

*B*ernard Darwin once summarised the appeal of Royal County Down by suggesting that it offered, 'the kind of golf that people play in their most ecstatic dreams.' Another celebrated English writer, Peter Dobereiner, described the Newcastle links as, 'exhilarating even without a club in your hand.' At one time or another Royal County Down has been adjudged more beautiful than Turnberry, more spectacular than Ballybunion, more natural than Royal Dornoch and more punishing than Carnoustie.

More beautiful than Turnberry and more spectacular than Ballybunion? Newcastle is where, in the immortal words of Percy French, 'the Mountains of Mourne sweep down to the sea.' Fringed by the impressive sweep of Dundrum Bay, towering sandhills appear wrapped in bright yellow gorse during spring, and in autumn are liberally sprinkled with purple heather. The views from the 4th tee and

the crest of the 9th fairway are quite mesmerising, while the 2nd, 3rd, 4th, 8th, 9th, 13th, 15th and 16th could all be described as sensational holes.

More natural than Royal Dornoch? Old Tom Morris (ably assisted by Mother Nature) was the original architect of both Newcastle and Dornoch. With its plethora of blind tee shots, Newcastle is the more old fashioned layout. The contours of its fairways and greens appear completely untouched by man – and surely no one could have created those wild, tussocky-faced bunkers!

And more punishing than Carnoustie? The greens at Newcastle are invariably smaller, the rough is more severe and Carnoustie's bunkers appear tame by comparison.

The most beautiful, most spectacular, most natural and most difficult links … Surely, there is none finer?

COURSE INFORMATION & FACILITIES

Royal County Down
36 Golf Links Road, Newcastle,
Co. Down.

Secretary: Peter Rolph.
Tel: 028 43723314. Fax: 028 43726281.
e-mail: royal.co.down@virgin.net

Golf Professional Kevan J. Whitson Tel: 028 43722419.

Green Fees:
Weekdays — £70. Weekends — £80.
Letter of introduction and handicap certificate required.
Some time restrictions. Visitors Mon/Tue/Thu/Fri.

CARD OF THE COURSE — PAR 71

1	2	3	4	5	6	7	8	9	Out
506	421	474	212	438	396	145	429	486	3507
Par 5	Par 4	Par 4	Par 3	Par 4	Par 4	Par 3	Par 4	Par 5	Par 36

10	11	12	13	14	15	16	17	18	In
197	438	525	443	213	464	276	427	547	3530
Par 3	Par 4	Par 5	Par 4	Par 3	Par 4	Par 4	Par 4	Par 5	Par 36

HOW TO GET THERE

Newcastle is 30 miles south
Belfast via the A24; 90
miles north of Dublin via the
to Newry, and 25 miles
of Newry via the

Londonderry

Donegal Northern Ireland Belfast

Galway Dublin

Eire

Shannon

Wexford
Waterford

Tralee

Cork

Royal County Down

Royal Portrush

*I*t is remarkable that a country as small as Northern Ireland should have two of the Top 12 Golf Courses in the World. But, in Royal County Down and Royal Portrush, and according to America's two biggest selling golf publications, it has precisely that. Arguments as to which is the better of the two links have raged for more than a century.

There are 36 holes at Portrush with the Dunluce and the Valley Courses, the former being the one on which the 1951 (British) Open Championship was staged.

Portrush was shaped by master architect Harry Colt. There are many who regard the Dunluce Course as Colt's finest achievement – notwithstanding that he was also responsible for Muirfield. As for Portrush's setting, let's just say that among the courses presently on the Open Championship rota, only Turnberry's scenery can compare. Portrush is situated on the Antrim coast, close to the Giant's Causeway, and even closer to Dunluce Castle from which the championship links takes its name. The most striking view of the links is to be gained from the main coa road that approaches Portrush from the east.

The front nine of the Dunluce is particularly outstanding. The most famous hole is undoubtedly the 5th, 'White Rocks a shortish par four that charges downhill from a spectacular tee to a green perched on the edge of the links, overlooking the sea. The 14th 'Calamity' often provides th defining moment of the back nine. It is a real 'death or glory' hole – a 210 yards par three with a tee shot across the edge of an enormous ravine.

COURSE INFORMATION & FACILITIES

Royal Portrush Golf Club
Dunluce Road, Portrush,
Co. Antrim.

Secretary/Manager: Wilma Erskine.
Tel: 01265 822311. Fax: 01265 823139.

Golf Professional Dai Stevenson Tel: 01265-823335.

Green Fees:
Weekdays — £70. Weekends — £80. (per round)
Letter of introduction and handicap certificate required.
Some time restrictions

CARD OF THE COURSE — PAR 72

1	2	3	4	5	6	7	8	9	Out
392	505	155	457	384	189	431	384	475	3372
Par 4	Par 5	Par 3	Par 4	Par 4	Par 3	Par 4	Par 4	Par 5	Par 36

10	11	12	13	14	15	16	17	18	In
478	170	392	386	210	365	428	548	469	3446
Par 5	Par 3	Par 4	Par 4	Par 3	Par 4	Par 4	Par 5	Par 4	Par 36

HOW TO GET THERE

...m Belfast take M2 North, ... on to A26, follow to ...trush. Links can be seen ...you enter town.

al Portrush
olf Club

Warrenpoint

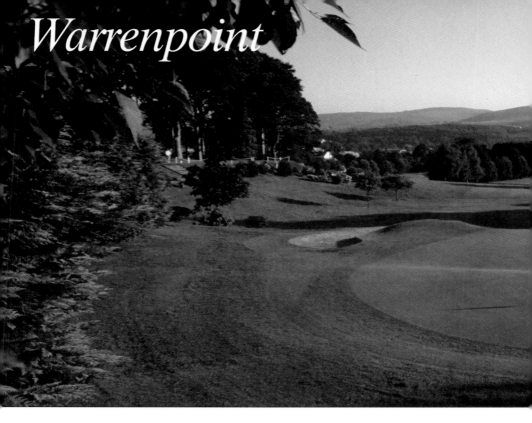

Northern Ireland has an array of outstanding parkland golf courses, the majority of which are located close to the capital, Belfast: Malone, Belvoir Park, Royal Belfast, Clandeboye and Lisburn are all located within 20 miles of the city centre. The country's finest parkland course beyond this area is probably Warrenpoint, which is situated close to (in fact overlooking) picturesque Carlingford Lough.

It is impossible to speak of Warrenpoint without mentioning Ronan Rafferty, who along with Fred Daley and Darren Clarke is one of Northern Ireland's three finest ever players. Great Britain and Ireland's youngest Walker Cup player (he was just 17)and the 1989 European Order of Merit winner (eclipsing Messrs. Faldo, Ballesteros, Lyle and Langer), Rafferty learnt his golf at Warrenpoint.

Set in the attractive grounds of the Hall Estate, Warrenpoint is distinguished by its unorthodox opening sequence – you don't play a par four until the 5th - for its variety of short par fours (particularly good are the 12th and 13th) and for its demanding last two holes. The 428 yards 17th and 418 yards 18th have a reputation for 'sorting the men from the boys', and a four-four finish here is always more than acceptable.

HOW TO GET THERE

1 from Belfast to Newry —
ual Carriageway from Newry
Warrenpoint. The course is
uated on the Dual
arriageway before
itering the town
ntre.

COURSE INFORMATION & FACILITIES

Warrenpoint Golf Club
Lower Dromore Road, Warrenpoint
Co Down BT34 3LN

Secretary: Marian Trainor
Tel: 02841 753695

Golf Professional: Nigel Shaw
Tel: 02841 752371

Green Fees:
Weekdays - £20 Weekends - £27
Weekdays (day) - £20 Weekends (day) £27
Handicap Certificate required — Restrictions apply

CARD OF THE COURSE — PAR 71

1	2	3	4	5	6	7	8	9	Out
517	181	530	526	316	153	412	348	315	3298
Par 5	Par 3	Par 5	Par 5	Par 4	Par 3	Par 4	Par 4	Par 4	Par 37

10	11	12	13	14	15	16	17	18	In
190	282	345	364	163	500	185	426	420	2875
Par 3	Par 4	Par 4	Par 4	Par 3	Par 5	Par 3	Par 4	Par 4	Par 34

North West

The North West

*T*he hauntingly beautiful county of Donegal, up in the left hand corner
of the emerald isle, is a place not on many golfer's maps. That's a
pity, for there is great golf to be found there. More importantly, it is a
landscape you could easily fall in love with. There are many areas of Ireland
that make you feel as if you're the only person in the whole of the island,
nowhere gives you this sense of isolation more than Donegal. Not surprisingly,
there are times when you can go to this region, play its golf courses and find
no one else on the course.

The best courses in the region are to be found at Murvagh, near Donegal
town, and at Ballyliffin in the far north of the county. These are links courses
par excellence. Ballyliffin offers two links courses which are totally different.
The Old Course at Ballyliffin has to be played by anyone interested in
traditional golf. Here you will find fairways that ripple and roll. That is
obvious from the first tee. The opening hole is called 'The Mounds' and that
is exactly what the fairway consists of, a series of mounds that can throw the
ball of at all sorts of strange angles. That sets the scene for the entire round,
and hole after hole seems to offer up the whole range of features you expect to
find on links courses. If the Old Course at Ballyliffin is a traditional links
course that reminds you of the way golf was meant to be played, then the new
Glashedy Links course is everything a championship layout should be. While
the old is fairly short by modern standards, the new course is a big golf course
in every sense of the word. You need to hit the ball a long way if you want to
play off the back tees on the Glashedy Links. That's not usually the case for
golf in Donegal, for the courses tend to be on the short side by modern
standards. That's normally not such a bad thing given that the wind is ever
present. However, one course that would never be called short is Murvagh.
This is a course that looks as if it was laid down a 100 years ago. In fact, it's
one of the newer courses in the area. Play it from the back tees at your peril,

because this is a course that includes all the hallmarks of links golf. Indeed, traditional links golf is what you will find in Donegal. From Northwest to Rosapenna, from Bundoran to Cruit Island and from Narin and Portnoo to Portsalon, everywhere you will find traditional seaside courses in some of the most hauntingly beautiful scenery.

Heading down the west coast of Ireland you soon reach County Sligo and a region immortalised by William Butler Yates. Laid out beneath the impressive gaze of Ben Bulben – Ireland's answer to Table Mountain – is the magnificent links of County Sligo, better known as Rosses Point. Some thirty minutes drive west of Rosses Point there is Enniscrone, a very underrated course, and beyond Enniscrone in County Mayo, a dramatic new links at Belmullet, called Carne. The best of the inland golf courses in the far west of Ireland is Westport, an attractive parkland course that basks on the shores of Clew Bay. Further south and into County Galway, the finest course is Connemara at Ballynonneely: a big course this, it is bordered by the Atlantic and encircled by the dramatic scenery of Connemara National Park.

The bohemian capital of the west of Ireland, Galway city, has a number of courses close at hand, the best of which may be the new Galway Bay Golf and Country Club at Orromore.

BALLYLIFFIN
CARNE
CONNEMARA
COUNTY SLIGO
DONEGAL
ENNISCRONE

GALWAY BAY
NARIN & PORTNOO
NORTH WEST
PORTSALON
ROSAPENNA
WESTPORT

North Wes

Page

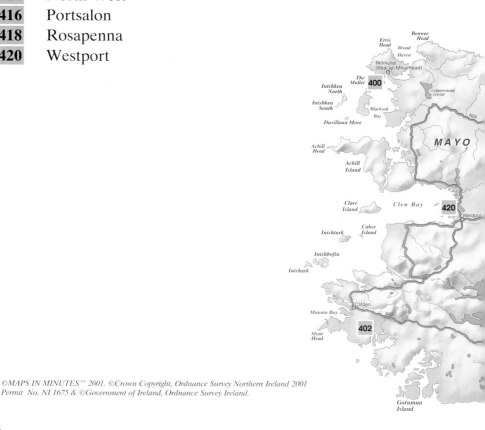

Ballyliffin

When a golf club is described as 'the Dornoch of Ireland' you can hardly ignore it; and when, on adding a further 18 holes that same club is christened 'the Ballybunion of the North', you are almost compelled to make a visit. Ballyliffin is the place in question and it is to be found near Malin Head on the northwestern tip of Donegal's Inishowen Peninsula.

It seems there were three reasons for the very flattering comparison with Royal Dornoch. Firstly, Ballyliffin's geography - Malin Head is the John O'Groats of Ireland and this is the country's most northerly situated golf club; secondly, the original 18 holes, now named the Old Links, is one of the world's most natural golf courses - its rippling fairways are especially fascinating; and thirdly, like Dornoch, Ballyliffin enjoys a remarkably beautiful and serene setting.

In 1995 Ballyliffin unveiled the Glashedy Links. Stretching to more than 7000 yards from the back tees and designed by Tom Craddock and Pat Ruddy, the new course is both formidable and thrilling to play. Writing in LINKS Magazine in November 1996, John Hopkins declared, "I have found the new Ballybunion." And he went on to suggest that the Glashedy Links "might be the best new links course to have been built this century."

'Almost compelled to make a visit'? How could you possibly think of missing Ballyliffin!

HOW TO GET THERE

velling from Belfast (and
rry) cross the Foyle Bridge
d take the A2 towards
ville, turning off for
rndonagh at Quigleys
nt/Carrowkeel. Ballyliffin
miles beyond
rndonagh.

COURSE INFORMATION & FACILITIES

Ballyliffin Golf Club
Ballyliffin, Clonmany, Inishowen,
Co. Donegal.

Golf Office:
Tel: 00 353 77 76119. Fax: 00 353 77 76672.
e-mail:ballyliffingolfclub@tinet.ie

Green Fees:
Weekdays — IR£25. Weekends — IR£30.
Letter of introduction and handicap card required.
Restrictions apply on weekends.

CARD OF THE COURSE — PAR 72

1	2	3	4	5	6	7	8	9	Out
426	432	428	479	177	361	183	422	382	3290
Par 4	Par 4	Par 4	Par 5	Par 3	Par 4	Par 3	Par 4	Par 4	Par 35

10	11	12	13	14	15	16	17	18	In
397	419	448	572	183	440	426	549	411	3845
Par 4	Par 4	Par 4	Par 5	Par 3	Par 4	Par 4	Par 5	Par 4	Par 37

Carne

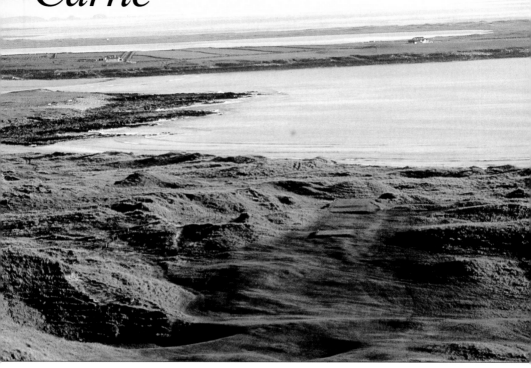

Y ou often get the sense of complete isolation playing in Ireland, as if you are playing at the end of the earth, as far from civilisation as possible. Nowhere in Ireland is this sense more profound than at Carne. The nearest town, Ballina, is 30 miles away.

Carne is about as far west as you can get on mainland Ireland. Any farther west and the Statue of Liberty would just about be visible. The course is situated on Mullet peninsula, on the edge of the Atlantic Ocean. Here you will find glorious views of Blacksod Bay and various islands out in the Atlantic.

Carne was built with one aim - to attract tourism. Those who have sampled its delights since the Eddie Hackett designed course was opened in 1993 have spread the

word. Carne is worthy of trekking to this isolated part of County Mayo, and more golfers are doing so every year.

So natural is the linksland, that there is feeling the course has been here for years. The greens, in particular, seem to belong to the land, as if the golfing greats have been pacing them since the turn of the century.

Huge sand dunes are the order of the day at Carne, and many are used to elevate the tees. This means that on most holes you can see the trouble that lies ahead. That's not to say you will avoid it, for the wind plays a big part in how well you play this course. Pray you get a calm day, otherwise you'll struggle to match your handicap. Just as well it only measures just over 6,600 yards.

COURSE INFORMATION & FACILITIES

Carne Golf Links
Carne, Belmullet
Co. Mayo.

Secretary Manager: Evelyn Keane Tel: 097 82292.
Fax: 097 81477.

Green Fees:
Weekdays — IR£22. Weekends — IR£22.
Weekdays (day) — IR£22. Weekends (day) — IR£22.

CARD OF THE COURSE — PAR 72

1	2	3	4	5	6	7	8	9	Out
366	183	376	473	378	363	162	365	327	2993
Par 4	Par 3	Par 4	Par 5	Par 4	Par 4	Par 3	Par 4	Par 4	Par 35

10	11	12	13	14	15	16	17	18	In
465	332	300	482	133	366	154	399	495	3126
Par 5	Par 4	Par 4	Par 5	Par 3	Par 4	Par 3	Par 4	Par 5	Par 37

HOW TO GET THERE

59 to Belmullet

Carne
Golf Links

Connemara

onnemara is another of those
Irish courses where you feel as if
you're at the very edge of
civilisation. Its hard to believe there is
actually a golf course in this remote part
of County Galway, yet here lies a fabulous
links some five miles beyond the town of
Clifden at Ballyconneely.

Eddie Hackett is responsible for
Connemara. He built the course in 1973,
taking full advantage of the huge rocks
which characterise the landscape. In
fact, Hackett was able to design the
course without moving a single rock, a
tribute to his skill as an architect. While
this is a bona fide links, you won't find
the type of sand dunes you would
normally expect. This means you are
more at the mercy of the winds that whip
over the course from the Atlantic Ocean.

And, yes, there is always a wind.

Calm days at Connemara are rare
indeed. You'll pray for such a day,
however, when you look at the scorecard,
for this is a very long golf course. Play it
from the back if there is no wind or you're
feeling brave, otherwise play from the
forward tees. To give you an example,
there are par fours of 475 yards (8th), 443
yards (9th), 432 yards (10th), 451 yards
(12th) and 452 yards (16th), plus the four
par fives measure 576 yards (7th), 523
yards (14th), 532 yards (17th) and 537
yards (18th). Be sure to make the most of
the front nine, as it is about 300 yards
shorter than the back nine.

Connemara provides superb views of
the Atlantic Ocean, and of an imposing
mountain range known locally as 'The
Twelve Bens'.

COURSE INFORMATION & FACILITIES

Connemara Golf Club
Ballyconneely, Clifden
Co. Galway

Secretary/Manager: Richard Flaherty..
Tel: 095-23502/23602 Fax: 095-23662
e-mail: links@iol.ie

Green Fees:
May/June/July/Aug/Sept — IR£35 Apr/Oct - IR£30
Jan/Feb/Mar/Nov/Dec — IR£22

Society Outing (20 people minimum)
July/Aug — IR£30. June - IR£28 May/Sept - IR£22
Jan/Feb/Mar/Apr/Oct/Nov/Dec — IR£18

CARD OF THE COURSE (metres) — PAR 72

1	2	3	4	5	6	7	8	9	Out
349	385	154	358	360	193	531	438	408	3176
Par 4	Par 4	Par 3	Par 4	Par 4	Par 3	Par 5	Par 4	Par 4	Par 35
10	11	12	13	14	15	16	17	18	In
398	171	416	196	483	367	417	491	496	3435
Par 4	Par 3	Par 4	Par 3	Par 5	Par 4	Par 4	Par 5	Par 5	Par 37

HOW TO GET THERE

m Clifden, continue to
yconneely where you will
 right (straight on for
ndstone), then turn right
in before the Pier, where you
find the golf club.

County Sligo

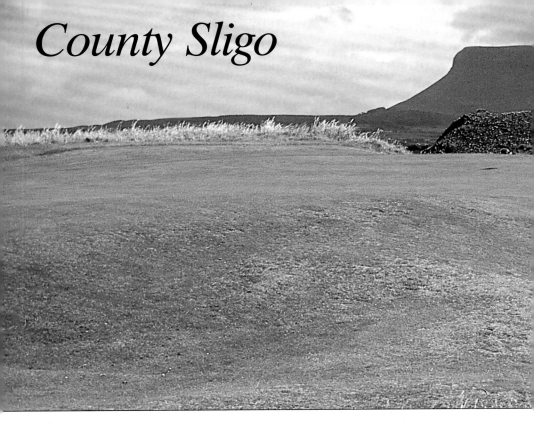

If you're going to play County Sligo, or Rosses Point as it's also known, then you might just want to consider brushing up on your knowledge of the verse of William Butler Yeats, Ireland's most famous poet.

The land around Sligo is Yeats' country. In fact he is buried nearby, within sight of Benbulben, the mountain that dominates the region and much of Yeats' poetry. You may not appreciate poetry, but rest assured that Rosses Point will have you waxing lyrical after just one round. This is a links course that has many fans; Tom Watson, Peter Alliss and Bernhard Langer – to name but a few – have all sung its praises.

There are many courses in Ireland with great views, and Rosses Point is no exception. From as early as the 3rd tee you are presented with stunning views of Drumcliffe Bay, the Atlantic Ocean, the Ox Mountains and Benbulben, Yeats' mountain. Enjoy the views on the 3rd, for after a bunkerless, medium iron par three, the real test that is County Sligo begins at the 5th. This hole is called 'the Jump' and is aptly named as you jump from the high ground around the clubhouse down into real golfing country. This par five hole cal for a shot to be played from a clifftop tee t a fairway lying far below you. This is true links land, amidst sand dunes, pot bunkers and elusive undulating greens.

County Sligo is the venue for the West Ireland Championship, a prestigious amateur event with many fine winners dating back to 1924. Oh, and Harry Colt had a hand in the design of the course – that should be enough to whet your appeti to visit Sligo Town.

HOW TO GET THERE

...m north west of Sligo city
Rosses Point village.

County Sligo
Golf Club

COURSE INFORMATION & FACILITIES

County Sligo Golf Club
Rosses Point,
Co. Sligo.

Acting Administration Manager: Teresa Banks.
Tel: 071 77134/77186. Fax: 071 77460.

Golf Professional: Leslie Roberson. Tel: 071 77171.

Green Fees:
Weekdays — IR£32. Weekends — IR£40.
Letter of introduction and Handicap certificate required.

CARD OF THE COURSE (metres) — PAR 71

1	2	3	4	5	6	7	8	9	Out
347	278	457	150	438	379	393	374	153	2969
Par 4	Par 4	Par 5	Par 3	Par 5	Par 4	Par 4	Par 4	Par 3	Par 36

10	11	12	13	14	15	16	17	18	In
351	368	486	162	394	367	196	414	336	3074
Par 4	Par 4	Par 5	Par 3	Par 4	Par 4	Par 3	Par 4	Par 4	Par 35

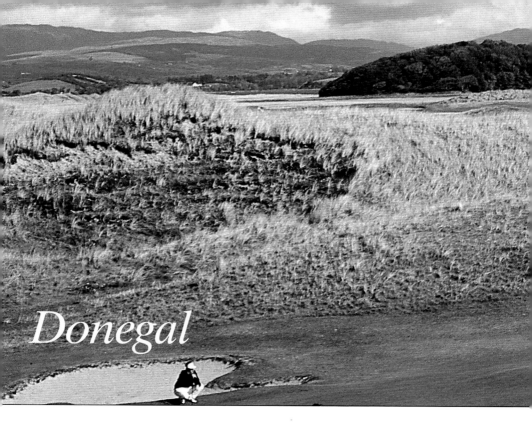

Donegal

*D*on't go to Donegal and miss Murvagh.
Those were the words of Christy
O'Connor Jnr. Now when such a
famous Irish golfer gives you advice, it pays to
listen.

Christy knows his stuff, for Murvagh is a
true hidden gem. Play it and you'll be
convinced it's been there for at least a 100
years. It hasn't – this cracking links course was
only laid down in 1973.

The ubiquitous Eddie Hackett was
responsible for Murvagh, and it's one of his
best. This is a true links course that will test
the best, especially from the back tees, where
the course measures over 7,150 yards.

The first four holes don't really give you a
taste of what's to come. Although they're good
holes, they are played over land that can't
really be called true links. Then comes the 5th.

Beginning with the 5th, you are into proper
links country, in amongst the dunes. The hole
is a beauty, too, a par-3 of 187 yards with a
high green. To come up short of the fifth
green is to roll back down into a collection of
bunkers, from where par is virtually
impossible.

Murvagh is man-sized golf. Although the
outward nine is longer than the inward by
more than two hundred yards, don't be fooled
into thinking the back half will be easier.

Coming home you face one of the longest
par-5s in Ireland. The 12th hole measures
almost 600 yards and calls for three wood
shots by most mortals. Then there's the 16th,
which is a par-3 hole of 240 yards. Most accept
a four here as a good score, that's how tough
the hole is from the back.

Play Murvagh from sensible tees unless
you've got some sort of sadistic streak in you.
And enjoy the fine views it offers of the
Atlantic and the mountains of Donegal- they'll
more than compensate for the troubles you'll
be experiencing if you're playing from the back
markers.

HOW TO GET THERE

ff the N15, main
onegal/Ballyshannon road.
miles from Donegal and
allyshannon.

Londonderry

Donegal

Northern
Ireland

Belfast

Galway

Dublin

Eire

Shannon

Tralee

Waterford

Wexford

Cork

Donegal
Golf Links

COURSE INFORMATION & FACILITIES

Donegal Golf Links
Murvagh, Laghey,
Co. Donegal

Administrator: John Mcbride
Tel: 073-34054 Fax: 073-34377
Email: info@donegalgolfclub.ie
Web: www.donegalgolfclub.ie

Green Fees:
Mon/Thur — IR£30 Fri/Sun — IR£40
Mon/Thur (day) — IR£30 Bank Holidays — IR£40

CARD OF THE COURSE (metres) — PAR 73

1	2	3	4	5	6	7	8	9	Out
485	423	193	441	172	469	391	502	368	3444
Par 5	Par 4	Par 3	Par 4	Par 3	Par 5	Par 4	Par 5	Par 4	Par 37

10	11	12	13	14	15	16	17	18	In
322	371	543	147	510	367	222	325	368	3175
Par 4	Par 4	Par 5	Par 3	Par 5	Par 4	Par 3	Par 4	Par 4	Par 36

Enniscrone

nniscrone is set to do a Portstewart. It is about to open six new holes which, when incorporated into the present layout, should establish Enniscrone as one of the very finest links in Ireland. Not that it isn't close already.

Situated at the point where County Sligo meets County Mayo, and somewhat wedged between the Ox Mountains and Killala Bay (a fisherman's paradise), Enniscrone enjoys a glorious setting; the links itself overlooks a vast pristine white beach.

The golf course was originally laid out by Eddie Hackett. It possesses many strong and characterful holes, its only weakness being the first few holes – particularly the 1st and 2nd which are both fairly

pedestrian par fives. They will not be part of the 'championship 18' when the new holes are ready for play (in 2001), rather they will be included in a newly created 'third nine.' As at Portstewart, the six new holes have been carved out of adjacent dramatic duneland. Enniscrone will become one of those rare links courses that golfers with high blood pressure should avoid playing.

In the current layout the most celebrated holes are the 9th and 10th – the former with its huge amphitheatre green, and the latter with its exhilarating downhill drive and rollercoasting fairway. Yes, they are classic links holes, and ones that provide a foretaste of what's to come when Enniscrone joins golf's premier league.

COURSE INFORMATION & FACILITIES

Enniscrone Golf Links
Enniscrone,
Co. Sligo.

Administrator: Anne Freeman.
Tel: 096 36297. Fax: 096 36657.

Golf Professional Charlie Mc Goldrick
Tel: 096 36666. Fax: 096 36657

Green Fees:
Weekdays — IR£25. Weekends: IR£34.
Weekdays (day) — IR£40.
Some time restrictions.

CARD OF THE COURSE — PAR 72

1	2	3	4	5	6	7	8	9	Out
551	535	395	534	170	395	374	170	345	3469
Par 5	Par 5	Par 4	Par 5	Par 3	Par 4	Par 4	Par 3	Par 4	Par 37

10	11	12	13	14	15	16	17	18	In
350	427	540	202	368	412	403	149	400	3251
Par 4	Par 4	Par 5	Par 3	Par 4	Par 4	Par 4	Par 3	Par 4	Par 35

HOW TO GET THERE

R297 Enniscrone/Ballina
ad, 13km Ballina Town.
km Knock airport.
km Sligo airport.

Enniscrone
Golf Links

Galway Bay

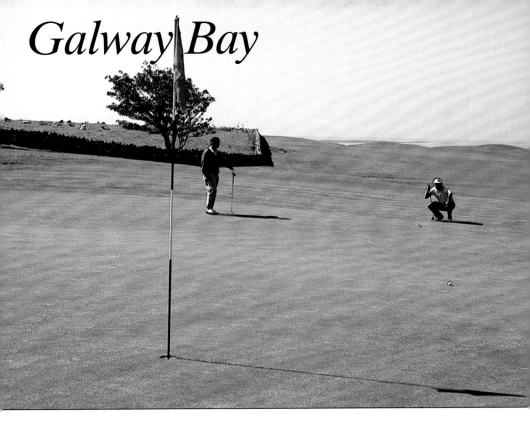

Christy O'Connor Jnr didn't need Peter McEvoy's help when he laid out the course that is Galway Bay Golf & Country Club. However, he didn't design all 18 holes. He called on the help of his famous uncle, Christy O'Connor Snr, allowing him to create one hole on his course. The result is the 176-yard, par-3 13th hole.

Chisty Jnr had always dreamt of designing a golf course in his home town. In fact, his eye had been on the land his course now occupies for some time prior to development. It's land that sits on the Galway Peninsula, with splendid views out over the Atlantic Ocean. As you can appreciate, the wind is often a factor at Galway Bay.

Although it has the Atlantic on three sides, Galway Bay is not a links course. You won't find high duneland here, or turf that is firm and fast. This is essentially a parkland course set beside the sea. However, like links courses you will find lots of bunkers. There isn't one green that is bunker free on the whole course.

Although it is quite open, Galway Bay is stiff test of golf. It's a big course in every sense of the word, measuring close to 7,100 yards, from the back tees, par-72, with long par-4s and 5s. Three of the par-4s measure 457-yards (2nd), 446-yards (10th) and 477-yards (18th). Thankfully the par-3s are of sensible distance, ranging from 149-yards to 188-yards.

While not a links course, Galway Bay is nevertheless set in beautiful landscape. Christy and his uncle have done well to creat a course that complements the scenery. But take a tip, play the course from sensible tees unless you're a big hitter – that way you'll enjoy the walk.

COURSE INFORMATION & FACILITIES

Galway Bay Golf and Country Club Hotel
Renville, Oranmore,
Co. Galway

Secretary/Manager: David O'Connor
Tel: 091-790-500 Fax: 091-790-510

Golf Professional Tel: 091-790-503

Green Fees:
Weekdays (May-Sept) — IR£30, (Oct-April) — IR£25
Weekends (May-Sept) — IR£35, (Oct-April) — IR£30

CARD OF THE COURSE (metres) — PAR 72

1	2	3	4	5	6	7	8	9	Out
486	362	370	136	323	434	126	386	374	2997
Par 5	Par 4	Par 4	Par 3	Par 4	Par 5	Par 3	Par 4	Par 4	Par 36

10	11	12	13	14	15	16	17	18	In
367	356	372	148	464	160	481	323	423	3094
Par 4	Par 4	Par 4	Par 3	Par 5	Par 3	Par 5	Par 4	Par 4	Par 36

HOW TO GET THERE

8 Limerick to Galway.
llow signs for and go through
anmore, take first on left, follow
ad for approx. 2 miles.
Dublin to Galway. Follow signs
and go through Oranmore,
n right at church
d follow road
approx.
niles.

Narin & Portnoo

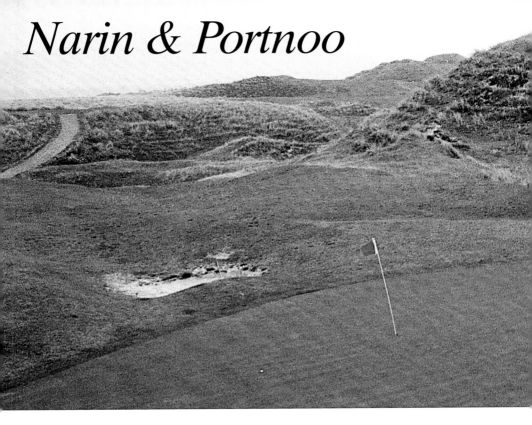

*P*lay the seaside courses in Donegal and you'll soon find there's nowhere to hide from the wind. That's especially true at the delightfully named Narin and Portnoo.

It's not a long course, but the wind can sometimes make it feel like a walk in purgatory, as if the devil was blowing at you through a straw. Holes that would normally call for a drive and pitch sometimes ask you to play a driver and 2-iron only to see the ball come up short.

Narin and Portnoo only measures 5,800 yards to a par of 69, but it will feel like 7,800 on some days. This is a totally natural course that seems to jut out into the Atlantic Ocean. Indeed the holes closest to the sea are the best on the course, although they can be a nightmare when the wind is howling. And here's the rub: you very seldom get a calm day in this part of Donegal.

Get your iron play in shape before you play golf in this remote part of Donegal, for Narin and Portnoo has six par-3s. There are some crackers, as the Irish would say, but best of the bunch may be the 16th. Called High Altar, the hole only measures about 120-yards. However you have to play to a green that drops off on all sides. In a gale you can be hitting a wood.

A word of warning – if the secretary says it's just a gentle breeze, sit in the clubhouse and enjoy a pint of the black stuff. There's lots of time for golf in Donegal.

HOW TO GET THERE

From Donegal town — follow main road to Glenties for 6 miles, then road to Dungloe for 5 miles. At Mass take the road to Narin/Portnoo.

Narin & Portnoo Golf Club

COURSE INFORMATION & FACILITIES

Narin & Portnoo Golf Club
Narin, Portnoo,
Co. Donegal

Secretary: Enda Bonner
Tel: 074-24668 Fax: 074-25185

Golf Professional Tel: 075-45107

Green Fees:
Weekdays — IR£17 Weekends — IR£20
Weekdays (day) — IR£17 Weekends (day) — IR£20
Weekends — booking only.

CARD OF THE COURSE (metres) — PAR 69

1	2	3	4	5	6	7	8	9	Out
289	450	171	416	356	187	292	130	294	2585
Par 4	Par 5	Par 3	Par 4	Par 4	Par 3	Par 4	Par 3	Par 4	Par 34

10	11	12	13	14	15	16	17	18	In
356	180	303	170	476	450	110	371	321	2737
Par 4	Par 3	Par 4	Par 3	Par 5	Par 5	Par 3	Par 4	Par 4	Par 35

North West

Northwest Golf Club will never host the Irish Open, or the Irish Amateur Championship for that matter. At just a little over 6,200 yards it isn't considered long enough to stage a tournament of note. Don't be fooled into thinking it's an easy course, though – it isn't.

Sure there are short holes at Northwest. Sure it only plays to a par of 70. Don't let looks deceive you, however. Northwest is a links course that can make you feel you play to a higher handicap than the one you showed up with. You'll realise that as you stand on the first tee looking at a tough par-4 that measures 440-yards. Making four at the first is no easy task, even for good players.

This is a truly natural little links course hard by the Atlantic Ocean. Not surprisingly,

the Atlantic's capricious winds play a big part in how well you score. On a calm day you can score very well if your swing is on song. On a windy day you will realise why Northwest is not to be taken lightly.

At Northwest you will find par-4s ranging from 343-yards (the 4th), to 443-yards (the 12th), a definite drive and long iron hole for most players. You will find only two par-5s on the layout and four par-3s. Shortest of the par-3s is the 16th, which stretches to only 93-yards. However, it is surrounded by sand so hitting the green is imperative.

Northwest is situated in County Donegal only 12 miles north of Londonderry and about two miles south of Buncrana. It's a popular holiday spot in the summer so make sure you phone ahead in the months of July and August.

HOW TO GET THERE

mile from Buncrana on
in Derry to Buncrana
ad.

North West
Golf Club

Londonderry

Donegal Northern
Ireland Belfast

Galway Dublin

Eire

Shannon

Tralee Wexford
Waterford

Cork

COURSE INFORMATION & FACILITIES

North West Golf Club
Lisfannon, Fahan,
Co. Donegal

Hon. Secretary: Dudley Coyle
Tel: 077 61027 Fax: 077 63280

Golf Professional Tel: 077 61715

Green Fees:
Weekdays — IR£15 Weekends — IR£20
Weekdays (day) — IR£15 Weekends (day) — IR£20

CARD OF THE COURSE — PAR 70

1	2	3	4	5	6	7	8	9	Out
440	346	162	343	407	358	424	139	524	3143
Par 4	Par 4	Par 3	Par 4	Par 4	Par 4	Par 4	Par 3	Par 5	Par 35

10	11	12	13	14	15	16	17	18	In
386	358	443	177	349	370	93	407	513	3096
Par 4	Par 4	Par 4	Par 3	Par 4	Par 4	Par 3	Par 4	Par 5	Par 35

Portsalon

For years visiting golfers came to Ireland and played the great courses on the Antrim Coast, went to the west of the Island and marvelled at Ballybunion and Lahinch, then went to Dublin and played Portmarnock, perhaps Royal Dublin, a few others and then went home. They never thought about exploring the Northwest corner of the Emerald Isle.

Golfers still largely ignore the beautiful county of Donegal. That's a pity because there is good golf to be found there.

Portsalon is one of those good golf courses in Donegal that doesn't get near the number of visitors it would do if it were located near Dublin, Killarney, Cork or Belfast. Like other courses in the region – Northwest, Rosapenna, Ballyliffin, Murvagh – Portsalon is a truly natural links, most of which is set in glorious duneland beside the Atlantic Ocean.

Established in 1890, Portsalon was in danger of virtual extinction until it was purchased by the members in 1986. Since then the course has made something of a comeback, with better care and attention given to what is a superb links.

The course only measures just under 6,000 yards to a par of 69, but like all the go courses in Donegal, some days the scorecard lies – a yardage chart at Portsalon on a wind day would be a complete waste of time. Her you basically have to rely on instinct when it comes to club selection. Those able to overcome their machismo and hit a 5-iron 120-yards, or a 9-iron 170-yards, will succeed at Portsalon.

Arguably the most memorable hole on the course is the 431-yard, par-4, 13th hole. It has been dubbed Matterhorn because an odd pointed rock formation has to be negotiated on the second shot.

COUNTY DONEGAL

HOW TO GET THERE

miles north of Letterkenny.
Ranelton, Milford,
ryheel and Portsalon.

Portsalon
olf Club

COURSE INFORMATION & FACILITIES

Portsalon Golf Club
Portsalon,
Co. Donegal

Secretary: Peter Doherty
Tel: 074-59459 Fax: 074-59459

Green Fees per 18 holes:
Weekdays — IR£20 Weekends & Bank Holidays — IR£25

CARD OF THE COURSE — PAR 69

1	2	3	4	5	6	7	8	9	Out
365	196	356	344	208	354	514	174	317	2828
Par 4	Par 3	Par 4	Par 4	Par 3	Par 4	Par 5	Par 3	Par 4	Par 34

10	11	12	13	14	15	16	17	18	In
351	323	186	431	155	388	285	526	405	3050
Par 4	Par 4	Par 3	Par 4	Par 3	Par 4	Par 4	Par 5	Par 4	Par 35

417

Rosapenna

W hen Frank Casey bought the Rosapenna hotel in 1981, the golf course was thrown in with the deal. For £500,000 Casey not only bought a good hotel overlooking the wild Atlantic Ocean, but purchased hundreds of acres of the finest duneland you could ever come across. Casey's acquisition also saved a course that was fading slowly and sadly into extinction.

Rosapenna was given the best possible start in life. This remote Donegal course was conceived by Old Tom Morris. Later it was remodelled at different times by James Braid and Harry Vardon. Some courses are lucky enough to have one Open Champion involved in their evolution, Rosapenna had three.

Unfortunately the trio did not have access to modern equipment, and so wild were the dunes at Rosapenna that only 10 holes could be constructed on proper

linksland before the course had to move inland. The holes in the dunes just got you into the rhythm of links golf before the final eight left you with the feeling that you had actually played two courses. In the old days you had. Modern technology has ensured that you now play proper links golf when you go to Rosapenna.

New holes have been created in the dunes to rival the first 10 holes. Casey called in another great architect. Although not an Open Champion, Eddie Hackett's work on numerous courses, links and otherwise, around Ireland made him the obvious choice to add to the work of Morris, Braid and Vardon. Rosapenna is now an excellent 27–hole complex that shouldn't be missed on any trip to Donegal.

What's more, the hotel serves excellent seafood. The lobster is reason enough to visit the Rosapenna Hotel - the golf just happens to be a mouth-watering bonus.

HOW TO GET THERE

Miles North of Letterkenny.

COURSE INFORMATION & FACILITIES

Rosapenna Golf Club
Downings,
Co. Donegal

Director: Frank T Casey
Tel: 074-55301 Fax: 074-55128

Golf Professional Tel: 074-55128

Green Fees:
Weekdays — IR£25 Weekends — IR£30
Weekdays (day) — IR£35 Weekends (day) — IR£45

CARD OF THE COURSE — PAR 70

1	2	3	4	5	6	7	8	9	Out
298	428	446	386	255	167	367	485	185	3017
Par 4	Par 4	Par 4	Par 4	Par 4	Par 3	Par 4	Par 5	Par 3	Par 35

10	11	12	13	14	15	16	17	18	In
543	427	342	455	128	418	216	358	367	3254
Par 5	Par 4	Par 4	Par 4	Par 3	Par 4	Par 3	Par 4	Par 4	Par 35

419

Westport

The delightful little down of Westport has been a magnet for visitors for years. People come here for a relaxing holiday, or to walk the rugged coastline, or trudge up a mountain to see the spot where St Patrick is said to have banished all the snakes from Ireland.

Croagh Patrick is the mountain in question, and every year thousands of worshippers ascend Ireland's Holy Mountain. This same mountain stands towering above the golf course at Westport, providing a unique backdrop.

A golf course is just what Westport needed to make it the ideal holiday destination in County Mayo, and Fred Hawtree has designed a course the town can be justifiably proud of.

Although the course sits by the sea, it is not a links course. This is basically pure parkland, with a good mixture of holes on lush terrain. Don't be lulled into a false sense of security by the opening nine, which are fairly straightforward. The course really comes into its own on the inward half.

Westport is long. From the back markers it stretches to 7,000 yards. That was long enough for the course to be selected as venue for the 1977 and 1985 Irish Amateur Close Championship, as well as the 1989 Irish Ladies Amateur Championship.

Although basically a parkland layout, Westport has one hole that wouldn't be out of place on any fine links course. The 15th is the hole in question, and it is simply stunning. It calls for a drive to be played over Clew Bay and then the hole bends round to the left back towards the water. Make par here from the back tees and you've had a result.

HOW TO GET THERE

5 miles from Westport
wn, on Newport Road. Turn
t on Newport Road after
aving Westport and
ntinue for approximately
miles.

Westport
Golf Club

COURSE INFORMATION & FACILITIES

Westport Golf Club
Carrowholly, Westport,
Co. Mayo

Secretary: Margaret Walsh
Tel: 098-28262 Fax: 098-27217
e-mail: wpgolf@iol.ie

Golf Professional Tel: 098-27481

Green Fees:
Weekdays — IR£19 Weekends — IR£24
Time restrictions apply.

CARD OF THE COURSE — PAR 73

1	2	3	4	5	6	7	8	9	Out
325	322	141	476	335	417	491	416	176	3011
Par 4	Par 4	Par 3	Par 5	Par 4	Par 4	Par 5	Par 4	Par 3	Par 36

10	11	12	13	14	15	16	17	18	In
490	392	184	390	160	510	342	300	490	3218
Par 5	Par 4	Par 3	Par 4	Par 3	Par 5	Par 4	Par 4	Par 5	Par 37

South West

The South West

*B*allybunion, Waterville Killarney, Tralee, Dooks and Beaufort. They're names that make you want to pack your clubs and head for Ireland, for the County of Kerry and the Southwest corner of the Emerald Isle. Golfers have been doing that for years, most making Killarney their base from which to explore Kerry and its famous ring. The Ring of Kerry is one of the great drives in the world. It's a journey that takes you around a peninsula that offers simply the most glorious views to be found anywhere in the world. Keeping your eyes on the road will be no easy matter. For golfers the drive is even more memorable, for you have to drive out this way to get to Dooks and Waterville, two links courses worthy of even the most boring car journey, let alone this scenic route. The two courses couldn't differ more, Waterville is a true championship layout, while Dooks is one of Ireland's true gems.

Waterville is a big golf course in every sense of the word, especially the back nine, which is the making of the course. On this loop you will encounter hole after challenging hole, culminating in a par-3 that is simply stunning. The tee of the par-3 17th is known as Mulcahy's Peak, after the man responsible for this fine links. The tee offers stunning views over the golf course, a spot Jack Mulcahy often visited to look over the land that would one day become one of the best links courses anywhere. If you have to play off forward tees on this hole, make sure you take a walk up to the top of the tee to have a look around. You may want to just sit there all day and soak in the scenery.

The scenery is also one of the major pluses at Killarney Golf Club. Killarney's two courses are dominated by the Magilicuddy Reeks, the tallest mountains in Ireland. Between the courses and the slopes of the Reeks lies Lough Leane. There is no finer place to play golf on a sunny day. However, the most famous course in this region is not known so much for its outstanding beauty as its outstanding golf course. Ballybunion is the course in question, and the Old Course there just has to be played at least once. Tom Watson is the man most

responsible for Ballybunion's popularity with American golfers. Watson thinks it's one of the best courses anywhere in the world. He's right. Ballybunion is traditional links golf at its very best.

While County Kerry undoubtedly possesses the finest and most famous courses in the south west of Ireland, County Cork is not without its gems. Indeed, in the Old Head Golf Links near Kinsale it has arguably the most spectacular new course in Europe. Old Head has to be experienced to be believed. According to Irish legend Joe Carr it is, 'the eighth wonder of the world in golfing terms'. The city of Cork is surrounded by good golf. The premier 'established' course is the Alister MacKenzie designed Cork Golf Club at Little Island, while the pick of the new layouts is Fota Island, followed by Lee Valley.

To the north of Kerry lie the counties of Limerick and Clare. The former has no links courses but there are two good parkland layouts near the city of Limerick, namely Limerick and Limerick County, and an outstanding new Robert Trent Jones creation at Adare Manor. The pride of County Clare is Lahinch, a classic links course with a series of oceanside holes that compare with the best of Ballybunion. Away from the grounds of Dromoland Castle and also at Shannon Golf Club, one of Ireland's most underrated parkland challenges.

ADARE
BALLYBUNION
CORK
DOOKS
DROMOLAND CASTLE
FOTA ISLAND
KILLARNEY

LAHINCH
OLD HEAD
RING OF KERRY
SHANNON
TRALEE
WATERVILLE

South West

Page

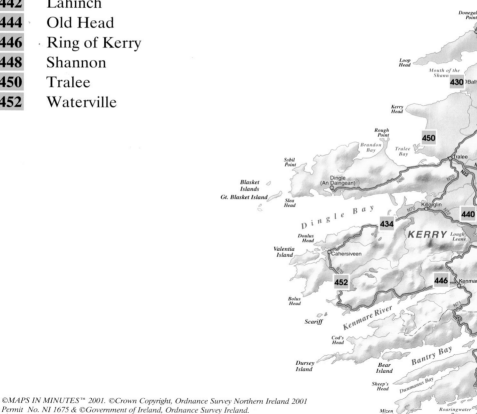

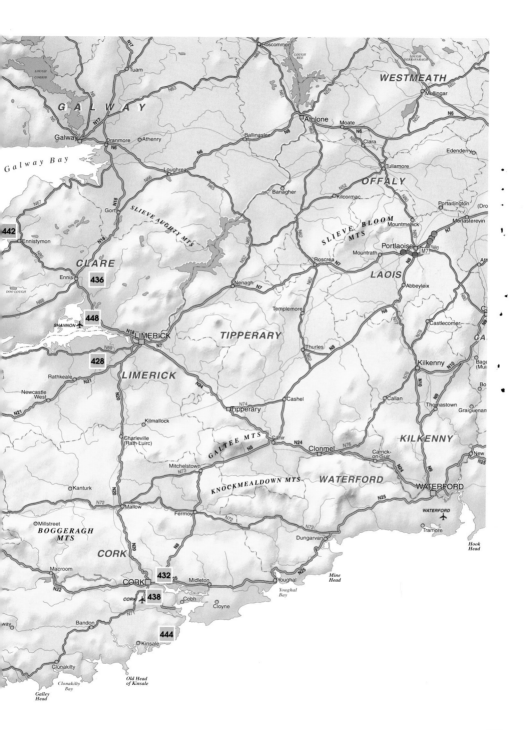

Adare

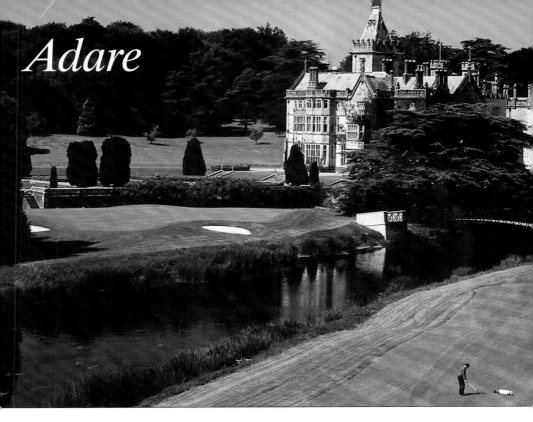

he village of Adare in County Limerick is just what you would expect of rural Ireland, a picturesque village standing on the banks of a river, the Maigue, with thatched cottages and a few pubs. There is also a stately home here, which was the one time ancestral home of the Earls of Dunraven. Now it's a splendid hotel, with an equally splendid golf course.

Adare Golf Club is the work of Robert Trent Jones, and ranks among the best inland courses in Ireland, even though it was only created in 1995.

What you will remember from your round at Adare is the 18th, the course's signature hole. It's a 510-yard, par-5 which calls for a confident third shot. For some 450 yards, the Maigue runs along the left hand side of the fairway, before it turns right to bisect the fairway before the green.

Two large trees on the right hand side of the fairway force you further left than you would like. From here you need a confident pitch to a green that isn't as large as you've been accustomed to throughout the other 17 holes.

Mature trees are to be found on some holes, while others are quite open. The course itself can be described as a gently rolling parkland with not much elevation, making it a joy to walk. You will find water on about 10 holes, in the shape of the Maigue itself, a small tributary, two ponds and a large lake. Besides the 18th, the greens are large. If you are prone to under clubbing your approach shots, then you may spend the day three putting.

A good, enjoyable course if played from sensible tees. Make sure you're playing well if you decide to play from the back tees, where Adare stretches to some 7,100 yards.

COURSE INFORMATION & FACILITIES

Adare Golf Club
Adare,
Co. Limerick

Golf Administrator:
Tel: 061-395044 Fax: 061-396987

Green Fees:
Weekdays — IR£75 Weekends — IR£75
Weekdays (day) — IR£100 Weekends (day) — IR£100

CARD OF THE COURSE - PAR 72

1	2	3	4	5	6	7	8	9	Out
433	413	403	180	419	205	537	427	577	3594
Par 4	Par 4	Par 4	Par 3	Par 4	Par 3	Par 5	Par 4	Par 5	Par 36

10	11	12	13	14	15	16	17	18	In
441	187	550	442	425	370	170	415	544	3544
Par 4	Par 3	Par 5	Par 4	Par 4	Par 4	Par 3	Par 4	Par 5	Par 36

HOW TO GET THERE

ocated 20 miles from
hannon Airport on the
alee/Killarney Road. The
otel and Golf course are
cated in the village of
dare.

Ballybunion

*P*lease excuse the blasphemy, but for well-travelled golfers, particularly those with a penchant for seaside golf, Ballybunion is 'God's own Country.' In fact, mere mention of the name Ballybunion to such folk is enough to set their pulses racing.

The reason is simple enough. Situated in a remote but beautiful corner of County Kerry, Ballybunion is the most spectacular links on the planet. Thirty-six holes weave their way amidst – and occasionally carve a route through – the largest and most extensive range of sandhills in the British Isles. It is thrilling, swashbuckling golf. Moreover, one of the two 18 hole layouts, Ballybunion Old Course, is regarded by no lesser a judge than Tom Watson as the world's greatest golf course. (The newer Cashen Course was designed by Robert Trent Jones and opened in the mid 1980s).

While the 2nd, 7th and 8th are marvellous holes, everyone remembers the back nine on the Old Course. And some golfers dream about the par four 11th. Bordered by huge dunes to the left and the Atlantic Ocean to the right, the fairway at this hole cascades down to a bunkerless green overlooking the sea.

The Old Course hosted its first ever Irish Open Championship in June 2000. What a golden summer for golfers: a US Open at Pebble Beach, The Open at St Andrews and an Irish Open at Ballybunion!

COURSE INFORMATION & FACILITIES

Ballybunion Golf Club
Sandhill Road,
Ballybunion, Co. Kerry.

Secretary: James J. McKenna.
Tel: 068-27146.

Golf Professional: Brian O Callaghan Tel: 068-27842.

Green Fees:
Weekdays — IR£60. Weekends — IR£60.
Weekdays (day) — IR£80. Weekends (day) — IR£80.
Letter of introduction and handicap certificate required.
Time restrictions apply. Early booking available.

CARD OF THE COURSE — PAR 71

1	2	3	4	5	6	7	8	9	Out
392	445	220	520	524	364	432	153	454	3495
Par 4	Par 4	Par 3	Par 5	Par 5	Par 4	Par 4	Par 3	Par 4	Par 36

10	11	12	13	14	15	16	17	18	In
359	453	192	484	131	216	499	385	379	3098
Par 4	Par 4	Par 3	Par 5	Par 3	Par 3	Par 5	Par 4	Par 4	Par 35

HOW TO GET THERE

rom Shannon Airport, take
ast road N69 to Ballybunion.
mile through town to Club
ouse.

Iragh Ti Connor

Iragh Ti Connor Country House is situated within its own walled garden at the top of main street, Ballybunion, two minutes from Ballybunion Golf Club.
It consists of 17 spacious bedrooms including 3 mini-suites each with its own individual character. The restaurant specialises in seafood, most notably lobster fresh from the sea tank.
Full bar facilities and private car parking are also available.

Contact Joan or John O Connor
Main Street, Ballybunion, Co. Kerry, Ireland
Tel: 353 68 27112 Fax: 353 68 27787
Email: iraghticonnor@eircom.net Web: golfballybunion.com

Cork

*A*ny fan of Dr Alister MacKenzie will want to pay a visit to Cork Golf Club at Little Island, for the creator of Augusta National is partly responsible for this course.

Cork Golf Club was formed in 1888 on a different piece of land to which the present 18 hole course occupies today. In 1898 the club moved to its present location beside the Lee Estuary where nine holes were laid out by Tom Dunn, the club's first professional. Thirty years later the club expanded to 18 holes and MacKenzie was called in to add the new nine and revise the existing holes.

Further changes were made to the course in 1975, when Frank Pennink was called in to make revisions.

Cork has been considered good enough to have hosted many important tournaments, including the 1932 Irish Open, the 1940 Irish Professional Championship and the Carrolls International in 1965. As well as these professional events, the club has been venue for many of the country's top amateur tournaments.

What these players faced at Cork are MacKenzie's trade mark - large, undulating greens. Indeed, play Cork without three putting and you can count yourself a good putter.

A limestone quarry has been incorporated into the golf course, and comes into play from the 6th hole, which calls for a short pitch shot to a green where the walls of the old quarry are very much in play.

The Lee Estuary also comes into play at Cork, especially at the par-4, 4th hole. This is a great two shotter which calls for your drive to cut off as much of the estuary as possible to allow you to reach the green in two at this 450-yard hole.

The closing holes are not quite as dramatic as those that come beforehand, but they are played in the most pleasant of parkland surroundings.

HOW TO GET THERE

miles east of Cork city, off
5 road.

Londonderry
Donegal   Northern   Belfast
          Ireland
          Dublin
Galway
Eire
Shannon
                    Wexford
          Waterford
Tralee
    Cork   Cork
                Golf Club

COURSE INFORMATION & FACILITIES

Cork Golf Club
Little Island,
Co. Cork

General Manager: Matt Sands
Tel: 021-4353451 Fax: 021-4353410

Golf Professional: 021-4353451

Green Fees:
Weekdays — IR£45 Weekends — IR£50
Letter of introduction required

CARD OF THE COURSE (metres) — PAR 72

1	2	3	4	5	6	7	8	9	Out
340	460	244	411	510	300	169	379	178	2991
Par 4	Par 5	Par 4	Par 4	Par 5	Par 4	Par 3	Par 4	Par 3	Par 36

10	11	12	13	14	15	16	17	18	In
374	454	289	157	397	383	323	360	387	3124
Par 4	Par 5	Par 4	Par 3	Par 4	Par 4	Par 4	Par 4	Par 4	Par 36

Dooks

It's very easy to by-pass Dooks Golf Club – not advisable, but very easy. Most golfers hurry past this fine little links course on their way to the mightier challenge of Waterville.

Thankfully enough golfers have slowed down and actually stopped to have a look at the Dooks course. Those who have returned to play have spread the word that this is a little gem of an 18-holer.

It wasn't always 18 holes, though. Founded in 1889, Dooks was a nine hole course until 1970, when the members decided to do something about it. This was in the days long before EEC money was available to upgrade Irish leisure facilities. Having little money with which to pay for the expansion, the club took a pragmatic approach. A committee of nine was formed and each was responsible for designing one hole!

For less than £3,000, the task was finished with the holes built by the members themselves. The result is terrific. True, Dooks wouldn't test the greatest golfers in the game not at just 6,000 yards. However, it's as much fun as you're likely to find anywhere.

Here you find a golf course that has the feel of a traditional links, one where you will find it hard to spot the new holes from the old (the new are the 4th through the 12th).

Undulating greens that are often raised put a premium on a good short game, so work on your chipping and putting beforehand.

Fine views over Dingle Bay and the mountains of Kerry are to be had here. Try to play it when the sun is setting – it's an enchanting experience.

HOW TO GET THERE

uated on N70 — between
onglin and Glenbeigh.
rn right at Canagh Bridge
d continue for 1 mile.

Dooks
Golf Club

COURSE INFORMATION & FACILITIES

Dooks Golf Club
Glenbeigh,
Co. Kerry

Secretary/Manager: Declan Mangan
Tel: 066-9768205. Fax: 066-9768476
E-mail: office@dooks.com

Green Fees:
Weekdays — IR£25
Weekdays (day) — IR35

CARD OF THE COURSE — PAR 70

1	2	3	4	5	6	7	8	9	Out
419	131	300	344	194	394	477	368	183	2810
Par 4	Par 3	Par 4	Par 4	Par 3	Par 4	Par 5	Par 4	Par 3	Par 34

10	11	12	13	14	15	16	17	18	In
406	531	370	150	375	213	348	313	494	3200
Par 4	Par 5	Par 4	Par 3	Par 4	Par 3	Par 4	Par 4	Par 5	Par 36

Dromoland

A trend in Irish golf in the late 80s and early 90s has been for stately homes and castles with large tracts of land to construct golf courses on the property. The stately homes become first rate hotels and those who want to wine and dine in style can also include a round of two of golf. All very civilised indeed.

Adare Manor, The K-Club, Mount Juliet, to name only three, spring readily to mind. Dromoland Castle is another.

Dromoland Castle dates back to the 16th century, and for a long time was the ancestral home of the powerful O'Brien clan of County Clare, descendants of Brian Boru, the 10th century Irish King. The castle is very much in view from the golf course, indeed it provides a spectacular backdrop to the 140-yard, par-3, 7th hole. The course itself is of the parkland variety set out over rolling ground, with very few trees that come into play.

Water comes into play at Dromoland, as does a river, so make sure you are not wayward. The course won't call for you to hit every club in the bag, and at around 6,200 you don't need to be a long hitter. Make sure you concentrate from the very beginning, though, as the front nine is som 400 yards longer than the back. You'll nee to be a good long iron or fairway wood player, too, as the outward half closes with a demanding 220-yard, par-3.

HOW TO GET THERE

From Shannon airport —
take N19, follow signs to
N18 Newmarket-on-Fergus.
3 miles past village entrance,
club is on right.

Dromoland Castle
Golf Club

COURSE INFORMATION & FACILITIES

Dromoland Castle Golf & Country Club
Newmarket-on-Fergus,
Co. Clare

Secretary/Golf Manager: John O Halloran
Tel: 061-368444/368144
Fax: 061-368498/363355

Green Fees:
Weekdays — IR£25 Weekends — IR£30
Weekdays (day) — IR£25 Weekends (day) — IR£30

CARD OF THE COURSE (metres) — PAR 71

1	2	3	4	5	6	7	8	9	Out
356	480	212	423	377	513	130	358	206	3055
Par 4	Par 5	Par 3	Par 4	Par 4	Par 5	Par 3	Par 4	Par 3	Par 35

10	11	12	13	14	15	16	17	18	In
268	440	317	110	358	257	347	153	414	2664
Par 4	Par 5	Par 4	Par 3	Par 4	Par 4	Par 4	Par 3	Par 5	Par 36

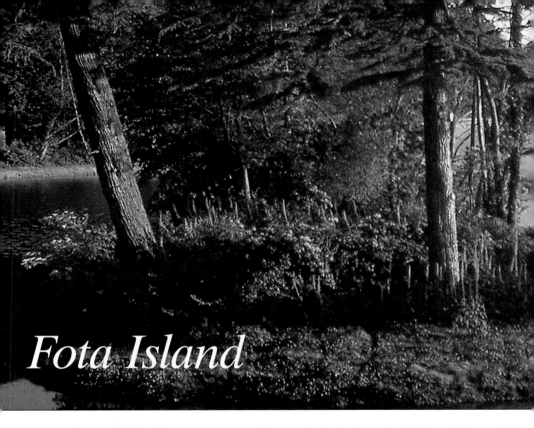

Fota Island

*T*ake one of Britain's top amateurs and one of Ireland best professionals, ask them to create their idea of a great golf course and what do you get? Fota Island, that's what. Although the course only opened in 1993 it has already hosted no fewer than three Irish Open Amateur Championships as well as the Irish PGA Championships.

Two time British Amateur Champion (1977-78) Peter McEvoy – the last British Amateur Champion to make the cut at The Masters incidentally – and four time European Tour winner Christy O'Connor Jnr are responsible for Fota Island, which lies about 15 minutes drive from Cork.

The golf course is one of the prettiest you will find in all of Ireland. It is situated next door to the Fota Island Arboretum and Gardens, so if you've got a green thumb you'll be well pleased.

Obviously McEvoy and O'Connor know a few things about good golf course design,

and they've brought that knowledge to Fota Island. This is a par-72 course that runs to nearly 6,900 yards, one that will require you to use every club in the bag. Indeed, if you play from the back tees you may find yourself staring down long iron second shots on a number of par-4s. There are no fewer than seven par-4s that measure 417-yards or longer.

Three of those long par-4s are to be found on the run-in, as 14, 15 and 16 measure 440, 455 and 417-yards respectively. Seventeen isn't much of a breather either – it plays to 209-yards!

McEvoy obviously learnt from his two visits to Augusta National to play in The Masters, for Fota's greens are quite undulating. However, they are built to the highest standard so that every putt rolls true.

Water comes into play quite a lot at Fota Island, so take lots of balls if you're a bit wayward.

HOW TO GET THERE

ke N25 east from Cork city
wards Waterford and
sslare. After about 9 miles
it for Fota Island/Cobh.
trance is 1500m
m N25 exit on
ht.

Londonderry
Donegal Northern Ireland Belfast
Galway Dublin
Eire
Shannon
Wexford
Tralee Waterford
Cork
Fota Island
Golf Club

COURSE INFORMATION & FACILITIES

Fota Island Golf Club
Carrigtwohill,
Co. Cork

General Manager: Kevin Mulcahy
Tel: 021-883700. Fax: 021-883713.

Golf Professional: Tel: 021-883710.

Green Fees:
Weekdays — IR£32 Weekends — IR£37
Weekdays (day) — IR£44 Weekends (day) — IR£49

CARD OF THE COURSE — PAR 72

1	2	3	4	5	6	7	8	9	Out
428	435	182	501	577	375	170	484	425	3577
Par 4	Par 4	Par 3	Par 5	Par 5	Par 4	Par 3	Par 5	Par 4	Par 37

10	11	12	13	14	15	16	17	18	In
502	201	425	183	440	455	417	209	492	3324
Par 5	Par 3	Par 4	Par 3	Par 4	Par 4	Par 4	Par 3	Par 5	Par 35

Killarney

*T*he town of Killarney is a natural starting point for visiting the famous Ring of Kerry and its spectacular scenery – the only problem is, once in Killarney you may never want to leave.

It's a town like no other in Ireland, one with a distinctly cosmopolitan feel. It's also overshadowed by the magnificent Magilicuddy Reeks, the highest mountain range in the Emerald Isle. Golfers are provided with the best view of these magnificent mountains, for only an enchanting lake, Lough Leane, separates Killarney Golf and Fishing Club's two courses from the Reeks.

The two courses are named Mahony's Point and Killeen, with the latter being the longer and more challenging. Indeed the Killeen course hosted the 1991 and 1992 Irish Opens, won both times by Nick Faldo.

While Mahony's Point takes a back seat to the Killeen course when it comes to staging big tournaments, don't think it's not worth

playing – it is. Just to play the last three holes is worth the green fee alone. The trio involves flirting with the water of Lough Leane – for the approach shot to the par-5 16th, and for the entire length of 17 and 18. The 18th, especially, will stick in your memory. Henry Longhurst once described it as the best short hole in the world. No wonder, it calls for a long iron or wood over the lake to find the putting surface.

Killeen also makes good use of the lake on some holes, especially at the first, third, fourth and fifth holes. However, the best hole on the course, and maybe of the entire complex, is the 13th, a long par-4 calling for an accurate second to be played over a stream set down in a little hollow to a long green that falls away to the left. Par here is a good score. But don't be too worried about your score the first time you play Killarney.

Enjoy the scenery, smell the flowers and pack your camera. You'll be enchanted.

HOW TO GET THERE

...ilometres west of Killarney
...wn — on Ring of Kerry Road.
...62 to Killorglin.

Killarney
Golf Club

COURSE INFORMATION & FACILITIES

Killarney Golf & Fishing Club
(Mahony s Point), Killarney,
Co. Kerry

Secretary: Tom Prendergast
Tel: 064-31034 Fax: 064-33065

Golf Professional

Tel: 064-31615 Fax: 064-33065
e-mail: kgc@iol.ie

Green Fees:
Weekdays/Weekends — Available on request
Handicap Certificate required

CARD OF THE COURSE — PAR 72

1	2	3	4	5	6	7	8	9	Out
341	404	431	141	448	360	169	532	296	3122
Par 4	Par 4	Par 4	Par 3	Par 5	Par 4	Par 3	Par 5	Par 4	Par 36

10	11	12	13	14	15	16	17	18	In
344	426	216	435	364	268	458	373	179	3042
Par 4	Par 4	Par 3	Par 5	Par 4	Par 4	Par 5	Par 4	Par 3	Par 36

Lahinch

Two legendary figures shaped the golf course at Lahinch: Old Tom Morris, arguably the greatest golf architect of the 19th century; and Alister Mackenzie, arguably the greatest golf architect of the 20th century. Given that Old Tom was initially responsible for, among others, Royal County Down, Prestwick and Royal Dornoch, and that Mackenzie created Augusta, Cypress Point and Royal Melbourne, it is hardly surprising that between them they crafted an extraordinary links.

Lahinch is known as 'the St Andrews of Ireland' – not because of the association with Old Tom, but because the Lahinch community lives and breathes golf. It is situated on the coast of County Clare, a short drive from the dramatic Cliffs of Moher. Any golfer making the pilgrimage to Ballybunion should visit Lahinch if nowhere else.

The Old Course (for there are now 36 holes) has been described as a cross between Ballybunion and Prestwick. The dunes at Lahinch are not as extensive as those at Ballybunion, although in places they are just as impressive. Midway through a round, between the 7th and the 12th, golfers play a sequence of holes that are every bit as thrilling as the back nine at Ballybunion.

Old Tom's influence and the similarities with Prestwick are most evident at the 5th and 6th, both of which feature blind shots. Not too many people raise eyebrows at the 5th as it's a par five, but the following hole is a par three!

Commentators are occasionally critical of Lahinch's finish, suggesting that it's an anti-climax. Nonsense! Lahinch charms and challenges from first to last.

HOW TO GET THERE

om the town of Ennis, take
e N67 to Ennistymon and
ahinch is two miles from
nnistymon
y the Sea.
is well
gnposted.

COURSE INFORMATION & FACILITIES

Lahinch Golf Club
Lahinch,
Co. Clare

Secretary/Manager: Alan Reardon
Tel: 065-7081003 Fax: 065-7081592

Golf Professional:
Tel: 065-81592

Green Fees (old course):
Weekdays — IR£45 Weekends — IR£45
Weekdays (day) — IR£50 Weekends (day) — IR£50

Letter of introduction required.

CARD OF THE COURSE — PAR 72

1	2	3	4	5	6	7	8	9	Out
385	512	151	428	482	155	399	350	384	3246
Par 4	Par 5	Par 3	Par 4	Par 5	Par 3	Par 4	Par 4	Par 4	Par 36
10	11	12	13	14	15	16	17	18	In
451	138	475	273	488	462	195	437	533	3452
Par 4	Par 3	Par 4	Par 4	Par 5	Par 4	Par 3	Par 4	Par 5	Par 36

Old Head

*T*here have been many new courses built in Ireland in the past 10 years, and many that can be considered true championship links. However, the most spectacular of the new breed is the Old Head Golf Links at Kinsale.

The Old Head has been laid out on a rocky promontory that juts out into the sea. You drive into the course through a narrow spit of land that opens out into what was formerly just poor farmland and a haven for birds. On all sides the land drops dramatically down to the sea, where the water crashes onto the dark rocks. The cliff edges have been fully incorporated into the design of the holes, so that no less than nine play along the very edge of the promontory.

There is no room for error on the holes along the edge of the Old Head. Even if you are a touch wayward you can find yourself reaching for another ball. There is just no safety area if you fire at some flags, for your ball will disappear into the depths of the sea. Best among the holes hard by the sea is the 16th. Here you play from a high tee to a green that is literally one step from a long drop to the rocks below. Push or slice the ball and you will be in trouble, deep trouble.

Even off the tee on some of the cliff holes you can find yourself reloading. The 12th, for example, is a dramatic par-5 that asks you to hit across fresh air towards an elusive fairway. A bird sanctuary is located on the cliff face to your left. Concentration can be just a trifle tough.

You have to play this course at least once. You won't find a course as dramatic anywhere else in Ireland.

COURSE INFORMATION & FACILITIES

Old Head Golf Links
Kinsale,
Co. Cork

Membership/Events Executive: Fiona MacDonald
Tel: 021-4778444

Golf Professional:
Tel: 021-4778444
Email: info@oldheadgolf.ie

Green Fees:
Weekdays and Weekends — IR£120

CARD OF THE COURSE — PAR 72

1	2	3	4	5	6	7	8	9	Out
420	387	153	407	405	488	164	496	449	3369
Par 4	Par 4	Par 3	Par 3	Par 4	Par 4	Par 5	Par 3	Par 4	Par 36

10	11	12	13	14	15	16	17	18	In
493	180	498	222	429	340	186	628	411	3387
Par 5	Par 3	Par 5	Par 3	Par 4	Par 4	Par 3	Par 5	Par 4	Par 36

HOW TO GET THERE

...ain Road from Cork to
...insale (R600). Through
...insale Town and take the
...ad to Garretstown/Old Head
...f Kinsale (R606).

Ring of Kerry

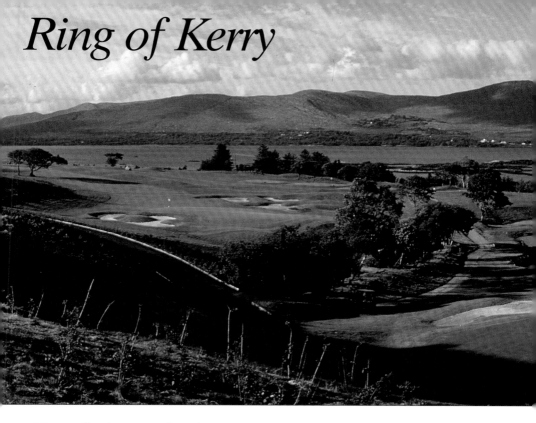

*U*ntil quite recent times it was suggested that golfing visitors to County Kerry should reserve one day for inland golf – either 18 or 36 holes at Killarney – and then spend the remainder of their time exploring the county's majestic links courses - specifically Ballybunion, Waterville and Tralee. Now golfers are strongly advised to keep two days for their inland sojourn.

The very new Ring of Kerry Golf and Country Club is the reason for the extension. Nestling between the soaring peaks of the Caha Mountains and the MacGillycuddy Reeks and overlooking Kenmare Bay, few golf courses in Ireland enjoy such a spectacular situation.

Ring of Kerry was one of the last designs of the late Eddie Hackett and some commentators regard it has his crowning achievement. Not only an excellent design, Ring of Kerry was built to the highest specifications and features sand-based fairways – so ensuring that the course drains quickly whenever the heavens open (and, let's face it, those lakes didn't get there by accident!). There are many outstanding holes at Ring of Kerry but among the best are the 6th (Ladies' View), the very strategic short par four 9th, and the par three 18th. Concluding the round with a short hole is unusual, though no different from the nearby Mahony's Point Course at Killarney. The 18th at Ring of Kerry isn't quite in the same league as that course's 'greatest par three finishing hole in golf', but generally speaking the course overall is just as good, and it is hard to pay Ring of Kerry a higher compliment than that.

HOW TO GET THERE

miles West of Kenmale
wn of the N70 Ring of
erry Road.

COURSE INFORMATION & FACILITIES

Ring of Kerry Golf & Country Club
Templenoe
Kenmale Co. Kerry Ireland

Secretary: Vincent Devlin
Tel: + 353 64 42000 Fax: + 353 64 42533

Green Fees:
Weekdays - £50 Weekends - £50
Weekdays (day) — 75 Weekends (day) - £75

Handicap Certificate required.

CARD OF THE COURSE — PAR 71

1	2	3	4	5	6	7	8	9	Out
386	381	179	541	454	383	186	505	307	3322
Par 4	Par 4	Par 3	Par 5	Par 5	Par 4	Par 3	Par 5	Par 4	Par 37

10	11	12	13	14	15	16	17	18	In
441	619	386	233	433	425	430	435	199	3601
Par 4	Par 5	Par 4	Par 3	Par 4	Par 4	Par 4	Par 4	Par 3	Par 35

Shannon

R elatively few golf courses were built in Ireland during the 1960s; one of the best, however, was the parkland course at Shannon in County Clare. John Harris was the architect responsible, and a more unlikely setting for a championship layout it is hard to imagine. Of course, Shannon wasn't as busy or as industrialised in the 1960s as it is today, but the land was essentially flat farmland - the perfect site for an airport runway and a few giant oil drums. Shannon Golf Club is laid out amidst all this, and yet, thanks to some magnificent landscaping, there are times when the golfer can feel 'miles from anywhere'. The number and the variety of trees and shrubs that have been planted since the course opened is staggering.

There is also one other very significant feature, namely the Shannon Estuary. It is visible from a number of holes and it comes into play most dramatically at the penultimate hole - Shannon's (more natural) version of the par three 17th at Kiawah Island!

The extensive landscaping is apparent as you play the first few holes; so too is the quality of the putting surfaces - Shannon boasts some of the best greens in Ireland. The outstanding hole on the front nine is undoubtedly the 8th, a glorious par five where the green is sited the far side of an attractive pond. The 17th is of course the most famous hole of all but the back nine also includes an excellent run of par fours from the 13th to the 16th.

COURSE INFORMATION & FACILITIES

Shannon Golf Club
Shannon,
Co. Clare

Secretary/Manager: Michael Corry
Tel: 061-471849 Fax: 061-471507

Golf Professional: 061-471551

Green Fees:
Weekdays — IR£22 Weekends — IR£27
Weekdays (days) — IR£22 Weekends (days) IR£27

Restrictions: Members time from 1-2pm
Pre-booking is advisable.

CARD OF THE COURSE — PAR 72

1	2	3	4	5	6	7	8	9	Out
373	493	407	170	320	501	369	498	458	3589
Par 4	Par 5	Par 4	Par 3	Par 4	Par 5	Par 4	Par 5	Par 4	Par 38

10	11	12	13	14	15	16	17	18	In
154	414	203	332	346	393	378	216	490	2926
Par 3	Par 4	Par 3	Par 4	Par 4	Par 4	Par 4	Par 3	Par 5	Par 34

HOW TO GET THERE

[Ta]ke the Shannon Airport
[ro]ad from Limerick City,
[co]ntinue past the airport and
[Go]lf Course is on the left
[00]0 yds from the Airport.

Tralee

*I*f you've seen the film, *'Ryan's Daughter'*, then you probably know that Tralee possesses one of the world's most glorious beaches, not to mention scenery that is unrivalled anywhere in Ireland.

The scenery hits you in all its glory from the moment you get to the first green and second tee. The vista is simply breathtaking and it is one that will enchant you for the rest of your round.

Arnold Palmer and Ed Seay are responsible for the layout at Tralee. Palmer had always wanted to create an Irish links course and was given the opportunity to do so in the early 1980s. Like the scenery, there are some holes that will take your breath away. The 2nd, for example, is a par five that runs along the clifftop, with a green placed perilously close to the edge – hit a wayward shot and it will land on the rocks far below! The 3rd hole is reminiscent of the 7th at Pebble Beach (albeit a longer version), where a shot is played to a green with the Atlantic Ocean dominating the backdrop. On the back nine you will no doubt find the par four 12th one of the most demanding two-shots in golf. At 434 yards it calls for a good drive followed by an extremely testing approach that must be played over a ravine to a plateau green. Make four here and you'll feel like you've birdied the hole. On the 13th you have to carry your shot over a deep chasm to find the putting surface – mercifully, it's only a 150 yard par three, but the bad news is that some days you have to hit a wood into the wind.

Still, if your round doesn't go quite to plan you can always admire the scenery!

HOW TO GET THERE

om Tralee, take the road to dfert. After 11 km, take the t turn to Spa/Fenit. After km, take the right turn to rrow Harbour and after the idge take the left fork.

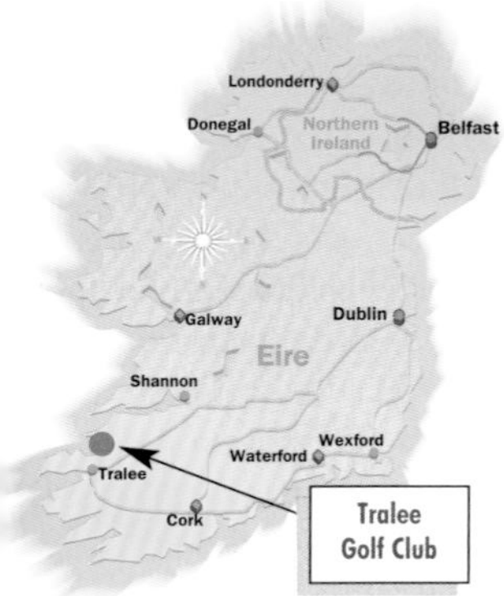

COURSE INFORMATION & FACILITIES

Tralee Golf Club
West Barrow, Ardfert, Tralee,
Co. Kerry.

Club Supervisor: Michael O Brien.
Tel: 066 36379. Fax: 066 36008.

Golf Professional: David Power.
Tel: 066 36379. Fax: 066 36008.

Green Fees:
Weekdays - £60, Weekends - £60. Not on Sunday
Handicap certificate required.

CARD OF THE COURSE (metres) — PAR 71

1	2	3	4	5	6	7	8	9	Out
368	542	183	388	391	389	143	354	451	3209
Par 4	Par 5	Par 3	Par 4	Par 4	Par 4	Par 3	Par 4	Par 5	Par 36
10	**11**	**12**	**13**	**14**	**15**	**16**	**17**	**18**	**In**
385	530	417	145	367	273	181	323	422	3043
Par 4	Par 5	Par 4	Par 3	Par 4	Par 4	Par 3	Par 4	Par 4	Par 35

Waterville

Jack Mulcahy was an Irish born American who, after making millions in the chemical business, sought a reason to return to Ireland for good. That reason became a golf course on the remote west coast of Ireland at Waterville.

Eddie Hackett was the man Mulcahy entrusted to create one of the finest links in all of golf. Built in 1973, it didn't take long for Waterville's reputation to grow. Now it's on the itinerary of every visiting American golfer.

Waterville is just about as natural a links course as you will find anywhere. True it starts slowly with the first and second being slightly inland, but by the time you get to the 417 yard, par 4, 3rd hole you know you're in for a treat. This hole is a slicer's nightmare, for the entire right hand side of the fairway hugs the Atlantic Ocean.

It is on the back nine that Waterville lives up to its premier billing. That's when you get to the meat of the course, so to speak. The 11th and 12th for example, are links holes that would grace any great seaside course. Eleven is a 496 yard, par 5 called Tranquillity which is played over a roller-coaster fairway through an avenue of tall dunes. It is one of the best par 5s in golf.

The 12th is called the Mass hole because priests used to say Mass in a large hollow immediately below the green during a time in Irish history when Catholicism was outlawed. You won't find priests today, but you may just pray that your ball reaches the plateau green.

Best view of the course is provided by Mulcahy's Peak, which is the teeing area for the superb par 3, 17th. Sit here for as long as you possibly can without holding up the group behind. The views are stunning. So is Waterville

COURSE INFORMATION & FACILITIES

Waterville Golf Links
Waterville,
Co. Kerry

Email: wvgolf@iol.ie
Web: www.watervillegolf.com

Manager: Noel Cronin.
Tel: 00 353 (0) 66-94 74102
Fax: 00 353 (0) 66-94 74482

Golf Professional Tel: 066-94 74102
Green Fees:

Weekdays — IR£100 Weekends — IR£100
Mon-Thurs before 8am & after 4pm IR£50
Handicap certificates required.

CARD OF THE COURSE — PAR 72

1	2	3	4	5	6	7	8	9	Out
430	469	417	179	595	387	178	435	445	3535
Par 4	Par 4	Par 4	Par 3	Par 5	Par 4	Par 3	Par 4	Par 4	Par 35

10	11	12	13	14	15	16	17	18	In
475	606	200	518	456	407	350	196	582	3690
Par 4	Par 5	Par 3	Par 5	Par 4	Par 4	Par 4	Par 3	Par 5	Par 37

HOW TO GET THERE

...uated half way on the Ring
Kerry. ¹/₄ mile off the main
...g off Kerry Road, on the
...ast.

The Midlands

The Midlands

*M*any of the 'Golfing Gems' featured in this book are either seaside courses (links and clifftop) or parkland courses situated within striking distance of the coast. There are no real heathland courses to speak of in Ireland, certainly there is no Woodhall Spa or Walton Heath, and until the early 1990s there weren't too many top notch parkland courses either. Not surprisingly then, most foreign visitors have tended to head straight for the coast – frequently to the west of Ireland but sometimes to Northern Ireland or North Dublin – and they have rarely ventured inland (Killarney, of course, like Gleneagles in Scotland, is the one great exception).

Since Links land is a precious and rare commodity these days, even in Ireland, the vast majority of new courses that have been built since 1990 have been parkland courses. True, a good number of these are located fairly close to Dublin, the most celebrated being The K Club and Druids Glen, but a number have also been created in the less fashionable regions of the 'Irish Midlands'. And such is the quality of Mount Juliet, Slieve Russell and Glasson, to name the leading three, that travelling golfers have now begun to journey further and further inland.

Singlehandedly, it would seem, Mount Juliet has put the south east of Ireland on the golfing map. Golfers inspecting the impressive Jack Nicklaus designed course at Thomastown have naturally enquired as to the quality of other courses in the vicinity, and so the likes of nearby Kilkenny (an above average 'traditional' parkland layout) and Carlow (a superb parkland-cum-moorland course) are at last being discovered.

To the north of Carlow at Tullow there is a visually striking new course laid out within the grounds of the Mount Wolseley Estate – it too is well worth viewing. Golfers heading west out of Dublin should try to fit a game in at Mullingar, a beautifully mature parkland course in County Westmeath, and towards the south of County Kildare, not too great a distance from

The K Club, another attractive new course wraps itself around 12th century Kilkea Castle.

So to Glasson and Slieve Russell, two courses located in areas far more renowned for their fishing than golf but which we strongly urge you to explore. While Mount Juliet, The K Club and Druids Glen may have received most of the commentators' accolades, Glasson near Athlone is more scenic that any of the illustrious trio (it has been described as 'the Killarney of the Irish Midlands') and Slieve Russell at Ballyconnell in County Cavan provides a strong and absorbing a test of golf. Glasson, then, is one for the romantic and Slieve Russell one of the brave. Together, Glasson and Slieve Russell underline the new depth and diversity of Irish inland golf; but as yet they remain largely undiscovered – they are the true hidden gems of the Emerald Isle.

CARLOW
ESKER HILLS
GLASSON
KILKENNY

MOUNT JULIET
MOUNT WOLSELEY
MULLINGAR
SLIEVE RUSSELL

The Midlands

Page

©MAPS IN MINUTES™ 2001.
©Crown Copyright, Ordnance
Survey Northern Ireland 2001 Permit
No. NI 1675 & ©Government of
Ireland, Ordnance Survey Ireland.

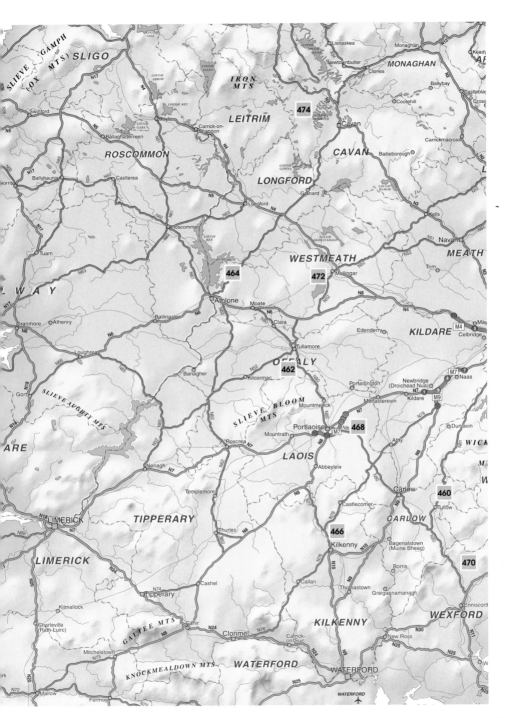

Carlow

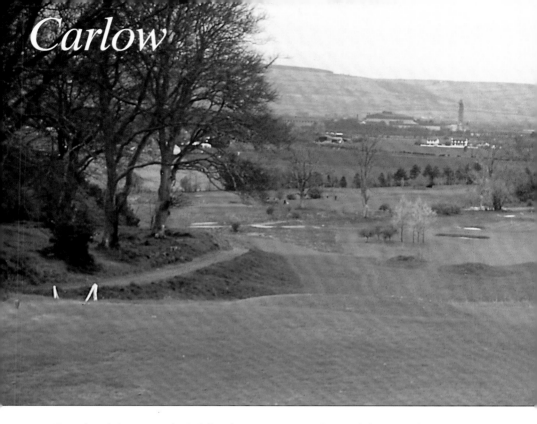

arlow is home to the Midland Scratch Cup every October. Such is the quality of this fine inland course that it nearly always attracts a quality field. Among the winners of this prestigious event is Peter McEvoy, who managed to shoot 11 consecutive rounds under 70. That's impressive, given that the course's SSS is 70.

There are only two par-5s on Carlow, the 5th and the 18th, and both offer good birdie opportunities. That's more than can be said about the par-3s, which are elusive birdie holes. Best among these is the 17th, an uphill par-3 which calls for more club than the 146 yards indicated on the card. The hole is well bunkered, so an accurate iron shot is need to find the putting surface if you are to have any chance of making a birdie or par.

The 17th is part of a good closing stretch that begins at the tough, 455-yard, par-4 14th hole. Play well over these holes and you have a chance of returning a good score. The trees, too, seem to encroach on the holes on the back nine, calling for straighter shots on the run in.

Of the holes on the front nine, the 8th is the one that will probably stay in your memory. The tee on this 426-yard, par-4 is the highest point on the course, and the drive must be played downhill through an avenue of tall trees that frame the fairway. A straight drive is a must.

Carlow is blessed with excellent turf, so that golf is usually playable 12 months of the year.

HOW TO GET THERE

5 miles north of Carlow
~wn on the Dublin Road
~19).

Carlow
Golf Club

COURSE INFORMATION & FACILITIES

 Carlow Golf Club
Deerpark,
Carlow

Secretary: Margaret Meaney
Tel: 0503-31695 Fax: 0503-40065

Golf Professional Tel: 0503-41745

Green Fees:
Weekdays — IR£20 Weekends — IR£25

CARD OF THE COURSE (metres) — PAR 70

1	2	3	4	5	6	7	8	9	Out
395	275	124	333	450	163	389	390	335	2857
Par 4	Par 4	Par 3	Par 4	Par 5	Par 3	Par 4	Par 4	Par 4	Par 35

10	11	12	13	14	15	16	17	18	In
273	381	334	150	415	334	393	134	450	2874
Par 4	Par 4	Par 4	Par 3	Par 4	Par 4	Par 4	Par 3	Par 5	Par 35

Esker Hills

Golfing visitors to Ireland have traditionally headed for the coast. The quality of the country's links courses, from Portmarnock and Royal Dublin to Ballybunion and Lahinch, is undoubtedly tremendous; however the Emerald Isle does contain an increasing number of inland gems and the Esker Hills Golf and Country club, which opened in 1996, is quickly establishing itself as one of the best of the newcomers.

Built over a unique and extraordinary piece of terrain known as 'the Eskers', and designed by Christy O'Connor Jnr., architect of the Irish midlands' other outstanding new course, Glasson, Esker Hills occupies a site of 150 acres and straddles a series of glacial ridges. Mother Nature has moulded the landscape into a series of valleys and plateaux which together with the existence of natural lakes and woodlands makes for ideal golfing terrain. It was this overwhelmingly natural environment that made such an impression on O'Connor: "Rarely on a first site visit have I been so impressed, not just by the beautifully contoured Esker Riada Hills, but the sweeping valleys, lakes and woodlands, and panoramic views of the pastoral landscape with the backdrop of the Slieve Bloom Mountains. This is destined to be one of the great Irish courses".

Christy's comments may be a little biased, but a trip to Esker Hills will very likely confirm his enthusiasm. It is an exceptional golf course - at once challenging (especially the 211 yards par three 11th and the 592 yards par five 16th), visually spectacular and great fun to play: the golfer who omits Esker Hills from his midlands' itinerary is missing a rare treat.

COURSE INFORMATION & FACILITIES

Esker Hills Golf Club
Tullamore
Co. Offaly. Ireland

Secretary/Manager: Donal Molloy
Tel: 0506 55999 Fax: 0506 55021

Green Fees:
Weekdays — £20 Weekends — £27

CARD OF THE COURSE — PAR 71

1	2	3	4	5	6	7	8	9	Out
491	392	479	404	174	525	394	357	221	3337
Par 5	Par 4	Par 4	Par 4	Par 3	Par 5	Par 4	Par 4	Par 3	Par 36

10	11	12	13	14	15	16	17	18	In
401	363	166	310	353	172	592	419	397	3275
Par 4	Par 4	Par 3	Par 4	Par 4	Par 3	Par 5	Par 4	Par 4	Par 35

HOW TO GET THERE

miles from Tullamore off
e main Tullamore to Clara
oad in Mid Ireland.

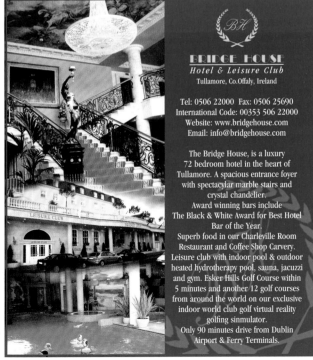

BRIDGE HOUSE
Hotel & Leisure Club
Tullamore, Co.Offaly, Ireland

Tel: 0506 22000 Fax: 0506 25690
International Code: 00353 506 22000
Website: www.bridgehouse.com
Email: info@bridgehouse.com

The Bridge House, is a luxury
72 bedroom hotel in the heart of
Tullamore. A spacious entrance foyer
with spectacylar marble stairs and
crystal chandelier.
Award winning bars include
The Black & White Award for Best Hotel
Bar of the Year.
Superb food in our Charleville Room
Restaurant and Coffee Shop Carvery.
Leisure club with indoor pool & outdoor
heated hydrotherapy pool, sauna, jacuzzi
and gym. Esker Hills Golf Course within
5 minutes and another 12 golf courses
from around the world on our exclusive
indoor world club golf virtual reality
golfing sinmulator.
Only 90 minutes drive from Dublin
Airport & Ferry Terminals.

Glasson

While Irish golf and great scenery almost go hand in hand, don't think that golf courses with great views are only restricted to the seaside. There's beauty to be found inland as well.

Glasson Golf and Country Club is just one of many excellent Irish courses where the scenery is quite simply spectacular.

Christy O'Connor Jnr is responsible for the Glasson layout, and he was blessed with 175 acres of land that provides some of the best views in all of Ireland. Glasson is situated beside Killinure Bay on Lough Ree, a large inland lake some 17 miles long which is connected to the River Shannon.

O'Connor Jnr has made good use of the land he was given to produce a par-72 course that measures just over 7,000 yards. (So good that the bay or the lough is visible from all 18 holes.) Here you will find a good variety of golf, including a good mix of long and short holes. The third is perhaps one of the best so called short holes. This a 219-yard, par-3 that has to be played over a swale to a plateau green with Lough Ree providing a superb backdrop. After two fairly generous opening holes, you know the game is on at the third. Glasson just gets better as you proceed to the 19th hole.

Christy saved his best efforts for the last half dozen holes, holes which provide magnificent views of the lough, especially from the back tee at the par-5 14th. Here the tee is situated on high ground, from where you are provided with a panoramic view of Killinure Bay. The bay even comes into play for the approach shot, as it lies near the left side of the green.

Don't worry about the golf – the walk will be just fine.

COURSE INFORMATION & FACILITIES

Glasson Golf & Country Club
Glasson, Athlone,
Co. Westmeath

Web: www.glassongolf.ie
Email: info@glassongolf.ie

Operations Manager: Fidelma Reid
Tel: 0902-85120 Fax: 0902-85444

Green Fees:
Mon-Thurs: IR£32 Fri/Sun: IR£35 Sat:IR£40

CARD OF THE COURSE — PAR 72

1	2	3	4	5	6	7	8	9	Out
396	552	219	406	199	559	410	432	412	3585
Par 4	Par 5	Par 3	Par 4	Par 3	Par 5	Par 4	Par 4	Par 4	Par 36

10	11	12	13	14	15	16	17	18	In
513	183	406	397	566	185	452	450	383	3535
Par 5	Par 3	Par 4	Par 4	Par 5	Par 3	Par 4	Par 4	Par 4	Par 36

HOW TO GET THERE

/₂ hours from Dublin/
alway/Shannon.
miles north of Athlone on
55. Turn left at Glasson
llage Restaurant
d Golf Club is
/₂ miles away.

Hodson Bay Hotel

ATHLONE, COUNTY WESTMEATH, IRELAND

Fairytale Lakeside Setting on the shores of Lough Ree adjacent to Athlone Golf Club. The Hodson Bay Hotel boasts 133 Deluxe Ensuite Bedrooms with breathtaking views of the lake and surrounding islands. The Award Winning L'Escale Restaurant serves fresh Irish produce daily specialising in fish. The lively Waterfront Bar and Buttery is the ideal 19th Hole. Other facilities include Garden Restaurant, Leisure Centre, Swimming Pool, Sauna, Steam Room, Children's Playroom With 10 Championship Golf Courses within 40 minutes drive the Hodson Bay Hotel is a golfers Haven. Other activities nearby include Boat Trips, Watersports, Horse Riding and many Historical Sites.

Tel: (0902) 80500 Fax: (0902) 80520
Email: info@hodsonbayhotel.com
Website: www.hodsonbayhotel.com

465

Kilkenny

Kilkenny's 18 hole golf course is no great distance from Mount Juliet and yet the two layouts are like chalk and cheese. Kilkenny Golf Club celebrated its centenary in 1986; its members have played on the present site since 1923 and it is a very typical Irish parkland golf course. Mount Juliet is a new golf course plucked from Ohio and planted in rural Ireland - very good, for sure, but (in the opinion of the traditionalists) not very Irish.

Kilkenny ranks among the top dozen or so of the country's established inland courses. Maybe it is not quite in the very top echelon, but it is well worth inspecting. And of course, the town of Kilkenny merits detailed investigation. This is one of Ireland's most famous 'small' towns and is steeped in history. Kilkenny was once the home of the Irish Parliament; its Castle, its churches and its numerous medieval buildings are fascinating.

But back to the fairways. Kilkenny opens with an inviting, downhill drive. The first major test comes at the 3rd, a long two-shotter, and this is followed by two handsome par fours. Along with the 4th and 5th, the finest hole on the front nine is the 7th, a gently curving dog-leg with a fiercely defended green. The 11th, which again sweeps from right to left is the outstanding par four on the back nine but the most memorable hole of all is the short 17th, where the tee shot must be fired across a gorse and tree filled chasm.

HOW TO GET THERE

utskirts of Kilkenny city just
ast Newpark Hotel.

Kilkenny
Golf Club

COURSE INFORMATION & FACILITIES

Kilkenny Golf Club
Glendine, Kilkenny
Co. Kilkenny

Secretary: Sean O Neill
Tel: 056-65400

Golf Professional: Tel: 056-61730

Green Fees:
Weekdays — IR£20 Weekends — IR£25
Weekdays (day) — IR£20 Weekends (day) — IR£25

CARD OF THE COURSE — PAR 71

1	2	3	4	5	6	7	8	9	Out
353	295	358	320	273	125	357	353	435	2869
Par 4	Par 4	Par 4	Par 4	Par 4	Par 3	Par 4	Par 4	Par 5	Par 36

10	11	12	13	14	15	16	17	18	In
183	395	447	354	441	172	350	153	310	2805
Par 3	Par 4	Par 5	Par 4	Par 5	Par 3	Par 4	Par 3	Par 4	Par 35

Mount Juliet

O f all recent Irish courses laid out on former country estates, Mount Juliet may just be the best. Nick Faldo certainly thinks so – he loves the place.

The main reason Faldo loves the golf course is that it's always in first class condition. The Englishman ostensibly moved to the United States so he could play on good quality courses throughout the year. If European professional tournaments were held on courses like Mount Juliet, he would probably move back home permanently.

Mount Juliet had the best start in life, because the best was brought in to design the golf course. Jack Nicklaus was entrusted with the task of making Mount Juliet the best inland course in Ireland.

Quite simply, Mount Juliet is a top notch course in top notch condition. You won't find better fairways and greens in all of Ireland. You'll be hard pressed to find a better selection of holes too. This a golf course laid out in beautiful parkland, with many ponds and mature trees.

Nicklaus has made excellent use of the land to shape the holes. Best on the front nine is the par-3, 3rd and the par-4, 4th. The former calls for a good tee shot over water to a green with lots of room on the right but little on the left. In other words, pray the pin is on the right when you get to the tee. The 4th calls for an accurate tee shot to a narrow fairway and then an approach to a green with water on the right. Many balls land on the left side of this green.

On the back nine the run of holes from the par-3, 11th to the par-3, 14th is as good a stretch as you will find anywhere.

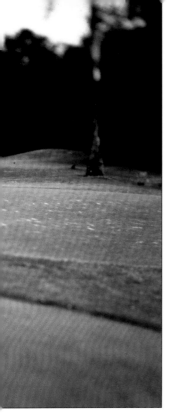

COURSE INFORMATION & FACILITIES

Mount Juliet Golf Club
Thomastown,
Co. Kilkenny

Director of Golf: Kim Thomas
Tel: 056-73062 Fax: 056-73069

Golf Professional Ted Higgins
Tel: 056-73070/1 Fax: 056 73069
Email: info@mountjuliet.ie

Green Fees:
Weekdays — IR£50 Weekends — IR£60 Low
Weekdays (day) — IR£75 Weekends (day) — IR£85. High
Weekdays (day) — IR£85 Weekends (day) — IR£100. Premium

CARD OF THE COURSE — PAR 72

1	2	3	4	5	6	7	8	9	Out
363	414	184	402	534	229	417	577	424	3544
Par 4	Par 4	Par 3	Par 4	Par 5	Par 3	Par 4	Par 5	Par 4	Par 36

10	11	12	13	14	15	16	17	18	In
546	168	417	436	197	371	433	515	474	3557
Par 5	Par 3	Par 4	Par 4	Par 3	Par 4	Par 4	Par 5	Par 4	Par 36

rom Dublin Airport head south
n M50, then M7 to NAAS,
M9 to Castledermot and
Carlow — follow main
Dublin to Waterford Road for
0 minutes
which leads
Thomastown.

MOUNT JULIET

ONE OF EUROPE'S GREAT COUNTRY ESTATES

*1,500 walled acres of unspoilt woodland, pasture and
formal gardens, secluded in the southeast of the
country, yet close to Dublin, London and continental cities.*

Enjoy an almost endless variety of outdoor pursuits amid the
magnificent scenery and pure country air of the estate. Mount
Juliet offers a truly unique sporting experience from the most
energetic activities to the more sedate. Built over 200 years ago,
Mount Juliet House still retains an aura of 18th century
grandeur, whilst the Hunters Yard & Rose Garden Lodges offer
more rustic and casual accommodation.

**Thomastown, County Kilkenny, Ireland
Telephone: 353 56 73000   Fax: 353 56 73019
email: info@mountjuliet.ie
Website: mountjuliet.ie**

Mount Wolseley

I f there isn't an annual match between Mount Wolseley in County Carlow and The Rolls of Monmouth Golf Club in Wales there should be. Mount Wolseley was the ancestral home of Frederick York Wolseley who gave his name to the famous Wolseley motor car; The Rolls of Monmouth is named after Charles Stewart Rolls who teamed up with Henry Royce to create you-know-what. Both Welsh and Irish estates now possess a first class 18 hole golf course: The Rolls opened in 1982 and Mount Wolseley, or rather The Mount Wolseley Golf and Country Club, took its bow as recently as 1995.

Course architect Christy O'Connor Jnr was given the brief to build a modern championship length layout and he clearly achieved as much.

On commencement O'Connor remarked, "This is an incredibly beautiful stretch of land where the addition of water at seven holes and an expansive tree planting programme will add to the challenge of a round of golf here at any time of year". Water is certainly a dominant feature of the new course and if there is a signature hole then it may be the 11th, a do-or-die par three which, from the back tees, requires a 200 yard carry across water to the green.

Situated on the edge of Tullow, Mount Wolseley is just 40 miles from Dublin and 55 miles from Rosslare. It is very accessible and there are some magnificent views of Mount Leinster and the Blackstairs to the south and glimpses of the Wicklow Mountains to the east.

HOW TO GET THERE

ituated 40 miles from Dublin
ke the Naas by pass on to
astledermont. Turn left on to
ullow Road it is signposted
Tullow.

COURSE INFORMATION & FACILITIES

Mount Wolseley Golf and Country Club
Tullow, Co. Carlow
Ireland

Secretary/Director: Ann-Marie Morrissey
Tel: 0503-51674 Fax: 0503-52123

Golf Professional: 0503-51391

Green Fees:
Weekdays — IR£25 Weekends — IR£30
Society Rates — 10% discount on groups of 20

Restrictions: Members have tee up to 10.30 and after 4.30

CARD OF THE COURSE — PAR 72

1	2	3	4	5	6	7	8	9	Out
411	447	447	273	499	210	542	440	191	3460
Par 4	Par 4	Par 4	Par 4	Par 5	Par 3	Par 5	Par 4	Par 3	Par 36

10	11	12	13	14	15	16	17	18	In
592	207	519	427	339	466	226	457	413	3646
Par 5	Par 3	Par 5	Par 4	Par 4	Par 4	Par 3	Par 4	Par 4	Par 36

Mullingar

Sylvan is an adjective commonly used to describe the setting at Mullingar, and when one adds the indisputable quality of the golf course and the friendliness of the welcome to the equation, it is easy to see why this is one of Ireland's most popular clubs to visit.

And yet, before the War the most accurate word to describe the Mullingar golfer - or at least the early Mullingar member - might have been 'pernickety'. This is because by the mid 1930s, less than 50 years after the club's creation, the golfers were already searching for a fifth home. Pernicketiness obviously paid off, though, for when they discovered the magnificently wooded site at Belvedere, situated just south of Mullingar and close to the peace and

beauty of Lough Ennell, they knew at once that they had struck gold.

Today the club annually hosts one of Ireland's premier amateur competitions, the Mullingar Scratch Cup: winners have included such famous names as Joe Carr, Peter Townsend, Des Smyth and Philip Walton.

The most celebrated hole at Mullingar is probably the 2nd, a long and difficult par three where the pin sits on a small, slippery table of a green flanked by pot bunkers on either side. The par fives are not especially frightening, each presenting a genuine birdie opportunity, while the two-shot holes possess considerable character and variety. A selection of the best par fours at Mullingar would likely include the 7th, 8th, 10th, 11th and 17th.

COURSE INFORMATION & FACILITIES

Mullingar Golf Club
Belvedere, Mullingar
Co. Westmeath

Secretary: Brian Kiely
Tel: 044-48366 Fax: 044-41499

Golf Professional: Tel: 044-40085

Green Fees:
Weekdays — IR£20 Weekends — IR£25

CARD OF THE COURSE — PAR 72

1	2	3	4	5	6	7	8	9	Out
338	189	389	486	186	330	453	343	338	3052
Par 4	Par 3	Par 4	Par 5	Par 3	Par 4	Par 4	Par 4	Par 4	Par 35

10	11	12	13	14	15	16	17	18	In
433	388	152	370	480	162	493	417	511	3406
Par 4	Par 4	Par 3	Par 4	Par 5	Par 3	Par 5	Par 4	Par 5	Par 37

HOW TO GET THERE

Golf Course is located 3 miles
from Mullingar town on the
Tullamore Road.

Marshbrook Manor
at The Well
Moate, Co. Westmeath

Beautiful Pre-famine Manor House situated in the
Real Centre of Ireland half way Dublin/Galway Road
on 41 acres of wooded and hilly land with river
running through it.

Phone: (0902) 81069
Fax: (0902) 81539

Slieve Russell

Deep in the countryside of County Cavan a remarkable hotel and championship golf course seemingly 'sprang from nowhere' in the early 1990s and now demands to be discovered. Ballyconnell is the place - a small town in a quiet, sleepy part of Ireland, one much more renowned as a fisherman's paradise than a golfer's, although this would appear set to change.

The unsuspecting traveller's first impression of the Slieve Russell Hotel is that it must be an incredible mirage. The knowledgeable golfer's lasting impression of Slieve Russell is that it is an extraordinary oasis. Designed by Paddy Merrigan and opened in 1992, Slieve Russell is now widely acknowledged as one of Ireland's finest new courses.

Two large lakes connected by a wandering stream are the dominant features of the layout and they are responsible for creating several outstanding and dramatic holes. Water, in fact, must be confronted as early as the 2nd, a marvellous swinging dog-leg where, after trying to avoid the lake to the left of the fairway with the drive, the approach must be played over the stream to a raised and two tiered green. Both the 2nd and rollercoasting 3rd are superb par fours, but Slieve Russell's quartet of short holes - especially the picturesque 16th - will probably leave an even greater impression on the mind of the first time visitor, as will the amazing par five 13th where for its entire length the fairway follows the curving edge of the second lake.

rom Dublin, follow the N3
rough Navan and Cavan
wn to Belturbet and then
llow the signs to
allyconnell village.

Slieve Russell
Golf Club

COURSE INFORMATION & FACILITIES

Slieve Russell Hotel, Golf & Country Club
Ballyconnell,
Co. Cavan

Golf Director: P J Creamer
Tel: 049 26444 Fax: 049 26474

Golf Professional: Liam McCool

Green Fees:
Weekdays — IR£28 Weekends — IR£36

CARD OF THE COURSE — PAR 72

1	2	3	4	5	6	7	8	9	Out
399	407	371	159	412	491	196	338	509	3282
Par 4	Par 4	Par 4	Par 3	Par 4	Par 5	Par 3	Par 4	Par 5	Par 36

10	11	12	13	14	15	16	17	18	In
393	168	434	502	356	426	165	369	519	3333
Par 4	Par 3	Par 4	Par 5	Par 4	Par 4	Par 3	Par 4	Par 5	Par 36

South East

The South East

*T*his corner of Ireland is famous for cut glass, for it is in this region that you will find Waterford. You will also find a few courses not far from the crystal factory that are well worth a visit. Until 1991 there were really only two courses to speak of in this area – Tramore and Waterford Golf Club. Mind you, they were courses you could speak volumes about. Waterford, for example, was designed by Willie Park and with later alterations by James Braid. Whenever two Open champions have a hand in the creation of any course, it is well worth playing.

In recent times the number of Irish courses has simply mushroomed. European money was responsible for this explosion, and many clubs have come into being throughout the island. The boom in Irish golf has not missed Waterford. There are at least four courses in the area that have been developed from 1991. (Who knows, by the time you read this there may be a few more). Dunmore East, Faithlegg, Waterford Castle and West Waterford have all come into existence in the '90s, making the region an attractive destination for visiting golfers. Waterford Castle is especially worthy of a visit. A Des Smyth designed layout, the golf course sits on an island in the River Suir. Don't worry if the odd boat passes you by, it'll only add to your round of golf.

To the east of County Waterford is Wexford, a county famous for its glorious unspoilt beaches and its favourable climate (the Sunshine Coast, they call it). Rosslare is the principal city in these parts and it is where many overseas visitors gain their first experience of Ireland. There are two good courses near Rosslare and its famous harbour, Rosslare Golf Club and St Helen's Bay – one is almost one hundred years old, the other is very new. St Helen's Bay is the new course: part links, part parkland, it was designed by Philip Walton. As for Rosslare, its principal architect was mother nature. It is an extremely natural looking links – old fashioned and brimming with character.

This region not one frequented by many visiting golfers, so you may find it easier to get a game here than in areas such as Dublin, Kerry and Northern Ireland, although with the number of good new courses, it's a safe bet that this area will soon be attracting more and more golfers. With airports at Waterford and Cork (no great distance to the west) and ferry terminals at Rosslare and Cork, it is very accessible.

FAITHLEGG
ROSSLARE
ST HELEN'S BAY

TRAMORE
WATERFORD
WATERFORD CASTLE

South East

Page

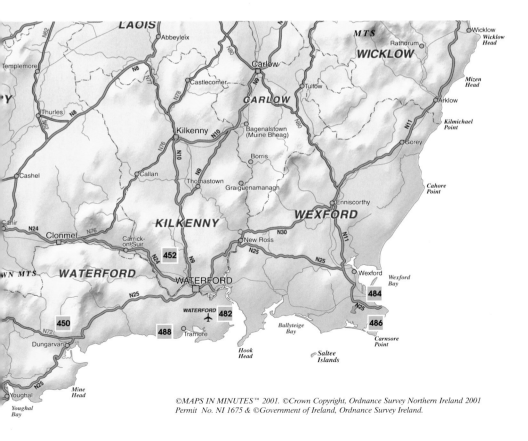

Faithlegg

*I*f you're going to play Faithlegg, then get lots of putting practice in beforehand. This lovely course in County Waterford is renowned for its undulating greens, placing pressure not only on the short game, but on your approach play as well. Paddy Merrigan is the man responsible for numerous three putts, for he designed Faithlegg.

Merrigan was given a great piece of land on the banks of the River Suir on which to create a golf course that runs to just over 6,700 yards with a par of 72. It's not a conventional 72, however, as the front nine plays to a par of 34, while 38 is the score the scratch man is supposed to match on the inward nine. As you would expect from the above figures, the inward half is much longer than the outward nine, by over 700 yards.

The difference in length of the two nines would seem to indicate that you should take advantage of the outward nine, but that's not as easy as it sounds. While it's over 700 yards shorter, it's basically because the nine comprises only one par-5 and three par-3s.

The first is fairly short at 293-yards, calling for a drive and a flick. The fourth, too, is no slog at 348-yards, but the other holes aren't easy by any means. There are three par-4s around 400-yards, and the par-3, 6th hole measures 205 yards.

The back nine is the complete reverse of the outward half, inasmuch as it contains only one par-3 and three par-5s. Don't expect to tear Faithlegg apart, though, as it's a fairly stiff test for most handicap levels.

Faithlegg is dominated by Faithlegg House, an outstanding building that was built in 1783. There are plans are to turn the magnificent building into a hotel at some point in the future.

COURSE INFORMATION & FACILITIES

Faithlegg Golf Club
Faithlegg, Cheekpoint,
Co. Waterford

Director: Ted Higgins
Tel: 051-382241 Fax: 051-382664

Green Fees:
Weekdays — IR£22 Weekends —IR£25
Weekdays (day) — IR£32 Weekends (day) — IR£35

CARD OF THE COURSE (metres) — PAR 72

1	2	3	4	5	6	7	8	9	Out
268	454	149	319	385	187	378	356	142	2638
Par 4	Par 5	Par 3	Par 4	Par 4	Par 3	Par 4	Par 4	Par 3	Par 34

10	11	12	13	14	15	16	17	18	In
448	362	401	455	465	339	150	395	404	3419
Par 5	Par 4	Par 4	Par 5	Par 5	Par 4	Par 3	Par 4	Par 4	Par 38

HOW TO GET THERE

 miles from Waterford. Take
Dunmore East Road towards
Cheekpoint village.

483

Rosslare

For many overseas visitors Rosslare is the gateway to Ireland. Situated not far from the busy ferry port is Rosslare golf links, and stories abound of touring golfers who have dropped in on the course, played 18 holes, and then never ventured beyond Rosslare for the remainder of their trip - the links is that good! Yet you rarely see Rosslare ranked among the top 30 or 40 courses in Ireland, which it surely deserves to be. The club is old enough and established enough but presumably it gets overlooked by critics because the links is forever being tinkered with, the layout forever being revised or refined.

Rosslare is 'The Island of the South East': a splendidly old fashioned links with some magnificent duneland terrain. The fairways twist and tumble in a manner very reminiscent of the north Dublin course. True, some holes are a little quirky, a little too blind for the purists, but Rosslare has enormous character. There are also some magnificent views - the course starts and finishes under a canopy of beautiful sea pines and almost half the holes are played very close to the sea.

Some solid hitting is required to master Rosslare's exacting finishing stretch, from the 15th onwards, but the most interesting sequence comes between the 4th and the 7th, and the last of these, a superb rollercoasting par five, is the best on the course. Other note-worthy holes are the 11th, 13th and 14th, all of which exude charm - a quality Rosslare has in abundance.

Rosslare Golf Links
Rosslare Strand
Co. Wexford

Secretary: Emily Ward
Tel: 00353 53 32203 ext 3 Fax: 00353 53 32263

Golf Professional: Johnny Young
Tel:00353 53 32032

Green Fees:
Weekdays — IR£25 Weekends — IR£35
Please ring for bookings. Tuesday — Ladies Day.

CARD OF THE COURSE — PAR 72

1	2	3	4	5	6	7	8	9	Out
382	194	542	373	443	335	554	177	414	3414
Par 4	Par 3	Par 5	Par 4	Par 3	Par 4	Par 5	Par 3	Par 4	Par 36

10	11	12	13	14	15	16	17	18	In
167	481	494	282	172	403	400	420	482	3301
Par 3	Par 4	Par 5	Par 4	Par 3	Par 4	Par 4	Par 4	Par 5	Par 36

HOW TO GET THERE

 miles from ferry terminal at
osslare Harbour, 10 miles
outh of Wexford town.

Rosslare
Golf Club

The Crosbie Cedars Hotel is a grade AA*** hotel situated in the heart of Rosslare. The hotel provides 34 elegant and tastefully designed en-suite bedrooms which include direct dial telephone, satellite colour TV, radio and tea/coffee making facilities.

Our delightful a-la-carte restaurant, with a capacity for up to 90 diners, serves an interesting menu of national & International cuisine. Our traditionally styled hotel also features the 'Bunker Pub' & 'The Tavern' ensuring a comfortable and relaxing stay for all. A haven of outstanding quality, offering true Irish warmth and hospitality. Ideal golf centre within easy reach of Rosslare golf course.

Golf rates and packages available.

Rosslare,
Co Wexford, Ireland

Tel: 053-32124
Fax: 053-32243

E-mail: info@crosbiecedars.iol.ie
Web: www.crosbiecedarshotel.com

St. Helen's Bay

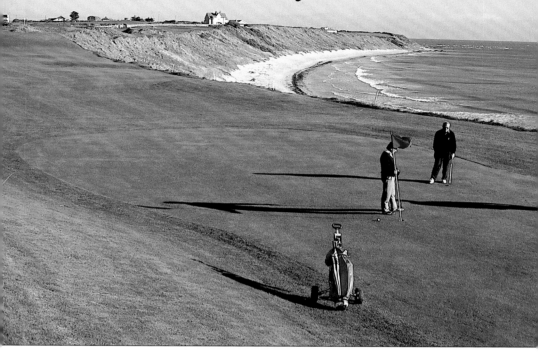

*M*any Irish courses are steeped in the island's history. On them you will find old castles, or towers or ruined ring forts, all sorts of relics from Ireland's colourful days of yore. Such is St. Helen's Bay.

Situated about three miles from Rosslare Harbour in County Wexford, St. Helens Bay has a 13th century tower near the 12th hole and nearly a mile of stone walls that date back to the Great Potato Famine, a devastating event in Irish history that claimed the lives of about one million people. The walls have been lovingly restored and incorporated into the design of the golf course, for example one of those old walls runs down the right side of the 18th fairway.

Like Seapoint near Dublin, the course is a mixture of parkland and links golf

rolled into one. Five lakes have been incorporated into the design, and thousands of trees have been planted to give definition to some of the holes.

European Tour professional Philip Walton is responsible for the design of St. Helens, and he has created a golf course beside one of the loveliest beaches you will find in all of Ireland. It's called Pirates Cove, for it was used long ago by the bad boys of the seven seas. The last two holes sit tight by this beach. Hook the ball at the last and you will be wishing you had thought to bring a bucket and spade, for the ball will be sitting on the sand.

St. Helens measures just under 7,000 from the back tees, but play it from more sensible markers for the wind always blows on this part of the Wexford coastline.

COURSE INFORMATION & FACILITIES

St. Helen's Bay Golf & Country Club
Kilrane, Rosslare Harbour,
Co. Wexford

Managing Director: Larry Byrne
Tel: 053-33234 Fax: 053-33803

Green Fees:

Weekdays — IR£25 Weekends — IR£28. (High)
Weekdays — IR£20 Weekends — IR£25. (Low)

CARD OF THE COURSE (metres) — PAR 72

1	2	3	4	5	6	7	8	9	Out
410	379	192	288	305	308	165	412	478	2937
Par 5	Par 4	Par 3	Par 4	Par 4	Par 4	Par 3	Par 4	Par 5	Par 36

10	11	12	13	14	15	16	17	18	In
488	175	406	419	299	567	368	192	240	3154
Par 5	Par 3	Par 4	Par 4	Par 4	Par 5	Par 4	Par 3	Par 4	Par 36

HOW TO GET THERE

From Port of Rosslare —
left 1 mile at Kilrane and
follow signs.
On N11 — 90 miles (Dublin)
right at Kilrane.

ST. HELEN'S BAY GOLF & COUNTRY CLUB

Luxury on site accommodation available. Two and three
bedroomed cottages (Bord Failte Approved 3***) beside the
beach, also tennis courts, bars and dining room. Ideal for
family holidays or golf outings.
Green fee and society friendly, playable all year round.
Only 5 minutes from Rosslare Ferryport.

Electricity – coin-operated meter, colour TV, washing machine,
linen provided, open fire, parking, sorry strictly no pets, shops
nearby, babysitting by arrangement, private garden.

St. Helen's, Kilrane, Rosslare Harbour, Co. Wexford
Tel: 053-33234 Fax: 053-33803

E-mail: sthelens@iol.ie

Website: www.sthelensbay.com

Tramore

Tramore Golf Club started out as a seaside course away back in 1894. However, the members have been gradually forced inland over the years.

Flooding from the sea forced the first move. Sea water broke through protective sand banks surrounding the original 9-hole layout, flooding the course. As a temporary measure, a new course was created inside the local racetrack until, in 1939, Tramore occupied the present site. The new location allowed the club to expand to the 18 holes which exist today.

Tramore was honoured in 1987 when the Irish Close Championship was held there. Eddie Power won the event that year, but being a member of the club he had the benefit of local knowledge. While the increased length of today's professionals might make it a bit short for the game's top players, at 6,700 yards Tramore is worthy of the game's top amateurs. Besides the Irish Close, the Irish Ladies Amateur Championship has been held there twice, in 1975 and '88. It's also a good course that all levels of handicap will enjoy.

Fairly flat with broad fairways and not too many bunkers, Tramore can offer up good scores. Excellent turf and equally excellent putting surfaces mean you should seldom find a poor lie or need to complain about bad greens. It doesn't pay to be too overconfident, though, for there are some tricky doglegs and holes that call for accuracy off the tee.

Many trees were planted when the course was created and now provide definition and a splendid backdrop for many of the holes.

COURSE INFORMATION & FACILITIES

Tramore Golf Club
Newtown Hill, Tramore,
Co. Waterford

Manager: James Cox
Tel: 051-386170 Fax: 051-390961

Golf Professional Tel: 051-381706

Green Fees:
Weekdays — IR£30 Weekends — IR£35
Weekdays (day) — IR£45
Pre-booking required.

CARD OF THE COURSE (metres) — PAR 72

1	2	3	4	5	6	7	8	9	Out
365	455	155	344	294	159	367	371	506	3016
Par 4	Par 5	Par 3	Par 4	Par 4	Par 3	Par 4	Par 4	Par 5	Par 36

10	11	12	13	14	15	16	17	18	In
174	366	315	366	406	117	500	346	449	3039
Par 3	Par 4	Par 4	Par 4	Par 4	Par 3	Par 5	Par 4	Par 5	Par 36

HOW TO GET THERE

Half a mile from Tramore on
Dungarvan Coast Road.

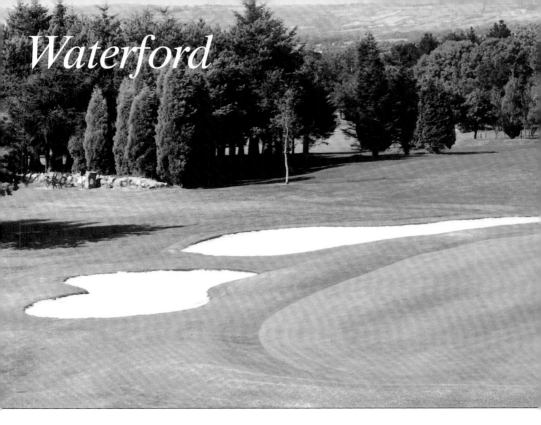

Waterford

Waterford is a town that people have long been drawn to. In the early days they were not always welcome. First it was the Vikings - a race not exactly renowned for their good manners. A few centuries later it was Cromwell's Roundheads, a particularly wretched bunch who named the spectacular hill that overlooks the town and its splendid bay, 'Mount Misery'. Crystal came to Waterford in 1783 about 130 years after Cromwell's Roundheads, and then 130 years after the Penrose Brothers founded their famous glass manufacturing business, golf came to Mount Misery.

Although only a few miles from the sea, Waterford is regarded as one of the finest inland courses in Ireland. Eighty per cent of it couldn't be described as anything other than classic parkland, but on the highest parts of the course - on the top of Mount Misery if you like - there is just a hint of a moorland type course, or even, if you stretch your imagination, a Formby-like links.

By no means is this a very difficult course but there is ample challenge nonetheless. The 1st demands an uphill drive to a blind target and is a testing opener. There are three short holes on the front nine, two of which demand tricky downhill tee shots. The 11th, 12th and 13th make for a most attractive run of holes and the finish is quite dramatic with a superb par three (the 16th) being followed by an almost driveable par four and a magnificient downhill 18th.

HOW TO GET THERE

2 hours drive via N9 from Dublin (exit left 1 mile from Waterford). 1 hour from Rosslare via N25 (exit right from dual carriageway entering Waterford).

Waterford Golf Club

COURSE INFORMATION & FACILITIES

Waterford Golf Club
Newrath, Waterford
Co. Waterford

Secretary/Manager: Joe Condon
Tel: 051-76748 Fax: 051-883405

Green Fees:
Weekdays — IR£22 Weekends — IR£25
Restrictions: Sunday — Mens Competition;
Tuesday — Ladies Competition

CARD OF THE COURSE — PAR 71

1	2	3	4	5	6	7	8	9	Out
384	334	119	380	370	361	164	494	170	2776
Par 4	Par 4	Par 3	Par 4	Par 4	Par 4	Par 3	Par 5	Par 3	Par 34

10	11	12	13	14	15	16	17	18	In
270	452	443	178	398	439	128	270	368	2946
Par 4	Par 5	Par 5	Par 3	Par 4	Par 5	Par 3	Par 4	Par 4	Par 37

Waterford Castle

aterford Castle is unique among Irish golf courses as the only way to get to it is via a ferry. The course is situated just a few miles to the east of the famous glass making city on an island in the River Suir estuary. A small ferry for about six cars takes you to the island.

Needless to say, there is also a castle on the island, an imposing edifice that dates back to the 11th century. It once belonged to the Fitzgerald clan, a powerful family in this part of Ireland in years gone by.

Waterford Castle was designed by Des Smyth, a veteran and seven time winner on the European Tour. Along with Declan Branigan, a former Irish International player who has collaborated with Smyth on other projects, the Irish pro has fashioned a good par-72 course in an idyllic setting.

Waterford Castle has matured quickly since it opened in 1992. Playing golf on an island is extraordinary in itself, but to be overlooked by an ancient castle and surrounded by beautiful trees on terrain that rises and falls – sometimes subtlety, sometimes dramatically – is a wonderful experience.

Among the outstanding challenges are the 2nd and 3rd – water threatens on both holes; the par five 13th, a superb swinging dog-leg, and the 16th, a long par three which runs alongside the estuary and where sailing boats are spotted more frequently than birdies.

COURSE INFORMATION & FACILITIES

Waterford Castle Golf Club
The Island, Ballinakill,
Waterford

Golf Administrator: Ann Dempsey
Tel: 051-871633 Fax: 051-871634

Green Fees:
Weekdays — IR£24 Weekends — IR£27
Weekdays (day) — IR£35 Weekends (day) — IR£40

Time restrictions apply.

CARD OF THE COURSE (metres) — PAR 72

1	2	3	4	5	6	7	8	9	Out
385	176	372	356	476	315	193	452	381	3106
Par 4	Par 3	Par 4	Par 4	Par 5	Par 4	Par 3	Par 5	Par 4	Par 36

10	11	12	13	14	15	16	17	18	In
160	346	415	463	343	468	187	368	353	3103
Par 3	Par 4	Par 4	Par 5	Par 4	Par 5	Par 3	Par 4	Par 4	Par 36

HOW TO GET THERE

N25 to Tower Hotel — turn
eft to Dunmore, East Road —
approx 2 miles to Waterford
Regional Hospital, through
roundabout, turn for
Waterford Castle
approx 300yds.

Dublin & North East

Dublin & The North East

"*I*n Dublin's fair city where the girls are so pretty" is the line to the famous song. Substitute golf courses for girls and you won't get many arguments. Let's face it, if you're going to go to Ireland, then you've got to go to Dublin, haven't you? What could be finer than strolling down O'Connell Street on a sunny day, or standing by the Liffey watching the world go by? The Irish have a term known as the "craic", as in "you'll enjoy the craic." It's a hard term to define, but it basically means enjoying yourself with friends and a few drinks. Nowhere will you experience the craic more than in the capital itself.

Dublin has always been a destination for golfers. Portmarnock, The Island, Woodbrook and Royal Dublin, all are good enough reason to visit Ireland's capital city. Not surprisingly though, as golf has boomed throughout the island, many of the best new courses are to be found near Dublin. Portmarnock Hotel, Luttrellstown Castle, St Margaret's, Druids Glen and The K Club, to name but a few, are all additions to an area already rich in good golf courses. Indeed, you could easily spend a month based in Dublin and never run out of courses to play. First and foremost you have to try to play Portmarnock. It's not easy to get on this fine old links, because it's on everyone's must play list. But if you can beg a round somehow then do so, for it's an experience not to missed. Play it and you soon see why so many Irish Opens have been held there. If you can't get on Portmarnock then fear not, for the Portmarnock Hotel course is reasonable compensation. It was designed by Bernhard Langer and the two time Masters winner has come up with a cracking links course that will suit all levels of golfer.

Perhaps the County that has seen the greatest number of good new courses built in the past decade is Wicklow, due south of Dublin. Druids Glen has probably become the most famous course in County Wicklow after staging three successive Irish Opens, but among the new inland courses there is also

Rathsallagh at Dunlavin and Powerscourt at Enniskerry. Also, near to Wicklow town there is a much heralded new links course called the European Club. The European overlooks Brittas Bay, as does the fine parkland-cum-clifftop course at Blainroe.

Immediately to the north of Dublin is where Portmarnock, Portmarnock Hotel Links and The Island are situated. Some forty miles north of Dublin is Drogheda in County Louth and due east of Drogheda is Baltray, a truly splendid links course (officially called County Louth Golf Club). Two other courses to note in County Louth are Seapoint, a fairly new links course which lies 'next door' to Baltray and, further north, Dundalk's attractive parkland course at Blackrock.

BLAINROE

COUNTY LOUTH

DRUIDS GLEN

DUNDALK

LUTTRELLSTOWN CASTLE

PORTMARNOCK

PORTMARNOCK LINKS

POWERSCOURT

RATHSALLAGH

ROYAL DUBLIN

SEAPOINT

ST MARGARETS

THE EUROPEAN

THE ISLAND

THE K CLUB

WOODBROOK

Dublin & North East

Page

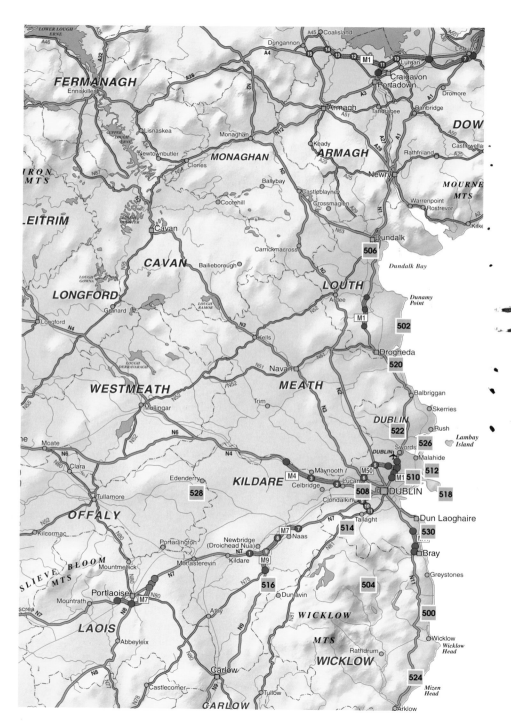

Blainroe

W icklow is one of, if not *the* most attractive county in Ireland. It may not possess the rugged beauty of a Galway, or the wilderness charm of a Donegal, but it has some spectacular mountain scenery - courtesy of the Wicklow Mountains - and a superb coastline. It also has a wealth of majestic trees (as anyone who has driven south from Dublin will confirm) and, equally importantly, several outstanding golf courses. One of the best places to sample the scenery and the golf is at Blainroe, just south of Wicklow town.

Blainroe is a very good parkland course, laid out on high ground overlooking the sea. The Wicklow Mountains pose imperiously on the horizon as the course meanders (and occasionally plunges) its way along avenues of trees sprinkled with large bunkers that bar entry to bold, undulating greens.

The routing is unusual in that eight of the holes (from the 2nd to the 9th) are separated by road from the remaining 10. The eight 'over the road' are characterised by dramatic changes in elevation - the 7th tee, for instance, is 300 feet above sea level. The best hole on the front nine is probably the par five 4th. On the clubhouse side of the road the terrain is less hilly and the quality of the holes superior. The final five are especially interesting, beginning with a Turnberry-like tee shot at the 14th with the drive needing to skirt the cliff edges, and a mighty par three which is played across a small lake.

COURSE INFORMATION & FACILITIES

Blainroe Golf Club
Blainroe,
Co. Wicklow

Golf Administrator: William O Sullivan
Tel: 0404-68168 Fax: 0404-69369

Green Fees:
Weekdays — IR£30 Weekends — IR£40
Weekdays (day) — IR£40 Weekends (day) — IR£50
Society Rates IR£20 Weekdays

CARD OF THE COURSE (metres) — PAR 72

1	2	3	4	5	6	7	8	9	Out
326	387	378	475	440	335	332	188	329	3190
Par 4	Par 4	Par 4	Par 5	Par 5	Par 4	Par 4	Par 3	Par 4	Par 37

10	11	12	13	14	15	16	17	18	In
339	346	388	351	296	199	408	108	445	2880
Par 4	Par 4	Par 4	Par 4	Par 4	Par 3	Par 4	Par 3	Par 5	Par 35

HOW TO GET THERE

From Dublin — N11 to Rathnew. Straight to Wicklow Town. Through Wicklow to coast road 3/4 miles outside town on coast road heading south. Blainroe Golf Course on left.

County Louth

Not far from Dublin, just north of the Town of Drogheda, lies a links course that has remained virtually undiscovered by the hordes of golfers who descend on Ireland every year. Yet County Louth at Baltray, which it is often called, is worth the 6,000 or 7,000 mile round trip many golfers make for the pleasure of teeing it up in Ireland.

Irish golfers know how good the course is, as do some foreigners. They know that the course initially laid out in 1890 and later redesigned by Tom Simpson in 1938 is worth the effort it takes to get there. Simpson was responsible for such other great courses as Cruden Bay, Royal Aberdeen and Ballybunion. That's enough to have any serious golfer seeking out County Louth.

It is on this course that the East of Ireland Championship has been held since 1941. This is a 72-hole amateur championship that has been won by some very good players indeed. Joe Carr won the inaugural East of Ireland, and went on to win 11 more times. Current European Tour pros Darren Clarke and Raymond Burns have also won the event.

What the players find when they get to Baltray is a links course with among the best greens in all of Ireland. The contouring of these putting surfaces is such that you'll have done remarkably well if you survive the round without one three-putt.

The par-3s at Baltray are particularly good, as each plays in a different direction. The two on the outward call medium iron shots but are played from exposed tees to plateau greens.

Of the par-4s, probably the most memorable is the 14th, a 332-yarder played off a high tee. It's not so much the challenge that makes this hole as the superb views over a long sandy beach and the distant Mourne Mountains near Royal County Down.

COURSE INFORMATION & FACILITIES

Co. Louth Golf Club
Baltray, Drogheda,
Co. Louth.

Secretary/Manager: Michael Delany.
Tel: 041 9822329. Fax: 041 9822969.

Golf Professional Paddy McGuire Tel: 041 9822444.

Green Fees:
Weekdays — IR£50. Weekends — IR£60.
Weekdays (day) — IR£50. Weekends (day) — IR£60.
Tuesdays all day and Wednesday afternoons (Ladies Day).

CARD OF THE COURSE — PAR 73

1	2	3	4	5	6	7	8	9	Out
433	482	544	344	158	531	163	407	419	3481
Par 4	Par 5	Par 5	Par 4	Par 3	Par 5	Par 3	Par 4	Par 4	Par 37

10	11	12	13	14	15	16	17	18	In
398	481	410	421	332	152	388	179	541	3302
Par 4	Par 5	Par 4	Par 4	Par 4	Par 3	Par 4	Par 3	Par 5	Par 36

HOW TO GET THERE

5 miles north east of town of Drogheda.

Co. Louth
Golf Club

Druids Glen

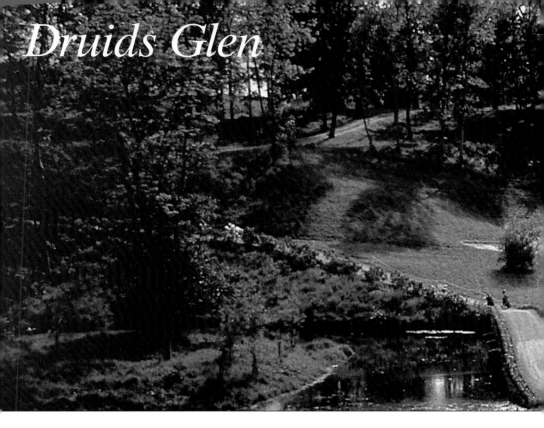

*T*he Murphy's Irish Open was held at Druids Glen for the first time in 1996. Colin Montgomerie was the winner that year and, not surprisingly, he loved the place. Montgomerie loves courses which put a premium on accuracy, but then he would do – he very rarely misses a fairway.

Course architects Pat Ruddy and Tom Craddock were given a brief to "build the best inland course in Ireland". Whether or not they have is matter of opinion – suffice it to say that Montgomerie probably thinks it is – but it's certainly one of the toughest.

Set on the Woodstock estate some 25 miles from Dublin, Druids Glen gets its name from a wooded valley said to be an ancient Druid spiritual site. In fact, the par-3, 12th hole is supposedly where the Druid's conducted their pagan ceremonies.

Montgomery won the first Murphy's Irish Open at Druids Glen with an aggregate score of 279, 5-under par. In days when European Tour events are won with scores in the minus teens, 5-under is quite high. It also tells you something about the course – it's extremely tough. You'll need to have every part of your game on song if you hope to play well at Druids Glen, especially from the back tees. You'll need to drive it long and straight, play your approach shots well and chip and putt to the best of your ability. Otherwise content yourself with a nice walk around an immaculate course set in pleasant surroundings.

HOW TO GET THERE

From the N11 south from Dublin take the slipway signposted Newtown Mount Kennedy & Newcastle Hospital. Keep following the brown finger signs to Gleann Na Draoite (which is Druids Glen in Gaelic). The course is situated approx. 30 minutes from Dublin City South.

Druids Glen Golf Club

COURSE INFORMATION & FACILITIES

Druids Glen Golf Club
Newtownmountkennedy,
Co. Wicklow

Golf Professional: Eamonn Darcy
Tel: 353-1-287 3600 Fax: 353-1-287 3699

Green Fees:
IR£75 per person Mon-Sun. (IR£65 — 20+ golfers)
From 19/10/98 to 15/4/99 — £IR75 per person
(green fee, 5-course dinner & wine)
From 16/4/99 onwards — £IR80 (green fee Mon-Sun.)
£IR65 20+golfers Mon-Sun

CARD OF THE COURSE — PAR 73

1	2	3	4	5	6	7	8	9	Out
427	174	330	417	492	456	392	152	369	3209
Par 4	Par 3	Par 4	Par 4	Par 5	Par 4	Par 4	Par 3	Par 4	Par 35

10	11	12	13	14	15	16	17	18	In
401	512	155	461	333	395	481	178	422	3338
Par 4	Par 5	Par 3	Par 4	Par 4	Par 4	Par 5	Par 3	Par 4	Par 36

Dundalk

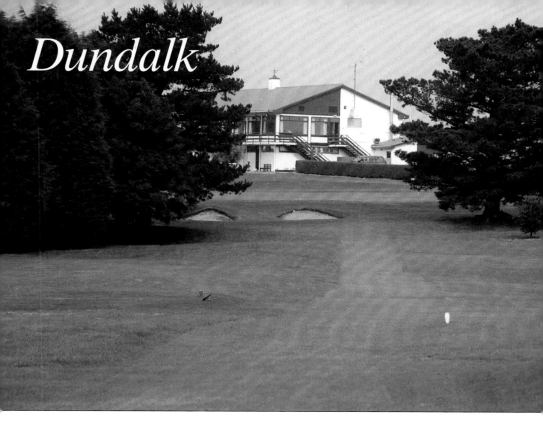

*A*nyone embarking on a 'Grand Tour of Irish golf', and who plans to journey between Baltray and Newcastle, will pass through the town of Dundalk. It may prove difficult to postpone the allure of a game on either of these great links but if a round can be squeezed in at Dundalk it will not disappoint. This is one of Ireland's finest inland courses.

Dundalk Golf Club was founded early this century. Since the 1920s the club has played over the present site at Blackrock, just south of the town. The current layout bears testimony to the skills of Dave Thomas and Peter Alliss who renovated and redesigned much of the course in the early 1980s. It is a very scenic parkland course and one that always appears green and lush. The Mountains of Mourne and the Irish Sea combine to provide a striking backdrop.

Careful placement of tee shots is the key to playing well at Dundalk. Thanks to Messrs Alliss and Thomas, the course is extremely well bunkered. It begins rather benignly but gets fully into its stride at the 5th, an attractive par three played to a green defended by water and sand. The best sequence is between the 7th and 12th, both of which are par fives. There is plenty of variety within this stretch and the final three holes ensure that interest is maintained right up to the final putt. After which, you either adjourn to the large, comfortable 19th, or resume that Grand Tour - and set sail for Newcastle.

COURSE INFORMATION & FACILITIES

Dundalk Golf Club
Blackrock, Dundalk
Co. Louth

Secretary/Manager: Joe Carroll
Tel: 042-21731 Fax: 042-22022

Green Fees:
Weekdays — IR£19.50 Weekends — IR£23.50
Weekdays (day) — IR£19.50. Weekends (day) — IR£23.50

Restrictions: 1 to 2.30pm

CARD OF THE COURSE — PAR 72

1	2	3	4	5	6	7	8	9	Out
355	357	367	404	156	452	485	304	158	3038
Par 4	Par 4	Par 4	Par 4	Par 3	Par 5	Par 5	Par 4	Par 3	Par 36

10	11	12	13	14	15	16	17	18	In
452	389	462	160	291	357	390	172	317	2990
Par 5	Par 4	Par 5	Par 3	Par 4	Par 4	Par 4	Par 3	Par 4	Par 36

HOW TO GET THERE

Two miles south from
Dundalk (N1) turn left for
village of Blackrock (signpost).

FAIRWAYS HOTEL

The Fairways is a 3* family-run Hotel situated two miles south of Dundalk mid-way between Dublin and Belfast. The Hotel is the ideal base to visit the many Golf Courses in the North East and is adjacent to Dundalk Golf Club. The Hotel facilities include:

- **100 Comfortable Bedrooms**
- **Carvery / Grill**
- **Modi's Restaurant**
- **Conference Centre**
- **Piano Lounge & Nite Club**

The Fairways Hotel · Dublin Road · Dundalk · Co. Louth

Tel: 042 9321500 · Fax: 042 9321511
E-mail Address: info@fairways.ie
Web Site Address: http://www.fairways.ie

Luttrellstown Castle

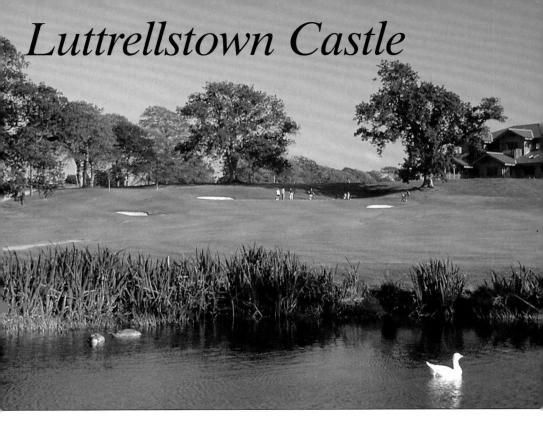

*I*n July 1993, within a few days of the opening of Luttrellstown Castle Golf and Country Club, a sprightly 91 year old was seen touring the course in a buggy. It was golf's 'Oldest Member', genial Gene Sarazen, and he was heard to remark, "This is one of the finest parkland courses I have ever seen".

No doubt Sarazen was somewhat intoxicated by a combination of the stately surroundings and some typically overwhelming Irish hospitality but his comments were sincere. What so enchanted Sarazen was the beauty of the setting – overlooked by an ivy-clad castle, a glorious assortment of trees adorn the site, including ancient oaks, limes and beeches – and the way the course blends so harmoniously with the landscape. Unlike many of the new Irish inland courses

Luttrellstown is not an 'American styled' layout. The water hazards, for instance, are not incongruous lakes but inhabited natural ponds, and there is no overt fairway mounding. After all, why would anyone want to shield the many magnificent vistas?

Skilfully designed by Nicholas Bielenberg, the course can be stretched to 7000 yards from the back tees. In 1997 Luttrellstown hosted its first major tournament, the Guardian (Ladies) Irish Open. There are several memorable holes, with a particularly strong sequence between the 7th and 12th (the par three 10th was Sarazen's favourite). The greens are among the truest and best conditioned in Ireland, while the clubhouse – built in Finnish pine – is one of the country's most stylish and relaxing 19th holes.

COURSE INFORMATION & FACILITIES

Luttrellstown Castle Golf & Country Club
Castleknock,
Dublin 15

Director: Graham Campbell.
Tel: 01-808-9988 Fax: 01-808-9989

Golf Professional
Tel: 01-808-9988 Fax: 01-808-9989
Email address: golf@luttrellstown.ie
Web Site: http://www.luttrellstown.ie

Green Fees:
Weekdays — IR£40 Weekends — IR£45
Group rates available on request.

CARD OF THE COURSE — PAR 72

1	2	3	4	5	6	7	8	9	Out
384	472	386	352	338	202	358	127	508	3127
Par 4	Par 5	Par 4	Par 4	Par 4	Par 3	Par 4	Par 3	Par 5	Par 36

10	11	12	13	14	15	16	17	18	In
171	325	526	403	396	415	153	486	375	3250
Par 3	Par 4	Par 5	Par 4	Par 4	Par 4	Par 3	Par 5	Par 4	Par 36

HOW TO GET THERE

N1 — Dublin City Centre, exit right at M50 (south), exit left for Castleknock — right at roundabout (Auburn Avenue), straight on at mini-roundabout, right at lights, left at MYOS Pub, right at lights, follow road.

509

Portmarnock

ortmarnock is Ireland's premier championship venue. In addition to hosting numerous Irish Opens, the links has staged the World Cup (in 1960) and the Walker Cup (in 1991) – American teams winning on both occasions. Somewhat surprisingly it has also been the venue for a British Amateur Championship and, somewhat ridiculously, it has never hosted the Ryder Cup.

Portmarnock is a magnificent links. Located just a few miles north of Dublin, it occupies a peninsula and is effectively surrounded by water on three sides. Being so exposed, the player is often at the mercy of the elements; indeed, Portmarnock can pose as tough a challenge as any links in the world.

From its championship tees the course measures in excess of 7100 yards. The links is both expertly and heavily bunkered and the rough really is rough. But Portmarnock, rather like Muirfield, is regarded as a very 'fair' links. There is, for instance, only one blind tee shot (at the 5th); the fairways do not undulate significantly, thus awkward stances are the product of poor golf not poor fortune, and as the course is arranged in two loops of nine there is a great sense of balance.

Perhaps the finest sequence at Portmarnock occurs between the 4th and the 8th, although the best and possibly most difficult hole of all is the par three 15th. It is played parallel to the shore and if the wind is whipping in off the Irish Sea you have to start your tee shot out over the beach! Ben Crenshaw has called the 15th, 'one of the greatest short holes on Earth.'

COURSE INFORMATION & FACILITIES

Portmarnock Golf Club
Portmarnock,
Co. Dublin.

Secretary/Manager: John Quigley.
Tel: 01 8462968. Fax: 01 8462601.
Golf Professional: Tel: 01 8462634.
Green Fees:
Weekdays — IR£75. Weekends — IR£95.
Letter of introduction and handicap certificate required.
Some time restrictions.

CARD OF THE COURSE (metres) — PAR 72

1	2	3	4	5	6	7	8	9	Out
355	346	351	403	364	550	168	364	399	3300
Par 4	Par 4	Par 4	Par 4	Par 4	Par 5	Par 3	Par 4	Par 4	Par 36

10	11	12	13	14	15	16	17	18	In
341	392	139	516	350	173	480	429	377	3197
Par 4	Par 4	Par 3	Par 5	Par 4	Par 3	Par 5	Par 4	Par 4	Par 36

HOW TO GET THERE

Follow M50 to Malahide and on to Portmarnock by the coast road.

MARINE
HOTEL

The Marine Hotel has welcomed visitors to Dublin since 1887. Located only 15 minutes from the city center and Dublin's International Airport, the hotel offers you something with a difference. The grounds of the hotel lead down to the shore of Dublin Bay and the views of the Dublin coast are second to none. The main DART line is right beside the hotel, giving convenient access to the City Centre and South Dublin.

The Marine has 50 bedrooms, a lively bar and atmospheric restaurant. Swimming pool and sauna are an added bonus.

Five golf clubs neighbour the Marine Hotel, including the championship links of Portmarnock and Royal Dublin Golf Clubs. Also within a short distance are the Island, Malahide and new Portmarnock Links golf course.

**Tel: 00 353 1 8390000 Fax: 00 353 1 8390442
Email: info@marinehotel.ie Web: www.themarine.ie**

Portmarnock Hotel Links

*T*he Portmarnock Hotel & Golf Links lies adjacent to Portmarnock Golf Club. The hotel, once the home of the Jameson (whiskey) family, became fully operational in June 1996. The new links was designed by Bernhard Langer, a three-time winner of the Irish Open, and the architect was Stan Eby. Together they have produced a masterpiece.

Perhaps the most immediately striking aspect of the links is how natural it appears. There is nothing flamboyant about the design, and it is refreshing to see that no fewer than five of the par fours measure less than 380 yards. The course flows, almost gracefully, from green to tee to green. As at St Andrews and Ballybunion Old Course, there are no lengthy walks in between holes.

The other very obvious feature is the quality and extent of the bunkering. There are almost 100 bunkers in total and each has been painstakingly and skilfully constructed with steep revetted faces, similar to Carnoustie and Muirfield. In fact, the Portmarnock Hotel links bears more of a resemblance generally to those two great Scottish courses than to neighbouring

Portmarnock. More specifically, the front nine is reminiscent of Carnoustie and the back nine of Muirfield, although it could be argued that the four final holes are more thrilling than those at either of the Scottish links.

In true Carnoustie style, then, the opening few holes demand a 'keep your head down' approach. The views are hardly distracting, but the challenge is very evident. The landscape becomes more appealing from the 8th hole onwards. Aside from the climactic finish, the 8th is possibly the finest hole on the course. The fairway dog-legs sharply to the left before tumbling in classic links fashion towards a severely sloping green perched amid some very wild-looking dunes. The great finish begins at the 15th, where the approach must somehow be threaded past (or over) a sea of deep traps. The 16th is played from a superbly elevated tee. The 17th is yet another formidable short hole – beware the very cavernous greenside bunker – and the 18th descends from a lofty tee to an amphitheatre green surrounded by towering sand dunes and devilish pot bunkers. The perfect stage for a winning birdie!

COURSE INFORMATION & FACILITIES

Portmarnock Hotel & Golf Links
Portmarnock,
Co. Dublin.

Director of Golf: Moira Cassidy
Tel: 01-846-1800. Fax: 01-846-1077.

Green Fees:
Non —Hotel Residents IR£60
Hotel Residents IR£38

CARD OF THE COURSE (metres) — PAR 71

1	2	3	4	5	6	7	8	9	Out
304	305	172	512	409	462	405	323	139	3031
Par 4	Par 4	Par 3	Par 5	Par 4	Par 5	Par 4	Par 4	Par 3	Par 36

10	11	12	13	14	15	16	17	18	In
467	406	316	135	312	345	354	171	365	2878
Par 5	Par 4	Par 4	Par 3	Par 4	Par 4	Par 4	Par 3	Par 4	Par 35

HOW TO GET THERE

From Dublin Airport turn left at first roundabout, Belfast Road — take inside lane, exit right to Malahide, look out for signs Portmarnock Hotel & Golf Links, 1¹/₂ miles turn left at lights.

Powerscourt

*T*here was a time when, on arriving in Dublin, the golfing visitor to Ireland couldn't wait to race off to the magical west. Now there has been some serious reappraisal. During the 1990s three outstanding parkland courses opened in County Wicklow, directly south of Dublin. The first was Rathsallagh, the second Druids Glen and the most recent is Powerscourt, situated just 12 miles south of the city at Enniskerry.

Powerscourt is probably the most celebrated estate in Ireland. Its name dates back to 1300 when the land was acquired by the Norman Le Poer family. In the 17th, 18th and 19th centuries the estate was owned by the Wingfields who built Powerscourt House and gradually developed the world famous gardens.

The course is approached via an avenue of towering beech trees. As soon as you turn into the golf club you are confronted by a handsome Georgian styled clubhouse. Powerscourt House is nearby and all around is rolling countryside. There is still one more striking feature - Sugarloaf Mountain: Wicklow's greatest peak dominates the horizon at Powerscourt.

The course architect, Peter McEvoy has placed an emphasis on subtlety and harmony and has not attempted to manufacture the spectacular. The course flows with the land and there are only two water hazards in the entire layout. As for the greens, they are beautifully contoured - or as Golf Monthly described them in 1996, "18 of the best shaped putting surfaces since God had a hand in shaping Prestwick".

COURSE INFORMATION & FACILITIES

Powerscourt Golf Club
Enniskerry,
Co. Wicklow

Golf Manager: Bernard Gibbons
Tel: 01 204 6033 Fax: 01 276 1303

Golf Professional: Paul Thompson
Tel: 01 204 6033 Fax: 01 276 1303

Green Fees:
IR£70 Every day.
Restrictions apply.

CARD OF THE COURSE — PAR 72

1	2	3	4	5	6	7	8	9	Out
384	444	131	295	191	461	336	401	306	2949
Par 4	Par 5	Par 3	Par 4	Par 3	Par 5	Par 4	Par 4	Par 4	Par 36

10	11	12	13	14	15	16	17	18	In
351	354	485	156	309	333	134	488	371	2981
Par 4	Par 4	Par 5	Par 3	Par 4	Par 4	Par 3	Par 5	Par 4	Par 36

COUNTY WICKLOW

HOW TO GET THERE

South of Dublin near Bray can be found the Powerscourt Estate at Enniskerry.

This charming hotel is just a short walk to the quaint village of Enniskerry and the world famous Powerscourt Golf Club and gardens.

We have 57 spacious bedrooms, private free car parking, excellent hill walking and nature trails nearby.

Located on the N11, 19km south of Dublin City and 15km from Dunlaoire Ferryport.

Members of
Logis of Ireland

Summerhill House Hotel

Enniskerry, County Wicklow, Ireland
Tel: +353 (0) 1 286 7928
Fax: +353 (0) 1 286 7929

515

Rathsallagh

*P*eter McEvoy and Christy O'Connor
Jnr are making a habit of producing
good golf courses. They teamed
together to create the magnificent Fota Island,
and they've done it again with Rathsallagh.

Set in beautiful rolling countryside in
County Wicklow some 30 miles from Dublin,
Rathsallagh is another in a long line of fine
parkland courses to be built in Ireland.
Mount Juliet, the K Club, Druid's Glen, the
list gets longer every year. Rathsallagh can
easily be added to that list. Nor is it inferior
amongst the aforementioned layouts.

McEvoy and O'Connor Jnr have created
one of the best conditioned courses you will
play anywhere. Built to USGA specifications,
Rathsallagh is normally always in good shape.
It's also one of the more demanding parkland
courses you are likely to play.

Measuring close to 7,000 yards,
Rathsallagh is not a course the high
handicapper should play from the back tees.
Anyone brave enough to play the course at its
full length had better be a good player, a very
good player.

Here you will find man-sized holes, with
at least four holes in excess of 450-yards. That
this course will be no pushover is obvious
from the very first hole, which is a genuine
three shot par-5 of 571-yards A lot of players
won't be attacking the pin with a mere flick of
the wedge. The fact that the second stretches
to 454-yards foreshadows the test that lies in
store.

However, while the length may have you
hitting longer irons than you feel comfortable
with, you should have no excuse around the
greens, which are among the best you'll find.
At Rathsallagh you don't have to hit your
putts, a good stroke should send the ball off
on a true line to the hole. If you can't putt at
Rathsallagh, you can't putt anywhere.

COURSE INFORMATION & FACILITIES

Rathsallagh Golf Club
Dunlavin,
Co. Wicklow

Chief Executive: Joe O Flynn
Tel: 353 (0) 45-403316 Fax: 353 (0) 45-403295
Email: info@rathsallagh.com
Web: www.rathsallagh.com

Green Fees:
Weekdays — IR£40 Weekends: IR£50
Restrictions apply at weekends.

CARD OF THE COURSE — PAR 72

1	2	3	4	5	6	7	8	9	Out
506	436	367	158	373	490	177	351	370	3228
Par 5	Par 4	Par 4	Par 3	Par 4	Par 5	Par 3	Par 4	Par 4	Par 36

10	11	12	13	14	15	16	17	18	In
438	510	355	134	332	374	516	170	426	3255
Par 4	Par 5	Par 4	Par 3	Par 4	Par 4	Par 5	Par 3	Par 4	Par 36

HOW TO GET THERE

Take M50 south from Dublin, N7 south to M7 south, exit to M9 south. At end of M9 continue on two-lane highway for 6 miles until signposts for Rathsallagh begin.

Rathsallagh House

Rathsallagh House is a four star Grade A Country House set on 530 acres of mature parkland and surrounded by the magnificent Rathsallagh Golf Club. To maintain a happy and relaxed atmosphere, there are only 29 en-suite bedrooms. The House is centrally heated throughout and has large open fires in the dining room, sitting rooms and bar. It has a heated indoor swimming pool, sauna, tennis court, billiard room and fully equipped conference room. Horse riding, clay pigeon shooting, archery and hunting are available by prior arrangement.

Rathsallagh House, Dunlavin, Co. Wicklow
Tel: + 353 (0)45 403112 Fax: + 353 (0)45 403343
Email: info@rathsallagh.com Website: www.rathsallagh.com

The Royal Dublin

Royal Dublin may be the closest thing in Ireland to the Old Course at St Andrews. Laid out over a narrow tract of land, it is the only one of Ireland's great links that stretches out and back in traditional 'Scotttish' style. Like St Andrews the land is essentially flat with subtle undulations. Wind and pin position dictate a player's strategy, the greens are kept firm and fast, and bump and run is king.

The golf club dates from 1885. Initially 'home' was a confined area in Phoenix Park, but in 1889 the club moved to its present site at Bull Island, still within the city limits. Bull Island is accessed by a wooden bridge and the duneland terrain is shared by golfers, bird watchers and botanists. It is an extraordinary domain.

A combination of greater length and the prevailing wind ensures that the inward nine is invariably the tougher half. However, the outward nine includes arguably the two best holes, namely the par four 5th and the par five 8th. The inward nine starts to bare its teeth at the 13th. This is a formidable two-shotter where the entrance to the green is cambered and very narrow – rather appropriately the hole is called 'Dardanelles'.

The most famous hole at Royal Dublin is the 18th, 'Garden', a right-angled par four. The approach must be fired directly over an Out of Bounds field (the eponymous garden) to reach the green in two. Royal Dublin has staged many important championships over the years and the closing hole has provided many dramatic finishes.

CARD OF THE COURSE (metres) — PAR 72

1	2	3	4	5	6	7	8	9	Out
361	445	363	163	423	180	322	440	164	2902
Par 4	Par 5	Par 4	Par 3	Par 4	Par 3	Par 4	Par 5	Par 3	Par 35

10	11	12	13	14	15	16	17	18	In
374	483	172	381	439	390	241	341	430	3251
Par 4	Par 5	Par 3	Par 4	Par 5	Par 4	Par 4	Par 4	Par 4	Par 37

HOW TO GET THERE

Royal Dublin is on an island 3
miles from the centre of Dublin
City. It is reached by a wooden
bridge off the main north
Dublin Bay road.

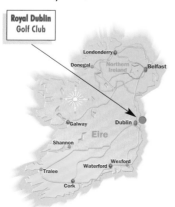

Seapoint

*L*ike his great playing competitor Christy O'Connor Jnr, Ireland's Des Smyth has been around golf long enough to know a few things about golf course design. It wasn't surprising then that he soon turned his hand to architecture. The members of Seapoint Golf Club are glad he did.

Smyth hails from nearby Drogheda, so he knew the land the course now occupies. It's land just beyond the beach where Smyth plays with his children when he's not lugging his sticks around the European Tour making a living.

Seapoint is on good links land perfect for golf. Indeed, it sits next door to County Louth, one of Ireland's unsung gems. Seapoint hasn't quite matured to the same standard as Louth – that would be asking a bit much. Nevertheless, it is a fine golf course that will please every level of golfer, from scratch player to high handicapper.

The land at Seapoint is pure, genuine links. However, the opening nine take on the appearance of a fine parkland layout. You won't find many water hazards on true links courses, but there are six on the first nine holes at Seapoint. There are also mature trees on some of the opening holes, further enhancing the feeling that you are playing a parkland course. Don't despair, for there are good links holes here to whet your appetite.

The back nine is more linkslike than the front, with many holes in good duneland. For example, the 180-yard, par-3, 17th hole plays along side the beach, and is one of the best seaside par-3s you'll find anywhere.

Smyth has designed a handful of good courses in Ireland, but Seapoint may be his best.

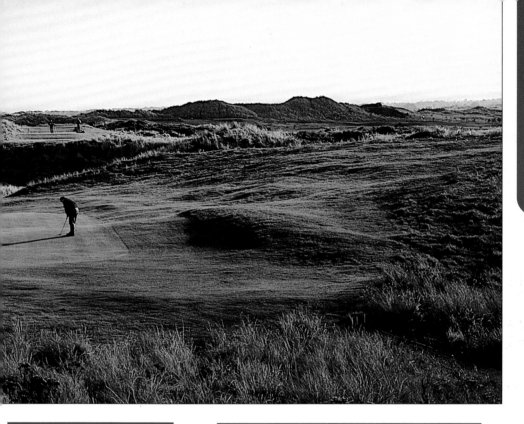

HOW TO GET THERE

From Dublin, head north on N1 to
Drogheda. Continue on N1 over
Boyne River to traffic lights.
Proceed straight over and after
300yds turn right to Termonfeckin
— once there go over hump back
bridge and turn
right for club.

COURSE INFORMATION & FACILITIES

Seapoint Golf Club
Termonfeckin, Drogheda,
Co. Louth

Manager: Kevin Karrie
Tel: 04198-22333 Fax: 04198-22331

Golf Professional Tel: 04198-22333

Green Fees:
Weekdays — IR£22.50
Weekdays (day) — IR£27.50

CARD OF THE COURSE (metres) — PAR 72

1	2	3	4	5	6	7	8	9	Out
356	494	405	386	182	336	405	466	185	3215
Par 4	Par 5	Par 4	Par 4	Par 3	Par 4	Par 43	Par 5	Par 3	Par 36

10	11	12	13	14	15	16	17	18	In
480	344	407	412	384	146	334	164	453	3124
Par 5	Par 4	Par 4	Par 4	Par 4	Par 3	Par 4	Par 3	Par 5	Par 36

St. Margaret's

P at Ruddy and Tom Craddock seem intent on making themselves the best golf design partnership in Ireland. They've already impressed with Druid's Glen, where the Irish Open has been held, and they've done an excellent job on St. Margaret's not far from the centre of Dublin.

It's not unusual to find water on many of Ireland's newer courses, but it is unusual to find one hole with three water hazards. That is exactly what you will find on the 525-yard, par-5 8th hole at St. Margaret's. This hole features a lake to the left off the tee, a lake to the right that comes into play on the second shot, and a third lake fronting the green. Needless to say it is one of the most unique holes in Irish golf, one that will remain in your memory long after your visit.

The 8th hole is just one of five par-5s at St. Margaret's. Along with four par-3s and nine par-4s, it makes par for the course 73. As you've probably gleaned from the description of the 8th, water features prominently on this course. Play it from the back tees on an off day and you will lose a lot of balls. Your last might be used on the 18th, where your approach shot has to flirt with a large pond fronted by a lake.

St. Margaret's has been built to the highest of standards, as is expected of any course Ruddy and Craddock put their names to. Conditions are first class, so good that the club hosted the top European women golfers when the Irish Holidays Open was held there in 1994 and 1995. Given the difficulty of the layout, it's not surprising that big hitting Laura Davies took the title both years.

HOW TO GET THERE

5 miles from Dublin Airport.
Take Belfast Road. Turn left at
next roundabout, follow road
for 4 miles and signs to the
golf course.

COURSE INFORMATION & FACILITIES

St. Margaret's Golf & Country Club
St. Margaret's,
Co. Dublin

Reservations Manager: Gillian Harris
Tel: 01-8640400 Fax: 01-8640289

Golf Professional Tel: 01-8640400

Green Fees:
Weekdays — IR£40 Weekends — IR£40
Weekdays (day) — IR£60 Weekends (day) — IR£60

CARD OF THE COURSE — PAR 73

1	2	3	4	5	6	7	8	9	Out
358	149	509	456	174	458	374	525	398	3401
Par 4	Par 3	Par 5	Par 4	Par 3	Par 4	Par 4	Par 5	Par 4	Par 36

10	11	12	13	14	15	16	17	18	In
395	366	474	194	402	180	535	512	458	3516
Par 4	Par 4	Par 5	Par 3	Par 4	Par 3	Par 5	Par 5	Par 4	Par 37

The European Club

*I*t is the proud boast of golfers at Mount Juliet that they play 'the course that Jack built.' Near Brittas Bay in County Wicklow we can now experience the links that Pat built. Whatever else Pat Ruddy achieves in his life, The European Club will stand as his monument to golf.

The word 'great' should be used very sparingly in relation to golf courses, but the links at Brittas Bay which opened as recently as 1993 is undoubtedly a great links. It has many great qualities. The sandhills are not quite of Ballybunion-like proportion, but they dwarf those at Portmarnock. Better still, the golf course never leaves the dunes. There is balance and consistency and no feeling of mild disappointment, as is sometimes expressed in relation to the final few holes at Lahinch and Newcastle – and indeed with regard to the first few at Portmarnock and Ballybunion.

The Irish Sea is the golfer's constant companion. You see it as you leave the 1st green, you hear it as you approach the 3rd and smell it as you stroll down the 7th – and you can almost touch it as you play along the 12th and 13th.

There are at least six genuinely great holes at The European Club: the beautifully flowing downhill 3rd, the 7th with its fairway bordered by haunting marshland, the 8th, the 11th, the 12th and the fabulous 17th which plunges through a secluded dune-lined valley.

One final treat – or is it a shock – awaits at the 18th. But who are we to spoil the surprise?

COURSE INFORMATION & FACILITIES

The European Club
Brittas Bay,
Co. Wicklow. Ireland

Secretary: Sidon Ruddy
Tel: 0404-47415 Fax: 0404-47449

Green Fees:
Weekdays and Weekends — IR£60
Weekdays and Weekends (day) — IR£80

CARD OF THE COURSE — PAR 71

1	2	3	4	5	6	7	8	9	Out
392	160	499	452	409	187	470	415	427	3411
Par 4	Par 3	Par 5	Par 4	Par 4	Par 3	Par 4	Par 4	Par 4	Par 35
10	**11**	**12**	**13**	**14**	**15**	**16**	**17**	**18**	**In**
417	389	459	596	165	401	415	391	445	3678
Par 4	Par 4	Par 4	Par 5	Par 3	Par 4	Par 4	Par 4	Par 4	Par 36

HOW TO GET THERE

M11 South 30 miles from Central Dublin. At Jack White's Inn, turn left into Brittas Bay. At T junction at Beach, turn right & go 1.5 miles to Links.

The Island

*A*lthough founded over a century ago, The Island Golf Club near Malahide is one of Ireland's greatest golfing secrets. There are several reasons for this, chief of which is the links' close proximity to Royal Dublin and Portmarnock, two very well established championship venues. Another is that until quite recently the principal mode of transport to The Island was by ferry.

In fact it isn't literally an island – the course occupies a peninsula, directly across the estuary from Malahide. The rather eccentric voyage discouraged many but for those with a spirit of adventure it merely added to the allure and charm of the links.

The Island enjoys some of the most naturally rugged terrain on the east coast.

It has been called 'the Lahinch of the east', and the sandhills dwarf those at Portmarnock. When the course was originally laid out (it is not clear by whom), little attempt was made to tame the landscape and the links was built right in amongst the dunes.

Although changes have occurred over the years (the ferry was discontinued in 1973 when a newly sited clubhouse opened) the course has kept its essential character. In 1990, the club's centenary year, a revised layout was unveiled. It included several new holes but also retained the best of the old layout, including the wonderful sequence between the 12th and the 15th, which tour the tip of the peninsula.

CARD OF THE COURSE (metres) — PAR 72

1	2	3	4	5	6	7	8	9	Out
396	363	405	320	336	300	403	282	159	2964
Par 4	Par 4	Par 4	Par 4	Par 4	Par 4	Par 4	Par 4	Par 3	Par 35

10	11	12	13	14	15	16	17	18	In
500	284	379	191	315	507	140	388	410	3114
Par 5	Par 4	Par 4	Par 3	Par 4	Par 5	Par 3	Par 4	Par 4	Par 36

HOW TO GET THERE

Take the main Dublin/Belfast Road. 3 miles past Swords take the road to Donabate/Portrane, and follow signs to the Island Golf Club.

527

The K Club

*I*f you're looking for a first class hotel and a first rate golf course near Dublin, then look no further than The K Club.

Arnold Palmer was the man called in to design a golf course on the land that borders the River Liffey and which surrounds Straffan House, now a five star hotel. He has done a good job, too. For while the hotel will cater to your every need, the course should satisfy your golf cravings.

The K Club is a good enough course to have hosted the Smurfit European Open for a number of years. That's really not too surprising – Dr Michael Smurfit owns the course and the hotel.

No expense was spared on The K Club. While they did have problems with drainage early on, these have been overcome. Parkland in nature, the course winds its way through the lovely estate. Not surprisingly, the holes along the River Liffey are the ones

that will remain in the memory.

The par-5, 7th and par-4, 8th holes sit by the river on the front nine, and of the two the 7th is perhaps the harder. This hole calls for a delicate third shot to be played over the Liffey. Hook at the next and you will be in Ireland's most famous river, for the river runs all the way down the left hand side of this fairway.

On the back nine the Liffey comes into play on the 17th. Here the river threatens any shot hit to the right hand side of the fairway. However, at no more than 395-yards long, the previous hole, the 16th, is perhaps the best on the course. Keep the ball away from the right side of the fairway off the tee and you should keep it dry. Although then you face a shot over water to find the green.

Besides the Liffey, there is a lot more water at The K Club. So take lots of balls.

528

HOW TO GET THERE

Take N4/M4 from Dublin airport, exit motorway for Naas. Continue for 5 miles, cross Clane Road and follow sign for Straffan, continue through village and hotel is on right.

COURSE INFORMATION & FACILITIES

The K Club
Straffan,
Co. Kildare

Director of Golf: Paul Crowe
Tel: 01-6017300. Fax: 01-6017399
Email: golf@kclub.ie

Golf Professional: Tel: 01-6017321

Green Fees:
Weekdays — IR£120 Weekends — IR£120
Group & residents rates available.

CARD OF THE COURSE — PAR 72

1	2	3	4	5	6	7	8	9	Out
584	408	173	402	213	446	606	375	434	3641
Par 5	Par 4	Par 3	Par 4	Par 3	Par 4	Par 5	Par 4	Par 4	Par 36

10	11	12	13	14	15	16	17	18	In
418	413	170	568	416	447	395	173	518	3518
Par 4	Par 4	Par 3	Par 5	Par 4	Par 4	Par 4	Par 3	Par 5	Par 36

Woodbrook

Woodbrook is on one of the most scenic spots near Ireland's capital. Situated at the holiday town of Bray, the Woodbrook course sits on high cliffs that provide fantastic views of Dublin Bay.

The golf course dates back to 1921, when it was just a nine hole course. Another nine were added in 1927, and the course gradually grew in reputation until it was a regular venue for Irish tournaments. For example, the Irish Open has been staged here a number of times, as well as the Irish Professional Championship, not to mention numerous amateur championships.

Although situated beside the sea, Woodbrook is not a links course but a pure parkland layout. Over the years, the club's committee has made a number of changes to toughen up the course. In other words, don't go there expecting to tear the place apart, there are a lot of tough holes at Woodbrook.

The best stretch of holes is to be found beside the cliffs after you start the back nine. For example, the 443-yard, par-4, 10th is a hole that should be given as much respect as it deserves. Only two perfect shots will reach the green.

The 14th is another that will require your utmost attention, for a slight lapse in concentration can see your ball on the beach a long way below the fairway.

Although there are some tough holes, Woodbrook does offer the chance of a good score. You will find quite a few par-4s that require just a drive and a medium or short iron. With the exception of the 194-yard, 2nd hole, the par-3s don't require you to hit towering long irons.

HOW TO GET THERE

From the south, take the road for Shankill as you enter Bray. From the city, take the first exit for Bray off the N11, turning left at the roundabout.

COURSE INFORMATION & FACILITIES

Woodbrook Golf Club
Bray,
Co. Wicklow

Secretary:
Tel: 01-2824799 Fax: 01-282 1950

Golf Professional Tel: 01-2824799

Green Fees:
Weekdays — IR£45 Weekends — IR£50

CARD OF THE COURSE — PAR 72

1	2	3	4	5	6	7	8	9	Out
502	194	383	449	576	401	482	385	157	3533
Par 5	Par 3	Par 4	Par 4	Par 5	Par 4	Par 4	Par 4	Par 3	Par 36
10	**11**	**12**	**13**	**14**	**15**	**16**	**17**	**18**	**In**
443	196	542	230	551	447	507	136	371	3423
Par 4	Par 3	Par 5	Par 3	Par 5	Par 4	Par 5	Par 3	Par 4	Par 36

Gems of Britain & Ireland
Alpha index of golf courses

Gems of Britain & Ireland
Index of golf courses by Country

ENGLAND & WALES

Gems of Britain & Ireland
Index of golf courses by Country

SCOTLAND

Gems of Britain & Ireland
Index of golf courses by Country

IRELAND